HISTORY OF THE
AMERICAN CINEMA
Volume 3
1915 – 1928

THE WEDDING MARCH (*Paramount, 1928*): *a window card.*

HISTORY OF THE AMERICAN CINEMA

CHARLES HARPOLE, GENERAL EDITOR

3
AN EVENING'S ENTERTAINMENT: THE AGE OF THE SILENT FEATURE PICTURE 1915 – 1928

Richard Koszarski

UNIVERSITY OF CALIFORNIA PRESS

Berkeley • Los Angeles • London

University of California Press
Berkeley and Los Angeles, California
University of California Press, Ltd.
London, England
First Paperback Printing 1994

Library of Congress Cataloging-in-Publication Data

Koszarski, Richard.
    An evening's entertainment: the age of the silent feature picture,
1915–1928 / Richard Koszarski.
      p. cm.
    Originally published: New York : Scribner ; Toronto : Collier
Macmillan Canada ; New York : Maxwell Macmillan International,
© 1990. (History of the American cinema ; v. 3)
    Includes bibliographical references and index.
    ISBN 978-0-520-08535-0 (pbk. : acid-free paper)
    1. Silent films—United States—History and criticism. 2. Motion
pictures—United States—History. 3. Motion picture industry—
United States—History. I. Title II. Series: History of the American cinema ; v. 3.
PN1993.5.U6H55   1994 vol. 3
[PN1995.75]
791.43'0973 s—dc20
[791.43'0973'09041]
                                                  93-40204
                                                  CIP

Printed in the United States of America

13   12   11
    10 9 8 7 6 5 4

The paper used in this publication meets the minimum requirements of
ANSI/NISO Z39.48-1992 (R 1997) (*Permanence of Paper*). ∞

Cover design by Ritter and Ritter, Inc.

Advisory Board

Coordinators

IAN JARVIE
York University

E. ANN KAPLAN
*State University
of New York
at Stony Brook*

JOSEPH L. ANDERSON
WGBH, Boston

TINO T. BALIO
University of Wisconsin—Madison

EILEEN BOWSER
Museum of Modern Art

HENRY S. BREITROSE
Stanford University

PETER J. BUKALSKI
*Southern Illinois University at
Edwardsville*

NOËL BURCH

JACK C. ELLIS
Northwestern University

RAYMOND FIELDING
Florida State University

DONALD FREDERICKSEN
Cornell University

MICHAEL GLENNY

RONALD GOTTESMAN
University of Southern California

JOHN G. HANHARDT
Whitney Museum of American Art

LEWIS JACOBS

GARTH JOWETT
University of Houston

JOHN B. KUIPER
University of North Texas

DANIEL J. LEAB
Seton Hall University

JAMES LEAHY
Slade School of Fine Art, London

JAY LEYDA†
New York University

JOHN MERCER
*Southern Illinois University at
Carbondale*

JEAN MITRY†

PETER MORRIS
York University

JOHN E. O'CONNOR
New Jersey Institute of Technology

EDWARD S. PERRY
Middlebury College

VLADA PETRIC
Harvard University

RAYMOND RAVAR
*Centre International de Liaison des
Écoles de Cinema et de Television,
Brussels*

ROBERT ROSEN
University of California, Los Angeles

DONALD E. STAPLES
University of North Texas

ALAN WILLIAMS
Rutgers University

VITALY ZHDAN
VGIK State Film School, Moscow

History of the American Cinema

Charles Harpole, general editor of the History of the American Cinema, is a cinema historian, filmmaker, and consultant. Author of *Gradients of Depth in the Cinema Image* and articles on cinema and mass media, he was written animation for Sesame Street and directed a film in Russia. He has taught at New York University, the University of Texas–Dallas, the University of Georgia, and Ohio State University. He now teaches, writes, and makes films in Florida, where he also helped found the Florida film festival.

The Cinema History Project and the *History of the American Cinema* have been supported by grants from the National Endowment for the Humanities and the John and Mary R. Markle Foundation.

Contents

Preface

*I*n 1976 the Royal Film Archive of Belgium asked 203 critics from around the world to name the most important American films of all time. Hundreds of titles were nominated, but of the top ten vote-getters, 80 percent were silent feature pictures released between 1915 and 1928. For this group of critics at least, the silent-feature era had set standards that would dominate motion pictures well into the video age.

Over the years, the history of this period has been interpreted by many different voices. For Benjamin Hampton, the development of industrial organization was the most significant achievement of the age. For William K. Everson, the films themselves are paramount. For Kevin Brownlow, the workers who created this art and industry are the necessary focus. David Bordwell, Janet Staiger, and Kristin Thompson characterize the period through its establishment of standardized production practices. The problem for any new history is how to build on each of these precedents—and many others as well—while offering a fresh perspective that avoids falling into whatever revisionism is fashionable this season.

The Belgian Film Archive poll offers only one instance of the high regard now accorded films of this period. But if there is no question today of the central importance of these films in the social and artistic development of the cinema, things were quite different at the time of their initial release. The very notion of a filmgoing experience was much more complex and extended far beyond that part of the show which came in a can. The intrusive operations of silent-film exhibitors would shock and appall a modern viewer. Today, the federal government acts to protect the integrity of film classics, and colorization of vintage product is a burning issue. In the 1920s, films were regularly sliced and diced by well-meaning exhibitors, projected at super speed to get past the dull parts, framed with vulgar theatrical pageants fore and aft (sometimes in mid screening, as well), and accompanied by a musical score that varied from intolerable to inconsequential.

These offenses gradually disappeared with the coming of sound, as the picture itself came to dominate the rest of the show. Soon they were nearly forgotten, at best remembered as quaint artifacts, simple period window dressing. But this is the way the intended audience saw GREED, THE BIG PARADE, and THE BIRTH OF A NATION. More important, it is the way the makers of these films *knew* the audiences would see them. To look at the films again without knowledge of this context is to ignore a major part of their creators' original design.

In a very important sense, it is these peculiar exhibition conditions which best characterize the era and separate if from what followed, and what had gone before. Accordingly, this volume of the Scribner *History of the American Cinema* takes the filmgoing experience itself as a prime focus. Chapters on the conduct and content of picture shows are central; chapters on technology, production practice, industrial organization, and critical thinking should be read against this context. The same is true for the two chapters dealing with key creative figures. While each contains a certain amount of biographical information, they are not intended simply as biographical essays, but as illustrations of larger issues or forces peculiar to the period that can be most clearly demonstrated by examining their effect on specific careers. Ian Jarvie has written that films themselves do not constitute film history but instead form useful entry points for the study of film history. We have tried to treat these lives in similar fashion.

For reasons of narrative continuity, one major topic has been omitted altogether in these pages: the development of talking-picture systems, which eventually would obliterate most traces of silent-picture practice. That discussion can be found in the next volume of this series. The focus here is the silent feature as public spectacle, one part of a filmgoing experience that left its mark on an entire generation.

It is worth noting that this generation included Theodore Huff, Seymour Stern, Jay Leyda, Herman G. Weinberg, Lewis Jacobs, George Pratt and many other scholars whose critical agenda would dominate the field for decades, and whose passion for cinema, born of childhood experiences in silent-movie houses, would prove among the era's most significant legacies. Today it is easier to research the silent period than ever before. While oral-history resources may be shrinking, we have unprecedented access to films and the research materials that support them. But no matter how closely we study these traces, our knowledge will always be secondhand. We can call up the documentation, but the firsthand experience is unrecoverable. For this reason, I feel fortunate to have been a student of Jay Leyda and Lewis Jacobs, to have listened as Seymour Stern and Herman G. Weinberg ruminated on their lifelong fascination with silent film, and to have counted George Pratt as a friend. George's comments on early drafts of these chapters were typically direct. His insights never let me lose sight of the fact that before the silent cinema came to rest in museums and universities, it was a dynamic presence in the lives of millions of daily viewers, himself included. I thank George for his enthusiasm and his memories, just as I thank all those who shared with me their recollections of working in the silent film industry, and whose names appear in the bibliography.

For conceiving this project, and guiding it through an often stormy decade, Charles Harpole deserves special congratulations. Eileen Bowser and Charles Musser, two exceptional scholars, have set new standards with their work on early cinema, and I am proud to share the same series with them. A very patient John Fitzpatrick saw all the books through to publication.

Anyone working in this field owes a particular debt of gratitude to William K. Everson, Kevin Brownlow, and Anthony Slide, who for so many years have interpreted American silent film for a new generation. A work like this would be inconceivable without their formidable contributions to build on.

My special thanks go to those curators, archivists, and librarians who have guided my inquiries at many great research centers, especially the Academy of Motion Picture Arts and Sciences, the American Film Institute Center for Advanced Film Studies, the UCLA Film, Radio, and Television Archives, the Cinema Collection of the University of Southern California, Department of Special Collections, the Wisconsin Center for Film and Theater Research, the Free Library of Philadelphia, the

George Eastman House/International Museum of Photography, the Motion Picture Division of the Library of Congress, the National Archives and Records Center, the Museum of Modern Art Department of Film, and the Billy Rose Theater Collection of the New York Public Library. Marc Wanamaker and the Bison Archives deserve special mention for skill, cooperation, and extraordinary picture research.

Thanks also to my colleagues at the American Museum of the Moving Image, especially JoAnn Hanley, David Schwartz, Donald Albrecht, and Eleanor Mish. Rochelle Slovin, director of the Museum, gave me the time to work on this volume during 1984–1985.

There are numerous others who have helped in so many ways over the years, including Jill Alexander, Mary Lea Bandy, John Belton, Robert Birchard, David Bradley, James Card, Paolo Cherchi Usai, Mary Corliss, Donald Crafton, Ted Crane, Raymond Fielding, Sam Gill, Robert Gitt, Carol Golterman, Stephen Higgins, Jan-Christopher Horak, Arthur Lennig, Brooks MacNamara, Patrick Montgomery, Paul Myers, Sol Negrin, Herbert Reynolds, Andrew Sarris, Anne Schlosser, David Shepard, Charles Silver, Paul Spehr, Dorothy Swerdlove, and Morgan Wesson. Thanks for many favors.

My wife, Diane, whom I first saw at a screening of Mauritz Stiller's GUNNAR HEDES SAGA, has helped me watch a great many silent pictures ever since—including every scrap of William S. Hart footage known to survive. Our daughter, Eva, has grown up with this manuscript, which was in progress long enough to allow her to help with the Charlie Chaplin material. Since I am closing with family history, I should note that it is generally recognized that much of my own enthusiasm for the movies is inherited from my mother. She doesn't remember the silent days, of course, but still appreciates a good Pola Negri picture. This book is dedicated to her.

RICHARD KOSZARSKI

HISTORY OF THE AMERICAN CINEMA

Volume 3

1915 – 1928

1

An Industry and an Art

*T*he home office of the Universal Film Manufacturing Company was located at 1600 Broadway, a midtown Manhattan office tower not far from several of Universal's eastern studios and the company's laboratory in Bayonne, New Jersey. On a cold Saturday morning in March 1915, two hundred of the company's employees gathered on a platform at Grand Central Terminal. Their boss, Carl Laemmle, was about to leave for the West Coast to open the company's vast new studio, to be called Universal City. Bundled up against the chill air, Laemmle arrived at the terminal in the tonneau of a flashy touring car, part of an entourage of honking horns and waving banners assembled by the studio press office. His thinning white hair made him seem older than his forty-eight years, and to many in the industry he was already "the old man," or "Uncle Carl," a diminutive Bavarian immigrant known for his broad smile and thick accent. Laemmle had started as an exhibitor in 1906, had moved into distribution, and since 1909 had been making his own films. When a group of independent producers coalesced as the Universal in 1912, Laemmle had come out on top, but the corporate pot was still bubbling. Pat Powers, a giant Irishman who served as treasurer and owned 40 percent of the stock, was also coming along for the ride. He too smiled for the cameras, but Powers wanted Laemmle out. The trip would give him an opportunity to confer with his allies and agents on the West Coast.[1]

To Laemmle, Powers was a known irritant, and corporate infighting a way of life. What bothered him most at the moment, however, was the United States Supreme Court. In a statement to reporters, Laemmle denounced the Court's recent decision in the Mutual case. Ruling that motion pictures were "a business pure and simple," the Court had denied the Mutual Film Corporation's argument that first-amendment guarantees protected their film THE BIRTH OF A NATION from prior restraint by Ohio censors. The immediate effect was to stop the showing of the film in the state of Ohio, but everyone in the industry knew that state and local censorship boards across the country could now act with impunity, treating their precious films like so much interstate baggage. Laemmle announced his strong support for the National Board of Censorship, an industry-sponsored body whose judgments were, in effect, powerless.[2]

Laemmle may or may not have seen THE BIRTH OF A NATION, which had opened in New York just two days earlier. Was he aware that many of its great battle scenes had been filmed at the Providencia ranch, picturesque acreage just east of his own studio and quite often the location of his own Western and Civil War Pictures?[3] In any case, he had certainly seen the daily reviews, which suggested a revolution in motion-picture content and style. As one "first-nighter" would put it:

> In dramatic and photographic technique it is beyond our present day criticism. . . . The true greatness of this production lies in its emotional appeal, an appeal so forceful that it lifts you out of your seat and thrills you as the speaking stage never did and [never] realized. And did any of us ever believe it could be done—like this? (*Motion Picture News*, 13 March 1915, quoted by Seymour Stern, *Film Culture*, Spring–Summer 1965, p. 147).

Universal had distributed occasional features as far back as 1912, but the company's prosperity was based on a "balanced program" of short subjects. How the clamor over THE BIRTH OF A NATION might affect future release schedules would be a major topic of concern at upcoming strategy sessions. Not only was the picture extraordinarily expensive ($110,000), but at twelve reels, it simply did not fit the established patterns of distribution and exhibition. No film exchange handled THE BIRTH OF A NATION, and no nickelodeon was showing it. Instead, it was running at Klaw and Erlanger's Liberty Theatre, one of a series of legitimate houses that both K & E and the Shuberts had recently announced would be given over completely to feature pictures.[4]

The previous April, Vitagraph had leased its own Broadway showcase, and a palatial theater called the Strand had caused a sensation when it opened its doors with a feature-picture program. Even the Hippodrome was starting a movie season for the spring and summer, with the films accompanied by its pipe organ, one-hundred-piece orchestra, and chorus of three hundred voices. It was clear that exhibition would be in upheaval for the next year or two, and Universal would have to make a gesture in the direction of long films. But Laemmle was convinced the short-film market was too well established ever to be abandoned.[5]

Of course, Laemmle and Powers were not the only VIPs leaving for the opening. Exchange manager M. H. Hoffman was going, at the head of a contingent of Universal's distribution chiefs from across the country. The exchange men and the exhibitors they serviced were the company's lifeline, and impressing them with such a gala was one way of demonstrating Universal's formidable size and strength. Hoffman would leave the company a few years later to start his own studio, Tiffany. Joe Brandt was going only as far as Chicago. He was Universal's general manager, a lawyer (like Hoffman), and the future president of Columbia Pictures. Laemmle's brother, Louis, was also in the party. (He did something for Universal, but no one could quite figure out what. In the years to come, nepotism at Laemmle's studio would become an industry joke, but some other producers were not far behind.) Least noted of the group was Julius Laemmle, the president's seven-year-old son. A few years later he would change his name to Carl Laemmle, Jr. For his twenty-first birthday his father would put him in charge of the studio, and he would produce ALL QUIET ON THE WESTERN FRONT (1930).[6]

A reception line of stars from Universal's eastern studios offered formal farewells at the platform. The first to shake Carl Laemmle's hand was Mary Fuller, star of the

Exhibitors and exchange operators on their way to the opening of Universal City, March 1915.

original serial picture, WHAT HAPPENED TO MARY (1912). Laemmle had hired her away from the Edison Company but was becoming quite ambivalent about the entire subject of stars. He was much more interested in serials, however, and had turned Universal into one of the industry's leading producers. Nonetheless, he saved Mary Fuller for two-reel dramas and melodramas. After her on the reception line came King Baggott, William Garwood, Hobart Henley, Matt Moore, Violet Mersereau, Harry C. Myers, Charles Ogle, and Ben Wilson, all names to conjure with in 1915 and all wondering whether the opening of the new California studio would mean the closing of their eastern stages and a long trek west. In fact it would take three years.[7]

Filming the proceedings for the *Universal Animated Weekly* was that newsreel's editor, Jack Cohn. With his brother Harry, and Joe Brandt, he would be part of the triumvirate behind Columbia Pictures.

The Lake Shore Limited pulled out of Grand Central and headed for Chicago, where more Universalites would join the party and a special train would be ready to take them all to the Coast. Laemmle had begun his theater and exchange operations in Chicago and had once been the largest distributor in the Midwest. In fact, servicing great numbers of small middle-American theaters was still the basic method of doing business at Universal. Chicago was a symbol for this company, not just a necessary transfer point.

The Universal Special left the Dearborn Street Station in Chicago on Sunday evening, stopped in Kansas City, and reached Denver by Tuesday. The local exchange operator was at the station with a circus band and seven open limousines. For eight hours the party saw the sights of Denver, was greeted by Governor Carlson on the steps of the capitol, and lunched at the Savoy in the company of Buffalo Bill Cody. Buffalo Bill and his Wild West troupe had perfected the modern method of bill-poster ballyhoo, but these movie people were prepared to extend his lavish local campaigns to a national level. The president of the Morgan Lithograph Company, P. J. Morgan, was also along for the trip. He supplied Universal with its posters now, but in later years Morgan would dominate the entire industry.[8]

At 7:45 that night the group left Denver's Santa Fe Station en route to the Grand Canyon, a side trip that took another day and a half. Typical tourists, they grumbled at the encroachments of civilization (the supposedly tranquil canyon "sounds like the Brooklyn express making up time under the East River," one quipped) but insisted on luxuriating in heated baths, despite the seventy-five-cent extra charge.[9]

By now the train was loaded with Universal executives and exchange managers, theater owners, and journalists. U. K. Whipple, the company's legendary newsreel cameraman, was on board with his entire outfit. Harry Vestal and his wife had been on since Chicago. He was chairman of Ohio's film-censorship commission, a post he would soon be forced to resign because of this little junket. One of the nation's first prominent movie reviewers, Kitty Kelly, was there to cover the event for the *Chicago Tribune*. *Billboard*, the Western Newspaper Union, the *National Magazine*, *Leslie's Weekly*, *Motography*, and the *Motion Picture News* all had representatives on the train. Among them were Robert Grau and Homer Croy, whose descriptions of filmmaking in this period were among the first attempts to suggest the real complexity of the industry's art and economics. The "youngest man on board" was Ned Depinet, twenty-four years old, an exchange man from Dallas who earned a reputation on the trip as a fancy dancer. Years later, he would become president of RKO Radio Pictures.[10]

It was on Saturday, six days after leaving Grand Central, that the Special deposited Laemmle and his crew in Los Angeles. Even without the sight-seeing, the California studio seemed very far from 1600 Broadway. Land and labor were cheap, but was it a good idea to set up the company's factory so far from executive supervision? The pluses appeared to outweigh the minuses, but the issue was hardly closed.

The general manager of Universal City, Isidore Bernstein, had met the train at San Bernardino. He brought along a bevy of "poppy girls" bearing gifts of flowers and fruit and rode with the party to the Santa Fe Station in Los Angeles. There a mounted escort of cowboys and Indians, whooping and hollering and firing their revolvers into the air, accompanied the visitors to their quarters at the Hollywood Hotel. The following day, Sunday, was spent sight-seeing at Busch Gardens and ogling the millionaires' homes along Pasadena's Grove Avenue. Bernstein had other things to attend to, however. Six weeks earlier the entire lot had almost been washed away by a flood, and tomorrow ten thousand visitors were expected for the grand opening.[11]

Of course, this was not Universal's first West Coast studio. In 1911 the Horsley brothers had established the Nestor studio in an old roadhouse on Sunset Boulevard—the first studio in Hollywood proper. The following year, when the Horsleys joined in the creation of Universal, their studio became the new firm's West Coast headquarters. Another facility was built at Edendale in 1912. Universal's West Coast "ranch" could produce 15,000 feet of negative (*i.e.*, finished product) per week, but a much larger facility was needed, capable of 30,000 to 40,000 feet, with enough room for a vast array of permanent standing sets—a motion-picture city.

Bernstein began looking for a suitable location and in 1914 acquired the 230-acre Taylor ranch in the San Fernando Valley, five miles across the Cahuenga Pass from the old studio. Stanley Anderson, the developer of Beverly Hills, handled the $165,000 purchase. The spring crop of oats was harvested, and on 18 June ground was broken for Universal City. William Horsley was put in charge of construction, and by the autumn of 1914 the western part of the lot had been leveled for stages and grading was completed for a network of roads, including a mile-long "Laemmle Boulevard" linking the back lot to the front gate. By October five hundred people were living on the property, seventy-five of them in teepees situated along the hills that provided the studio's dramatic backdrop. Bernstein took advantage of this permanent population to obtain for "Universal City" a ranking as a third-class city, with its own post office and voting precinct. The city's first birth occurred in December, to the wife of a cowpuncher foreman. She named her son Carl Laemmle Oelze.[12]

Filming proceeded even during construction, and approximately fifty films were shot here before the formal opening. Most important of these was DAMON AND PYTHIAS (released 21 December 1914), a four-reel production intended to challenge the popular Italian spectacle films. As the winter rainy season progressed, it became obvious that Universal City needed an indoor stage, so Horsley converted a structure he had originally intended as a garage. It was still being hung with Aristo Arcs and Cooper-Hewitt lamps when the great flood hit.[13]

A river meandering through the property, usually a tepid stream, had been swollen by excessive winter rains. On the night of 30–31 January a gale caused it to surge over its banks, undermining every building on the lot and demolishing all the pre-1914 structures. Seven hundred laborers were called in to help repair the damage, estimated at $130,000. Among the standing sets destroyed were the Indian temples built for Francis Ford's serial THE MASTER KEY (1914–1915). Release of its final chapters had to be delayed until they could be reconstructed.[14]

As Universal City's opening date approached, its competitors sought to get their own strengths on the record as well. The American Studio, up the coast at Santa Barbara, was said to be employing four hundred people. Selig's ace director, Colin Campbell, was returning to their West Coast studio after a location trip to the Canal Zone. Edwin Thanhouser had just returned after three years to take charge once more of the company he had founded. And Sigmund Lubin was opening the largest artificially lit stage in the world at his studios outside Philadelphia. If Universal wanted to boast of its size and wealth, Vitagraph would not be outdone. The week Laemmle opened his new city, Vitagraph announced its own capital investment as $5 million, with real-estate holdings alone of $1 million. Every week, twelve hundred Vitagraph employees in Brooklyn, Los Angeles, and Paris spent $70,000 of the company's money, while its laboratories churned out 1,500,000 feet of release prints.[15]

Universal was about to open a producing plant of unprecedented size, capable of generating great amounts of film at limited cost. Special projects like THE BIRTH OF A NATION had no place in this scheme, and even ordinary feature-length films were not easily accommodated. Laemmle was prepared to leave the high road to the competition, but would his cut-rate policies justify the overhead of this new plant? Universal's West Coast stars would greet him at the gates of the city on Monday. Could they carry the company into the new era that was obviously coming?

On Monday, 15 March the visiting party left the Hollywood Hotel in a fleet of

Visiting a set during the opening-day festivities at Universal City, 15 March 1915.
Directors Otis Turner and William Worthington; studio general manager Isidore
Bernstein; executives Pat Powers, Carl Laemmle, and R. H. Cochrane; Western star
Anna Little.

buses and drove up through the hills above Hollywood. Seen from Lankershim
Boulevard, Universal City was a white city, fresh paint and stucco gleaming in the
California sunshine. True, these were only the administration buildings, the studio's
public face, but one year ago nothing had stood here but a chicken ranch. At 10:15
the chief of police of Universal City, Laura Oakley (who doubled as a Western star),
made a simple presentation: "Mr. President, acting for the west coast studios, I am
pleased to present you with this golden key, a key which will permit you to open the
gates of this wonder city." Laemmle turned the key, the band struck up "The Star
Spangled Banner," and Pat Powers ran the stars and stripes up the flagpole. Laemmle led his army of executives and exchange operators through the gates, followed by
a cheering crowd of ten thousand. They marched between two ranks of Universal
stars until they reached another flagpole, where R. H. Cochrane, vice-president and
Laemmle's silent right hand, raised a special Universal City flag. The band played "I
Love You, California," and Laemmle, Cochrane, and Powers were showered with a
hail of flowers tossed by their employees.[16]

Not far behind the administration buildings was the main stage, in fact a great
open-air platform three hundred feet long. The stage was divided into segments on
which various companies could simultaneously shoot a number of different silent

films. A dramatic company filming on one set might be flanked by a comedy unit rehearsing to their left and a construction crew knocking together sets on their right. Sunlight was the only illumination, moderated by a series of overhead diffusion screens that could limit the amount of light pouring down on the actors. When it became too cloudy for uniform photographic results, a banner with the words DON'T SHOOT was run up a pole and all production companies stopped filming. Beneath this stage were various traps and water-tight pits, while one corner housed a revolving turntable and another a rocking setup. For an open-air stage, it was state-of-the-art, but even in California Cecil B. DeMille and other filmmakers were already making use of improved arc lighting to allow them to shoot indoors at all hours of the day.[17]

This stage now became the scene of a mass review, where Laemmle and his party inspected the companies "in true military fashion." When this was finished the resident cowboy-and-Indian cavalry mounted their own review.[18]

After lunch, a few things began to go wrong. Director Henry McRae's "101" Bison Company staged a flood scene in which 60,000 gallons of water poured from a reservoir, sweeping away a Western town. Marie Walcamp rode through the waves to warn the inhabitants. But there was a little too much force to the inundation, and Walcamp was almost swept away too. As the flood reached the crowd, Carl Laemmle jumped atop an automobile to keep his feet from getting wet, but a number of other guests needed to be sent to the wardrobe department for a change of dry clothes. No one mentioned the January flood, at least not in print.

There were five hundred cars parked on the lot at the moment, and the crowd was said to have swollen to twenty thousand. Streetcars and buses had been delivering more and more visitors all day. Universal City was establishing itself as a tourist attraction, even comparing itself directly to the Panama-Pacific Exposition in San Francisco. Visitors continued to come in large numbers in the days following the opening, and soon Laemmle was charging them to get in and building special stands from which they could watch the action on the main stage. That night, a grand ball was held in William Horsley's new studio, a converted garage decorated with banks of flowers and lit by the eerie glow of Cooper-Hewitt tubes.[19]

Tuesday morning was given over to a general inspection of the buildings and grounds, and after lunch, Eddie Polo, a circus stuntman now working with Francis Ford's company, had his crew demonstrate a series of daring leaps from a high parapet. The location was "The Wall of Lucknow," part of a large standing set originally built by Ford for THE CAMPBELLS ARE COMING (1914), which had survived the rainy season. Henry McRae's unit followed this with a full-scale rodeo, taking good advantage of Universal's resident cowboys and Indians.

Frank Stites, Universal's stunt pilot, had been scheduled to take off earlier in the day for a bit of exhibition flying. But news of the crash of another aviator, his friend Lincoln Beachey, so upset Stites that at the last moment he refused to go up. Later in the day he reconsidered, although what induced him to change his mind was never made clear. Stites took off, crashed, and was killed before thousands of horrified spectators.[20]

Stites's death effectively ended the celebration. The visitors drifted away, and for a long time Stites's fall was read as an omen by many in the industry. Played down in the press, it was the single indelible image many of those at the opening would carry away with them.[21]

Activity at the factory studio went on as scheduled for the rest of the week. As one

Henry McRae's "flood scene" accidentally inundates much of the back lot during opening-day festivities at Universal City.

observer noted, "If Universal City has a motto it is this: We must never let the 'footage' fall behind." Laemmle and Cochrane were hearing constant rumors that Pat Powers was about to instigate a coup, but they were at a loss to understand how. The press carried reports that Vitagraph, Lubin, Selig, and Essanay would join together to establish a single booking agency for spectacular films, a powerful new combination. By the end of the week, Universal had another thirty reels of film ready for release.[22]

2

Going to the Movies

We sell tickets to theaters, not movies.
                                    —*Marcus Loew*

During the 1915–1928 period, the experience of viewing a film was far different from what it would be at any time before or since. Exhibitors considered themselves showmen, not film programmers. The feature motion picture was only one part of their evening's entertainment, supplying about 68 percent of the total "attraction," according to one 1922 exhibitors' poll. Indeed, 24 percent of theater managers in this survey found that it made absolutely no difference at the box office whether the feature attraction was any good or not. Consequently, while exhibitors always hoped for a strong feature, they did not feel wholly dependent on that part of their show which arrived in a can. Nor were they above "improving" their film subject by any means at their disposal.[1]

The Theater

In 1928 Harold Franklin, then president of West Coast Theatres, Inc., described the various categories of motion-picture theaters in operation at that time. Most impressive was "The Super," seating thousands, the last word in architecture and decoration. The Roxy and the New York Paramount were his examples. "De Luxe First Run" houses were to be found more frequently, centrally located to cater to an entire metropolis, and probably offering a stage presentation along with the film. "Neighborhood Theatres" were located in residential areas, and their size and magnificence were determined entirely by the nature of the surrounding population. These usually played second-run films. After them were third-, fourth-, and fifth-run houses, whose service and standards were left undefined. "Vaudeville Picture Houses" ran a film with five or six acts of vaudeville but were distinct from straight vaudeville theaters, and "Double Feature Houses" offered their patrons two successive feature-length pictures ("like asking a person to read two novels in the same evening," Franklin carped). Finally, one could still find those small-town legitimate houses which would present a film when the need arose. There were an estimated 20,500 screens across the United States.[2]

Although the "picture palace" occupies an important position in the lore of the era, relatively few such theaters existed. The *Film Daily Yearbook* noted sixty-six major first-run houses in 1927, only seventeen of which grossed as much as $1 million annually. It would appear that a great many Americans were still patronizing neighborhood and subsequent-run houses.[3]

Despite the opening of such elaborate motion-picture theaters as John Kunsky's Columbia in Detroit (1911) and the Regent in New York, designed by Thomas Lamb (1913), storefront theaters of three hundred seats were still being built in 1915.[4]

Photoplay magazine offered the following costs for such a house:

Original Starting Costs

seats @ $2.75 each
screen @ $150
indirect lighting
   chandeliers (6) @ $200
   wall sconces @ $30
electric sign in front of lobby @ $75
projector $275 (should have two)
city license $100

Weekly Operational Costs

rent $100 (monthly)
advance for first week's film rental $35
   (total film costs about $60 per week)
cashier $10
operator $20
pianist $15
usher $5
advertising $10–15
plus electricity, repairs, carbons, tickets,
   film shipping[5]

Although *Photoplay* concluded that such theaters would no longer be economical because they were too small to take advantage of popular films, a large number apparently survived well into the 1920s. The *Motion Picture News* found that the average size of a 1916 movie house was 502 seats, a figure that had increased only to 507 by 1922, despite a boom in the construction of large theaters after the war.[6]

In 1915, many movie theaters still wore the flashy nickelodeon-style ornamentation of an earlier day, bedecked with garish displays of electric lights and gaudy facades in cast iron or terra-cotta, ordered by catalogue from such dealers as the Decorators Supply Company of Chicago. The *Architectural Record* attacked such decorative schemes as "illiterate trashiness" and published a useful, no-frills essay on moving-picture theater design by John Klaber in the November 1915 issue. Sensibly, Klaber starts with the central problem of the booth and the screen. Projection booths should be fireproof, preferably of brick, terra-cotta blocks, or reinforced concrete. Three examples are given: a six-by-eight-foot booth with one projector, a nine-by-eight-foot booth with a projector and a stereopticon, and a twelve-by-eight-foot booth with two projectors and stereopticon. Each machine should have its own lens port and lookout port. The stereopticon projected illustrated song slides, local advertisements, and announcements of coming attractions, while the second projector had become necessary in the best houses to eliminate the waiting time between reel changes during multiple-reel films.[7]

Klaber's first choice for a screen is a plaster wall, finished with dull enamel or whiting, and tinted slightly blue. If the screen needs to be moved, muslin may be used, but this is not recommended, since it is not as brilliant, tends to become soiled, and wafts about in drafts. A dull-finished aluminum screen is also proposed, but for "the most brilliant effect," a frosted plate-glass mirror is suggested, available in sizes as large as 13½ by 18 feet. A screen image of 9 by 12 feet will give a clear and "approximately life size" picture for up to one hundred feet, but one should not place it too high off the floor, "in order that the figures may appear to walk on the ground and not in the air."

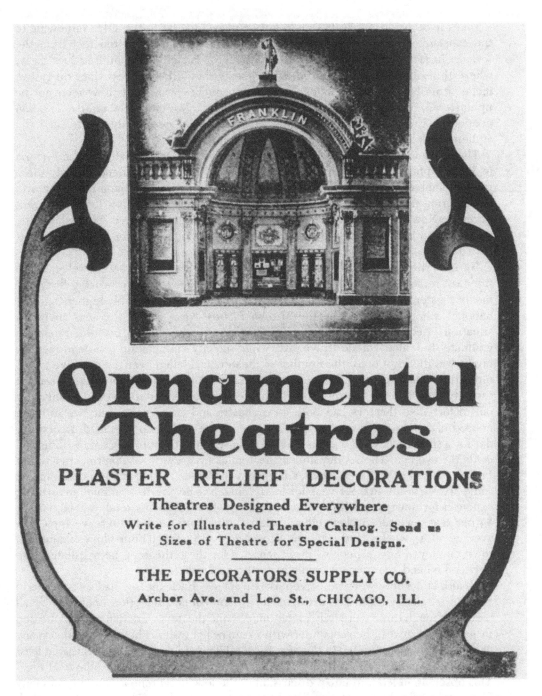

The Decorators Supply Company offered prefabricated ornamental theater facades to readers of the Moving Picture World (10 July 1915, p. 419).

Because of distortion, seats should not be placed too far to the side, and owing to the constant vibration of the image, none should be less than ten feet from the screen. In fact, the best seating will be about seventy to one hundred feet away, where this vibration is minimized. These seats should be not less than thirty-two inches from back to back, or less than twenty inches wide, but they need not be upholstered, "as the performances are usually short." Nor is any elaborate decoration needed on the interior, since changes between reels are usually short, "and the audience has little time to admire the auditorium."

The long and narrow design Klaber seems to favor is best illustrated by the Victoria in Philadelphia, which contained over eight hundred seats arranged in forty-three rows of nineteen or less, with two aisles, all squeezed into a 48-by-200-foot structure. Considering that he is writing a year after the opening of Thomas Lamb's elegant Strand in New York, Klaber's suggestions seem positively primitive. Yet it should be remembered that the average house of the period was far nearer Klaber's designs than Lamb's.

By 1919 short performances with time-consuming reel changes were relegated to the most remote situations. A good-sized town like Toledo, Ohio, boasted forty-five movie theaters with an average seating capacity of 811 (considerably higher than the national average reported by the *Motion Picture News*, since this was an urban situation). According to a study of Toledo's theaters conducted by John Phelan, a graduate student at Toledo University, while the city's population had been increasing (it was then 250,000), the number of theaters had fallen over the past five years, indicating a shaking out of some older and smaller houses. Of the town's total seating capacity of 55,132, the fourteen largest theaters accounted for 20,000 seats. Only four out of forty-five theaters had both an orchestra and an organist, but two of those housed elaborate $20,000 pipe organs. Attendance in Toledo averaged 45,000 per day for a six-reel show, at a price ranging from seven to thirty-nine cents with fifteen cents the average. The six downtown theaters alone drew 75,000 patrons per week. Phelan figured that annual movie admissions in Toledo averaged $10 per capita, or some sixty-seven visits per year for every citizen. The theaters' annual advertising expenses for newspapers, billboards, posters, and other media totaled $166,000, or $3 per seat per year. Ticket sellers, ushers, attendants, and cleaners were paid an average of $15 weekly, but projectionists earned $18 to $35. Four film exchanges in town employed fifteen people. Profit margins for these theaters, he calculated, ran between 60 and 100 percent annually, with small risk.

Health and safety were perceived as real issues. Each theater had an average of three fire exits and five fire extinguishers. Thirty-nine projection booths were all metal, although three were only metal-lined. Nine theaters were dangerously heated by gas or coal stoves, the remainder with steam or hot water. Phelan noted that many of the theaters were located in the vicinity of saloons and dance halls, and that at least six "make a specialty of catering to the questionable and suggestive phases of life." This observation led him into a discussion of the low moral tone and nudity in many films, especially those that purported to attack social vices: "They contain so much portrayal of the vice itself and portray it with such lingering detail that the spectacles, instead of making immorality disgusting, defeat their avowed purpose by arousing either morbid curiosity or downright passion."[8]

A comparative survey of theater sizes across the country in 1919 was provided by H. D. H. Connick in a report to the investment firm of Kuhn, Loeb & Co. Here the nation's fifteen thousand theaters were divided according to admission prices and seating capacity:[9]

            4,100 charging 10¢, 300 seats average
            6,000   "   15¢, 450   "   "
            2,400   "   18¢, 600   "   "
            2,500   "   25¢, 1,100 seats and over

The increasing unprofitability of small houses in the immediate postwar years was graphically demonstrated by theater owner Frank J. Rembusch, who compared operating costs at one of his small Indiana theaters in February 1922 with the same house's record exactly ten years earlier (table 2.1). With seventeen years in the business, Rembusch complained that "the times are the toughest in my experience."

The year 1922 was a poor one for other theater owners as well, with nearly three-fourths of the exhibitors reporting worse business than in 1919, 1920, or 1921. This slump was documented by an extensive survey conducted by the Babson Statistical Organization for the *Motion Picture News,* with the cooperation of Columbia University's Department of Photoplay Production. Questionnaires were sent to ten thousand of the nation's estimated fourteen thousand exhibitors, although no figure was ever given on the number of questionnaires returned. Nevertheless, this sampling is the most detailed we are likely to find for this period (table 2.2). The poll also discovered that 52 percent of theaters had no exhibitor competition—they were the only film show around. Despite this fact, nearly one-third had been forced to lower prices recently. Small theaters continued to provide the backbone of national film exhibition. Nearly 64 percent of all theaters seated five hundred or less, while not even 9 percent seated over a thousand. While 62 percent were open for more or less the entire week, 30 percent did business only on three days or less. When the hot weather arrived, business evaporated.

In 1923 the *New York Times* reported that while one-third of the population was concentrated in 190 large cities, these cities contained only one-fourth of the country's motion-picture theaters. Although the average size of the country theaters was smaller (city theaters were found to have an average seating capacity of 750, against a national average of around 500), their preponderant numbers still provided the bulk of the nation's seating.[10]

Even at the time, little attention was paid to this silent majority of picture houses. When F. H. Richardson reported on the status of "village theaters" to the Society of Motion Picture Engineers, he sketched a sorry story, but one, he implied, that was of merely local significance.

> These "theaters" eke out a precarious existence for the most part by renting the very cheapest possible junk service, paying small attention to decoration, the comfort of their patrons, or to ventilation. Some man or boy with little knowledge or experience is hired to "operate" old, worn out projectors, using the minimum possible screen illumination. . . . As a rule their projection equipment is antiquated, badly worn, and very thoroughly inefficient. The screen very often is basically very poor, and usually its surface is more or less dirty with the accumulations of months, if not years. Ventilation is largely a matter of imagination. The music is

TABLE 2.1 TEN-YEAR COMPARISON OF OPERATING COSTS
FOR A THEATER OWNED BY FRANK J. REMBUSCH

Showings

1912	1922
6 days (no Sundays)	7 days

Box Office Receipts—Gross

$364	$ 506

Film Service Expense

Gen. Film Co., per week, 1912	$ 50
Several Companies, 1922	$ 225

General Expense

	1912	1922
Water	$ .25	$ 1
Light and Heat	10.00	35
Rent	30.00	30
License		3
Express and Inc.	4.00	8
Total	$44.25	$ 77

Competition

1912	1922
1 Pic. Theater	1 Pic. Theater
1 Op. House	Basketball

Attendance

1912	1922
Weekly paid admissions	
at 5 cents	at 20 cents
7,280	2,530

Labor Expense

	1912	1922
Musician	$12	$ 35
Cashier	6	12
Accounting		8
Operator (Projectionist)	12	25
Manager	18	30
Ticket Taker		4
Usher		4
Janitor	12	18
Singer (illustrated songs)	25	
Totals	$85	$ 136

Advertising

1912	1922
$12	$ 52

Weekly Profits—Gross

1912	1922
$170	$ 12

(One dollar in 1912 perhaps equal to two of 1922. Depreciation, insurance and taxes not included.)

Summary of Percentages

Increases	%
Box Office increase	45
Film Cost increase	350
Labor increase	60
General Expense increase	80
Advertising increase	300
Length of Program increase	200

1922—Open one day more.

Decreases	%
Number Paid Admissions	200
Profits	1,300

1912—Owner works one hour daily.
1922—Owner works unceasingly.

SOURCE: *Film Daily Yearbook of Motion Pictures* (1922–1923), p. 245.

Rembusch does not give the size of the house, but since it was operating in 1912 in a town of ten thousand people, it would not have had more than a few hundred seats.

supplied by a girl who drums on a decrepit old piano, apparently with the idea of creating as much noise as possible. The films are rainy, battered old junk ("Importance of the Village Theatre," *Transactions of the SMPE* 23 [October 1925], p. 85).

Projection problems were so widespread that only specialists bothered to take note of them. While small exhibitors loaded the pages of the *Exhibitor's Herald* with complaints about the films they were forced to show, few admitted their own shortcomings. The editor of *American Projectionist* visited the booth of a small suburban theater in 1926 by climbing up a steep wooden ladder through an eighteen-inch trap door. The room was nine feet square and six feet high, lined in sheet metal. Unglazed projection ports twelve inches square and observation ports five inches square (set at the same level) provided the ventilation and a small fan the only air circulation. The ceiling was ten inches above the lamp housing and covered with a layer of white ash. The projectors were held together with baling wire, cords, and rubber bands, since the management would not invest in spare parts. The show had broken down four times that week, and audiences were screaming to replace the projectionist, an apparent "tubercular case" who had taken the job because there was nothing else available.[11]

Although the job might be boring, unhealthy, and dangerous, working as a projectionist seemed to many an easy way to break into the movies. While some unscrupulous "schools" graduated scenario writers and cinematographers, others targeted the exhibition end of the business. One victim reported paying $50 for a four-week course with a guaranteed job. His "school" featured poor equipment and worse instructors, but by memorizing the questions he was able to pass the required

TABLE 2.2   STATISTICS OF THE MOTION-PICTURE INDUSTRY—1922

Seating Capacity			Days of Operation		
Seats	*Theaters*	*(%)*	*Days*	*Theaters*	*(%)*
0–250	26.88		1	6.87	
251–500	36.91		2	13.01	
501–1000	27.44		3	10.38	
1001–1250	3.20		4	5.42	
1251–1500	2.37		5	2.33	
1501–2000	2.23		6	30.13	
over 2000	0.97		7	31.87	

Admission Charges			Seasonal Attendance		
Price	*Matinee (%)*	*Evening (%)*	*Season*	*Best (%)*	*Worst (%)*
10¢–24¢	83.79	56.44	Spring	20.16	16.05
25¢–49¢	15.24	40.30	Summer	7.20	61.09
50¢–99¢	0.73	3.07	Fall	48.29	3.35
$1.00 +	0.24	0.19	Winter	24.34	19.51

SOURCE: L. C. Moen, "Statistics of the Motion Picture Industry," *Motion Picture News*, 2 December 1922, p. 2772. The results of this poll, which appeared in the *Motion Picture News* between 18 November and 16 December 1922, are reproduced in *Film Daily Yearbook of Motion Pictures* (1922–1923), p. 231.

"PREPAREDNESS" FOR PICTURE PALACES

You know how the tender passages are always blotted out by this silly silhouette on the screen?

You have also heard of this little device they used to hold our grandparents' heads still while they were having their pictures "took?"

Well, this is the idea—make every couple that can't produce a marriage license at least six months old, sit in seats equipped with these contraptions and give the man behind a chance.

Then just think of the war measures that could be made use of in the photoplay. Wouldn't poison gas be about right for the nut who insists upon reading the sub-titles, etc., aloud?

Why not utilize the lovely uniforms the ushers wear by forming a firing squad to take care of the boobs who supply the kissing sounds?

Suggested to the Board of Strategy
by GALE

And finally—wouldn't the periscope put the photoplay pests out of commission—the lady who removes her hat in fifteen minutes flat, the human Zeppelin that floats athwart your rapt gaze just at the climax and all of the fell crew?

Motion Picture Operator's License
FORT WORTH, TEXAS

No. 87 Grade First May 2 1918

License Is Hereby Granted to E. L. Young
to pursue the occupation of Motion Picture Operator within the Corporate limits
of the City of Fort Worth, Texas.

Said E. L. Young having this day appeared
before Examining Board provided by City Ordinance No. 400 and duly demonstrated his ability to operate Motion Picture Machine.

R. E. Benton

City Electrician.

This License subject to re-
vocation at the pleasure of the
Board of Examiners.

By

The city electrician of Fort Worth, Texas, was empowered to examine and license motion-picture machine operators (projectionists). By 1918 these men were already the first unionized film industry workers.

test. The guaranteed job was at a fleapit theater whose run-down equipment he was unable to operate, and he was promptly fired. This situation proved to be a setup between the school and the theater manager. Protesting through the union was no help because it already had one hundred members out of work. Only after studying a projection manual he found in the public library did he succeed in locating a job in a small country theater. While incompetent graduates of cinematography schools were unlikely to get the chance to spoil the photography of a real film, projectionists with similar qualifications were regularly turned loose on unsuspecting audiences.[12]

With such working conditions, one wonders how the number of catastrophic fires were kept as low as they seem to have been, since a great deal of professional care was needed when handling the inflammable nitrocellulose film. Once started, such conflagrations were hard to control. On 22 May 1923 overheated film caused a fire in a Mexicala theater, which resulted in fourteen deaths, $2 million in property damage, and one thousand people losing their homes.[13]

The end of the silent period was marked by a surge in theater construction involving modest houses as well as picture palaces. The 1928 *Film Daily Yearbook* reported 967 theaters erected in 1926, nearly all of them film theaters, and offered a financial plan for a typical 1,000-seat house (see table 2.3). One has only to compare these figures with the sorry statistics offered by Rembusch five years earlier to see why the boom in theater construction extended beyond the operation of downtown showplaces. The greater profitability of the 1927 example comes not just from the

TABLE 2.3   FINANCIAL PLAN FOR A 1,000-SEAT THEATER

Building Cost

Ground	$20,000	
Construction	80,000	
Heating and ventilating	6,500	
Electric	6,000	
Carrying charges during construction	3,000	
Interior decorating	2,500	
Marquise [*sic*]	1,000	
Architect's fee	6,000	
TOTAL CONSTRUCTION		125,000
Seats	8,000	
Organ	12,000	
Booth equipment	3,500	
Draperies, carpets, etc.	2,000	
TOTAL FURNISHING		25,500
TOTAL BUILDING COST		$150,500

Financing

Mortgages	$100,000	
Cash in property	25,000	
Cash on acct., equipment	3,500	
Deferred payment	22,000	
TOTAL		150,500

Annual Income

1,000 seats filled 4× per week @ 25¢	52,000	
Rent of two stores @ $75/month	1,800	
TOTAL		53,800

Annual Expenses

6% $100,000 mortgage (approx.)	6,000	
Taxes, water, rent, etc.	2,000	
Film cost ($150/wk)	7,800	
Salaries: manager	50	
organist	40	
ushers	40	
cashier	20	
janitor & projectionist	50	
	200/wk	

Total salaries	10,400	
Advertising ($60/wk)	3,120	
Heat and light ($40/wk)	2,080	
Depreciation/replacement	3,000	
TOTAL EXPENSES		$34,400

Profit

Profit first year	19,400	(Income less expenses)
Less equipment payment	11,000	
NET PROFIT FIRST YEAR		8,400
Profit second year	19,400	
Less equipment payment	11,000	
NET PROFIT SECOND YEAR		8,400
Profit succeeding years		$19,400

SOURCE: George S. Falkenstein, "Financial Plan for a 1,000-Seat Theatre," *Film Daily Yearbook of Motion Pictures* (1928), p. 928 (reprinted from *Exhibitor's Herald*).

Nitrate fires in theaters, studios, and film exchanges were a constant hazard. Director James Durkin stands amid the ruins of the Famous Players Twenty-sixth Street Studio in Manhattan, destroyed by fire on 11 September 1915.

added nickel charged but from the 40 percent rise in weekly attendance that occurred in the five-year interval.

Still, the most visible mark of this boom was unquestionably the select number of
downtown showplaces, the picture palaces that left so strong an impression on several generations of American filmgoers. "The United States in the twenties was
dotted with a thousand Xanadus," wrote theater historian Ben Hall.

> Decreed by some local (or chain-owning) Kubla Khan, these pleasure
> domes gave expression to the most secret and polychrome dreams of a
> whole group of architects who might otherwise have gone through life
> doomed to turning out churches, hotels, banks, and high schools. The
> architecture of the movie palaces was a triumph of suppressed desire and
> its practitioners ranged in style from the purely classic to a wildly aban-
> doned eclectic that could only have come from men who, like the Khan
> himself, "on honeydew had fed, and drunk the milk of Paradise" (*The Best
> Remaining Seats* [New York: Bramhall House, 1961], p. 93).

At first, many of the great film palaces drew on the examples of such elaborate
turn-of-the-century spectacle theaters as the New York Hippodrome. This monstrous
hall, opened in 1905, combined the most modern stage equipment with interior
decoration of rare opulence—at a cost of nearly $4 million to its backer, John "Bet a
Million" Gates. But unlike New York's Metropolitan Opera House or Adler and
Sullivan's Auditorium Theatre in Chicago, the Hippodrome was not designed to
serve an elite audience. Instead, it hoped to fill its 5,200 seats by attracting a huge
and continuing volume of patrons. As we have seen, as early as 1915 statistics indicated that the small theater was an essentially uneconomical proposition. Simple
economic pressures impelled a move to larger and larger playhouses, which soon
grew to rival the Hippodrome itself in scale, and surpass it in decoration.[14]

The sudden emergence of lavish motion-picture houses in the mid-teens was a
shock to patrons of the legitimate stage. In April 1914 *New York Times* theater critic
Victor Watson covered the glittering opening of the Strand, Broadway's first lavish
picture house: "If anyone had told me two years ago that the time would come when
the finest looking people in town would be going to the biggest and newest theater
on Broadway for the purpose of seeing motion pictures, I would have sent them down
to my friend, Dr. Minas Gregory, at Bellevue Hospital. The doctor runs the city's
bughouse, you know."[15]

These picture palaces soon differentiated themselves from earlier legitimate
houses, as well as from the modest film theaters described by John Klaber in 1915.
Their large and distinctive facades (remotely descended from the nickelodeons)
served to announce their special form of entertainment with elaborate marquees and
bursts of electrical signage. Unlike large opera houses or concert halls, their performances tended to be continuous, so arrangements needed to be made for handling
waiting multitudes. This situation led to the design of vast lobbies, often more
opulent and intriguing than the auditorium interiors themselves. A few of the new
design features of the picture palaces were more prosaic, such as the placement of the
projection booth. For best effect, these could not simply be tucked into a disused
balcony, a lesson some were still learning as late as 1926. That year, MGM staged the
Los Angeles premier of BEN-HUR at the Biltmore, a legitimate house, with the

Atmospheric theaters mimicked a variety of exotic styles, as here in the Aztec The-atre, San Antonio, Texas. From "The Showman," a special theater supplement to Motion Picture News, 4 March 1927, p. 746.

The steep projection angle employed in this booth would have resulted in severe keystoning distortion onscreen. Nonetheless, James R. Cameron in the second edition of his Motion Picture Projection *(1921) highlights the installation as "An Up-to-Date Projection Room" (p. 88).*

projectors hanging in the second balcony. The steep angle of projection caused so much distortion that "the elongated heads and necks of our screen favorites is [sic] indeed horrible to behold."[16]

In the absence of reserved seating, crowd-control devices were ingenious. Each seat at the Roxy was wired to a central console, so the house staff could immediately direct patrons to new vacancies. If there were still no seats available, customers could pass the time in comfortable lounges, decorated with imported antiques, or the reconstructed interiors of millionaires' mansions. It was not unusual for a very elegant house to offer a fully staffed nursery, or even a hospital.[17]

The trademark of the picture palace, especially in the silent era, was the elaborate theater organ known as "the Wurlitzer Unit Orchestra," or more commonly, "the mighty Wurlitzer." This instrument had the ability to multiply the octave pitches of each rank of pipes, and as theaters vied with one another for the most splendid console, audiences often found themselves blown out of their seats. Some of these theaters were staffed with orchestras of over one hundred pieces, rivaling the size of the finest symphonies, but only at a picture palace could a theatergoer hear Jesse Crawford play the Wurlitzer.[18]

Among the most significant innovations in these large picture houses was something that appealed to neither eye nor ear. According to one historian, Balaban and Katz were able to dominate the Chicago film scene largely through the introduction of air conditioning in their theaters beginning in 1921. This convenience allowed them to operate throughout the summer, negating the seasonal attendance swings suffered by their rivals (see table 2.2).[19]

The design of most of these houses was in the hands of a small group of specialized firms. Some tended to work for specific chains, others became known for their signature design treatments, and a few came to dominate theater construction in entire cities or territories. Thomas Lamb was among the first widely recognized picture-palace designers. Often working in the tradition of Robert Adam, Lamb was responsible for such important New York houses as the Regent (1913), the Strand (1914), the Rialto (1916), the Rivoli (1917), and the Capitol (1919). "Lamb softened formal classicism by coating nearly every surface with delicate floral bas-relief," wrote historian David Naylor. The great classicist of picture-palace designers, he ultimately came to design most of the houses in the Loew's chain.[20]

The firm of Rapp and Rapp was just as closely associated with Chicago and the Balaban and Katz circuit. Their Chicago Theatre (1921) was the flagship of the chain, although its French Renaissance decor was probably surpassed by the Tivoli, which they built on the South Side of town the same year. Renowned for their "Sun King style," Rapp and Rapp were among the first to reflect the great size (and cost) of their houses by increasing the scope and scale of decorative ornamentation. The New York Paramount (1926) was probably their best-known eastern house.[21]

More fantastic still was John Eberson, whose "imitations of exotic environments" were the most fanciful and individualistic of picture palaces. These "atmospheric" theaters were not simply developments of some historical style but witty concoctions of fantasy and reality that borrowed freely from any and all traditions. The Houston Majestic (1923) was the first of these, a theater built to represent an ancient Italian garden, with a ceiling made to look like an open sky across which traveled stars and cloud formations. Eberson was at his best in the Chicago Capitol (1925) and the Miami Olympic (1926), and few who visited it would forget his Loew's Paradise (1929), with its surreal treatment of the Italian Renaissance.[22]

There were others, notably B. Marcus Priteca, designer for the Pantages chain on the West Coast, and C. Howard Crane, a prolific worker who hit his stride at the end of the silent era with theaters like the United Artists in Los Angeles. But most houses simply echoed the neoclassical, baroque, or atmospheric styles developed by the top firms. Exotic theaters in less fashionable modes, like Grauman's Egyptian (1922) and Chinese (1927), San Antonio's Aztec (1926), or the Navajo-inspired Kimo in Albuquerque (1927), offered occasional variants on the traditional revival approach. A theater designed in a contemporary style, like the art deco Carthay Circle in Los Angeles (1926), was almost unheard of.

The greatest of silent picture palaces was unquestionably the Roxy in New York, the 6,214-seat "cathedral of the motion picture," which opened just in time to see the end of the silent cinema. Unlike most of its great rivals, the Roxy was not intended as part of a chain. Instead, it was a promotion successfully floated by Herbert Lubin, a failed motion-picture producer. Lubin conceived the idea of the world's largest theater, raised the initial financing, and enticed S. L. "Roxy" Rothapfel (sometimes "Rothafel"), the most prominent showman in pictures, to come over from the Capitol. (One week before the opening Lubin sold his interest to William Fox, who was looking for a New York flagship for his chain.) Rothapfel worked closely with the architect, Walter W. Ahlschlager, and the designer, Harold W. Rambusch, to ensure that the building set a standard for opulence. Ben Hall characterized this standard as

A rendering of the Roxy Theatre prepared by the office of the architect, W. W. Ahlshlager, 1927.

"an exuberant grafting of Renaissance details on Gothic forms with fanciful Moorish overtones." The exterior suggested the cathedral of Valladolid, and the interior "the inside of a great bronze bowl." Patrons who were not intimidated by a trip under the massive, five-story tall rotunda faced a squadron of ushers drilled by a retired Marine Corps captain. The statuary, the carpeting, the mural decorations, all worked together to create an effect of overwhelming grandeur, but the frame had grown far more important than any picture. This was no accident, but the conscious plan of the theater's manager and owners.[23]

According to the director of the Publix Theatre Managers Training School:

> People come to the motion picture theater to live an hour or two in the land of romance. They seek escape there from the humdrum existence of daily life. Civilization has crowded from their lives other places where formerly they could get mental rest and imaginative release. . . . However, people realize with gratitude that for a small charge they can be picked up on a magic carpet and set down in a dream city amidst palatial surroundings where worry and care can never enter, where pleasure hides in every colored shadow and music scents the air (John F. Barry, "The Motion Picture Theatre," quoted in *Theatre Historical Society Annual* 3 [1976], p.3).

He might have mentioned that they could also see a film, but to the showmen of the era this fact was hardly an indispensable part of the evening's entertainment. As John Grierson wrote in 1926, with only a touch of irony:

> I think the big theaters have dislocated the cinema world for the moment, and I have a mind to say that the pictures are not good enough for the theaters. Too often I have been ushered into one of these palaces like a princelet, and mounted the great staircase like a modern Jacob, only to find the picture so trivial that I had to unusher myself and descend five minutes after. The hospitality was excellent, the meal terrible. The mountain was laboring hugely and giving birth to mice ("The Industry at a Parting of the Ways," *Motion Picture News*, 13 November 1926, p. 1842).

The Audience

Unfortunately, we have better information on the location of theaters and the makeup of theater programs than on the audiences who patronized them. Even in the crudest terms, estimates of the number of paid admissions are not reliable before 1922. Prior to this date, most figures given are extrapolations from federal admissions-tax receipts, which lump together all forms of entertainment. The standard figures provided by the *Film Daily* show a rising curve that begins to climb sharply after 1925 (fig. 2.1).

Who were these people? By 1919 theater men and sociologists alike had begun conducting their own surveys, although for very different ends. The attendance of children at motion-picture shows had been a concern of reformers since nickelodeon days, and studies by non-industry groups tended to center on the impact of films on

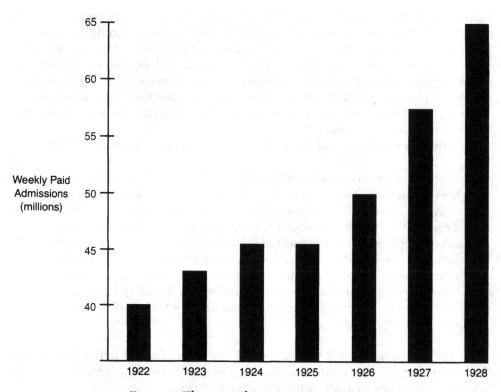

Fig. 2.1. Theater Admissions, 1922–1928*

this sector of the population. Within the industry, exhibitors were most concerned to poll audience preferences, hoping to use the information to help them in programming or in negotiating with their suppliers.

The Phelan study in Toledo suggested that this audience was relatively young. One exhibitor reported that two-thirds of his daily attendance consisted of young people aged ten to twenty. Since unaccompanied children younger than seventeen were not permitted by law, Phelan used that age as a reference point. His survey of managers indicated that 40 percent of their audience were males above seventeen, 35 percent were females above seventeen, and 25 percent were children under seventeen. The managers admitted that half of these children were unaccompanied. That same year Harold Corey, writing in *Everybody's Magazine*, claimed, "The backbone of today's business is the attendance of young people from seventeen to twenty-three years of age. At twenty-three other interests develop."[24]

A decade later, Alice Miller Mitchell analyzed the filmgoing habits of 10,052 grade-school- and high-school-age children in Chicago. Mitchell also concluded that as children grew older, they attended the movies less frequently, with fifth- through eighth-graders attending more heavily than high-school students. The Mitchell study was among the first to attempt a statistical correlation between motion-picture attendance and criminal activity. Here one can read of the reformatory inmate who committed a series of holdups because "I *had* to have money for the movies." This young felon attended the pictures almost every day (when at liberty), and his favorite films were THE BIRTH OF A NATION and THE PHANTOM OF THE OPERA (1925). Mitchell also reveals that 27.2 percent of Chicago's juvenile delinquents went to the

*SOURCE: *Film Daily Yearbook of Motion Pictures* (1951), p. 90.

movies five to seven times a week, while only 0.4 percent of local Boy Scouts did the same. More significant is the fact that the vast majority of children (69.2 percent) attended neighborhood theaters almost exclusively, avoiding the downtown Loop and its picture palaces. Indeed, only 3.3 percent of Chicago Boy Scouts might ever be found in a Loop theater, if these figures are to be believed. This means that the smaller neighborhood houses were the ones most heavily dependent on the patronage of children. "If it were not for the children, I should have to close my theater as 85 per cent of my audience is made up of them," one exhibitor admitted. Mitchell provides convincing accounts of the many ruses used by young Chicagoans to gain admission, along with the assertion that over 20 percent clogged the theaters by sitting through at least two shows.[25]

Children's attendance figures reported by Mitchell at the end of the silent era (when general audience figures were rising) are among the heaviest of any survey in this period. She found 64.1 percent attending once or twice a week and 9.7 percent attending three or four times. By comparison, a 1915 study in Portland, Oregon,

Children made up a significant portion of the audience in small neighborhood theaters, which used garish poster displays to attract them to daily program changes of Westerns and serials. This photo was taken outside a small New York theater in 1924.

showed only 28.4 percent of children attending twice a week and 5.6 percent going three times. In Portland in 1915, 9.5 percent of children did not go to the movies at all, while only 1.7 percent abstained according to the Mitchell study a dozen years later.[26]

The largest children's sampling was undertaken in 1923 by the Russell Sage Foundation, the National Board of Review of Motion Pictures, and Associated First National Exhibitors. It surveyed 37,000 high-school students in 76 cities across the country (table 2.4). The last part of the survey turned up interesting geographical biases. Boys and girls of central, eastern, and western states voted overwhelmingly for THE FOUR HORSEMEN; boys and girls in New England and girls in the South preferred WAY DOWN EAST; boys in the South supported THE BIRTH OF A NATION. A strong preference is apparent for the films of D. W. Griffith, whose work constitutes one-third of the entire list.

When asked about their favorite actors, the boys predictably voted for action and Western stars (Fairbanks was on top), while the girls supported romantic heroes (Valentino). But Wallace Reid came in second on both lists, unique in his ability to appeal strongly to both sexes.

That same year a more localized poll was conducted in Evansville, Indiana, and published in *The Educational Screen*. While the general preferences given in the Russell Sage study appear again, the Evansville survey included grade-school as well as high-school students and revealed significant shifts in attendance between these groups. In a sampling of 1,645 high-school and 3,354 grade-school students, it was found that the boys' average weekly attendance dropped from 1.6 to 1.3 times per week when they entered high school, while that of the girls rose from 1.5 to 1.6. This is one of the few early pieces of evidence indicating an increasing feminization of film

The aura of luxuriant efficiency sought by picture-palace operators was assured by teams of uniformed service employees. From Harold B. Franklin, Motion Picture Theatre Management *(New York: Doran, 1927), p. 136.*

SERVICE EMPLOYEES

TABLE 2.4 RESULTS OF NATIONAL HIGH SCHOOL STUDENTS' POLL, 1923

Film Attendance	Boys	Girls
Films attended each week (average)	1.23	1.05
Attend twice per week or less (%)	83	88
Attend more than four times per week (%)	2.6	0.9
Attend with friends (%)	49	53
Attend alone (%)	26	7
Attend with family (%)	25	40

Favorite Class of Story	Boys (%)	Girls (%)
Western and frontier	30.0	15.6
Comedies	27.0	19.4
Detective stories	18.6	10.7
Love stories	11.5	27.4
Society life	5.5	18.3
Serials	4.8	4.2
Sad-ending stories and tragedies	2.6	4.4

Type of Movie Criticized	Boys (%)	Girls (%)
Slapstick (or vulgar)	23.8	34.5
Not true to life	20.6	12.0
Mushy (oversentimental)	18.2	10.6
Bad artistically	18.2	8.8
Immoral (sex)	10.5	11.2
Murder and shooting	8.1	21.6
Brutality	0.8	1.3

"Best Picture They Had Ever Seen" (Poll)	Boys	Girls
1. THE FOUR HORSEMEN OF THE APOCALYPSE (1921)	2,111	2,394
2. WAY DOWN EAST (1920)	927	2,648
3. THE SHEIK (1921)	751	2,137
4. OVER THE HILL (1920)	999	1,432
5. THE BIRTH OF A NATION (1915)	1,646	784
6. THE THREE MUSKETEERS (1921)	1,421	445
7. A CONNECTICUT YANKEE (1921)	658	339
8. THE OLD NEST (1921)	220	669
9. HUMORESQUE (1920)	291	598
10. HEARTS OF THE WORLD (1918)	390	283
11. ORPHANS OF THE STORM (1922)	196	420
12. SMILIN' THROUGH (1922)	78	536
Total	9,688	12,685

SOURCE: *Film Daily Yearbook of Motion Pictures* (1924), p. 351.

audiences beginning in the high-school years. There are few reliable statistics on the proportion of women in silent-film audiences, but the Evansville survey suggests that males gradually lost interest during their teens. In 1920 W. Stephen Bush reported in the *New York Times* that 60 percent of film audiences were women, but in 1927 the *Moving Picture World* set the figure as high as 83 percent.[27]

While fan magazines organized popularity polls as circulation-building devices, industry surveys attempted to gain hard information that could inform bidding and other industry practices. The Kinema Theatre in Fresno, California (population 45,000), conducted one of the most methodical such surveys in 1924, distributing questionnaires to its patrons, hiring investigators to canvass 1,600 townspeople, and carrying out a special "across the tracks" survey among the town's German- and Russian-speaking communities, from which the theater drew much of its audience.[28] This allowed the management to compare the tastes of regular theatergoers with those of the community at large. For example, in terms of genre preference, regular theatergoers had a far higher opinion of comedies than the average resident, while foreign-speaking audiences favored them most of all (table 2.5).

Attendance statistics in Fresno seem very high, with 74.4 percent of regular theatergoers attending once or twice a week, while 31 percent of the general community showed up just as frequently. According to the small "across the tracks" sample (thirty interviews), 80 percent of foreign-speaking residents attended once or twice a week. It would be interesting to know what other entertainment options were available in Fresno in 1924. Patrons of the Kinema Theatre (which was a 1,400-seat house, the largest in town) were asked what special features of this theater appealed to them:

music	28.3%	pictures	10.0%
courtesy	18.5%	lighting	5.3%
seat comfort	17.7%	prestige	4.8%
beauty	15.1%		

These figures seem characteristic of many picture houses in this era. The Kinema was able to differentiate itself from its rivals primarily through its musical program, with its general opulence another important factor. Only 10 percent of its patrons came because they preferred the line of pictures shown there.[29]

TABLE 2.5   FRESNO SURVEY, 1924: GENRE PREFERENCES (%)

Genre	Filmgoers	Community	Foreign-speaking
Mystery	22.2	—	—
Melodrama	21.1	48.6	18.4
Comedy	18.5	6.8	42.1
Historical	15.1	22.4	37.0
Sex Drama	11.9	—	—
Costume	10.1	22.0	2.5

SOURCE: *Film Daily Yearbook of Motion Pictures* (1925), p. 59.

The samples are not directly comparable. No one would admit a preference for sex dramas in a face-to-face interview, and the mystery option was offered only in the theatergoers' questionnaire.

TABLE 2.6 HEPNER SURVEY, 1928: GENRE PREFERENCES (%)

Genre	General public	College students	Both groups
Comedy	20	25	22
Melodrama	20	18	19
Historical	21	17	19
Mystery	15	23	18
Sex drama	15	8	13
Western	5	6	5
Costume	4	3	4

SOURCE: *Film Daily Yearbook of Motion Pictures* (1929), p. 896.

In 1928 Professor H. W. Hepner had his students conduct another survey, using a questionnaire very similar to that of the Fresno study. The sample of 600 was 58 percent male, and 41 percent of respondents were college students. When they were asked, "What features about your favorite theater appeal to you?" the results were similar to those in Fresno four years earlier:[30]

music	43%	beauty	4%
seat comfort	24%	lighting	3%
pictures	17%	courtesy	3%
prestige	6%		

One can speculate on how the high percentage of college students might have affected the rising importance of the film (or the declining importance of courtesy). The significance of the musical portion of the show has also shown a marked increase, however.

For certain questions, the response of the college students was broken down separately, as in the obligatory genre question, "What kind of pictures do you like best?"(table 2.6).

The students' preference for comedies and mysteries, and relative lack of interest in dramatic and historical subjects, suggests the response of the regular theatergoers in the Fresno survey; however, no statistics are offered here on frequency of attendance. Nor is any attention given to the tastes of children in either poll, although, as we have seen, they made up a significant portion of the silent-film audience.

While these data are scattered and incomplete, they suggest that, when asked, children claimed to prefer Westerns (boys), love stories (girls), and comedies; college students favored comedies and mysteries, and the theatergoers of one small California town preferred mysteries, melodramas, and comedies. The only group that expressed any preference for serious drama was made up of those who did not go to the movies very often. Were these avowed feelings actually translated into box-office support for comedies and melodramas and neglect of serious dramas and costume pictures? It is very difficult to judge with certainty which films in this period were the best box-office performers. In the early years of features, most pictures would have been sold outright by producers, as was the case with THE BIRTH OF A NATION, generally assumed to be the biggest box-office success of the silent era. While surviving records tell us how much money was returned to its producers, there is no way

Six-sheet, three-sheet, and even twenty-four-sheet posters advertise the run of THE BIRTH OF A NATION *at the Majestic Theatre, Peoria, Illinois, 9 January 1916.*

of knowing what amount was actually paid in at box offices, because no such records were kept. That is the figure we would need to know in order to gauge the "popularity" of THE BIRTH OF A NATION.

Eventually, distributors demanded a percentage of the box-office take, but such records do not survive for all releases. Even when they do, it is dangerous to make comparisons among the releases of various firms. For example, a Universal picture would have to sell far more seats to net its producers $100,000 than would an MGM film because an MGM release would have immediate access to the downtown Loew's picture palaces, while Universal could only buy into such a situation at unfavorable terms. In addition, Universal's distribution apparatus was more heavily oriented to the country theaters, where admission prices were lower. So even if we had reliable figures giving the net returns on all films of this period, we would still be unable to judge how many seats were sold. And only this "voting with the feet" could show us the impact on the general public of particular films and stars of the day.

James Mark Purcell, in an unpublished study, has attempted to correlate the available figures and combine them with such other data as exhibitors' reports appearing in the trade papers. For this book he has provided an approximate ranking of the most popular attractions of 1922–1927:[31]

1922

1. ROBIN HOOD
2. ORPHANS OF THE STORM
3. TESS OF THE STORM COUNTRY
4. BLOOD AND SAND
5. OLIVER TWIST
6. DR. JACK
7. SMILIN' THROUGH
8. ONE EXCITING NIGHT
9. FOOLISH WIVES
10. MANSLAUGHTER

1923

1. THE COVERED WAGON
2. THE TEN COMMANDMENTS
3. THE HUNCHBACK OF NOTRE DAME
4. SAFETY LAST
5. WHY WORRY?
   ROSITA

1924

1. THE IRON HORSE
2. THE SEA HAWK
3. THE THIEF OF BAGDAD
4. HOT WATER
   GIRL SHY
5. AMERICA

1925

1. THE BIG PARADE
2. THE GOLD RUSH
3. THE FRESHMAN
4. DON Q, SON OF ZORRO
5. THE PHANTOM OF THE OPERA
   THE MERRY WIDOW
6. THE LOST WORLD
   CHARLEY'S AUNT

1926

1. BEN-HUR
2. WHAT PRICE GLORY?
3. BEAU GESTE
4. FOR HEAVEN'S SAKE
   THE BLACK PIRATE
   SON OF THE SHEIK

1927

1. WINGS
2. THE JAZZ SINGER
3. KING OF KINGS
4. THE KID BROTHER
5. THE GAUCHO
6. UNCLE TOM'S CABIN

These listings indicate that, for this period at least, the dominant genres were period spectacle and comedy. Except for some of the comedies, there are very few films here with contemporary settings. If audiences did have an aversion to historical costume dramas, it must have been to the wave of imitations that followed these successes. Harold Lloyd and Douglas Fairbanks appear as the most consistently popular stars, and the only film that could possibly be called a sleeper is CHARLEY's AUNT, a Sydney Chaplin comedy that appears to have done quite well in the non-urban areas. The fact that there are so few surprises here demonstrates just how tightly knit all aspects of production, distribution, and exhibition had become. There was little opportunity now for the innovative little picture from an unexpected corner. THE MIRACLE MAN, said to have been the top grosser of 1919, would not have reached so many screens by the end of the silent era.

The Show

The high rates of attendance in this period, with most of the population turning out once or twice a week, could only be fueled by constant changes of program. While so-called pre-release engagements of a few major spectacles such as THE TEN COMMANDMENTS, WINGS, or BEN-HUR tied up some theaters for months, even most picture palaces typically changed their feature every week. For example, Grauman's Chinese Theatre in Los Angeles ran THE CIRCUS from 28 January through 11 May 1928. But down the street at the larger Egyptian Theatre, this same period was devoted to one-week runs of BABY MINE, MY BEST GIRL, LOVE, WEST POINT, THE DOVE, THE LAST COMMAND, THE STUDENT PRINCE, THE SHOWDOWN, THE BIG CITY, CHICAGO, SORRELL AND SON, LEGION OF THE CONDEMNED, THE CROWD, THE DIVINE WOMAN, and SADIE THOMPSON. And, away from the big first-run houses, even more frequent changes were the rule. The *Motion Picture News* found in 1916 that only 3 percent of theaters ran their program an entire week, while 36 percent changed six times per week. The average number of changes per week was five, a figure that had gradually decreased to three and a half by 1922, when 10 percent of theaters kept a film for an entire week.[32]

This move from daily to weekly changes began as soon as feature-length pictures had established themselves in the market. Walter W. Irwin, in charge of distribution for VLSE (Vitagraph-Lubin-Selig-Essanay) in 1915, offered figures suggesting that the new system of weekly changes could be far more profitable—providing that

TABLE 2.7 PROFITABILITY OF DAILY AND WEEKLY CHANGES (1915)

	Daily Change		Weekly Change	
Average receipts/day	$300		$550	
Film rental/day		25		50
Advertising/day		50		100
Overhead/day		100		100
Total expenses		175		250
Profits	$125		$300	

SOURCE: Lanning Masters, "Marketing the Movies," Harper's Weekly, January 1916. Irwin claimed that his figures came from a specific southern theater.

theaters could afford to double their film-rental and advertising budgets (table 2.7).

Despite these attractive statistics, the Connick report, in 1919, continued to show high turnover rates. Of 15,000 theaters cited, only 160 (1 percent) were said to lease films for an entire week, 2,500 (16 percent) were leasing for half a week, and the balance were changing daily. These figures were provided by Famous Players–Lasky, whose clientele would have been more "upscale" than most.[33]

With such frequent changes, word-of-mouth publicity was of little value. Monthly fan magazines might be able to create some advance interest, but the daily reviewers had little influence. For this reason, one-quarter of exhibitors felt that the quality of the feature was of no importance to the box office. Audiences would arrive anyway, drawn to a particular theater by its unchanging amenities: comfort or music. If a particular film was bad, there was little time for such news to be circulated, and soon

The Rialto, an 800-seat Stanley theater in Germantown, Pennsylvania, featured a daily change of program in 1916. Postcards sent to a mailing list of eager patrons announced the week's attractions. A Paramount release was shown on Monday, Wednesday, and Friday; a Universal on Tuesday; and a Triangle on Thursday and Saturday. The theater was closed on Sunday.

DISTINCTIVE CREATIONS

Rialto

Booked Thru Stanley Company

GERMANTOWN AVE. and TULPEHOCKEN ST.

Week COMMENCING MONDAY APRIL 17th	
SUPERB **MONDAY** PICTURE	**MARGUERITE CLARK** In a Drama of Circus Life **"STILL WATERS"**
BLUEBIRD **TUESDAY** PICTURE	**MARIE WALCAMP** In Adaptation of Booth Tarkington's **"THE FLIRT"**
FEATURE **WEDNESDAY** EXTRAORDINARY	**SESSUE HAYAKAWA** The Celebrated and Popular Japanese Actor in **"THE TYPHOON"**
TRIANGLE **THURSDAY** PICTURE	**BESSIE BARRISCALE** And WILLIAM DESMOND in **"Bullets and Brown Eyes"**
FAMOUS **FRIDAY** PICTURE	**LOU-TELLEGEN** In Picturization of "The Red Mirage" **"THE UNKNOWN"**
TRIANGLE **SATURDAY** PICTURE	**DOUGLAS FAIRBANKS** In a Remarkably Interesting Production **"His Picture in the Papers"**
Matinee Daily at 2.30	**10c.** Admission **10c.** ANY TIME — Evenings Continuous 7 to 11

something else would be running in its place anyway. Given such conditions, the immediate appeal of certain stars was very important. Beyond that, the weekly grosses might be affected by the quality of exhibitor stunts and advertising.[34]

Silent-film-era advertising followed patterns established by nineteenth-century circuses and traveling shows. Paid newspaper ads were small, a heavy emphasis was placed on large and colorful posters, and exhibitor stunts were employed wherever possible. When the European war closed access to the Bavarian quarries that had supplied stones for lithography, the printing process for advertising posters in America became photomechanical. This situation temporarily reduced quality, but made such posters cheap and easy to print. The burgeoning motion-picture industry of the late teens took full advantage of these new conditions to order print runs of unprecedented size. The formats adopted by the American Printers' Congress in 1911 had become standard by the feature-picture era. The "one-sheet" (27" x 41") was by far the most common issue, posted singly or in combination in any convenient location. "Three-sheets" (41" x 81") and "six-sheets" (82" x 81") were reserved for poster hoardings around town, although in the early days they might appear in front of theater lobbies on specially built display stands. Small-town theaters continued to crowd their sidewalks with such large posters throughout the silent era. The "twenty-four-sheet," reminiscent of the advertising campaigns of Buffalo Bill's Wild West show at the turn of the century, was reserved for billboard use.[35]

The Morgan Lithograph Company of Cleveland, Ohio, was the most important supplier of such paper, typically running 8,000 to 12,000 one-sheets, 300 three-sheets, 300 six-sheets, and 1,000 twenty-four-sheets if the need arose.[36] Most of these posters were intended for use away from the theater, and a line of smaller advertising cards was created for use within the theater itself. These included lobby cards (11" x 14"), usually issued in a set of eight, inserts (14" x 36") and half-sheets (22" x 28"). Window cards (14" x 22") were cardboard stand-ups intended for posting in friendly shop windows, and a blank space was left at the top to indicate the theater location and date. It was not unusual to have a choice of designs available within each format. For example, Harold Lloyd's THE FRESHMAN offered a pair of one-sheets, with "style A" featuring Lloyd and Jobyna Ralston in a traditional romantic two-shot and "style B" showing a humorous close-up of Lloyd alone. Three-sheet "A" featured the basted-tuxedo gag, while the "B" style emphasized the college angle. Exhibitors were expected to choose whichever combinations would be most effective with local audiences. This "paper" was to be purchased directly from the film exchange (in later years specialized agencies would lease such material on a regional basis). Pressbooks describing these items, and including prepared publicity copy for insertion in local papers (even prepared reviews), were sent to exhibitors well in advance of the show date.[37]

One of the most elaborate campaigns was mounted for Universal's THE PHANTOM OF THE OPERA, which offered a choice of eight different one-sheets, six three-sheets, a pair of six-sheets, and four different twenty-four-sheets. How many of each were printed is unknown, but in 1919 that studio distributed 158,000 posters of all kinds for BLIND HUSBANDS, including 191 billboard-sized twenty-four-sheets in New York City alone.[38]

The quality of the design involved was a constant issue throughout this period. At times, studios would hire well-known illustrators in an effort to emphasize the artistry of their productions. During 1914–1915 Mutual announced that they had em-

The pressbook for Harold Lloyd's THE FRESHMAN (*Pathé, 1925*) *offered posters in a range of sizes and styles.*

ployed Scotson Clark, and Metro had a large department that is said to have included Edward Penfield. But the advertising men found the "artistic designs" to have inadequate drawing power. An article included in the pressbook for one of Paramount's 1923 releases confronts this situation rather bluntly:

> Not long ago a big picture company put out a 24-sheet which met with the approval of all the art critics, professional and amateur. It was a beautiful thing, the head of the star lithographed from a painting by one of the best known artists in the world, not alone America. One of these art critics, an amateur, come up to us [sic] and said, "Why don't you get out something like that?"
>
> We replied that we didn't want to.
>
> "Now that's a real poster," he said. "Look at the expression, the coloring, the slight cubist design in the background. It's a work of art."
>
> We had to admit it.
>
> Then we asked him a question. "Did you see the picture?"

The critic admitted that he had not, although he had recently attended a Thomas Meighan film after seeing the nondescript poster put out to advertise it. The lesson is clear: "Paramount's policy is to make paper that will draw the people to your box-office. We don't care how we do it just so it is done. If the ugliest poster in the world will keep them flocking we will give you the ugliest poster in the world." This language must have seemed very demoralizing to the poster staff, which, the same article tells us, included William Hannaman, a window-card specialist; Frederick Jehle, "a genius at colors"; and Joseph Fronder, designer of the posters for THE COVERED WAGON (1923), "one of the best portrayers of animals since the immortal Bonheur."[39]

No matter what their policy on high art, most studio advertising departments continued to maintain a staff of house artists. But gradually poster printers like Morgan came to take on more of the work themselves, dividing the design tasks in order to create an anonymous house style—one person handling portraits, another lettering, a third backgrounds and figures. By the late twenties, a poster with a strongly personal style, like John Held, Jr.'s, designs for TIN HATS or BATTLING BUTLER (both 1926), would be a rare exception.[40]

While the poster remains a key element of motion-picture advertising today, the heavy use of exhibitor stunts employed by showmen in this period has long been out of favor. Harry Reichenbach was justly considered the king of movie press agents due to the audacity (and success) of the stunts he devised in the late teens and early twenties. It was Reichenbach who promoted THE RETURN OF TARZAN (1920) by sneaking a lion into New York's Belleclaire Hotel, then leaving the management with the problem of evicting him. It was Reichenbach who convinced several New York papers that a group of supposed Turks he had registered at another Manhattan hotel were really in town searching for a lost virgin. This eventually caused the police to drag the lake in Central Park (just in time for the release of Universal's THE VIRGIN OF STAMBOUL [1920]), and the state legislature to prohibit the dissemination of false information to the press. In a more subtle vein, Reichenbach was credited with restoring Rudolph Valentino's sagging popularity by the simple expedient of urging the star to grow a beard. The ensuing tabloid commotion was inevitable. By 1924

John Held artwork for Tin Hats (*MGM 1926*), *as seen on the cover of the* Motion Picture News (*13 November 1926*).

Reichenbach would claim that such stunts were "now practically passé, because of the many amateurish attempts made which ended in crude failures," but few seem to have believed him that time.[41]

Throughout the twenties, pressbooks and trade papers were filled with suggestions for bizarre "exploitation tips." An exhibitor might be urged to rush an ambulance to his theater, which would carry off on a stretcher a "raving maniac," driven crazy from laughing at the comedy featured inside. Ukelele competitions, elaborate parade floats, and mysterious contests and giveaways seem to have been standard local fare. Trade papers were filled with photos and letters from exhibitors across the country proudly displaying some new exploitation stunt. Nor was such garishness reserved for the smaller theaters. At the end of 1927, Jesse Lasky offered a prize of $300 for the best campaign devised for any Paramount picture. The winner was Charles Amos, manager of the Florida Theatre in St. Petersburg, whose 2,400-seat house competed with ten others in the same town.

Two weeks before Clara Bow's Hula (1927) was to be screened, Amos put a twenty-four-sheet atop a downtown building, illuminating it each night with a powerful searchlight. A dozen small cutouts of Clara Bow in costume were placed in soda fountains, beach stands, and shop windows, and as the play date approached these

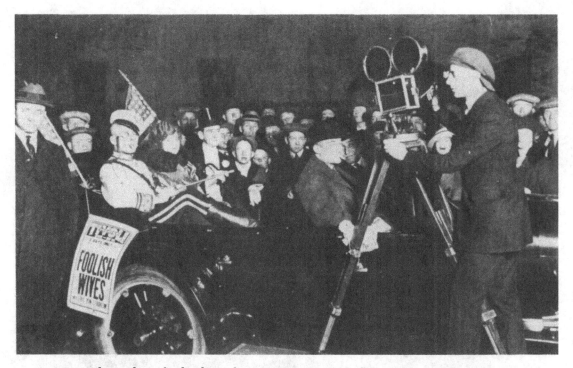

Actors dressed as the leading characters in Universal's Foolish Wives *arrive at Manhattan's Tivoli Theatre, a typical stunt used here to promote a five-day run of the film in 1922.*

displays were tied in with a music store's large window display, where an electric Victrola played Hawaiian music every night. A life-sized cutout of Clara Bow, mechanized to do the hula, was placed in a variety of locations around town. Its real grass skirt, fresh flowers, and shimmying action attracted considerable attention, but the police refused to intervene. As the premiere approached, Amos dropped a forty-foot banner from the roof of his theater, had advance programs inserted into every St. Petersburg dry-cleaning package, and placed announcements on the rear of every taxicab in town. In addition to screening the film's coming-attractions trailer during his regular program, he dressed eight local girls as Hawaiians to produce a "live novelty trailer." In winning the prize, Amos was cited for the low cost of these stunts as well as for their subtlety. And all this was for a two-day run on 12 and 13 October 1927. To gauge the impact of such a campaign on St. Petersburg, remember that Amos was simultaneously promoting a couple of other pictures for showing that same week, while his ten rivals were also doing their best to capture some of the local film audience.[42]

Today it is hard to weigh the value of such exhibitor stunts, but they were highly regarded at the time. It was even considered possible for stunts alone to make a theater competitive. The *Motion Picture News* reported in 1920 that the small Grand Circus Theatre in Detroit, long buried by competition from two of John Kunsky's downtown picture palaces, had staged a major comeback when a new manager gambled heavily on stunt decoration and unusual lobby displays. For the showing of Nomads of the North (1920) he transformed the theater facade into a replica of a

Canadian-wilderness cabin, surrounded by tree and animal cutouts, and plastered with posters and banners. A "pictorial forest fire illusion" was the finishing touch. Fueled by such exploitation, the Grand Circus was able to compete successfully with larger and more comfortable theaters featuring elaborate musical presentations and the finest first-run films.[43]

The one element that linked all silent-movie exhibitions (and that remains the most difficult to recapture for modern audiences) was the musical setting. Music was played to accompany the films, but it also existed by itself as a separate item on the program. This tradition dated from the earliest appearance of projected films on music-hall programs and survived even the storefront nickelodeon era in the form of songs illustrated by lantern slides, an immensely popular added attraction.

The problem of a proper musical accompaniment for the feature was widely discussed throughout this period, since it affected not only the big downtown palaces but the thousands of smaller theaters scattered across the country. The 1922 *Motion Picture News* survey revealed that 29.47 percent of all theaters answering provided some form of orchestra, 45.95 percent boasted an organ, and 24.58 percent accompanied their films only with a piano. But 15 percent of those surveyed failed to answer this question at all, suggesting to the *News* that these houses probably employed no live music at all. Of those reporting an orchestra, the following sizes were indicated:

2 pieces	11.05%	5–10	28.73%
3 "	22.09	11–15	3.32
4 "	13.26	16–25	2.21
5 "	18.24	25–50	1.10

These figures, of course, relate only to those theaters reporting an orchestra; by this account less than 2 percent of the nation's theaters reported an orchestra of over ten pieces in 1922.[44]

Formal musical accompaniment of silent films was a specialized craft that developed, and disappeared, within a decade and a half. Unlike the scoring of sound pictures, its creative center was the theater, with producers offering much help only on the most elaborate releases. House conductor-arrangers needed to have their orchestras ready to accompany a new film every time the program changed, which generally meant at least once a week. While the largest theaters maintained huge music libraries (the Roxy started by purchasing Victor Herbert's personal archive), even the small-town piano player had access to volumes like Erno Rapee's *Motion Picture Moods*. This work was so indexed that the performer could quickly flash from "mother love" to "fire-fighting" as the occasion arose. Such volumes would help if a musician had to face his or her subject cold, but generally accompanists could count on at least some guidance from the distributor.[45]

A completely original orchestral score was the finest, most expensive, and rarest of musical settings. George W. Beynon, in his *Musical Presentation of Motion Pictures* (1921), cites Robert Hood Bowers' score for A DAUGHTER OF THE GODS (1916) as the most memorable up to that time. It took months to write and rehearse, longer than it took to make most feature pictures. More common were "semi-original" scores that combined original themes with stock melodies. Joseph Carl Breil's music for THE BIRTH OF A NATION juxtaposed "The Ride of the Valkyries" with Breil's own love theme "The Perfect Song," famous again years later as the radio theme for "Amos 'n

The T&D Theatre, "Where Pictures and Music Are Proud of Themselves," was a 1,200-seat house in San Jose, California. Its display advertising emphasized the special qualities of its musical presentations (San Jose Mercury Herald, 6 March 1921).

Andy." Arranged for forty pieces, this music was unprecedented in its effective synchronization with the action, a fact that so impressed Beynon that he cited it six years later as "a criterion; no subsequent score has transcended its beauty or comprehensiveness."[46]

Other scores for Griffith pictures, including Carli Elinor's for HEARTS OF THE WORLD (1918), Breil's for INTOLERANCE (1916), and Louis F. Gottschalk's for BROKEN BLOSSOMS (1919), were equally notable, with Griffith taking a personal interest in the arrangement of each. Such scores could be written more quickly and rehearsed more easily, since large segments were simply adapted from existing music already familiar to the musicians. A study of the silent-motion-picture music preserved in the Music Division of the Library of Congress suggests that a favorite orchestration included a flute, an oboe, two clarinets, a bassoon, two French horns, two trumpets, a trombone, drums, and strings. Such disparate films as BEAU GESTE (1926), BROKEN BLOSSOMS, THE THREE MUSKETEERS (1921), and AMERICA (1924) follow this pattern, although one sees occasional variants. Victor Schertzinger's score for CIVILIZATION (1916) used a pair of saxophones instead of clarinets, while Mortimer Wilson's for THE THIEF OF BAGDAD (1924) added harp and tympani. Of Sigmund Romberg's score for FOOLISH WIVES (1922) only a portion of the piano arrangement survives.[47]

Also available were scores that were compiled entirely from stock melodies, and these appear to have been the most common (and the cheapest) of fully orchestrated scores. Yet the extent to which large numbers of exhibitors were prepared to deal with such scores is unclear. In the late teens Paramount entered into an arrangement with the music publisher Schirmer to print scores for 116 films. All lost money because of "lack of support" from exchanges and exhibitors, Beynon notes.[48]

Some films were supplied with an assortment of "musical settings," a group of standard selections loosely placed in a folder. These familiar numbers could be worked out with a minimum of rehearsal time. More popular were "musical cue sheets," suggestions to the conductor giving the approximate time and a short description of each scene. The conductor could then turn to his music library for a full orchestration. By 1921 the cue sheet was the format most frequently supplied to theaters. Through a careful study of the cue sheet, a conductor did not need to screen a film in advance to prepare his own orchestration of stock melodies, a great advantage given the frequency of program changes. A derivative of the cue sheet called the "musical suggestion synopsis" offered the summarizing function of a cue sheet but allowed the conductor to use his own ideas for arrangements.

It must be kept in mind, however, that while modern notions of "authentic" silent film accompaniment are usually based on the evidence of these surviving documents, the scores actually testify to the wishes of producers and distributors, not actual performance practice in most theaters. Abraham H. Lass accompanied silent films at Brooklyn's Eagle Theater from 1923 to 1926. His 1971 recording "Play Me a Movie" is of a very different character than other revival accompaniments by Arthur Kleiner or Carl Davis, for example, whose orchestrations are extremely tightly scored. According to Lass:

> Like most of the neighborhood movie pianists, I never pre-viewed any of
> the pictures. Some motion picture producers supplied cue sheets for each
> picture. These cue sheets provided appropriate music for every scene.
> But I rarely got to see them. They were usually lost in transit or mislaid

by the management. So I was thrown entirely on my own musical resources and perforce became an "instant composer." As each scene flashed
on the screen, I had to decide what music to play for what was *probably*
about to happen, and for what actually did happen (which frequently
wasn't exactly what I had anticipated would happen). Fortunately, the
subtitles and the fairly broad and obvious acting telegraphed enough cues
to me so I could hazard a reasonable guess (Abraham H. Lass, "Piano-
Player for the Silent Movies." Liner note for Asch Records AH 3856
[1971]).

The film industry's voracious musical appetite was soon recognized by the American Society of Composers, Authors, and Publishers (ASCAP), which charged theaters a fee of ten cents per seat per year for access to the catalogues of the fifty leading
publishers. This proved to be a gold mine. By 1926 the chairman of ASCAP's administrative committee could say, "The motion picture theater is the foremost employer of musicians and music—it pays more money for music than any other industry
in the world. Almost more than all others put together."[49]

Nonetheless, some theaters wished to avoid this tax, so obliging distributors supplied cue sheets with alternate selections of "tax-free" music drawn from public-
domain material. In Lady Windermere's Fan (1925), for example, when
Moskowski's "Valse Célèbre" is the suggested taxable selection, Lehar's *Merry
Widow* waltz might be substituted. Theaters resorting to the tax-free route provided
good homes for familiar melodies, but it would not be long before so restricted a
catalogue descended into cliché and self-parody.[50]

Just as with the development of poster design, a battle was soon raging between
populists and classicists in silent-film scoring. George W. Beynon suggested that a
music library should be filled mainly with "concert classics . . . preferably of short
length," and that Beethoven, Liszt, and Berlioz would almost always be preferable to
the hackwork of "photoplay series" composers. The exception was in "agitatos and
hurries," where the hacks were supreme.[51]

By contrast, the *Moving Picture World* only a few years earlier had attacked the
whole idea of offering the classics to film audiences:

> Considering the fact that the average motion picture audience is made up
> largely of people who are unable to appreciate classical music, it seems
> that the moving picture theater is the place for but little classical music.
> It might be safe to say that eighty per-cent of moving picture audiences
> are more bent on hearing the selections and songs that have appealed
> more to our emotions and sentiments. As for example, how many patrons
> of the theater know the "Hungarian Rhapsodie" by Litz [*sic*] or Chopin's
> "Nocturne in G Major"? (Samuel W. Thornton and F. Hyatt Stout, "Mu-
> sic and the Pictures," *Moving Picture World*, 3 April 1915, p. 106).

This was the opinion of a pair of theater pianists, but only a short time later, introducing the works of classical composers would become a minor competition among
the best downtown houses.

What one heard in the smaller theaters was another matter. *The Musician* complained that movie music was the only live music some children ever heard and that
they were not being well served in the average theater:

The instrument is generally old, out of tune, strings dusty, and incapable of producing the correct vibrations. The stool has no back and the pianist plays for hours with the muscles of her back becoming constantly more strained. The light, both night and day, is poor and inadequate, forcing the pianist either to play by memory, ear, or incorrectly by notes which she strives to make out.

During the performance, children in the front row would be kicking their feet wildly (just inches from the piano bench), and the boys would whistle along with the melodies, "generally rag-time, and tawdry at that." The performance of the exhausted and underpaid pianist was predictable:

The lights go out, the first picture appears on the screen, accompanied by a loud pound from the piano; then a series of runs through which the loud pedal is weighed down to its utmost; this bad pedaling is now quite a feature; the pedal is put down at the beginning of a piece and it is safe to say that it is released scarcely half a dozen times, and then more through accident than intention; there is not even the remotest effort at phrasing of any nature (K. Sherwood Boblitz, "Where 'Movie Playing' Needs Reform," *The Musician*, June 1920, pp.7, 29).

A year later, Leopold Godowsky had found little improvement:

The best picture seeps through in the course of time to the smallest of the dime houses . . . but the girl at the piano knows no change or progress in her efforts. She has learned a book of selections and they go for every picture. The continual playing of "The Maiden's Prayer," "Humoresque," and "Hearts and Flowers" is demoralizing. The effect on the emotion of the public is deplorable—it's a narcotic. . . . When I hear the sad melange of emotions in the music which is offered to small town folk, day in and day out and weeks without number and without change, I am almost for a censorship of certain selections ("Criticizes Music in Small Cinemas," *New York Times*, 16 November 1924).

Godowsky was speaking professionally: his son was the holder of several key color-film patents and his daughter a popular film star, so he had more reason to be concerned with the movies than the average concert artist. Unfortunately, he felt that the music he had heard in theaters in Central America, Java, and Turkey was superior to that in small American houses.

In later decades, many who wrote of their experience as part of the silent-film audience were recalling their childhood days in these small neighborhood or country theaters, which seem to have left far deeper an impression than the relatively more sophisticated performances offered in the downtown houses. Essayist E. B. White recalled:

When Anita Stewart went into an early-twentieth-century love sequence, or "mushy business" as it was called in my circles, the pianist was ready for her. He may have been busy with a waltz in E-flat, but with the stealthy arrival of Love on the screen he slipped quietly into D-natural and worked his way into Dvořák's "The Old Mother," wooing us till the tiny goose pimples disturbed our flesh and we almost swooned with beauty and tender desire. . . . If he began to coast after six or seven hours of playing, he would hear loud cries of "Music!" or (if it were a college town) "Better music!" ("Mood Men," *Reader's Digest*, July 1938, p. 87).

There is one further aspect of these accompaniments that deserves mention, namely the survival, until well into the feature era, of onstage lecturers and "ex-

The Bell Electric Piano, a mechanical instrument that provided "good music" in many smaller picture houses during the early feature period (Motion Picture Magazine, *January 1915, p. 152A*).

plainers." As late as 1920, the *New York Times* found five theaters catering to immigrant audiences on the Lower East Side that included a live "presenter" as part of the show. These men and women were on hand not to translate the titles into the language of an immigrant audience, but instead to read the English titles and provide dramatic commentary and explanation throughout the picture: "From behind, the man—he steps up to the lady and grabs her pocketbook. '*Ganef!* Robber! Help! *Ganef!*' she screams." The theater managers felt that this served as a language lesson for their patrons, but the lecturers felt differently. Audiences would complain if too much Yiddish was introduced, they said, citing a growing lack of familiarity with this tongue in the neighborhood. What the audiences really seem to have come for was the interpretive presentation (something most historians ascribe only to the Japanese *benshi* tradition). There are few records of such performances, and it is impossible to know how widespread the use of "presenters" might have been in this period, or whether the practice existed at all outside of certain immigrant neighborhoods. As late as 1926, *benshi* imported from Japan were touring West Coast theaters with performances of Japanese silent films, but they did not accompany non-Japanese films. In any case, the surviving New York presentations in 1920 were quite involved, requiring pre-screening, careful selection and arrangement of material by the "presenters," and a suitably dramatic performance. If displeased, audiences would whistle, stamp their feet, or rhythmically clap their hands.[52]

In larger theaters decorum would prevail, but to modern ears the orchestral arrangements heard there might seem as cliché-ridden as anything found in the single piano houses. Lang and West, in their *Musical Accompaniment of Moving Pictures,* present a lengthy synopsis of the prepared score for Maurice Tourneur's THE ROSE OF THE WORLD (1918), a Paramount release. The action is set in British imperial India, and an original love theme and a Hindu motif are provided, interwoven with popular melodies and light classics. While watching Tourneur's film, the audience heard Massenet's *Élégie,* "Somewhere a Voice Is Calling," "Home, Sweet, Home," two different segments of the *William Tell* Overture, Nevin's "The Rosary," and, accompanying scenes of the return to England, "Sailor Beware!" This program is cited as exemplary.[53]

Still, one wonders how much of their attention the musicians could devote solely to the feature. The traditional picture-palace routine, as perfected by the Balaban and Katz chain in Chicago, also required the orchestra to accompany the shorts, play an overture, support a soloist, and deal with the inevitable large-scale, live stage presentation. The following review of the week's attraction at the Chicago Theatre is revealing:

> 9:15 "Rachmaninoff Selection," overture, directed by Joseph Koestner in the probably vacational absence of Adolphe Dumont and not quite so well.
>
> 9:25 Newspicture views of local baby contest with B-K hookup, followed by shots of Gertrude Ederle swimming the channel.
>
> 9:30 Vincent O'Donnell, boy tenor late of Gus Edwards' corps, singing a couple of numbers he has sung too often in these parts, working in one.
>
> 9:31[*sic*] "The River Road," Bruce scenic, run off with violin lift by Eugene Dubois, veteran first fid at this theater. These things go big at the Chicago.

9:41 Jessie Crawford at the organ playing a probably original (good whether or not) number called "Ain't It a Grand and Glorious Feeling," with slides that might have been drawn by Briggs, who gets a credit line for the number. The number, featuring "Hello, Aloha," is way above the stuff most picture shows are offering with their billion dollar organs. So is Crawford.

9:46 "Sidewalks of New York." Nathaniel Finston's Publix presentation. Finston was ace director for B + K here for years, but his name on the film [sic] didn't elicit a ripple. The act is like the rest of those sightseeing-bus things but more so in that Finston even stuck "Glow Worm" into it. Nor did he fail to provide another of those expository introductory songs which mean so little in these big houses, as he should know.

10:05 "Fine Manners," Paramount picture. Later: "Excess Baggage," Educational comedy ("B-K Routine Still Hits at the Chicago," *Exhibitor's Herald*, 28 August 1926, p. 50).

Exhibitor's Herald saw fit to review this show at length because it already seemed a "last stand" for this mix of entertainment. The other Loop theaters had begun to replace their potpourri programs with jazz-band performances, which were cheaper to mount and more consistent in tone.

The presence of a newsreel, comedy, and scenic on the bill at the Chicago was characteristic of balanced programs in this period. In 1922 the percentage of theaters using such auxiliary attractions was found to be as follows:[54]

two-reel comedy	72.78%	scenic or travel	22.00%
news weekly	58.72	screen magazine	21.09
one-reel comedy	46.22	two-reel drama	13.54
serial	34.76	vaudeville	5.99
animated cartoon	22.72	prologue	2.47

Although it was passed over quickly by the reviewer, it should not be thought that the Rachmaninoff selection at the Chicago was just a musical warm-up. The energy and imagination devoted to even a simple overture at these first-run theaters is enthusiastically recalled in Beynon's account of an early (pre-1921) presentation of the *William Tell* Overture:

With house-lights full and stage-lights up, the Andante movement opened the overture. Gradually the dimmer brought the house lights down as the movement progressed, until the entire theater was in utter darkness when the orchestra reached the Allegro. Then the storm began, intermittently at first, but increasing in force. Lightning flashed and thunder rolled. At this instant, a picture showing a dilapidated homestead deluged with rain was projected upon the screen. This made a pretty effect and concentrated the attention of the audience. As the storm died down, the rain slowly diminished in the picture, the sun came out, and while the orchestra proceeded into the Andante, sheep were seen coming over the horizon. The scene was held until the finish of the movement, which brought the sheep and shepherd into a close-up, and faded out. Immediately the Allegro vivace was

NEW YORK CITY

Rialto Theatre—
Overture—Selection from "La Traviata," by Rialto Orchestra, Hugo Riesenfeld and Leon Vanderhoof conducting.
Current Events—Rialto Magazine.
Vocal—Aria from "La Gioconda," sung by Antonio Rocca, tenor.
Feature—The Furnace—Realart.
Special—Shadow song from "Deborah," by Grace Hoffman.
Comedy—His Wife's Caller—Sunshine.
Organ Solo—"Toccata in C," played by John Priest.

Strand Theatre—
Overture—"Il Guarany" by the Strand Symphony Orchestra, Carl Edouards and Francis W. Sutherland conducting.
Current Events—Strand Topical Review.
Vocal—"Ah Moon of My Delight" from "A Persian Garden," song by Richard Bold, tenor.
Feature—Dinty—Marshall Neilan.
Vocal—"Sweethearts" from "Sweethearts," sung by Mary Mitchell, soprano.
Organ Solo—"Melody of Peace," Ralph H. Brigham and Herbert Sisson, organists.
Next Week—Dangerous Business—Constance Talmadge.

Rivoli Theatre—
Overture—"The Bat" by Rivoli Orchestra, Frederick Stahlberg and Joseph Littau conducting.
Current Events—Rivoli Pictorial.
Novelty—Falstaff's Dream, interpreted by Emanuel List, basso profundo and male chorus.

PLAYING AT THE AMERICA THIS WEEK

Clara Kimball Young

"MID-CHANNEL"

"Four Times Foiled"

AMERICA

Vera Meyers, Grace Eastman, Martha Shelby and Paul Oscard, dancers.
Feature—The Life of the Party—Roscoe Arbuckle.
Special—Thanksgiving Ballet, Martha Shelby and Grace Eastman, dancers.
Comedy—A Tray Full of Trouble—Chester.
Organ Solo—Finale from "Third Sonata," played by Prof. Firmin Swinnen.
Next Week—Heliotrope—Paramount.

Capitol Theatre—
Overture—To Thanksgiving by the Capitol Grand Orchestra, Erno Rapee, conductor. Tableau—Landing of the Pilgrims at Plymouth Rock, Choral interpolation by the Russian Cathedral Choir.
Current Events—Capitol News.
Novelty—Wooden Shoe Dance by Marjorie Thompson and Gladys Waite.
Educational—The Quaint Isle of Marken off the coast of Holland.
Special—Polevtsian Dance and Finale of Second Act from "Prince Igor," by Capitol Ballet Corps, Capitol Grand Orchestra and Russian Cathedral Choir.
Feature—The Great Lover—Goldwyn.
Organ Solo—Capitol Grand Organ, Dr. Alfred Robyn, organist.
Next Week—The Mark of Zorro—Douglas Fairbanks.

Criterion Theatre—
Second week of "Idols of Clay" with Mae Murray.

LOS ANGELES

Grauman's Theatre—
Overture—"The Glow Worm."
Current Events—From Pathe and International News.
Organ—Spooks.
Solo by Henry Murtaugh.
Novelty—Topics of the Day—Pathe.

Comedy—The Scarecrow—Keaton.
Musical—In an Attic.
Tenor and basso soloists sing three numbers.
Feature—Conrad in Quest of His Youth—Thomas Meighan.

Tally's Broadway Theatre—
Overture—"The Bohemian Girl."
Current Events — International News.
Musical—Violin solo.
Novelty—Screen Snapshots.
Vocal—Solo Miss.
Soprano solo by local artist.
Feature—Are All Men Alike—Viola Dana.

Miller's Theatre—
Current Events — From Pathe and Gaumont.
Feature—Madame Peacock—Nazimova.
Presented with a prologue with an effective stage setting. Leonard Van Berg sings "Moments."
Comedy—Dear Departed—Pathe.

Superba Theatre—
Current Events — International News.
Current Events—International News.
Comedy—Twin Crooks—Century.
Short subject—Forest Runners.
Vocal—Goodbye to You.
Solo by Lew Farris.
Feature—Fixed by George—Lyons and Moran.
Next Week—Honor Bound.

Kinema Theatre—
Overture—Operatic selections.
Current Events — International News.
Cartoon—Bray.
Musical—Springtime.
Rendered as vocal solo with organ accompaniment.
Scenic—Banana Special—Bruce Educational.
Comedy—The Song—Mermaid—Educational.
Feature—Good References — Constance Talmadge.
Given with a prologue in which a deck of yacht is provided as a stage setting and from which three songs by a male quartette in sailor costumes is rendered.
Next Week—So Long Letty.

California Theatre—
Overture—"Musical Moments," consisting of selections from various operas with the projection of a novelty film showing clay models of the composers together with words and music of the selection being played at the time the film is being run.
Current Events—From Pathe and Fox Newsreels.
Organ—Motion Charles playing "Coral Sea," with a scene showing sea views being presented at the same time.
Educational—Adopting a Bear—Bray Goldwyn.
Piano — Chopin's "Polonaise," played by Clare Forbes Crane.
Feature—Just Out of College—Jack Pickford.
Comedy—A Flyer Wedding—Monty Banks.

Clune's Broadway Theatre—
Current Events—Selznick News.
Scenic—Chumming with a Chipmunk.
Cartoon—Jerry on the Job—Bray Goldwyn.
Feature—The Soul of Youth—Realart Special.

Symphony Theatre—
Overture—"Down South."
Current Events—Fox News.
Comedy—His Noisy Still—Sunshine.
Cartoon—Farm Efficiency—Mutt and Jeff.
Feature—The Texan—Tom Mix.
Presented with a prologue in which Western plains stage setting is provided. Paul Patton does a rope spinning act and sings cowboy songs.

RIALTO
ALL THIS WEEK
"THE FURNACE"
The Story of a Millionaire Who Married An Actress
HAROLD LLOYD
"High and Dizzy"
RIALTO ORCHESTRA

"With First Run Theatres," a regular feature of the Motion Picture News, *indicates the importance given to musical presentations in these key showplaces (4 December 1920, p. 4227).*

picked up by the orchestra. The lights slowly came up and, as the overture ended in a grand finale, the theater was flooded with light. It provided entertainment of a high order (*Musical Presentation of Motion Pictures* [New York: Schirmer, 1921], pp. 127–128).

The *William Tell* Overture was in fact one of the most frequently heard pieces of music in the silent-film theaters. According to Hugo Riesenfeld, musical director of the Rivoli and the Rialto, the ten most popular overtures were *Tannhauser* (Wagner), *William Tell* (Rossini), the *1812* Overture (Tchaikovsky), the *Second Hungarian Rhapsody* (Liszt), the *Light Cavalry* Overture (von Suppé), the *Marche Slav* (Tchaikovsky), the *Merry Wives of Windsor* (Nicolai), *Orpheus in the Underworld* (Offenbach), *The Queen of Spades* (von Suppé), and the *Irish Rhapsody* (Victor Herbert).[55]

In addition to the overture, it was obligatory for any large theater to offer a major production number, somewhat in the style of a lavish Broadway revue. At times, the tendency was to overproduce such entertainments, swamping the film presentation. Ben Hall describes the opening of Major Edward Bowes's Capitol Theatre in 1919,

Finale of the "Topsy Turvey Revue," the stage presentation that accompanied THE DIVINE WOMAN *at New York's Capitol Theatre in January 1928.*

which, in addition to the usual film shorts and a few warm-up selections featuring Arthur Pryor's seventy-piece orchestra, presented an eleven-act revue before the feature. Staged by Ziegfeld producer Ned Wayburn, this extravaganza featured original music by George Gershwin (including "Swanee," soon picked up by Al Jolson), ballets, rope-twirlers, and soloists like Mae West. The feature picture, HIS MAJESTY, THE AMERICAN, with Douglas Fairbanks, reached the screen at 11:20 P.M. Attacked in the press for its "unwarranted ostentation" and "misdirected talents," the Capitol streamlined its presentation policy the following season, when S. L. Rothapfel was brought in. He reduced the number of acts and emphasized one large production number, often related in some fashion to the weekly feature. On the West Coast such "prologues" had already been introduced by Los Angeles showman Sid Grauman, first at his Million Dollar Theatre in 1918, and later with even more ceremony at his Egyptian and Chinese theaters in Hollywood. The latter were the sites of many of the industry's most lavish picture premieres (a stunt Grauman is usually credited with perfecting).[56]

This "prologue idea" was soon widely imitated, although few theaters could equal Grauman's imagination or Rothapfel's resources. When presenting Fatty Arbuckle in THE LIFE OF THE PARTY (1920) at the Rivoli, Hugo Reisenfeld preceded it with "Falstaff's Dream," a ten-minute prologue whose main themes were lifted from *The Merry Wives of Windsor*. "The choice of number and title were appropriate because of the girth of the hero of the picture as well as of the Shakespearean character," noted one critic.[57] The implied commentary provided by a thematic prologue probably reached its height in Rothapfel's notorious 1921 prologue to THE CABINET OF DR. CALIGARI. Not only did the number frame the movie fore and aft, mimicking the film's formal structure, but it left the audience with the news that Francis was now happily married and working as "a prosperous jeweler in Holstenwall."[58]

In middle-sized theaters, the need to do something to keep up with such presentations soon strained the management's capabilities. Robert E. Sherwood complained that audiences who came to see a film were often "compelled to sit around while several talented recruits from the local high school danced the Sylvia Ballet." In one midwestern theater, he saw a prologue to SCARAMOUCHE (1923) that "was apparently supposed to be Elizabethan England, except that there was one young lady dressed as Cleopatra and a man who appeared to represent General Robert E. Lee. The chorus sang 'Look for the Silver Lining' from *Sally*."[59]

Some studios attempted to ease this problem by supplying their own prologue designs for middle-sized houses. Universal imported the German designer-director Paul Leni to work on this scheme, and Leni's ingenious and inexpensive design for the presentation of a 1926 revival of OUTSIDE THE LAW (1921) at New York's Colony Theatre was published in the studio house paper, *Universal Weekly*, as one of a series.[60]

But the prologue idea had already run its course by this point, and in 1927, Frank Cambria could announce that "the prologue, which at one time took first place in novelty film presentations, . . . is today practically discontinued, because in many instances the prologue hurt the picture, being a sad attempt to reproduce a scene from the picture." Cambria saw unit shows, which he had developed for Balaban and Katz, replacing the feature-specific prologues. He was then working for Publix Theatres in New York, designing unit shows like "Way Down South," "Alpine Romance," and "Opera vs. Jazz." Staged at a cost of $20,000 to $50,000 each, these units

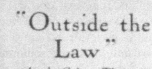

Universal suggested that exhibitors might restage for themselves the Colony Theatre's prologue to the 1926 reissue of OUTSIDE THE LAW, *and provided detailed instructions in their house organ* (Universal Weekly, *29 May 1926, p. 22).*

toured a circuit of eighteen Publix houses and often ran sixty to seventy-five minutes.[61]

The apotheosis of the Cambria style was the "Pageant of Progress" devised by John Murray Anderson for the opening of the New York Paramount in 1926. Aware of the self-importance of the new theater, as well as (apparently) Terry Ramsaye's recently published history *A Million and One Nights,* Anderson highlighted "The Pre-History of the Screen" and celebrated Edison's 1896 screening at Koster and Bial's Music Hall, a few blocks down Broadway from the Paramount. As a climax, a mammoth congratulatory finale celebrated the completion of the theater: "The Paramount Theatre stands at the Crossroads of the World wherein the Aladdin Lamp of the Camera, and the magic carpet of film, have built an Empire of Delight, and its boundaries are the limits of the Earth."[62]

Managing such an empire was a unique entrepreneurial problem. The showmen in charge of the nation's picture palaces often acted as if they believed Roxy's publicity and felt a personal responsibility to live up to it. It was not enough simply to sign up with the best available distribution chain and put on the most elaborate stage production. Despite the fact that the film came to them in a can, managers of first-run theaters regularly attempted to improve this portion of their show as well.

The Eastman Theatre in Rochester was not only that city's largest motion-picture house but one of the most elegantly appointed theaters in the country. Designed by McKim, Mead, and White, and sponsored by George Eastman himself, the 3,200-seat house opened in 1921. Its management was so self-conscious about its responsibilities that, beginning in 1925, it reported on them to the annual convention of the Society of Motion Picture Engineers. What is most interesting about these reports is the emphasis placed on the composition of the show, and the theater's treatment of its films as just another troublesome item on the bill. The Eastman was far larger than any of its rivals in this city of 330,000, and its director, Eric T. Clarke, felt that he needed to attract one-eighth of the population each week and make steady patrons of many of these customers. This meant that the Eastman emphasized family fare much more strongly than, say, a Broadway house in New York City, which served an extended entertainment district and a large population of transients. By 1925 the Eastman could still claim THE FRESHMAN (1925) as its biggest hit.[63]

The Eastman's standard bill included an eight-minute overture, a ten-minute news weekly (edited by the management from four rival "news services"), a ten-minute live act, and a ten-minute comedy or novelty film. The individual running time of any item on the bill might vary, but the feature would always be kept to eighty minutes or less, since the house followed a strict two-hour program policy. If the feature was too long, Clarke had three options: he could reduce the number of items on the program, shorten the films, or project the films faster than usual. Oddly enough, he never suggested even a slight lengthening of the entire program's running time, indicating the importance of standard show times to the filmgoing habits of his regular patrons. Another thing he refused to do was drop one of the program items. The fact that he was prepared to cut down his films and project at inappropriate speeds suggests an essentially different approach to first-class presentation than would be the case only a few years later. But the belief in a "balanced program" was almost mystical among silent-picture-palace managers, who clearly saw this part of their business as closer to the work of vaudeville managers than operators of legitimate houses.

The audience reacted in kind. Clarke claimed that 50 percent of his patrons arrived

during the running of the feature and stayed through the show to catch the beginning, suggesting the attendance pattern of a vaudeville house. He criticized producers for being insensitive to this situation and attacked films that were difficult to
follow if one missed the first couple of reels. To counter this problem, he always
skipped the first half-hour when pre-screening films for possible selection.

The Eastman Theatre was part of a small Rochester combine that also included the
Picadilly (2,200 seats) and the Regent (1,800).[64] Clarke would contract in advance
with various distributors for about 200 features per year to be used interchangeably
among these theaters. He could expect only about half to emerge as top-quality films,
and fifty of these would appear at the Eastman. The remaining 150 would be allo-
cated to the Regent and the Picadilly, with the weakest titles playing only split
weeks. An exclusive policy of first-run double features was successfully introduced at
the Picadilly in 1927, leaving that theater with a two-hour-and-twenty-four-minute
program and no stage show.

Clarke realized that he had an advantage in being able (essentially) to pick and
choose among the season's releases when most large houses were stuck with whatever the parent chain had in release that week. He felt that the reason many of the
New York palaces presented such elaborate stage shows was to "bolster up weak
features" that he was able to "palm off" on the Regent or the Picadilly. This was his
argument for mounting a less spectacular program than might be expected in so large
a theater. In fact, he was a bit smug about his policy:

> All deluxe theaters in New York live on the remains of Rothafel's policies.
> His has been the one original mind in deluxe presentation. When he,
> graduating from a 5,000 seat theater, opens one seating 6,200, his com-
> petition are tempted to follow his ways. The Capitol, having a better line
> of pictures than the Roxy can get, contents itself to increasing the orches-
> tra to 85 men. The Paramount slaps on massive acts of tinsel and gaudi-
> ness. The Roxy itself is not immune to the disease. There they slash away
> at the 11,960 feet of WHAT PRICE GLORY? until it can be run in 90
> minutes. Why? Well, anyhow they made room for a prologue lasting for
> half an hour. . . . The situation has grown top-heavy. Rothafel with his
> immense reputation can doubtless get away with it, for the public knows
> that he gives a show, and the public will come whatever the weakness of
> his feature picture. Already others like Hugo Riesenfeld are talking about
> the "dignity of the simplicity of presentation" and making capital of the
> opposite ("An Exhibitor's Problems in 1927," *Transactions of the Society
> of Motion Picture Engineers* 31 [September 1927], p. 453).

Clarke outlines the ways in which the Eastman Theatre was carefully tailoring its
stage shows to the screen presentation, even employing an in-house "scenario editor"
and staff merely to work on structure. His warnings about the danger of presenting
a weak film within an ostentatious frame (which echo the complaints of John Grierson) seem to predict the rejection of the Roxy style that followed a few seasons later.
In fact, his pioneering use of first-run double features and strong support for the
establishment of specialized "art cinemas" to serve the tastes of sophisticated audiences suggests that Clarke was one of the more thoughtful and innovative managers
of the day. But Clarke had one glaring weakness (at least to modern eyes): an

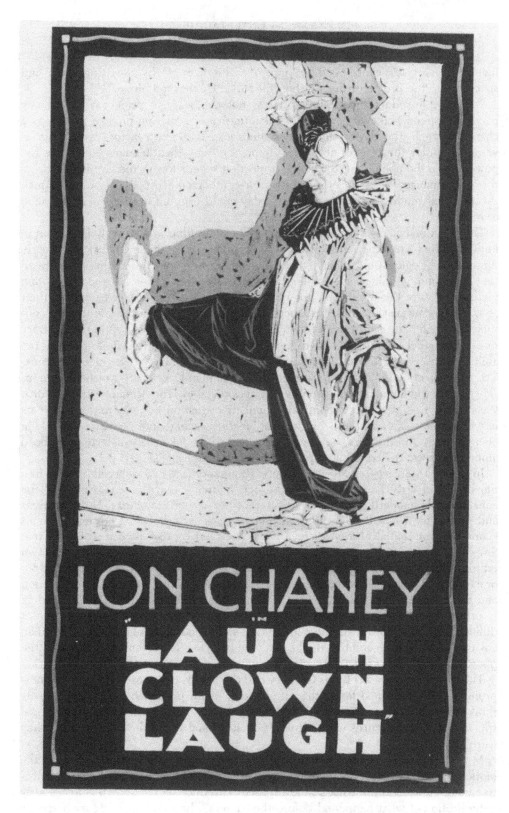

LON CHANEY
IN
"LAUGH
CLOWN
LAUGH"

Many important theaters rejected the studio-supplied poster material and commissioned their own designs. This poster for LAUGH, CLOWN, LAUGH *(MGM, 1928) was created for the Eastman Theatre, Rochester, New York, by Batiste Madalena.*

incessant, even arrogant, need to "improve" his features by recutting them and speeding up the projector during the dull parts. He was not alone.[65]

Until the introduction of talkies, it was not necessary to project a film at any particular speed. Likewise, the physical integrity of a motion-picture print was a chancy thing in the days before the soundtrack. These two factors were seen as variables under the control of the exhibitor, with any theater manager having the power, even the obligation, to change projection speeds to suit the circumstances of the performance. Recutting the film was a cumbersome process, but even small theaters that might use a film only for a day could drop an entire reel if the need arose.

The question of a proper projection speed for silent films is extremely important in understanding the experience of early film audiences, and the intentions of early filmmakers. Logic would dictate that films should be projected at the same speed they were photographed, and modern audiences have been trained to accept motion pictures in only this way. But pre-1927 audiences had no reason to expect their stylized shadow plays to be reproduced in this manner. Since the nineteenth century, they had been accustomed to moving-picture toys replicating action at arbitrary rates, and Heyl, Muybridge, and Reynaud worked in this tradition. In fact, the ability to observe in slow motion was the essential element of Muybridge's Zoopraxiscope. Projectionists in the nickelodeon era commonly projected either faster or slower than the taking speed, as circumstances dictated. The *Moving Picture World* was already finding cause to complain about this situation in 1909, and a few years later *Photoplay* was absolutely outraged at "*picture racing*, an evil existing mainly in cheap, poorly-run theaters, but which once in a while pokes its sinisterly rapid head among the seats that retail at a quarter or a half a dollar."[66]

In 1917 the Society of Motion Picture Engineers (SMPE) decreed that "a film movement of sixty feet per minute through motion picture mechanisms shall be considered as standard speed." This 16-frames-per-second standard for both cameras and projectors was still being touted as late as 1922, in the third edition of James Cameron's influential *Motion Picture Projection*, but by that time it was clear that few cameramen or projectionists were adhering to it. F. H. Richardson, projection editor of the *Moving Picture World*, claimed that it was impossible to project at 60, or even much below 70, without creating a distracting flicker. He felt that projection and taking speeds needed to be identical, but that managers ordered overspeeding in order to squeeze in more shows. "This one thing has . . . done more to render difficult the popularization of the photoplay as a high class form of entertainment than any or all other causes combined," he declared in 1920. "It has tended to cheapen the photoplay and to prevent its drawing at high prices."[67]

The following year Carl Louis Gregory told the SMPE that most theaters were now projecting "a great deal faster than it is taken," with predictable results: "I really think the public has become so educated to seeing pictures run faster than normal speed, that if the pictures were actually run at normal speed they would think they were slow."[68]

M. W. Palmer, an electrical engineer at the Paramount Astoria studio, stunned the motion picture engineers in 1923 by suggesting that projection speed was a subjective issue. "I don't think what you are trying to produce on the screen is necessarily a duplication of what happened before the camera," he told them. "It is an artistic presentation, and it is not necessary that it should be mechanically accurate."[69]

The society moved to change its standards and conducted a series of stopwatch

Cameraman Alvin Wyckoff cranks the Pathé camera with his right hand while operating the panning crank with his left. Director Cecil B. DeMille and screenwriter Jeanie MacPherson look on at right. The cranking speed is arbitrary.

tests on "a number of well known cameramen," who "tried to stick pretty close to a speed of sixty feet per minute." They then held a series of projection tests in Chicago that convinced them to adopt a projection standard of 80. "Apparently the mind is not satisfied when the projection speed is exactly the same as the taking speed," noted J. I. Crabtree of the Eastman Kodak Research Laboratory. Richardson and other supporters of "normal" projection speed were outraged. Dr. W. E. Story asked "why we propose a taking speed which will give a distortion in action." But, the society maintained this standard of shooting at 60 and projecting at 80 for the rest of the silent era.[70]

Oddly enough, the cinematographers were the group most pleased by the adoption of this standard. For years they had argued that projectionists were overspeeding merely to get in extra shows, and not, as the operators claimed, because cameramen had increased their own cranking speeds over the years. When F. H. Richardson suggested in 1923 that cameramen were varying their speeds and cranking as high as 80, cinematographer Victor Milner attacked his "appalling ignorance." Milner insisted that two turns per second of the camera crank produced an automatic rate of 65. John Boyle in 1925 and Dan Clark in 1926 continued to insist that cameramen were cranking as usual at their traditional speed of 60. Even the few mechanized cameras introduced in this period, like the Bell & Howell Eyemo (1925), were set at a standard of 60.[71]

All this information seems to indicate that 60 was, in fact, the usual camera speed at this time, but investigations by Kevin Brownlow and David Gill demonstrate otherwise. In preparing dozens of different silent films for their Thames Television series *Hollywood*, Brownlow and Gill transferred the material on a variable-speed telecine machine called a Polygon. Despite the SMPE tests, equipment calibrations, and testimony of the cameramen, these researchers found practically no one cranking at 60 after this "standard" had been adopted in 1917. Civilization, produced in 1916, was already varying between 60 and 75, according to the Polygon tests. Brownlow indicates camera speed on Robin Hood as 71, The Four Horsemen of the Apocalypse as 75, What Price Glory? as 82, and The General as 90. One of the few exceptions was G. W. "Billy" Bitzer, cameraman for D. W. Griffith, who cranked some sections of The Birth of a Nation as low as 45 and kept below 60 for most of his career.[72]

Since the most popular cameras of the day, such as the Bell & Howell 2709, had no film-speed indicator, it was impossible for most cameramen to know their exact cranking speeds, so all protestations on the part of Milner, Boyle, or Clark must be guesswork. Richardson and the projectionists, it seems, were correct in their original assessment of gradually increasing camera speeds.

But the projectionists were not content to maintain even this new standard. Implicitly agreeing with the SMPE that audiences expected their films to move briskly, they continued to push their own speeds upward. When the *American Projectionist* published a wall chart for its readers in 1923, it listed speeds from 66 to 126, although operators were warned not to run over 100 for more than a minute "for your own sake and the sake of the business generally."[73]

A study of musical cue-sheets issued by distributors gives us an indication of the speed at which distributors hoped their films would be shown, and by 1921 most of these seem to have settled at or near 90. First National announced in 1926 that they would indicate the proper film speed on each reel band, but projectionists were no more likely to follow these suggestions than the dictates of the SMPE.[74]

So what speeds were theaters using? The *American Projectionist* called 85 "a fair average speed" in 1926, but there were many exceptions. Indiana theater owner Frank Rembusch claimed that projection speed had jumped to 100 as an answer to rising camera speeds. One Texas theater had a scheduled rate of 110, and an MPPDA investigation found one in Atlanta running its comedies at speeds up to 120, so fast "it was almost impossible to read the titles." Another Atlanta theater would run a seven-reel show in forty-five or fifty minutes on Saturday nights to increase the number of shows. "Speeding . . . is practiced both by large theaters as well as small ones, probably more so by large ones," the study concluded. Indeed, the largest theaters often set the pace here, for their motorized projectors could easily be set to project at a rate that would soon exhaust the manually cranking projectionist in a small country house. Adjusting a lever on the Powers mechanical speed control, for example, made the film automatically run at any speed from 40 to 140.[75] Table 2.8 shows some of the standard projection speeds of the era, with frame-per-second equivalents.

"I have been in the projection room of the Capitol Theatre and four o'clock was the time for completing the program," one observer in New York reported. "There was

TABLE 2.8 FILM PROJECTION SPEEDS

Ft./Min	Frames/Sec.
60	16
75	20
90*	24*
105	28
120	32

* Standard sound projection speed.

a signal from the orchestra leader to speed up projection and the finale of the picture was shown at a hundred and twenty feet a minute, obviously detracting from its presentation." Sound-film pioneer Earl Sponable surveyed New York projection booths when he affiliated with Western Electric in 1927. His early tests had been done at 85, but he was unable to find any theater in the city projecting at that speed. He found the current average to be 105, with peaks of 120 on Sundays to slip in another show. Such overspeeding was not only inelegant but dangerous. A 1927 investigation showed that the majority of film fires took place in the late afternoon and early evening, times when the projection speed frequently reached 120. The *American Projectionist* argued that a film should be dropped instead of overspeeding to this degree, but as we have seen, managers had their own reasons for rejecting this suggestion.[76]

Of course, the Eastman Theatre was equally guilty of overspeeding, something it justified as a natural part of its program presentation. Their standard projection speed was 90 to 100, with THE TEN COMMANDMENTS run at 100, for example, because it was too long to fit the procrustean bed of their daily schedule. They would also regularly cut all the films on the bill, trimming the two-reel comedy to 1,200 feet and the news weekly to 800 feet and excising about 1,000 feet from every feature. The managing director, music director, and projection director would preview each feature, decide on the speed and running time, and indicate on a file card what was to be cut. The print arrived about four days before the show date, and the projection director would spend between six and seven hours making cuts, taking out "minor incidents which do not have a direct bearing on the story and unnecessary detail or padding, of which there is usually great sufficiency." This he insisted he would do as long as producers continued to release films of over 7,000 feet. The next three days were spent scoring the film and preparing the colored projection effects for which the Eastman was famous.[77]

Despite such callous behavior, the Eastman's management was capable of criticizing Rothapfel for his treatment of WHAT PRICE GLORY?, from which three reels were eliminated. They considered themselves above such behavior, just as they considered themselves superior to the filmmakers whose work they played. Once, D. W. Griffith, whose films were traditionally shot at very slow speeds, confided to Clarke that his cameramen were now cranking "with the idea that the picture would be exhibited at 90 feet per minute." Clarke told the SMPE, "Among ourselves, we believe his productions go best when run nearer 100 feet per minute. . . ."[78]

As might be expected, by the time the Eastman had restored its 1,000 feet of cuts, the once-pristine print contained a significant number of splices. This procedure was

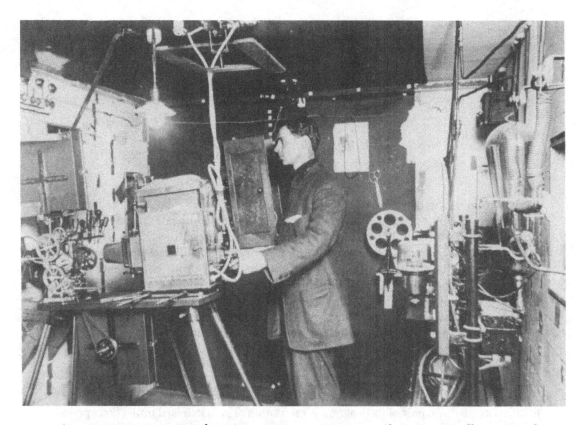

A projectionist poses with a Powers No. 6 Cameragraph in a typically cramped projection booth, about 1915.

repeated by other first-run houses across the country, and with a maximum of sixty-five prints being struck for the average release, the visible wear and tear on all circulating copies was soon quite extreme. While there were no soundtracks to spoil, these intentional splices were serious problems, for 75 percent of all print damage was due to faulty splicing. The *American Projectionist* estimated in 1926 that not one theater in a hundred possessed a mechanical splicing block. Torn-off film was simply rolled up and stuffed back into the shipping case. A survey of three hundred projection booths across the country found hasty splices made with straight pins, gum, safety pins, and wire. A reel hiding such materials could maul the fingers of an unsuspecting film-exchange worker operating a high-speed rewind.[79]

By 1926 most exchanges used mechanical splicing blocks, but even that did not guarantee the delivery of usable prints to the theater. The projection-booth log of Boston's Lancaster Theatre from June to August 1927 records the fact that the 411,653 feet of film received from the exchanges contained 6,892 splices, or about 17 splices per reel. Of these splices, 211 needed to be remade in the booth for the following reasons: loosened (133), unmatched perforations (10), damaged perforations (5), wide or curled splice (51), crack along splice (12). This theater reported that film would frequently arrive in a tangled mass in its shipping case because the exchange reels had come apart in transit.[80]

Exchanges were accused of improperly waxing prints, simply rubbing raw paraffin over the reel instead of using a proper waxing machine. This practice would gum up the projectors, increasing the already serious problem of scratching caused by the proliferation of bad splices. In fact, unless a film was absolutely first-run, severely scratched prints were the rule. The Motion Picture Producers and Distributors of America (MPPDA) found that most of the damage to film was sprocket damage caused by overspeeding or improper splicing. Such footage was discarded and rarely replaced. After splices and scratches, additional problems included mutilation of the ends of the film for "signal purposes," and fire damage. Projectionists would punch holes, mark crosses, even glue sheet tin to the perforations to help signal reel changes (the latter technique involved a primitive electric-bell system). The use of a cue sheet was considered the proper way to time a reel change, but many houses had no patience with such niceties.[81]

By the time these prints had reached the smallest theaters, they were in miserable condition. One such exhibitor complained in the *Motion Picture News* that his exchange defined as "good-running condition" anything that would travel through the projector: "I've been compelled to turn down films right from the express, by looking in the box, with each of the five reels half gone and looking like miniature reels. . . . Of course, you can make it go through the machine, but what about the story of the picture after half of it is gone?"[82]

Viewing conditions in most modern cinemas are far from ideal. The depressing sameness of multiplex houses, the careless attitude of management and staff, the infuriating quirks of automated booths, all suggest to modern audiences that if no one else cares about the presentation, why should they? Over the decades many forces have acted to concentrate the audience's attention on the feature alone, thus leaving theaters completely at the mercy of their current attraction's drawing power. The theater has effectively subtracted itself from the motion-picture equation. But would even the most nostalgic viewer wish to exchange current viewing conditions for those of the silent era? The convenience and affordability of the old neighborhood theater could hardly outweigh the battered prints, clichéd musical accompaniment, and careless projection that awaited the patron. And a trip downtown to luxuriate in the comfort of a grandiose picture palace was more an architectural treat than a cinematic one. Here, one was at the mercy of those theater managers who felt compelled to "improve" every reel that passed through their fingers. Cutting more severely than any censor, overspeeding more violently than an episode of "Fractured Flickers," these first-run theaters made an understanding of the filmmakers' intentions nearly impossible. Many of these abuses would be eliminated when the talkies made tampering with the films more difficult, but during the silent era simply watching a film could be one of the most unnerving parts of going to the movies.

3

Corporate Organization

1915–1917: *World and Triangle*

*I*n 1915 the "West Coast Number" of the *Motion Picture News* was filled with information on the new studios sprouting in California. But if an exhibitor leafing through this paper turned instead to the weekly release charts, he or she could find far more subtle evidence of industry turmoil.[1]

Available product was being offered in two distinct formats. The industry's oldest firms, and a few younger rivals, were marketing program releases of short films, one to three reels in length, which were issued like clockwork on a daily schedule. Another page listed the offerings of a half-dozen feature distributors, whose products were generally four to six reels in length and were not necessarily tied to specific release dates. If the birth of a new production system was being chronicled elsewhere in the *News*, these release charts plotted the end of a distribution scheme that was rapidly approaching irrelevance. Out of the dozens of producers listed, only a handful would survive three years hence, and most of those in significantly changed form. As for the daily change of program releases, its remaining tenure could be measured in months.

At the start of 1915, short-film programs were still being supplied by three major and two minor distributors. The General Film Company, the distribution arm of the old Motion Picture Patents Company, was still handling the product of Biograph, Edison, Essanay, Kalem, Lubin, Mina, Selig, and Vitagraph, with episodes of the Hearst-Selig newsreel available twice weekly. A few years earlier their "unlicensed" competition had offered their films through the Motion Picture Distributing and Sales Company, but that front had split into two competing programs, Mutual and Universal. Mutual now included the releases of American, Beauty, Broncho, Domino, Kay-Bee, Keystone, Komic, Majestic, Princess, Reliance, Royal, and Thanhouser, with an episode of the Mutual Weekly available each Thursday. Universal's line included the Big U, "101" Bison, Eclair, Gold Seal, IMP, Joker, Laemmle, L-KO, Nestor, Powers, Rex, Sterling, and Victor brands, with their newsreel available on Wednesday. Two minor services, Kriterion and United, were energetic but ephemeral.

The single page devoted to "Feature Releases—Current and Coming" was remarkably incoherent and incomplete for a journal of record. Nearly one-sixth of the space was devoted to the Pathé Exchange program, which did not even handle long films. Each week they issued an eight-reel program, of which the "feature" was a two-reel serial episode (here, THE EXPLOITS OF ELAINE) supported by various short dramatic, documentary, or cartoon subjects. This use of the word "feature" to describe the main item on a program, not simply a film of four or more reels, dated from the nickelodeon era and was already disappearing by 1915. Five other distributors made up the balance of the page. Alliance Films Corporation was a loosely knit grouping of minor independent producers, among them the Masterpiece Film Company and the Oz Film Company (Frank Baum's operation, which that week was offering THE NEW WIZARD OF OZ). Continental Features was the feature arm of the Mutual program, handling the longer product of Reliance-Majestic, Thanhouser, and the rest. Fox Film Corporation offered their own productions, including A FOOL THERE WAS, ANNA KARENINA with Betty Nansen, and THE NIGGER, a miscegenation melodrama with William Farnum that was currently doing big business at the New York Hippodrome. Paramount Pictures handled the Bosworth, Famous Players, and Lasky Feature Play Company releases, as well as the product of the Blazon Film Company and Oliver Morosco. World Film Corporation distributed its own productions as well as those of a few small independents.

Metro Pictures Corporation is nowhere on this list, although their full-page advertisement appears on page 9. Vitagraph, Lubin, Selig, and Essanay were also releasing and advertising features, but the calendar omits them as well. These four firms were about to combine their distribution operation into the VLSE organization.[2] THE BIRTH OF A NATION was still being road-shown by the producers and was not available on the open market. The *Motion Picture News*, in trying to adapt its program-release calendar to cover features, as yet had no way to account for much of this product.

Out of this hodgepodge, an industry analyst might have been most attracted by the growth of two new firms quite characteristic of the early feature period: the World Film Corporation and the Triangle Film Corporation (formed that September out of the remnants of Mutual). Janet Wasko, in her study of American film-industry financing, names these two organizations as the first motion-picture companies financed through securities issued by prominent Wall Street investment-banking firms. Prior to this, individual financiers such as Otto Kahn or Crawford Livingston had dabbled in specific projects with their own money, but industry conditions were still too chaotic to interest the banking community at large. Whatever funds could not be generated internally were raised from individual investors, but the motion-picture business was an attractive nuisance for would-be capitalists, trapping many by pointing to the example of a successful few. "Thousands of people are being led to invest in these companies, which will either fail outright or go into the hands of receivers, and will never return a fraction of the money that was paid into the treasury," wrote one analyst in 1915. "It were best to investigate the picture company that would make love to your money as you would the qualifications of a young man who comes to marry your daughter, for there are no greater returns to be gotten from the film business than shrewd investment may discover in other lines of industry."[3]

The World Film Corporation had originally been organized by Cleveland theater owner Emanuel Mandelbaum, who, with the financial backing of two Wall Street bankers, W. A. Pratt and Van Horn Ely, set it up as a distribution agency for independent features in 1914. Within a few months, Mandelbaum was out and World

Poster for THE EXPLOITS OF ELAINE: EPISODE 13, THE DEVIL WORSHIPPERS
(*Pathé, 1915*).

was involved in production on its own, following a merger with the Equitable Pictures Corporation, recently created to produce films for former Vitagraph star Clara Kimball Young. Equitable's president, mail-order magnate Arthur Spiegel, had arranged financing through Moritz Rosenthal with the Wall Street firm of Ladenburg, Thalman, and Company. As vice-president and general manager, Lewis J. Selznick, an aggressive jewelry salesman with minor film experience, was in overall charge of operations; it was Selznick who induced theatrical producer Lee Shubert to become a major investor in World. In addition to the Equitable line, World also handled the product of Peerless (owned by Eastman raw-stock agent Jules Brulatour), Daniel Frohman's Frohman Amusement Company, and Broadway impresario William A. Brady. Most of World's product was produced at Fort Lee, New Jersey, in either the Peerless or the Paragon studio. Here, Selznick and Brulatour, taking advantage of the collapse of French filmmaking activities in the United States in 1914, assembled an amazing group of French directors, designers, and cameramen. Eclair and Pathé had stopped production in America, and Solax ceased operating as an independent producer-distributor, with the result that many French technicians were thrown onto the U.S. market. Selznick snapped up the best, including directors Maurice Tourneur, George Archainbaud, Émile Chautard, and Albert Capellani, cameramen René Guissart and Lucien Andriot, and the great designer Ben Carré. Technical conversation on the sets was often carried on in French, although World employed a good deal of domestic talent as well.[4]

When combined with the acting talent and literary properties available through the Shubert connection, the result could be extremely sophisticated, as Maurice Tourneur's THE WISHING RING (1914) still demonstrates. The Ballet Russe, then appearing as a Shubert stage attraction, was worked into the plot line of THE DANCER'S PERIL (1917), while Barry O'Neil directed a version of Frank Norris' novel *McTeague* in 1915 (called LIFE'S WHIRLPOOL) that prefigured von Stroheim's GREED of a decade later.[5]

Nonetheless, friction with some of the same bankers he had brought into the company in 1914 forced Selznick out of World in 1916, and he was replaced by William A. Brady. Under Brady's tenure, the studio seemed to lose its competitive edge by holding too closely to the theatrical line that its more aggressive rivals, especially those on the West Coast, had begun to abandon. The studio's films were beginning to seem a little old-fashioned, although a picture such as Maurice Tourneur's lovely A GIRL'S FOLLY (1917) remains extremely valuable today for its view of filmmaking activities in this era.

In 1918 Brady went into independent production, and the following year Selznick was able to purchase the remnants of the company, now a fiscal wreck, and merge it with his own Selznick-Select organization. As Wasko suggests, the collapse of World, and the loss of considerable sums to its investors, acted to intensify Wall Street's aversion to motion-picture securities.[6] But the disintegration of the Triangle Film Corporation was even more damaging.

Harry Aitken, a Wisconsin insurance man, had been instrumental in forming the Mutual Film Company in 1912, largely by attracting the interest of two Kuhn, Loeb bankers, Felix Kahn and Crawford Livingston. The main independent rival to Laemmle's Universal, Mutual was in the process of flying apart just at the time the *Motion Picture News* issued its West Coast survey in April 1915. As president of Mutual, Aitken had been under constant pressure from two of Mutual's other corporate

The cover of the program booklet for the first Triangle presentation at the Knicker-bocker Theatre, 23 September 1915.

heads, Samuel Hutchinson and John Freuler, owners of the American Film Manufacturing Company, while Adam Kessel and Charles Baumann, whose New York Motion Picture Company controlled the product of Mack Sennett and Thomas Ince, generally supported Aitken's policies. Aitken's major coup was the signing of D. W. Griffith for his own Majestic label in 1913, but he soon came under increasing attack from Freuler and Hutchinson, who felt that he was favoring Griffith's product over other Mutual releases, namely their own. The final break came when the Mutual board forced Aitken to cover, out of his own pocket, $40,000 that Mutual had invested in the production of THE BIRTH OF A NATION. This personal investment not only made Aitken a fast fortune but convinced him that the future lay in the production of lavish features. Freuler and Hutchinson somehow talked Kahn and Livingston into withdrawing their support from Aitken (despite the ongoing success of THE BIRTH OF A NATION), and at the May 1915 annual meeting Freuler ousted him as president.[7]

Taking Kessel and Baumann with him, Aitken then abandoned Mutual and made a financial agreement with Smithers and Company. He was able to guarantee the continued participation of Griffith, Ince, and Sennett, the industry's three most noted producers, who would form the nucleus of the new concern, to be called the Triangle Film Corporation. Smithers underwrote a $5 million stock offering, and Triangle, introduced at $5 per share in July 1915, reached $8.75 by September, when the first Triangle program opened at New York's Knickerbocker Theatre.[8]

Aitken's idea now was to acquire showcase theaters in the major metropolitan areas that could highlight the new Triangle releases; the films would then pass to affiliated theaters that had contracted with Triangle's exchanges. This bold attempt at vertical integration began to unravel almost immediately, however. Aitken's importation of expensive Broadway stars proved ill-timed and ill-advised. It appears to have been modeled on Adolph Zukor's 1912 scheme of "Famous Players in Famous Plays," but even Zukor had largely abandoned this policy by 1915; audiences had already indicated that they preferred *screen* stars in their movies. The traditional example here is Aitken's payment of $100,000 to Sir Herbert Beerbohm-Tree for just two films, MACBETH (1916) and OLD FOLKS AT HOME (1916), both of which were notable box-office failures. On the other hand, despite an initial salary of $2,000 per week, Douglas Fairbanks proved quite profitable for Triangle from the moment his first film, THE LAMB, anchored the premiere Triangle program on 23 September 1915.[9]

Aitken had depended on Griffith's help in handling these stage imports, but Griffith was so busy with the production of INTOLERANCE that he never directed a single Triangle release and limited himself to nominal supervision of the work of his assistants. While the Sennett and Ince productions were popular, exhibitors resisted the higher advance prices they were expected to pay for them. These costs did not show on the screen. Ince spent only $8,356.12 on William S. Hart's THE DISCIPLE (1915), a five-reel feature; Hart himself was being paid just $300 per week. But Hart could work only fifty-two weeks a year, and Triangle's overhead demanded more. Kessel and Baumann so mismanaged their end of the business that Aitken had to buy them out in 1916, by which time Triangle's stock had already dropped to $2.[10]

The following year Triangle's chronic cash problems were so great that all three of its key producers moved to the Paramount program. Griffith wrote Aitken that Triangle was "conceded to be the worst managed business in Film History." Ultimately, Aitken was reduced to peddling reissues of Fairbanks and Sennett films and contemplating ways to squeeze another dollar out of THE BIRTH OF A NATION. Coming on the heels of the World Film fiasco, Aitken's failure soured Wall Street on motion-picture stocks for some time to come.[11]

1917–1919: Paramount, First National, and United Artists

The Paramount Pictures Corporation, the immediate beneficiary of Triangle's collapse, had not fallen into this position by accident. In fact, the success of Paramount was in many ways an illustration of Adolph Zukor's ability to refine and perfect schemes already introduced by men like Harry Aitken or William Fox (just as Aitken's failure with the "Famous Players" idea illustrates his inability to handle a production policy once successfully introduced by Zukor).

W. W. Hodkinson, an independent West Coast exchange operator, first conceived the idea of Paramount after observing the success of the General Film Company's national distribution system. The product of Zukor's Famous Players Film Company, as well as that of the Jesse Lasky Feature Play Company, constituted the bulk of those features then available on the open market (VLSE, Fox, and some others were handling their own distribution). They were offered on a "states rights" basis, with local distributors or exchange operators contracting for territorial exhibition rights. Hodkinson joined with other local distributors from New York, Boston, Pittsburgh, and Philadelphia and incorporated the Paramount Pictures Corporation on 8 May 1914. One week later this corporation entered into a five-year distribution agreement with Zukor, Lasky, and Bosworth, Inc. (an alliance of actor-producer Hobart Bosworth and Broadway impresario Oliver Morosco, financed by Los Angeles capitalist Frank C. Carbutt). By combining nationally, advances could be guaranteed for future productions that would be much higher than what might have been raised in separate states rights contracts, thus encouraging the production of more ambitious films. In exchange for exclusive distribution rights and 35 percent of the rentals, Paramount agreed to advance $20–$25,000 for each five-reel film and pay for the cost of prints and trade advertising. In 1915 this contract was extended to twenty-five years.[12]

Despite the great success of the organization for all involved, Zukor was uncomfortable about being, technically, a cog in the Paramount wheel. In addition, Hodkinson, remembering Aitken's recent failure at merging production and distribution, resisted Zukor's urgings to turn Paramount into a producing organization. Accordingly, Zukor and Lasky took control of Paramount by buying out the interests of several of the original incorporators on 21 May 1916 and forced Hodkinson to resign on 13 June. Zukor and Lasky then combined their production organizations as the Famous Players–Lasky Corporation on 29 July and acquired the stock of Bosworth and Morosco that November. What had begun as a move to consolidate power in the hands of the distributor had, under Zukor, become the world's most impressive producing concern, as the *Film Daily* put it, "the United States Steel Corp. of the motion picture industry."[13]

Having eliminated Hodkinson, the aggressive Zukor went to work on his new partners. Samuel Goldfish, one of the founders of the Lasky Company, was to serve as chairman of the board of Famous Players–Lasky, with Zukor acting as president. Friction between the two was immediate, and Zukor demanded that Jesse Lasky

"Out goes the library lamp." Paramount's national advertising campaign was intended to build product loyalty and trademark identification. Names of individual films or stars were not required (Motion Picture Magazine, April 1918, p. 86).

choose between them. Despite the fact that Goldfish was his brother-in-law, Lasky lined up behind Zukor. Goldfish cashed in his interest for $900,000.[14]

The combined star rosters of the Famous Players and Lasky operations were already considerable, but in 1917 Zukor was able to add the defecting talents once handled by Triangle. At a time when star prominence was the single most important factor determining a film's box-office success, Zukor had cornered the market. In a 1918 popularity poll conducted by *Motion Picture Magazine*, the six top stars on the list—Mary Pickford, Marguerite Clark, Douglas Fairbanks, Harold Lockwood, William S. Hart, and Wallace Reid—were all under contract to Zukor.[15]

Using this leverage, Paramount was able to insist that prospective exhibitors interested in, say, the Pickford films, acquire them in large blocks along with a quantity

Stars worked diligently to build up their followings. This personal response to a fan's request for photographs was written only to say that the pictures would follow in a later mailing. Mary Pickford's signature, however, is a rubber stamp.

Los Angeles, Cal.
May 13, 1915

My dear friend Mr Hoffman:

      It was very kind of you to write me your appreciation of my work. I sincerely thank you for the compliments you paid me.

      As soon as my pictures arrive from the photographer's I will gladly forward you one.

      Trusting I may have the pleasure of hearing from you again sometime, I am

Sincerely,
Mary J Pickford.

of less attractive titles. These block-booking arrangements typically included groups of from 13 to 52 or even 104 titles. Paramount salesmen offered a variety of different product lines, from the top-quality Artcraft releases of Pickford, Fairbanks, and Hart to the more modest Realart productions, in which stars such as Bebe Daniels were being developed. Because these films had not yet been produced, exhibitors were required to "buy blind" from a sketchy prospectus or campaign book. The system was similar to the program policy employed in nickelodeon days. But from the exhibitor's point of view, it was ill suited to current conditions, because audiences had become far more selective in their filmgoing habits (if only to patronize the films of one star over another). As best they could, all of Zukor's competitors soon adopted variants of this policy, with the notable later exception of the United Artists Corporation.[16]

In 1921 the Federal Trade Commission began an investigation of block-booking practices that continued intermittently until 1932. The ensuing case, *Federal Trade Commission* v. *Famous Players–Lasky Corporation, et al.*, yielded seventeen thousand pages of testimony covering all sides of this issue. The major producer-distributors defended themselves by arguing that the policy was simple wholesaling, that the sale of individual films was uneconomical, and that exhibitors still had the right to buy specific titles. Supporting the claims of independent producers and theater owners, the government charged coercion, denied the majors' economic arguments, and insisted that the situation was a straightforward example of unfair trade practices. A cease and desist order was issued in 1927, which the majors chose to disregard while the matter worked its way through the U. S. Circuit Court of Appeals.

Before waiting for the government to come to their rescue, many of the nation's most powerful theater owners had already banded together to form the First National Exhibitors Circuit. The rapid increase in picture-palace construction that followed the opening of the Strand in 1914 soon created a class of "first-run" theaters that proved crucial to the successful exploitation of new feature products. After the publicity of a run in one of these two hundred or so key theaters, a film would eagerly be sought by exhibitors outside the downtown areas. But if a film had no first-run record, it was almost impossible to sell it to the outlying houses.

Nonetheless, the owners of these key theaters (who often controlled chains of local theaters as well) felt themselves threatened by Zukor and Paramount, who compelled them to accept product on increasingly costly terms. As scattered retailers, they had little bargaining power, and only the Stanley Company in Philadelphia was able to deal with Paramount on its own terms, owing to the almost monopolistic control it exercised over local theater programming. Squeezing these exhibitors from the other side was the knowledge that many prime locations were already overseated, with so much local competition that even a popular (and expensive) feature might play to half-empty houses.[17]

A plan to organize these exhibitors was hatched by Thomas Tally, a pioneer Los Angeles showman, who together with J. D. Williams promoted the First National concept in 1916–1917. This was essentially a national organization of states rights franchisees. Films would be acquired by First National, with costs apportioned among the various franchise holders according to the value of their territories (table 3.1).[18]

The formation of the new organization was announced in New York in April 1917. Its two dozen original stockholders controlled about one hundred theaters, but subfranchises were offered to outlying exhibitors.

By April 1919 First National controlled 190 first-run theaters and approximately 40 subsequent-run houses, not counting some 366 theaters which were controlled under subfranchise agreements. In January 1920 the total number of theaters controlled by First National had increased to 639; of these 224 were first-run houses, 49 were subsequent-run houses, and 366 were outlets operated by subfranchise holders (Howard Lewis, *The Motion Picture Industry* [New York: Van Nostrand, 1933] p. 17).

Benjamin Hampton claims that the number of screens eventually aligned with First National was as high as five or six thousand, a figure that would have given them control of nearly half the nation's theaters. Whatever the figure, most of these exhibitors had once carried the Paramount program, and when these theaters began to supply their own product, Zukor was faced with an effective boycott.[19]

But it was not simply aggravation with the Paramount sales policy that drew so many theater owners to First National. In July 1917 it was announced that Charlie Chaplin had signed with the new company. Although his first release, A DOG'S LIFE, was not available until April 1918, the mere news of this acquisition was enough to

TABLE 3.1 ASSOCIATED FIRST NATIONAL EXHIBITORS CIRCUIT PERCENTAGES

Territory	Percentage
S. California, & Arizona	$2^{27}/_{56}$
Nevada, Hawaii, N. California	$3^{2}/_{14}$
Alaska, Wash., Ore., Mont., N. Col., New Mexico, Utah, Wyoming, S. Idaho	$3^{3}/_{4}$
Western Canada	2
Illinois	$8^{1}/_{4}$
Indiana	$3^{1}/_{8}$
Kansas, Iowa, Nebraska	$4^{3}/_{4}$
Michigan	$4^{1}/_{4}$
Minn., Wisconsin, N. & S. Dakota	5
Missouri	$3^{1}/_{4}$
Ohio	7
New England	8
Maryland, D.C., Delaware	$2^{1}/_{4}$
New Jersey	$3^{5}/_{8}$
New York	$14^{1}/_{2}$
West Virginia, Western Pennsylvania	$4^{1}/_{8}$
Eastern Pennsylvania	$4^{3}/_{4}$
Eastern Canada	$3^{1}/_{8}$
Ga., Fla., Ala., Va., N. & S. Carolina	$3^{1}/_{8}$
Louisiana and Mississippi	$1^{3}/_{8}$
Texas, Oklahoma, Mississippi [sic]	$4^{1}/_{2}$
Kentucky, Tennessee	$1^{7}/_{8}$

SOURCE: *Film Daily Yearbook of Motion Pictures* (1925), p. 698.

Similar states rights percentage allocations were adopted by other distributors, but the percentages were constantly changing. First National's own allocations changed from time to time, and while this 1925 table is not atypical, it has some idiosyncrasies of its own.

A picture-postcard view of Charles Chaplin's Hollywood studio, built to suggest a row of Tudor cottages.

start a rush. First National had been able to lure Chaplin from Mutual not simply by offering him more money but by setting him up as his own producer, with his own Hollywood studio on the corner of Sunset and La Brea. They would advance $125,000 for the production of each of eight two-reelers, with an additional $15,000 per reel if Chaplin chose to produce a longer picture. First National paid for prints and advertising, took 30 percent of the gross to pay for distribution expenses, and split the remaining profits equally with Chaplin. Now that they had changed hats and become (essentially) producers, the First National franchise-holders stopped complaining about high star salaries and became the first to offer a million-dollar contract. They became the second as well, when they lured Mary Pickford away from Zukor himself.[20]

For almost a year First National had negotiated with Pickford, whose Paramount contract approached expiration in 1918. Zukor, already feeling the effects of this exhibitors' revolt, calculated that he could not raise Pickford rentals high enough to match First National's offer. According to Benjamin Hampton, Zukor offered Pickford $250,000 simply to retire from the screen for five years (an incident that does not appear in Zukor's autobiography), but Pickford is said to have declined.[21]

In addition to Chaplin and Pickford, First National eventually signed D. W. Griffith, Louis B. Mayer, B. P. Schulberg, and Joseph Schenck, who brought with them such stars as Lillian Gish, Constance and Norma Talmadge, Anita Stewart, and Katherine MacDonald. Starting from an exhibition base, First National had successfully grown to include distribution and production as well. Adolph Zukor made the obvious countermove in 1919: from production and distribution he would move into exhibition.[22]

On the advice of Walter Irwin, who had successfully been merchandising the weak Vitagraph-Lubin-Selig-Essanay (VLSE) product and now had accepted a Paramount vice-presidency, Zukor decided to attack First National's franchise-holders on their own ground. As Irwin later testified before the Federal Trade Commission (FTC), Paramount could destroy First National if it would go into each one of the First National cities and build, or threaten to build, the finest and largest theater in the city. Many of these exhibitors, weakened by the strain of carrying the large Chaplin and Pickford contracts and suffering cash shortages on account of theater closings imposed during the influenza epidemic, were in no mood to battle Paramount over the issue.[23]

On 18 April 1919 Famous Players–Lasky acquired a half-interest in Grauman's Million Dollar Theatre in Los Angeles; on 7 May they obtained a controlling interest in New York's Rialto and Rivoli Theaters. This gave Paramount its own showcase in the most prominent East and West Coast exhibition sites. S. A. Lynch, a Paramount partner, sent his so-called "dynamite gang" through the South, intimidating exhibitors into selling out to Southern Enterprises, Inc., a Paramount subsidiary operated for this purpose.[24]

The general manager of the Saenger Amusement Company, a major Louisiana chain, complained bitterly in a full-page trade advertisement:

> The methods they are using are as near Bolshevism as anything I know of. They hope to gain a hold for each tentacle of their octopus by threats and brute financial force, and the independent exhibitor who has worked years to get his theaters in paying class and has striven night and day to make motion picture fans of his town's population is a mere pawn in the operation of this huge octopus and classed by it as worthy of no consideration (quoted in Gertrude Jobes, *Motion Picture Empire* [Hamden, Conn.: Archon, 1966], p. 220).

Zukor bought into Saenger on 22 June 1920. He had already taken over the Black New England Theatres on 27 January and had bought out the Stanley Company of America the previous 1 August. With these interests, he not only acquired some of the nation's most important theater chains but gained control over three of the key First National franchise-holders. The rumor that he had silently acquired E. H. Hulsey's interests in Texas and Oklahoma (he had) demoralized the rest of the First National board, who were no longer sure which of their number was now in the enemy camp. This move so distressed Thomas Tally that he sold out all his theater interests, save his one Los Angeles flagship.[25]

Much of this expansion had been financed by a $10 million stock issue underwritten by Kuhn, Loeb in 1919. The rumor that Zukor intended to buy up every major theater in the country, combined with the knowledge that Wall Street millions were behind him, did a great deal to soften up the opposition. By 1921 Zukor had acquired 303 theaters, only a fraction of the 14,000 then operating, but significant because most of Zukor's houses were first-class, first-run theaters. Since only some two hundred key theaters existed, Zukor had gained an effective monopoly, according to the complaint of the Federal Trade Commission. The way these theaters were acquired, and their function in denying screen time to independent producers, became the second part of a lengthy FTC investigation that would continue throughout the decade.[26]

Despite the fact that Zukor had acquired several seats on the First National board, he had not been able to put First National out of business. While the FTC investi-

By 1926 First National's trade advertising was almost indistinguishable from that of the other studios. Their "unbeatable flow of . . . sure-fire performance" was led that season by Ken Maynard, Colleen, Moore, and Johnny Hines (*Motion Picture News*, 13 November 1926, p. 1834).

gation developed, Zukor's hands were effectively tied, and First National continued acquiring strong program material. It merged in 1921 with Associated Producers, a distributing combine handling the work of Thomas H. Ince, Allan Dwan, George Loane Tucker, Mack Sennett, Marshall Neilan, Maurice Tourneur, J. Parker Read, and King Vidor under the new name Associated First National. In 1923 it constructed its first studio complex, an elaborate facility in Burbank financed by several million dollars' worth of stock issued by Hayden, Stone, and Company. Sam Katz of the powerful Balaban and Katz chain in Chicago tried to organize support among the members to merge all the company's scattered interests into one tightly knit organization. But the unwieldy First National Board hesitated. By 1926 Zukor had managed to buy out Balaban and Katz, crippling First National for good, and had merged many of the components (including the Balaban and Katz chain itself) into his new Publix Theatres Corporation.[27]

"Now that the inventors, cameramen, exchangemen and exhibitors had taken their fling at motion picture control," wrote Terry Ramsaye, "it was the actors' turn." At the January 1919 convention of the First National Exhibitors Circuit, a wild rumor circulated concerning Adolph Zukor's latest attempt to eliminate his rival: a direct merger of First National and Paramount. Mary Pickford and Charles Chaplin were then both releasing through First National and would have fallen under the control of Zukor if the deal had gone through. Chaplin appeared before the executive committee to ask for an increase in his budget allotment, because, with A DOG'S LIFE and especially with SHOULDER ARMS (1918), he was spending far more on production than he had originally estimated. The committee refused. "I believe it has something to do with this motion picture convention," advised his brother, Sydney, who served as his financial manager. For Pickford, it was enough that "the trade papers reported that the men ruling the industry were planning to clamp the lid down on the salaries of actors." Realizing that, whatever the results of the merger discussions, events were reducing them to pawns in a far larger power struggle, Chaplin, Pickford, and Douglas Fairbanks (whose Paramount contract was nearing an end) decided on an immediate preemptive move. They quickly involved D. W. Griffith and William S. Hart (both then releasing through Paramount) and ostentatiously announced to the press an ambitious scheme to set up their own producing and distributing organization. According to Chaplin's later testimony, the announcement was a simple ruse: "It was not our intention to go through with the project, however. Our objective was only to stop exhibitors from signing a five-year contract with this proposed merger, for without the stars it would be worthless."[28]

But the response was so dramatic that the scheme quickly took on a life of its own. Pickford, Fairbanks, Griffith, and Chaplin signed the United Artists incorporation papers on 17 April 1919. Hart, who had already talked of retirement, did allow himself to sign again with Zukor, taking full advantage of the situation to raise his fee to $200,000 per picture. Because Hart was releasing six films a year by this time, he immediately moved into the million-dollar class, in addition to avoiding the corporate squabbles and financial problems that plagued the United Artists members for years to come.

Unfortunately, Pickford and Chaplin still owed films on their existing First National contracts before they could begin releasing through United Artists. Griffith, in order to raise his share of the initial United Artists financing, actually signed a three-picture contract with First National, thus keeping himself tied up until 1920. Only Fairbanks was immediately free, and the first United Artists release, HIS

MAJESTY, THE AMERICAN, was a Fairbanks picture, just as the first Triangle release had been four years earlier.[29]

Hiram Abrams, an experienced marketing executive who had served as president of Paramount after Hodkinson's dismissal, was appointed general manager of the new firm. Some historians, especially Benjamin Hampton, have claimed that the essential concept of United Artists was actually brought to Abrams by a young associate of his at Paramount, B. P. Schulberg, to whom he agreed to give half of his share if he could convince the top stars to sign. But by the time the final papers were drawn, Schulberg was out, only to bring suit on this issue in 1920. In his history of United Artists, Tino Balio notes that Abrams denied all Schulberg's claims, which were said to be based on an oral agreement between them. The case was settled out of court for an undisclosed sum. In any event, the existence of the Schulberg–Abrams argument implies that the impetus for an organization of film artists came not from the artists themselves but from one or another distribution executive.[30]

The early history of United Artists was extremely troublesome. Without automatic access to any theaters of its own, the firm needed to break the stranglehold of Paramount and First National (it was not entirely a coincidence that Paramount began its theater-buying spree the day after the incorporation of United Artists). The

D. W. Griffith, Mary Pickford, Charles Chaplin, and Douglas Fairbanks sign the United Artists incorporation papers on 17 April 1919. Attorneys H. T. Banzhof and Dennis F. O'Brian hover discreetly in the background.

United Artists members also needed to raise production money in advance, and they attempted, with little initial success, to get it from the theater owners themselves. Fearing a possible takeover attempt, the four partners refused to go public with their stock, but given the investment community's opinion of "independent" producers (those with no firm access to theaters), even this group would have had trouble raising money on Wall Street.[31] Said Mary Pickford in 1923:

> I have to worry so much about distribution now that my ability as an actress is impaired. Producers have so bottled up the best theaters that it is often impossible to get a showing of my pictures in them. I will retire from the business if the conditions become worse. . . . Key cities mean two-fifths of the returns. If the market is closed by block booking the producers owning theaters will eliminate the people who are seeking to make big pictures and conditions will lapse into the state of three years ago (quoted in William Seabury, *The Public and the Motion Picture Industry* [New York: Macmillan, 1926] p. 60).

While United Artists was originally to release twelve films per year, only seven were issued in 1920, their first full year of operation. To help fuel the distribution machinery, pickups from other producers needed to be acquired. A subsidiary named Allied Producers was established to handle work by such lesser lights as Charles Ray and Max Linder, but it proved unattractive. The partners quarreled among themselves over their own distribution practices, Griffith preferring to handle road-show engagements of his films personally, then turning them over to United Artists after he had already skimmed the better part of their potential earnings. Chaplin released nothing through United Artists until the end of 1923, and then only the commercially unsuccessful A WOMAN OF PARIS. A few big hits—WAY DOWN EAST (1920), ROBIN HOOD (1922), and THE GOLD RUSH (1925)—were outweighed by many unprofitable releases. Between 1919 and 1927 the United Artists Corporation claimed a loss in all but two years, and even those "profits" amounted to less cash than Adolph Zukor would have paid Mary Pickford in a month. United Artists' inability to distribute films efficiently on an individual basis must have seemed an object lesson to Zukor and the other block-booking proponents then under investigation by the FTC.[32]

At the end of 1924 Joseph Schenck was hired to reorganize the company, made an equal producing partner, and elected Chairman of the Board. He brought with him the contract of his wife, Norma Talmadge, who was by this time selling more tickets than Pickford. Moving immediately to increase the flow of product, Schenck signed Rudolph Valentino, Buster Keaton, Gloria Swanson, and producer Samuel Goldwyn. Such acquisitions had more publicity value than practical success. Keaton's films failed at the box office, Swanson became bogged down in the QUEEN KELLY fiasco, and Valentino died just before the release of SON OF THE SHEIK (1926). Goldwyn proved irascible and difficult, but his films were successful enough that he was elected a producing partner in 1927. By then Griffith was already gone, his own financial problems driving him back into a contract with Zukor.[33]

Schenck had begun to act on his own merger plans as well and attempted to join with Metro-Goldwyn-Mayer in 1925, but Chaplin, fearing the size of the prospective combine, rejected the idea. In creative terms, Chaplin may have been right, but the U.A. partners lost millions by failing to acquire a piece of MGM at the start of the

Mayer and Thalberg years. By the end of the silent period, Schenck had to content himself with a tentative expansion into exhibition by acquiring first-run houses for United Artists in a handful of key cities and reconstructing their distribution apparatus via the United Artists Theatre Circuit.

1919–1927: *Metro-Goldwyn-Mayer, Fox, Universal, and Warner Bros.*

If Joseph Schenck had been able to complete the merger with MGM, he would have been adding his forces to the industry's most sensational new combine. Metro-Goldwyn-Mayer Pictures Corporation was the production arm of Loew's, Inc., a theatrical enterprise organized and controlled by Marcus Loew. His action in effecting the Metro-Goldwyn merger in 1924 was the most significant move to date in the industry's increasing centralization, as well as another example of the fallout produced by the Paramount–First National battle. Entering the industry with a penny arcade, Marcus Loew gradually expanded to include nickelodeons and even legitimate theaters (mostly in the New York area) for which he programmed a mixture of vaudeville and motion pictures. Among Loew's many partners in various theatrical ventures were Nicholas and Joseph Schenck, the latter of whom he placed in charge of the booking of live acts for the Loew's circuit and the other theaters handled by the Marcus Loew Booking Agency. The Loew's circuit was small-time vaudeville, less prestigious than the big time of the B. F. Keith or Orpheum circuits, and gradually the film item came to dominate the program at Loew's theaters.[34]

By 1919 Loew had an interest (through various partnerships) in approximately fifty-six theaters. On 18 October of that year Loew's, Inc., was organized to consolidate the various enterprises under his direct control. Fueled by a $9.5 million loan underwritten by Montgomery and Company and Van Emburgh and Atterbury, it was immediately listed on the New York Stock Exchange. In January 1920 the new Loew's, Inc., acquired all the stock of the Metro Pictures Corporation, a producing and distributing organization that ran its own system of exchanges and operated studios on both coasts.[35]

Loew's move into production was a clear response to Zukor's policy of theater acquisition begun earlier in 1919. But despite one phenomenal initial success, the acquisition of Metro was not to be the answer to Loew's problems. Metro had been organized in 1915 as an outgrowth of the ill-fated Alco Film Corporation. Al Lichtman, once one of Zukor's partners in Famous Players, had formed Alco as an exhibitors' combine, almost a precursor of First National. But the organization foundered, and its disgruntled component members, short of expected product, reorganized with Richard Rowland as president and Louis B. Mayer as secretary.

The new Metro handled the product of various minor producers, including B. A. Rolfe, Quality Pictures, and Popular Plays and Players (which made Olga Petrova and Florence Reed pictures in a converted church on West Thirty-eighth Street in Manhattan). Louis B. Mayer, an important New England theater operator when he became involved in Metro, further enhanced his status by acquiring the local distribution rights to THE BIRTH OF A NATION. By 1917 he decided to go into production on his own and hired Anita Stewart away from Vitagraph. Because Stewart's Vitagraph contract was still valid, the ensuing legal tangle forced considerable delays, and

Production and exhibition chiefs meet on the set of Metro's THE FOUR HORSEMEN OF THE APOCALYPSE: *writer June Mathis, director Rex Ingram, corporate head Marcus Loew, theater owner Sid Grauman, and studio manager Joe Engel.*

their first film, VIRTUOUS WIVES, was not completed until late in 1918. Following a quarrel with Rowland regarding the film's distribution, Mayer quit Metro and signed with First National.[36]

At this point, Metro, having bought out many of its weakest members, was in very poor shape, while the stronger franchise holders had gone over to First National. Rowland's production policy wavered between inexpensive program pictures and elaborate specials with stars like Alla Nazimova, but Metro did not have the distribution base to exploit either alternative properly. In development when Loew acquired Metro in 1920 was an ambitious adaptation of THE FOUR HORSEMEN OF THE APOCALYPSE, masterminded by the studio's canny scenario editor, June Mathis. The film version's reputed $4.5 million gross would make it one of the super-hits of the silent era, and not long after its premiere, Loew matched its success by opening his elegant Loew's State Theatre in New York City (designed by classicist Thomas Lamb).[37] His theatrical holdings continued to prosper, but Metro Pictures failed to repeat the success of THE FOUR HORSEMEN, despite the acquisition of Jackie Coogan, Buster Keaton, and even producer Louis B. Mayer again (all independents distributing through Metro's exchanges). Unloading the operation would have left Loew without any ready source of films, and in any case, this practice would have gone counter to the expansive spirit of the age.

On 16 May 1924 Loew merged Metro with an even shakier producer-distributor, the Goldwyn Pictures Corporation.[38] After Samuel Goldwyn had been voted out in 1922, the company that bore his name continued to deteriorate. The new production head, Abe Lehr, brought over June Mathis as scenario editor, but her insights were of little practical help. While twenty-eight films had gone into production in 1921, only seven went before the cameras in 1922. The figure rose to fifteen the following year, but this was still not enough to keep the lights burning in the Goldwyn exchange system. Mathis did hire some of Hollywood's finest directors in an effort to improve the quality of Goldwyn releases—Marshall Neilan, King Vidor, and Erich von Stroheim—but catastrophic problems with GREED and BEN-HUR demonstrated how weak the management at Goldwyn really was.

Bosley Crowther writes that Goldwyn chief Joe Godsol failed in an attempt at a merger with First National (they built their own studio instead) and watched the company's stock drop from 22 in the spring of 1923 to 8¼ by the end of the year. Loew, who could hardly resist such an undervalued plum, acquired control through a simple exchange of stock, without any cash changing hands.[39]

Among the items included were the fine Goldwyn lot in Culver City (originally the Triangle lot), a distribution contract recently negotiated with William Randolph Hearst's Cosmopolitan Pictures, the services of the aforementioned directors, and Goldwyn's theater and exchange interests, which included control of New York's Capitol Theatre, the largest in the country. Replacing the Goldwyn management seemed to be the only problem, and to do this Loew brought in, as part of the deal, Louis B. Mayer, then operating his own Los Angeles studio on Mission Road.

The imposing facade of the MGM studio, originally built for Triangle by Harry Aitken. King Vidor's THE BIG PARADE, *then playing at Grauman's Egyptian Theatre, is advertised in a banner stretched across Washington Boulevard.*

In fact, to run the new studio Loew acquired what was known as "the Mayer group," which included not only Mayer but attorney J. Robert Rubin and production head Irving Thalberg, who had been working for Mayer since February 1923. This group was under personal contract and in addition to salaries would divide 20 percent of the profits of all films produced under their regime.[40] Harry Rapf, not one of the official group, was an immediate addition to the studio's executive cadre.

Their first move was to assert firm control over the disparate forces brought together by the merger. They refused to restore the cuts already made by the Goldwyn management in GREED; they changed directors and stars on the nightmarish BEN-HUR production and eventually recalled the entire company from Italy; they censured (and possibly blacklisted) troublemakers like Neilan. But for those who would play by the rules—directors such as King Vidor or Clarence Brown—they offered unprecedented material support and the fabulous distribution potential of the Loew's chain. For the favored few, a measure of artistic freedom could be achieved, but it was clear from the beginning that it was the executive office that would have the last word at MGM, an attitude underscored by Thalberg's increasing reliance on a producer system by the end of the silent period.

Marcus Loew lived to see little of the success of his brainchild. He died in 1927, and control of his empire passed to his chief lieutenant, Nicholas Schenck. A few years earlier, Schenck's brother, Joseph, had suggested a merger of MGM with United Artists. In 1929, Nicholas would make his own merger attempt by gathering together enough shares from the Loew estate and other interests to sell out Loew's, Inc., to a bitter rival, William Fox.

That deal was never consummated, but for most writers it remains William Fox's most significant claim to a place in their histories. Of far greater practical significance, however, were his battles with the Motion Picture Patents Company in 1912, while he was still a local exhibitor and the owner of the Greater New York Film Rental Company. Like Marcus Loew, Fox operated a series of second-class vaudeville houses in which films had become a major part of the bill. To ensure his film supply, he went into production as early as 1914, when the establishment of Box Office Attractions made him "the first movie man successfully to embrace in one organization all branches of the industry."[41]

Fox's first film, LIFE'S SHOP WINDOW (1914), was an instant success in a product-hungry market, but it was with Theda Bara that his organization really struck gold. Reorganized as the Fox Film Corporation on 1 February 1915, the new organization expanded production rapidly. It leased the old Willat studio in Fort Lee, New Jersey, as its main production center but operated many scattered studios in places like Hoboken, New Jersey, Flushing, New York, and Edendale, California. Fox's control over this production-distribution-exhibition combine was unique. Financed by a group of New Jersey investors headed by John F. Dryden, president of the Prudential Insurance Company, Fox was able to maintain majority control of this empire in his own hands, a claim neither Zukor, Laemmle, Loew, nor any other mogul could make.[42]

For a decade, Fox avoided the race for prestige driving Paramount and First National. With Theda Bara, William Farnum, and Tom Mix, he produced melodramas and action pictures to please the patrons of his unpretentious houses. One experiment with lavish spectacle, A DAUGHTER OF THE GODS (1916), starring swimming champion Annette Kellerman and directed by Herbert Brenon, was an error

The use of mobile cameras was only one aspect of Fox's SUNRISE that revolutionized Hollywood production techniques: chief cameramen Karl Struss and Charles Rosher behind the Mitchell cameras at the left, director F. W. Murnau seated at the center, his assistants Edgar G. Ulmer and Herman Bing seated at the right.

Fox did not repeat. Presaging Irving Thalberg, Fox took the film away from Brenon and cut it himself. More typical was OVER THE HILL (1920), a sentimental tale of filial ingratitude that earned $3 million in rentals, according to Fox. He claimed to have written the script and produced it personally.[43]

Unsophisticated films like OVER THE HILL brought continuing profits into the coffers of the Fox Film Corporation, but by 1925 even Fox had begun to worry about the increasing expansion of Paramount, First National, and Loew's. Fox's international theater holdings were vast, but according to Gertrude Jobes, by the late teens his domestic chain was limited to twenty-six lower-quality vaudeville picture houses. In 1925 he moved to rebuild his holdings with the creation of the Fox Theater Corporation. Stock in this organization, and in the Fox Film Corporation itself, was now offered to the public for the first time. With the proceeds of this issue, entire theater chains were acquired, including the Poli circuit, the Midwest circuit, and the West Coast Theatres, previously an important First National franchisee. By the end

TABLE 3.2   SIXTEEN-YEAR SUMMARY OF FOX FILMS PRODUCTION
COSTS AND GROSS RENTALS

Year	Pictures	No. of Negatives	Gross Rentals	Ratio of Costs to Rentals (%)
1914	4	$ 53,250	$ 272,401	23.9
1915	36	767,243	3,208,201	30.4
1916	52	1,289,785	4,244,558	41.6
1917	70	2,964,696	7,118,172	44.0
1918	73	3,212,689	7,300,301	31.2
1919	69	2,929,069	9,380,883	19.5
1920	71	4,317,403	12,609,725	34.2
1921	65	4,783,210	13,715,000	34.9
1922	66	4,350,083	12,327,957	35.3
1923	51	4,821,456	11,242,629	42.9
1924	46	3,610,433	9,926,025	36.4
1925	42	5,226,809	11,750,515	44.5
1926	51	8,328,252	14,274,234	58.3
1927	46	8,558,101	17,012,875	50.3
1928	55	10,379,365	22,626,747	45.9
1929	53	16,142,216	30,803,974	52.4
Total	851	$81,734,055	$187,810,297	43.5

SOURCE: *The Motion Picture Almanac* (1931), p. 67, and *Upton Sinclair Presents William Fox*, p. 69.

The column "Gross Rentals" includes all rentals from pictures released during the respective years, regardless of the fact that these rentals were received over a period of about two years. Pictures released in 1930 were not included because they were still being exhibited when the table was compiled. In addition, twenty pictures had not yet had their foreign release, which accounted for 33 percent of total gross rentals.

of the decade Fox would control over five hundred houses. He bought the Roxy from its developers just before opening night and took over the Yaraab Temple, would-be home of Atlanta's Shriners, which he rechristened the Atlanta Fox. This Arabian Nights spectacle, called "the most overpowering [atmospheric] theater of all" by historian David Naylor, is one of the last great picture palaces still surviving in the post-studio era. Some of the other theaters crafted by Fox were not so lucky. The San Francisco Fox, "the largest and grandest movie palace ever built on the west coast," was decorated with museum-quality art and antiques personally acquired by Mrs. Fox on her European shopping tours, but like the East Coast jewel of the Fox empire, the Roxy, it has long since disappeared.[44]

But Fox was not just picking up real estate. His acquisition of Theodore Case's sound-on-film process, as well as the European Tri-Ergon patents, put him in a commanding position to dominate the coming age of talking pictures. Impressed by Paramount's big-screen Magnascope effect (which enlarged the screen image to giant size) he set his own technicians to work perfecting a 70-mm process ultimately marketed as Fox Grandeur. Most telling of all, he drastically altered the style of the most ambitious Fox Film productions. The decision to acquire hundreds of upscale theaters meant that Fox could no longer depend entirely on the familiar melodramas and Westerns that had carried the studio for a decade. He sent his chief lieutenant, Winfield Sheehan, to supervise production operations on the West Coast and ordered a massive expansion of the studio facilities at Western Avenue and at Fox Hills, the newly acquired hundred-acre tract in Beverly Hills, California (table 3.2).[45]

His success with The Iron Horse in 1924 (a Western but a prestige Western, itself inspired by Paramount's The Covered Wagon [1923]) led to such powerful historic epics as What Price Glory? (1926) and Three Bad Men (1926). But Fox's boldest move was the importation of Germany's most respected director, F. W. Murnau. That Murnau's The Last Laugh (1924) had been a catastrophe at the American box office failed to daunt Fox, who not only allowed Murnau a free hand in the production of Sunrise (1927) but encouraged the studio's other contract directors—solid Americana types like John Ford, Raoul Walsh, and Frank Borzage—to study Murnau's style and take from it what they could. The results were such brilliant amalgams of German and American style as 7th Heaven (1927), Street Angel (1928), The Red Dance (1928), Hangman's House (1928), and The River (1928).

These dark and introspective works marked a significant change in Fox's most prestigious releases, but in fact, such experimentation was only icing on the traditional Fox cake. While Murnau and his crews were busy re-creating "swampscapes" inside the Western Avenue stages, Tom Mix still rode the range at Fox Hills. Bertha the Sewing Machine Girl (1926), The Return of Peter Grimm (1926), and Mother Machree (1928) upheld traditional Fox values for traditional Fox exhibitors, and the Fox Film Corporation was able to absorb its experiment in expressionism without affecting overall profitability.

A different situation evolved at Universal. Like Fox's operation, the studio run by Carl Laemmle was highly successful in serving the needs of small exhibitors in the pre-1925 period. Westerns, melodramas, and short comedies, spiced with an occasional prestige effort, made the product of both companies rather similar in this period, and very different from that of Paramount, First National, or Metro-Goldwyn-Mayer. But Universal had special problems of its own, inherited from its early days as a consortium of independent producers organized in opposition to the Motion Picture Patents Company.

By the time Universal City opened in 1915, only the tenacious Pat Powers still contested Laemmle's hold over the company. Most of the internal dissension was gone, but a rational method of organizing the studio's vast output (fifty-four reels a week by 1916) eluded the company until the arrival of Irving Thalberg. Carl Laemmle often used the Woolworth metaphor to describe his position in the motion-picture business, and the most successful years of his administration did see Universal profit through the merchandising of vast quantities of cheap goods. But this "nickel-and-dime" philosophy was ultimately responsible for the studio's abrupt decline in the early sound years and Laemmle's departure not long after. Universal, while well situated in 1915 with a fine new studio and an aggressive distribution system, soon found itself falling behind its competition in the use of stars, the ownership of theaters, and even the introduction of feature pictures.[46]

Despite the fact that Universal had distributed three of the most successful early features—Paul J. Rainey's African Hunt (1912), Traffic in Souls (1913), and NEPTUNE'S DAUGHTER (1914)—Laemmle resisted the move away from a "balanced program" of short subjects much longer than any of his competitors. In a 1915 editorial headlined "Quit Using Dope!" he attacked feature-length pictures as "overdone" and claimed that the public was already tiring of them. Two years later he was still promoting his "regular service" program of one-, two-, and three-reel pictures, attacking feature-length films, and decrying the lavish presentation policies of the downtown theaters as wasteful. What is especially odd is that throughout this period Universal was offering not only the regular service program of short subjects but an entire range of feature pictures, some handled through their own exchanges and some distributed via states rights release. Promotions for each were carried in the studio house paper, alongside these continuing editorial attacks on the feature. Not until mid 1917 did Universal stop offering this full program of shorts, and the production of two-reel Westerns and comedies remained a staple there throughout the silent era.[47]

Laemmle had earlier been responsible for the promotion of Florence Lawrence and Mary Pickford, which gained him some credit for "launching" the star system. But in 1915 his experience with a line of "Broadway Features"—starring such theater imports as Jane Cowl, Nat Goodwin, and Florence Reed—completely soured him on stars, and he spent the rest of his career grumbling about them. While Aitken, Zukor, and others moving heavily into the production of features continued to promote the star, Laemmle resisted long enough to leave his studio almost bereft of big-name talent by the postwar period.

In the late teens Universal was known as a giant factory where work was easily attainable but working conditions (especially salary) remained substandard. During this period, John Ford, Rudolph Valentino, Rex Ingram, Lon Chaney, and Mae Murray all spent considerable time at Universal, but just as they began to establish themselves, Laemmle let them get away, lured elsewhere by promises of greater control, money, or both. By 1919 he had even lost Lois Weber, his most important director during the war years, although in this case her subsequent career, at First National and Paramount, was brief and unfortunate.

Historians have often noted the fact that Universal was heavily committed to women directors during the late teens. Lois Weber, Ida May Park, Cleo Madison, Ruth Stonehouse, Elsie Jane Wilson, Grace Cunard, and Ruth Ann Baldwin were all directing there by 1917. Because most of these women were hired before the establishment of the military draft, the shortage of manpower resulting from the war was not the reason for this situation. Laemmle's low pay scale and vast production needs might have been part of the explanation (as it was years later at Roger Corman's New World Pictures), but Universal was certainly not the only cheap studio in town. Idiosyncratic personal judgments seem to have played an important role in Universal's hiring policies. Laemmle was very fond of Lois Weber, for example, and when she fell on hard times in later years, he gave her work directing screen tests and doctoring scripts. The early Weber films had paid off handsomely, and perhaps he enjoyed continuing the gamble.[48] This well-known gambler's instinct (promoted in the trades as "Laemmle luck") seems to have induced him to hire Erich von Stroheim as a director at a time when von Stroheim's only reputation was that of a stock villain in World War I atrocity pictures. Von Stroheim's films, especially FOOLISH WIVES (1922), became the studio's tentative entries in the growing postwar competition for prestige pictures. Ultimately, von Stroheim proved more trouble than he was worth, and the man given the responsibility of putting him in his place, Irving Thalberg, emerged as Universal's most significant contributor to the rise of the modern studio system.

Thalberg was another of Laemmle's hunches, appointed general manager of the studio before he was old enough to sign checks.[49] Breaking von Stroheim was his way of demonstrating that control would henceforth be centered in the front office, not

Advertised as "the first million-dollar picture," Erich von Stroheim's FOOLISH WIVES *helped establish a new image for Universal in the postwar era.*

scattered among various production units as it had been during the late teens. For a time, Thalberg was also able to ward off the conflicting and confusing orders that issued from New York, contradictory signals which had made the position of all previous general managers quite impossible.

For example, in a letter to Thalberg dated 5 December 1922 Laemmle expresses disappointment regarding THE SHOCK (1922), has faint praise for THE STORM (1922), complains about various cost overruns, second-guesses Thalberg's choices of writers and directors, predicts that Wallace Worsley will turn THE HUNCHBACK OF NOTRE DAME (1923) into another "flivver," and urges, "Irving, turn over a new leaf, do business along conservative lines, and be cocksure you are right before you go ahead with anything."[50] Within a few months, he had lost Thalberg to Louis B. Mayer.

Two Thalberg projects, THE HUNCHBACK OF NOTRE DAME and MERRY-GO-ROUND (1923), were major financial successes for Universal in 1923–1924 and encouraged Laemmle to increase the quality of the general run of Universal features. He brought in Al Lichtman as general sales manager, and Lichtman announced to the sales force, "I have come to the conclusion that exhibitors want bigger pictures, and will pay to get them." In line with this policy, Laemmle reorganized his operation in 1925, selling $3 million worth of stock in Universal Pictures, Inc., a holding company that controlled the studio, its exchanges, and a small theater circuit called the Universal Chain Theaters.[51]

But Universal's move into domestic theaters had come too late (their foreign holdings were already considerable, however). In 1926 Robert H. Cochrane, the company's vice-president, complained that Universal was suffering from the lack of first-run houses and noted that, when their lease on New York's 539-seat Cameo Theatre expired four months hence, they would have no first-run theater in that city available to them.[52] As it happened, the theaters acquired proved so ineffective that Universal began to sell off the chain in 1927.

To create the elaborate films needed to meet this supposed exhibitor demand, Universal leaned heavily on its European connections. Not only was Laemmle a major owner of German theaters, but he was involved in European coproduction and in 1926 had even tried to merge with the German production firm UFA. Fox may have acquired Murnau, but Universal's exotic European talent was the most broadly based of all the Hollywood studios. By the end of the silent era, E. A. Dupont, Paul Leni, Paul Fejos, Dimitri Buchowetzki, Conrad Veidt, and Edgar G. Ulmer were all on the Universal lot. With such films as THE MAN WHO LAUGHS (1928) and LONESOME (1928), they offered new stylistic models for familiar Universal genres. Even a little Western like WILD BLOOD (1928), nominally featuring Rex, King of the Wild Horses, contains more than its share of superimpositions and hand-held subjective camerawork. But the lack of effective exhibition outlets, combined with increasing production costs, strangled Universal's profits by the end of the 1920s. A film like THE CAT AND THE CANARY (1927) might do very well at the box office, but as Carl Laemmle could hardly help noticing, the box office usually belonged to someone else.

There was one studio, of course, whose role in the history of silent film was remarkably small but that ultimately succeeded in upending the entire medium: Warner Bros. Harry, Sam, Albert, and Jack Warner had been touring exhibitors in the store-show era, exchange operators (who were forced to sell out to the General Film Company), and states rights distributors. Their infrequent early efforts at production reached a peak with MY FOUR YEARS IN GERMANY (1918), taken from ambassador James W. Gerrard's best-seller, which successfully exploited a tide of wartime patriotism.

Through the aid of Motley Flint, vice-president of the Los Angeles Trust and Savings Bank, the brothers obtained a cash loan of $1 million, some of which went into their new Hollywood studio at Sunset and Bronson. Production activity was minimal, however: one film in 1920, three in 1921. On 4 April 1923 they reorganized as Warner Bros. Pictures, Inc., and began a more ambitious production program that included acquiring the rights to a series of David Belasco properties and, more successfully, initiating a series of features starring a dog, Rin-Tin-Tin. Even more than at Fox or Universal, Warners releases in this period were characterized by outdated society melodramas and soap operas. Such films had little appeal in urban centers, but the brothers were essentially states rights specialists and were able to market their films successfully to the thousands of theaters located outside the big cities or otherwise unaffiliated with the major chains.[53]

With "expand or die" as the industry watchword, Warners decided to acquire theaters and raise the general level of their releases. They made the startling move of hiring Ernst Lubitsch and John Barrymore, and in December 1924 they bought their first theater—in their hometown, Youngstown, Ohio. Thirteen more theaters followed the next year. As with so many other studios, 1925 proved to be a year of expansion driven by Wall Street investment. Forming a close association with Waddill Catchings and the firm of Goldman, Sachs, Warners floated a $4 million stock issue. On 23 April 1925, they acquired control of the Vitagraph Company of America. Nearly moribund as a producer, Vitagraph did operate thirty-four domestic and twenty foreign exchanges as well as large studio facilities on both coasts. The brothers were now directly involved in exhibition, but they needed an edge of some sort if they intended to compete with the larger, better-financed, and longer-entrenched chains of their rivals. To this end they formed the Vitaphone Corporation of America on 25 June 1925.[54]

The Vitaphone process was a sound-on-disc system developed by Western Electric that Sam Warner felt could supply inexpensive canned musical accompaniments for features, thus eliminating the salaries of house orchestras in the growing Warners chain and providing a potent attraction for the small outlying houses that the Warners had serviced for so many years. Since March 1925 Warner Bros. had operated radio station KWBC in Los Angeles, and the microphone held no terrors for them.

While the recorded musical sound track of DON JUAN gained some acclaim at its 6 August 1926 premiere (as did the accompanying program of all-talking shorts), not until Warners used some dialogue in a feature picture did the talking film demonstrate that it might supplant the silent picture as the industry standard. It is easy to exaggerate the impact of the premiere of THE JAZZ SINGER on 6 October 1927. Silent films did not disappear overnight, nor did talking films immediately flood the theaters. Wiring for sound proceeded at a brisk pace, but it was limited by the realities of the manufacturing process. Two years later, silent films with stars like Greta Garbo and Lon Chaney were still opening and still playing to excellent business.[55] Nonetheless, 1927 remains the year that Warner Bros. moved to close the book on the history of silent pictures, even if their original goal had been somewhat more modest.

*   *   *

William Auerbach-Levy's stylized poster design for THE JAZZ SINGER (1927) *omits any mention of music, sound, or the Vitaphone.*

From 1915 to 1928 the structure of the American motion-picture industry had changed dramatically, and one of the major reasons behind this change was the way in which the industry was financed. In 1915 *Motion Picture* magazine had simply warned its readers to stay away from motion-picture investment schemes.[56] This was the standard line at the time, based on observed industry instability and the lack of any business methods that Wall Street analysts might understand as rational. As internal pressures forced film industry executives to seek capital in the marketplace, they tried to entice investors by making their organizations seem more businesslike and by promoting the notion that the cinema was one of the nation's industrial giants.

The first goal could be accomplished in a relatively straightforward, if time-consuming, manner. *The Commerce Monthly* announced in September 1924:

> The motion picture industry is slowly getting out of the class of a game and more in the class of a business. A settling-down process has been taking place during the past two years, resulting in the establishment of three fundamental principles: first, that production costs cannot be enlarged indefinitely without straining the financial basis of production to the breaking point; second, that sound financial methods are indispensable for the progress of the industry; and third, that public approval and good will are its most valuable assets (quoted in "A Banking Endorsement of the Industry," *Film Daily Yearbook* [1925], p. 55).

Barron's reported in 1924 that "the principal objection bankers make to producers' methods is not so much in the sum of money they spend in staging a story, as in their failure to keep within agreed limits." Three years later, analysts at *Forbes* pointed to Famous Players–Lasky as one firm that had nearly eliminated this problem. They reported that Famous Players–Lasky was generally within 2 percent of its annual production budget each year and that, out of a dozen costly features in the $1.5 million range, there was a difference of only $3,000 between the initial budget and the actual cost. "That looks as though the industry were on a business basis," they noted with approval. Even better, the studio had adopted uniform bankers' forms, ironed out the seasonal spurts of production that had made it impossible to predict cash flow, and eliminated most production waste. "Lasky has figures to show that his factory, which he calls a 'studio,' averages 90% of capacity," *Forbes* noted.[57]

In fact, according to Famous Players–Lasky comptroller Richard Saunders, writing in the *New York Times* in November 1926, it was this slow recognition that "certain of the prominent companies [had] built up proper organizations, along recognized industrial lines," which triggered the massive flow of Wall Street money in 1925–1926. Because theater attendance remained at a flat 46 million per week in 1924 and 1925, it was clearly greater efficiency, not increasing audiences, that attracted these investors.[58]

Howard T. Lewis, in his 1933 study *The Motion Picture Industry*, shows that funded debt grew substantially in the industry throughout the 1920s, from less than $10 million in 1921 to over $300 million in 1930 (table 3.3). More significantly, this debt as a percentage of total invested capital rose from 12 to 36 percent in the same period. The nearly 100 percent increase in this debt load over 1925–1926 coincides with the major stock issues floated that year by most of the major motion-picture firms.

To quote Richard Saunders again, 1925 "might be viewed as the year in which the motion picture industry became definitely recognized as stabilized and the stocks of the leaders regarded as safe investments."[59] Harry Aitken and Lewis Selznick had learned, to their chagrin, that bringing in outside investors had liabilities as well as

TABLE 3.3   GROWTH IN INVESTED CAPITAL 1921–1930
(UNIT: $1,000)

Year	Funded Debt	Capital Stores, Reserves, and Surplus	Total Invested Capital
1930	$305,586	$544,400	$849,986
1929	227,066	425,599	652,665
1928	128,537	278,804	407,341
1927	105,465	165,798	271,263
1926	71,578	157,909	229,467
1925	35,935	129,182	165,117
1924	25,266	97,465	122,731
1923	22,703	77,723	100,426
1922	15,966	73,572	89,538
1921	9,691	68,539	78,230

SOURCE: *The Motion Picture Industry* (Poor's Analytical Services, 1932), reprinted in Howard T. Lewis, *The Motion Picture Industry* (New York: Van Nostrand, 1933), p. 24.

benefits, and in the years to follow, most other producers would be forced to confront the same dilemma.

The larger context of industry boosterism, against which this influx of capital took place, plays an intriguing, if uncertain, part in this story. Was the motion-picture business one of America's industrial giants? Most analysts of the time appeared to see it that way and advised their clients accordingly. In January 1916 the *New York Times* reported that motion pictures ranked "fifth in importance among the industries of this country," behind agriculture, transportation, oil, and steel. In fact, the glowing tone of this piece might almost seem a paid insertion on the part of the industry: "The ramifications of the film industry are almost limitless," it sighs.[60]

As early as 1919, however, this "fifth-largest industry" claim was coming under direct attack, with one analyst proposing "the top ten" as a more likely supposition. The argument would rage around this issue throughout the silent era, because even within the industry not everyone was pleased with the attention garnered by the more lavish of these claims. The *Motion Picture News* found them "so absurd that it is difficult to understand their wide acceptance." Worried that legislative and public-interest groups would take a harder line with the film industry if they considered it a colossus, the *News* tried to promote a low-profile approach and hired the Babson Research Organization to collect accurate data in 1922 (although they never did propose a different industrial ranking).[61]

When Will Hays came on the scene, one of his first duties was to "restore the bankers' confidence in the industry" after a series of notorious scandals, and among the ways he accomplished this was through a continuing promotion of the industry as large, stable, and secure. His 1929 book *See and Hear* claimed that the motion-picture industry was "well among the first ten industries in the country," and for the period, this assessment was on the modest side. *Barron's* had reported in 1924 that the movies were in seventh place among America's leading industries, and the *Wall*

Street News put film in the fourth slot in 1926. Carl Laemmle claimed in 1927 that United States Commerce Department statistics listed the film industry in eighth place, but most commentators were not so specific about the source of their information. E. E. Quantrell, vice-president of Halsey, Stuart, and Company, wrote in the *Banker's Monthly* for October 1927 that the U.S. Bureau of the Budget had ranked film as the fourth-largest industry. Of course, Halsey, Stuart was deeply involved in industry financing at this point, but other analysts should have been more objective.[62]

The wide acceptance of such figures continued as late as 1966, in Gertrude Jobes's *Motion Picture Empire*, the first attempt in many years at a history of the industry. Chapter headings included "America's Fifth Industry (1914 to 1918)" and "America's Fourth Industry (1920 to 1934)." But most recent scholarship is decidedly more conservative on the relative size of the motion-picture business. Even in 1944 Mae Huettig claimed that "in so far as size of industry is measured by dollar volume of business, the motion picture industry is not only not among the first ten, it is not even among the first forty. It is surpassed by such industries, to name only a few, as laundries, restaurants, loan companies, investment trusts, liquor, tobacco and musical instruments." Using data from the Bureau of Internal Revenue's 1937 *Statistics of Income*, Huettig placed the film industry forty-fifth in volume of business.[63]

Huettig's was not the first revisionist assessment, although it remains the most influential. As early as 1931 the French critic Lucien Lehman, in a caustic study entitled *American Illusion*, had put the industry in seventy-fifth place, based on the value of annual production. Lehman argued that factoring in the profits of theater companies was like including stationery stores in an account of the printing industry. While this attitude displays a serious lack of understanding of the connection between the production and exhibition ends of the American film industry, the real problem is that Huettig and Lehman were applying different criteria from those used by their predecessors. They chose to count different returns, and their application of statistics was very selective.[64]

In any case, the crucial issue during the 1920s was the perceived position of the industry, a status that might draw the interest of government regulators but would certainly attract its share of investment interest as well. Whatever the truth of the matter, the movement into Hollywood of such vast amounts of capital suggests that the business community at large was reasonably convinced.

4

Making Movies

Breaking into the Business

*B*y 1915 the motion-picture industry had achieved a certain sophistication in the way it produced, marketed, and exhibited its pictures. Significant economic and industrial forces now acted to standardize these procedures, although filmmaking in the silent era could hardly be thought of as routine. What remained in a primitive and even chaotic state was the most elementary aspect of the filmmaking process: recruitment and training of new personnel. This is not to say that there was any shortage of activity in this area. Many volumes of self-instruction were published, schools abounded (some of them even legitimate), and magazine advertisements enticed men and women out to the studios. But the results of all this activity were negligible. Some actors and directors successfully came from the legitimate stage (many more were unsuccessful), and a few short-story writers and romantic novelists found new careers as photoplaywrights.

If memoirs and oral histories are to be believed, accident and bizarre coincidence seem to have been responsible for a disproportionate number of major careers. Allan Dwan, an electrical engineer, arrived to install Cooper-Hewitt lamps at the Chicago Essanay studio and stayed to write and direct. Raoul Walsh had most recently been working as a cowboy. Lois Wilson was a beauty-contest winner. Robert Flaherty was an explorer. The tremendous expansion of the industry within a single generation had created employment for thousands, but without a usable tradition there seemed no rational way to master the various professional skills involved. Relying on the theater as a model had limited application, and in the most technical areas, such as editing or cinematography, guideposts were nonexistent. Such fields soon came to be dominated by men and women who entered them just out of school and grew up with the medium, like Arthur Miller and Lee Garmes behind the camera, or Dorothy Arzner and William Hornbeck at the editing bench.[1]

Organized schooling seems to have had almost no success in preparing young hopefuls for motion-picture work, despite a surprising amount of effort. Columbia University demonstrated a commitment to film studies throughout this period but without any notable acceptance from either the industry or the academy. In 1914 Columbia introduced film as a teaching aid in the Journalism School and extended its use the following year into economics, science, history, psychology, and English-

The study of screenwriting and cinematography was advertised along with play money and podiatric remedies in the January 1915 issue of Motion Picture Magazine *(p. 156).*

literature classes. Victor O. Freeburg (author of *Disguise Plots in Elizabethan Drama*) lectured on film at Columbia from the fall of 1915 to the spring of 1917 and eventually produced a pair of sophisticated texts, *The Art of Photoplay Making* (1918) and *Pictorial Beauty on the Screen* (1923). Frances Taylor Patterson began as "instructor of Photoplay Composition" in the summer of 1917 and continued into the talking era. While Freeburg essentially defined screen art in graphic terms, Patterson had a stronger interest in narrative, and her three books are almost completely concerned with the niceties of plot construction. The avowed purpose of her class was to help foster public appreciation of film and offer prospective screenwriters a "short cut to success."[2]

When America entered World War I, the U.S. Army Signal Corps established a training school at Columbia University to provide instruction in the making of medical and historical-record films. Among those who passed through this program, either as students or as instructors, were Josef von Sternberg, Alan Crosland, Ernest B. Schoedsack, Irvin Willat, and Lewis Milestone. These men, and others, later looked back on their Signal Corps service as a valuable shared experience, but what they might have gained directly from this schooling is unclear. Efforts to continue a course in film production after the war were defeated because Columbia refused to support it with proper equipment or facilities and because according to one faculty member, "the funds to pay competent instructors were inadequate."[3]

Other attempts to shape film as an object of university study in this period ranged from Vachel Lindsay's lectures at his alma mater, the University of Chicago, to a series conducted by Joseph P. Kennedy at Harvard's Graduate School of Business Administration. An increasingly sophisticated amateur film movement (especially after the introduction of the 16-mm Bell & Howell Filmo in 1923) did make use of many of these manuals and scenario models, but they seem to have had little effect on the industry as a whole.[4]

When established programs like the one at Columbia failed to satisfy the demand for film production courses, a rash of private technical schools arose, most derided by the industry as mere "sucker traps." Such instruction was aimed largely at four major crafts: acting, writing, cinematography, and projection. Directing, while always given lip service in the various "Breaking into the Movies" manuals, was so hard to conceptualize that little energy was devoted to promoting it as a way of making a living. For example, one 1921 manual limits its discussion of directing to this observation: "Next in line is the director, who takes the scenario and sets out to make the picture. There is a shortage of directors at present, and for that reason, salaries are particularly high in this line, but of course, direction is a profession which takes many years of study. . . ."[5]

Prospective actors and actresses appear to have been the most widely victimized of these hopefuls. Relatively harmless instructional manuals like *Motion Picture Acting* (1916) offered for study "191 posed photographs of motion picture stars, showing 499 different expressions and emotions." Readers of Mae Marsh's *Screen Acting* (1921) learned that circumstance, hard work, and native talent developed before the camera were the keys to screen success—a dictum broad enough to discourage no one.[6]

Publicity regarding the "effortless" rise of many movie favorites encouraged large numbers of men and women to see themselves as potential screen material. This route was perceived as far easier than stage stardom as well as more accessible to the young and impressionable (Lillian Gish, Mary Pickford, Norma Talmadge, and others became major film stars while still in their teens). *Motion Picture* reported various "fakes and frauds" directed at such young hopefuls. In one common "scam," magazine advertisements would solicit "directory entries" (for a fee) that would be circulated to the studios. Because films were not cast in this fashion, the use of such directories by unknowns was worthless.[7]

For a time, many film studios followed the pattern of popular literary magazines in accepting unsolicited story contributions. A torrent of books on the writing and selling of photoplays was patterned after similar volumes in more established fields. For example, A. Van Buren Powell's *The Photoplay Synopsis* (1919) was the latest in one series that already included *Writing the Short Story, Writing for Vaudeville, The Technique of the Mystery Story*, and others.[8]

Organizations like the Palmer Photoplay Corporation offered a "complete Course and Service in Photoplay Writing." For a fee of ninety dollars (less for cash), students received two textbooks (including the *Photoplay Plot Encyclopedia*, which discussed the thirty-six dramatic situations in terms of motion-picture style), three sample film scripts (including Lois Weber's FOR HUSBANDS ONLY [1918]), a subscription to the *Photoplaywright*, the right to staff criticism of five submissions, and a series of booklets or "lectures" with titles like "Photoplay Elements of Situation Comedy" by Al Christie, or "The Necessity and Value of Theme in the Photoplay" by Jeanie MacPherson. Cecil B. DeMille, Thomas H. Ince, Lois Weber, and Rob Wagner served as Palmer's "advisory board."[9]

A rival operation, the Photoplaywrights' League of America, provided no written texts but offered to act as agent for its members in the sale of scripts. Criticism of manuscript submissions and legal and financial advice were also available. Sada Cowan and J. Grubb Alexander were among the "professional members" listed in its brochure.[10]

With the availability of good 35-mm motion-picture cameras on the open market, even the once-mysterious field of cinematography became accessible to ambitious amateurs. Ernest A. Dench advised "the ambitious young man or woman determined to break into the studios as a regular Motion Picture photographer" that many local opportunities already existed. He suggested establishing a service to film weddings, children, pets, and other domestic subjects, the production of advertising or industrial films, occasional work as a newsreel stringer, or even the establishment of one's own local newsreel. Creating an "amateur photoplay society . . . is no more expensive than is dabbling at ordinary photography on a moderate scale," Dench claimed. "Those with acting ability can figure in the cast, while the member possessing the most dramatic aptitude should be made the director. The talented weaver of stories would be the right man for scenario editor, provided he studied a book on photoplay writing and mastered the technique of photoplay construction. Last, but by no means least, you should do justice to the position of camera-man."[11]

Camera skills might be acquired at the New York Institute of Photography, which offered a classroom program as well as a correspondence course. It promoted its own 35-mm cine camera, the Institute Standard, especially for such semiprofessional work, and issued various texts through its Falk Publishing Company.[12]

These were the glamorous areas of the motion-picture industry, but the ten thousand local projectionists (1920 figures) were also fair game for unscrupulous educators. Sink-or-swim training seems to have been the conventional route here, something that was not the case in cinematography or editing, where an apprentice-ship system developed. It was not uncommon for the ill-trained graduates of "pro-jection schools" to find themselves alone in a booth with no idea of how to put on the evening's show.[13] Unfortunately, these were the men ultimately responsible for the quality of the show seen by the public, the weakest link in the chain apparently being the last.

New York and Hollywood

Southern California was clearly recognized as the major American production center by 1915, although the generic use of the term "Hollywood" to describe nearly all such activity had not yet developed. With studios scattered from Santa Monica to Edendale to Pasadena (and north to San Francisco and east to Phoenix), most com-mentators spoke of the area "in and about Los Angeles" as the "Mecca of the Motion

Selling Los Angeles real estate at the Sphinx Realty Company, late 1920s.

Picture." By 1924, however, a Hollywood mythos was clearly emerging. Perley Poore Sheehan, a popular screenwriter, issued a bizarre tract called *Hollywood as a World Center*, which combined elements of small-town boosterism, industry braggadocio, and occult transcendentalism (known locally as "new thought"). For Sheehan, "The rise of Hollywood and its parent city, Los Angeles, has world-wide significance. It is a new and striking development in the history of civilization. . . . This flooding of population to the Southwest has its origins in the dim past. It is the culmination of ages of preparatory struggle, physical, mental and spiritual. In brief, we are witnessing the last great migration of the Aryan race." Going beyond traditional American disdain for the eastern cities, Sheehan saw the birth of Hollywood as the dawn of the Aquarian age and described a New Jerusalem that would reveal to all mankind the "Universal Subconscious."[14]

In the absence of any traditional moral, intellectual, or religious framework, such philosophizing was quite popular in Hollywood in the boom years of the immediate postwar era, especially among the circle around Nazimova, Valentino, and June Mathis. Before it faded from fashion, one could see its traces in such curious films as the Mathis–Valentino YOUNG RAJAH (1922) or Sheehan's original story THE WHISPERING CHORUS (1918) for Cecil B. DeMille. But its representation in specific films is far less important than the gauge it provides to help measure the emotional and intellectual distance between Hollywood and the traditional centers of American culture. The physical isolation of the place—five days by rail from the corporate home offices—very quickly inculcated a special "Hollywood" way of looking at life that generations of audiences would instantly recognize. European films tended to be produced in and around traditional centers of national culture—Paris, London, Vienna, Rome, Berlin—but this community of desert exiles made something very different of the American cinema. Of course, such films won the contempt of American critics for many years, but audiences worldwide (and some foreign critics, such as Louis Delluc) felt otherwise. Movies from Hollywood would become the first American cultural export to conquer the world.

Equating American film production in this period with Hollywood production is, however, somewhat misleading. That colony was a factory town, producing the motion-picture industry's major product, while executive operations, newsreel production, and even much of the animation industry remained in the East. Kevin Brownlow, in *Hollywood: The Pioneers*, gives a flavorful account of early West Coast units seeking and finding "sun, space, and somnolence." The fact that Los Angeles was renowned as "the nation's leading open-shop, nonunion city" also did not hurt, keeping wages to half what they might have been in the East.[15]

The concentration of feature production in Hollywood during the teens was widely noted at the time, especially because few could have predicted the rapidity of this migration. Although visiting companies had worked in Los Angeles since 1908, much of the outlying area was still largely a wilderness in 1915, lacking equipment houses, prop and costume shops, a steady supply of professional actors, or even basic sanitation and safety. Thomas H. Ince and a group from his studio were robbed "stagecoach style" by four masked gunmen on "the lonely road near Inceville" in March 1915. Three years later, Erich von Stroheim was still carrying a revolver under the seat whenever he and his fiancée drove the dangerous Cahuenga Pass to Universal City. In this light the stories told by Cecil B. DeMille, Allan Dwan, and others, regarding the need for sidearms to protect themselves from Patents Company thugs, might conceivably have a more mundane explanation.[16]

The shortage of open space was a major drawback of the eastern studios, but few were as cramped as Cosmopolitan, located at 127th Street and Second Avenue in Manhattan. First National shot PARADISE *here in 1926.*

Florida was not always an easy solution to the eastern studios' problems with winter production. On a chilly beach near Jacksonville, the Thanhouser unit poses for a gag photo on 15 February 1916.

It was generally accepted that the West Coast studios were producing 125 reels of film per week in 1915, including everything from split-reel comedies to THE BIRTH OF A NATION. Knowledgeable estimates put this figure at between 62.5 and 75 percent of total American production.[17] Despite the fact that the bulk of domestic production had already moved to the West Coast, it was only in 1914–1915 that the makeshift facilities used by most of the producers were replaced by permanent installations comparable to the eastern studios, most notably the American Studio in Santa Barbara and Carl Laemmle's Universal City.

The comparatively large segment of production remaining in the East maintained its position throughout the early feature years, when the proximity of Broadway plays and players caused firms such as Goldwyn and Famous Players to increase the output of their New York and Fort Lee studios. This situation survived until the winter of 1918–1919, when problems with coal rationing forced nearly all the companies then operating in the East to consolidate operations in their West Coast facilities. Paramount-Artcraft closed in Fort Lee but kept operating at their Fifty-sixth Street studio in Manhattan; Universal closed all their eastern studios except their Coytesville, New Jersey, operation; Goldwyn, Metro, and Fox moved everyone to the West Coast; Vitagraph kept only a small operation in the East. Only World Film remained, because "their coal is not only all purchased, but delivered."[18]

This forcible relocation was strongly resisted by many filmmakers who found California unsuitable as a production center, but not until after the Armistice could anything be done about it. As soon as wartime restrictions were lifted, a boom in studio construction swept the New York area (for various reasons this renaissance bypassed Fort Lee, which soon disappeared as a production center). D. W. Griffith, who had filmed Hollywood's most stupendous films, THE BIRTH OF A NATION and INTOLERANCE, created a new studio for himself on the Flagler estate in Mamaroneck, just north of New York City. The East was where "the money and the brains" were, he said, as he proceeded to film WAY DOWN EAST (1920), ORPHANS OF THE STORM (1922), AMERICA (1924), and other costly features in Mamaroneck.[19]

William Randolph Hearst transformed Sulzer's Harlem River Park and Casino into the vast Cosmopolitan studio, a beer-hall-to-movie-lot conversion that also occurred at the smaller Mirror studio in Glendale, Queens. At Cosmopolitan, Marion Davies starred in such lavish epics as WHEN KNIGHTHOOD WAS IN FLOWER (1922), LITTLE OLD NEW YORK (1923), and JANICE MEREDITH (1924), an underrated Revolutionary War spectacle.[20]

Vitagraph increased the pace of its New York operations, while Goldwyn and Metro reopened their eastern studios. Fox came back as well, opening a large new studio on West Fifty-fifth Street in Manhattan, where Pearl White and Allan Dwan worked from 1920. This facility continues in operation today as the Cameramart stages. The Talmadge sisters had their studio on East Forty-eighth Street, and various rental studios abounded, hosting such New York–based stars as Richard Barthelmess. By September 1920 the *Exhibitors Trade Review* headlined "Producers Say California Has Been Filmed Out—Are Looking for New Producing Centers." The paper reported that all the major companies were now making films in the New York area and that California's weather remained its sole compelling asset.[21]

That month the most important of the new eastern studios opened, the Famous Players–Lasky studio in Astoria. Over the next seven years, this studio would produce 127 silent features, serving as home base for those Paramount stars who preferred to work in the East, such as Gloria Swanson (nine films) or Bebe Daniels

Sidewalks being laid for the new Famous Players–Lasky studio in Astoria, New York, 1920. The imposing edifice seems intended to suggest a railroad terminal, not a movie studio.

Filming A SAINTED DEVIL on the backlot of the Famous Players–Lasky Astoria studio in 1924. Careful placement of the camera will obscure the bulk of the main studio building, while the use of a trick effect will suggest a South American landscape. The building at left is now the American Museum of the Moving Image.

(fourteen films). Such recruits from the stage as W. C. Fields and Louise Brooks began their "Hollywood" careers in Astoria, while Rudolph Valentino and D. W. Griffith saw the studio as a means of escaping the factory conditions on the West Coast. Astoria was at its most active in 1926, when the 26 features produced there constituted 40 percent of the entire Paramount program.[22]

However, by 1922 Hollywood's share of American production stood at 84 percent, with 12 percent remaining in New York and 4 percent filming elsewhere. The East Coast had several large studios and ample rental space for the smallest companies. What it lacked was a significant group of middle-level producers, an area almost completely monopolized by Hollywood. New York boosterism reached a peak soon after, when *Barron's* predicted that "the motion picture business of the next decade will be mostly in sight of the tower of the Woolworth building"—a piece of advice that its readers would have done well to ignore. Such enthusiasm on the part of New York–based industry analysts reflected the positive feelings of those East Coast stars and executives whom they encountered while dining at the Colony or "21." It ignored the efforts of the larger and more powerful West Coast branches to centralize production under their own control, the increased costs of doing business in New York (Los Angeles was still relatively free of labor unions), and continuing problems with inclement weather. While the advantages of California sunlight were no longer crucial, problems with New York's rain and snow remained an issue, especially for a system that made heavy use of large standing sets. "Weather destroyed sets on the back lot time and again," wrote Jesse Lasky of the Astoria operation, which he temporarily closed in 1927. Other New York studios had already reduced operations, and by the close of the silent era, Hollywood was unchallenged as the center of American production.[23]

But what of that 4 percent produced outside either Hollywood or New York? With 748 features released in 1922, this suggests that some 30 feature pictures (and a proportionate number of shorts) were filmed elsewhere. Even allowing for a handful of imports, the number is still significant. The bulk of these films were made by small local producers without access to national distribution. Many remained unseen. Some were sold on a states rights basis and never played in a key theater or won the attention of an urban reviewer. For historians, these regional productions are the *terra incognita* of the American film industry. Local historical societies treasure vague records of production in Ithaca, Providence, Ogden, and Augusta, for example, but so little information survives that most historians simply omit this activity altogether.[24]

Writing Pictures

No matter what the location of the studio, the tremendous quantity of film generated each week required vast amounts of original (or at least semi-original) story material. The ad hoc practices of the earliest days of filmmaking had long been abandoned by most producers, although even as late as 1915 some directors could not resist a lucky opportunity. Henry Otto, directing for Flying A in Santa Barbara, noticed several hundred blackbirds sitting on telephone wires. He filmed them, then concocted a script in which the birds caused "wire trouble."[25]

In general, though, it was well understood that regular release schedules de-

The rough-hewn open-air stage of the Wharton Company in Ithaca, New York, was typical of regional film-producing facilities in the early feature period. Pearl White and Irene Castle worked here.

manded a dependable flow of production and that scenario departments were needed to process scripts and synopses. A few writers, such as Ince's C. Gardner Sullivan or Thanhouser's Philip Lonergan, had steady positions generating large amounts of story material to order, but in 1915 the free-lance scenario market was still quite significant. Producers solicited manuscripts in much the same fashion as literary magazines. The *New York Dramatic Mirror* carried the "For Photoplay Authors, Real and Near" column, edited by William Lord Wright. Readers of the 3 February 1915 issue were told that the Universal editorial department was giving assurances that it would read all manuscripts, so long as they were typed, carried a synopsis, and came with a stamped, self-addressed envelope. Requests for submissions were often quite specific:

> World Film Corporation, Fort Lee, New Jersey, is in the market for five-reel subjects running to not less than two hundred scenes. Stories must have original plots—not necessarily with what is known as "punch," but depicting a young innocent girl in country life. No costume plays considered, nor those dealing with crime or crooks. American stories preferable (William Lord Wright, "For Photoplay Authors, Real and Near," *New York Dramatic Mirror*, 3 February 1915, p. 30).

The *Photoplay Author* was a monthly publication brimming with articles on art and technique, profiles of photoplaywrights, and a tipsheet called "The Photo Play Mar-

THE editor regrets that the enclosed is not available for
production and wishes to thank you for your courtesy
in submitting the same to us.

Due to the large number of scenarios received daily it
is impossible to give detailed criticism. The Company
desires and is in the market for clean, original comedies
dealing with new complications and situations.

Yours very truly,

CHRISTIE FILM CO.

Managers of
NESTOR COMEDIES
Universal Films

A stock rejection card for unsolicited manuscripts used by the Christie Film Company around 1915. Note that more suitable submissions are still encouraged.

ket." In one issue, the Holland Film Manufacturing Company of Dorchester, Massachusetts, put out a call for one- and two-reel comedies and comedy-dramas, the New York Motion Picture Company advised authors to send their material directly to scenario editor Richard V. Spencer, and Edison announced a contest for the most suitable conclusion to a prospective one-reeler.[26]

Contests and similar schemes were constantly floated, in an effort to broaden the range of available materials, but without much success. One such contest promoted by Edison was directed at colleges across the country. Out of 337 scenarios submitted, only 8 were judged of produceable quality (the winner was "Jack Kennard, Coward," submitted by Harvard's William Marston). The conclusion of the Edison editors was that a dependence on amateur scenario writers was doomed to failure.[27]

The small amount paid for original scenarios was hardly conducive to high-quality submissions. The *Photoplay Author* complained that writers accepting three dollars for a two-reel script were depressing the market: "At the present scale $35 is fair, $50 is better and $100 per reel good money. Most of the purchases are made at $50 or less per reel."[28]

As late as 1923, Douglas Brown reported to the Society of Motion Picture Engineers that "the completed script of a feature picture costs the producer less than two thousand dollars." This sum did not, however, include the cost of any story rights involved, and beginning in 1919–1920 such costs began to soar for any property considered a sure success (essentially Broadway hits that already seemed to work in scenario form). "Apparently a season's run in New York automatically makes a play worth about $100,000 to the film producers," said the *New York Times* in 1920, with only slight exaggeration. Even before talkies, the existence of a usable Broadway playscript made a property far more interesting to film producers. For example, F. Scott Fitzgerald's *The Great Gatsby* reached the screen in 1926 via a 1925 stage version by Owen Davis, not directly from the original novel.[29]

Prominent screenwriter Frances Marion reported in 1924 that the average price

Trade advertisements for professional screenwriters, 1925 Film Daily Yearbook of Motion Pictures (*p. 444*).

for a successful play was $20,000. She offered the following list of high-priced properties:[30]

TURN TO THE RIGHT	$225,000
WAY DOWN EAST	175,000
A TAILOR-MADE MAN	105,000
THE FIRST YEAR	100,000
TIGER ROSE	100,000
DADDIES	100,000
THE GOLD DIGGERS	100,000
MERTON OF THE MOVIES	100,000
THE VIRGINIAN	90,000
DOROTHY VERNON OF HADDON HALL	85,000

This move toward the acquisition of pretested material clearly related to the collapse of the free-lance market. Submissions had grown so heavy that no quality control could be maintained. "When manuscripts come in they are handed over to the reading department," wrote an anonymous scenario editor in the *Bookman* in 1919. "This is a room where half a dozen women at an average salary of ten dollars a week, without the competence of a stenographer or salesgirl, sit all day making first choice of the material the editor is to see." According to this source, the women all had little scenarios of their own to promote, "consciously or unconsciously" stolen, which they schemed to place with their bosses, even to the extent of suppressing incoming material.[31]

Lawsuits by disgruntled authors were another problem, although one 1914 decision by a Los Angeles court dismissed charges of scenario-stealing against Hampton Del Ruth. "I have been given to understand that scenarios cannot be copyrighted," said the judge, incorrectly. "After looking into the question of scenarios I have decided they are of no value, and therefore dismiss the case."[32]

The virtual elimination of the free-lance market was among the most significant production changes of the immediate postwar era. Writing credits went to such contract employees as Jane Murfin, Lenore Coffee, Charles Kenyon, Jeanie MacPherson, Waldemar Young, and Jules Furthman, skilled wordsmiths with backgrounds as reporters or short-fiction writers. The flood of Broadway playwrights that would engulf Hollywood in the talkie years was hardly in evidence before 1927, when dialogue skills were not a requirement.

The Producer System

Janet Staiger describes the central producer system as "the order of the day" by 1914 and invokes Thomas H. Ince's operation for the New York Motion Picture Company as the traditional example. Script material was recast into continuity form, which allowed careful preplanning of all production activities. Actors needed to appear only when required; props and costumes could be scheduled on a dependable basis, and the logistics of complicated location trips (or studio shoots, for that matter) might be clearly predetermined. By closely monitoring the scripting and editing process, a central producer like Ince—or Mack Sennett—could guarantee a uniform standard of quality without having to attend personally to the filming of each scene.[33]

Thomas H. Ince built Inceville on the shores of the Pacific, at the point where Sun-set Boulevard meets the sea. This 1918 photo shows the studio as little more than a collection of ranch buildings, partially covered stages, and a few standing sets.

While this pioneering demonstration of organizational efficiency does mark Sennett and Ince as important innovators, their systems were primitive in comparison to those employed later in the silent period by more mature studios such as Paramount or MGM. In fact, the collapse of Ince's entire operation on the death of its central producer suggests that his studio was more an extended workshop than a true factory. Systems that could outlast their innovators reflected a higher level of organization and took several more years to develop.

In 1925 the new Metro-Goldwyn-Mayer studio produced a thirty-minute promotional film to demonstrate the power and scale of their factory operations. In true industrial-film fashion, they lay out the shape of their physical plant, boast of the capacity of their electrical powerhouse, and awe us with a staggering array of statistics. What is most interesting, however, is the way the film organizes and presents the studio workers. Dozens of cinematographers line up on a studio lawn, cranking away on Mitchells and Bell & Howells. They are matched by an equally formidable array of writers, directors, scenic artists, carpenters, electrical workers, cutters, even shippers packing MGM prints off to distant exchanges. Seen in control of this army of artists and technicians are three men, each busy behind a desk—Louis B. Mayer, Irving Thalberg, and Harry Rapf. Finally, we see a telegraph key that allows them to stay in constant touch with New York, where an unseen Marcus Loew and Nicholas Schenck call the ultimate shots.[34]

This little film is especially revealing because it consciously deemphasizes the glamour of the studio's employees and underscores the tight, pyramidal control exercised by the top executives. MGM's stars are reduced to a few charming close-ups. MGM's directors appear in a vast and nearly anonymous group. A title card announces, "Browning, Seastrom, Vidor, Niblo, von Stroheim, von Sternberg, . . ." but the names and faces do not really connect. All that matters is *studio and system*: clearly that is the message being communicated to the stockholders or theater owners who made up the film's original audience. To some later historians, this industrial self-consciousness must seem a simple admission of the way the business actually worked, the "real tinsel" underneath the usual phony tinsel.[35]

Production of fodder for the nation's movie screens—many hundreds of pictures annually—was clearly generated by just such a system. Yet even Staiger suggests that the leading works of the age, the product of the most powerful stars and filmmakers, remained under individual control to a great degree.[36] The most memorable work of many of the key filmmakers discussed in chapter 8, Griffith, Weber, von Stroheim, Cruze, Lubitsch, DeMille, Neilan, and Ingram in particular, was created via a simpler director-unit system, where projects were developed from script level through editing by individual creative directors and their personal staffs. In the final analysis, these were the films that created the models for new styles or genres that were then mass-produced (often more lucratively) by the factory studios. While the central-producer system certainly generated the bulk of American production in this period, those films that really mattered, to audiences of the time as well as to posterity, were often the dogged creations of an antiquated workshop system that somehow managed to survive well into the 1920s.

Just how efficient could this newer central-producer system be? One 1917 company was able to keep the costs of their five-reel features to three or four thousand dollars "by shooting players from one set to another with the speed of a Ford car assembly," but Taylorized efficiency was seldom as dramatic as this. A financial paper like *Barron's* looked for predictability as well as profitability, and here a studio like Famous Players–Lasky was at its best. "Their financial comptroller was formerly a cashier of the National Bank of Commerce. He has several young New York University statisticians associated with him," that paper reported approvingly. Of the last 164 films released by the company, only nine had failed to pay their expenses. Four of these were Arbuckle films, caught up in the scandal; one was an "English production"; and two others were only marginal failures.[37]

Richard W. Saunders, the comptroller referred to above, outlined for the *New York Times* many of the recognized industrial practices that were, by 1926, beginning to attract large numbers of investors. These practices ranged from the traditional habit of forcing theater owners to pay in advance to a relatively new method of writing off negative costs in a standardized, monthly fashion.[38]

When Saunders boasted to *Forbes* that Famous Players–Lasky had finally eliminated the seasonal peaks and slumps of production, he was making one of the manager's proudest boasts. These fits and starts had long been an embarrassment to those in the industry who had to deal with Wall Street, especially during extreme slumps, like that of the winter of 1923–1924. Then, Famous Players–Lasky stock dropped 12⅜ points when the management announced a total suspension of production, laying off nine hundred studio workers and putting contract players on half salary. Other studios cut back as well. By the end of the silent era, such economic swings no longer seemed an issue (fig. 4.1).[39]

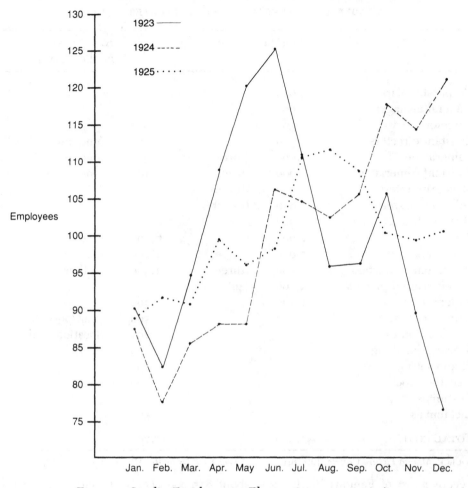

Fig. 4.1. *Studio Employment Fluctuation, 1923–1925**

How Much to Make a Picture?

There was great interest, both inside and outside the trade, in establishing some sort of "average cost" for a standard program feature. In July 1917 the *Motion Picture Classic* published a "conservative average" budget based on information from three different production companies. The *New York Dramatic Mirror*, a trade paper, offered its estimate for a similar production that same month (table 4.1).

In retrospect, the budget proposed by the *Dramatic Mirror* seems to represent less an average price than a rock-bottom one. In any case, generalizations about average picture costs in this period are of little practical use because budgets rose so rapidly during the first dozen years of features, while even within a single studio or genre, costs could vary widely on different productions. As Samuel Goldwyn, who moved from Famous Players–Lasky to First National and then to United Artists during these years, told the *New York Times* in 1926, "In the old days the average

*The graph shows the average number of workers employed by sixteen "identical" companies. Data from *Monthly Labor Review*, Feb. 1927, pp. 66–69.

TABLE 4.1 "AVERAGE COST" ESTIMATES, 1917

	Motion Picture Classic		New York Dramatic Mirror	
Corporate salaries	$ 5,000		$ —	
General manager	3,000		—	
Director	2,500		3,000	
Assistant directors	1,300	(two)	300	(one only)
Cameramen	1,200	(three)	300	(one only)
Assistant cameramen	600	(three)	100	(one only)
Stage carpenters	250	(three)	—	
Other employees	1,800	(twenty)	—	
Overhead expenses	900		—	
Star	12,000	(two)	6,000	(one only)
Near stars	5,000	(three)	1,200	(one leading man)
Prominent characters	2,500	(three)	1,300	("other principals")
Other salaried players	3,000	(40)	—	
Supers, etc.	1,100		300	
Transportation	1,200		500	(transportation)
& location exp.			200	(location rental)
Scenario handling	—		1,000	
Studio settings	—		1,000	
Negative stock	—		1,000	
Costumes	—		1,000	
Incidentals	—		500	
TOTAL COST	$41,350		$17,700	

SOURCE: *Motion Picture Classic*, July 1917, p. 19; *New York Dramatic Mirror*, 7 July 1917, p. 9.

negative cost of Famous Players was about $15,000. The distributors gave us an advance of $25,000. Today the average negative cost of Paramount productions is $300,000. The average negative cost of United Artists productions is from $750,000 to $800,000. The other two big companies are confronted with an average cost of between $240,000 and $260,000."[40]

The average cost of Famous Players–Lasky releases had increased twenty-fold over thirteen years, but knowing a studio's "average" production cost may not, in fact, be very revealing. In 1921, for example, Universal spent $34,211.79 on THE WAY BACK, a five-reel program feature. The cost of FOOLISH WIVES, an unusual "special jewel feature," made that same year, was thirty times this amount (see tables 4.2 and 4.3).

Despite the tremendous differences in scale between the production of THE WAY BACK and FOOLISH WIVES, it is clear that staff salaries were a significant part of the budget of both pictures. In 1924 *Barron's* offered the following statistics to explain where the production dollar went, figures that were generally accepted throughout the industry:[41]

Actors' salaries	25%
Director, cameraman, and assistants	10
Scenario and stories	10

TABLE 4.2

UNIVERSAL FILM MANUFACTURING CO.

Pacific Coast Studios

STATEMENT OF PRODUCTION COSTS
For Week Ending 2-1-22.

DIRECTOR: Paton   PICTURE NO: 3723 REELS: 5

TITLE: ''THE WAY BACK''   DATE STARTED: 12-23-21

FEATURING: Frank Mayo   DATE FINISHED: 1-16-22

CHARGES:	PREVIOUSLY REPORTED	THIS WEEK	TOTAL TO DATE
Stock Talent Salaries	3205.00		3205.00
Pict. Talent Salaries	1979.20		1979.20
Extra Talent Salaries	895.25		895.25
Directors Producing "	1333.30		1333.30
" Writ'g & Edit'g "	1666.70	400.00	2066.70
" Staff "	1298.75	120.45	1419.20
Continuity Writers' "	525.00		525.00
Editors' & Cutters' "	267.45	102.85	370.30
Negative Raw Stock	1450.89	118.65	1569.54
" Laboratory Chgs.	322.13	31.73	353.86
Positive Raw Stock	992.25	38.43	1030.68
" Laboratory Chgs.	321.40	14.88	336.28
Wardrobe Pur. & Mfg.	98.20		98.20
" Hire & Expense	58.54		58.54
Rent Studio Ward. Equip.	252.41		252.41
Prop Pur. & Mfg.	44.92	3.75	48.67
" Hire & Exp.—Misc.	653.47	13.64	667.11
" " & " Horses			
" " & " Special	40.00		40.00
Rent Studio & Prop. Equip.	606.90	17.09	623.99
Scenery	4744.24	256.12	5000.36
Auto Transportation	585.22		585.22
Traveling & Maintenance	330.70	2.00	332.70
Location Fees & Expense	25.00		25.00
Scenarios	2500.00	1000.00	3500.00
Light, Labor & Current	2153.31	226.90	2380.21
Rent Studio Elec. Equip.	1056.60	195.00	1251.60
Ranch Salaries & Exp.	1.00		1.00
Directors' Bonus			
Arsenal Salaries & Exp.	45.40		45.40
Misc. Unclassifled Exp.	179.02		179.02
New York Title Charges			
Overhead Charges	4000.00		4000.00
Still Prints & Negatives	38.05		38.05
TOTALS,—	31670.30	2541.49	34211.79

SOURCE: Author's collection.

Sets (manufacturing)	19
Studio overhead (including cutting, titling, etc.)	20
Costumes, gowns, etc.	3
Locations (and transportation)	8
Raw film	5

This negative cost factored into the total profit picture as follows:

Negative cost	40%
Distribution (U.S. and foreign)	30
Cost of positive prints	10
Administration and taxes	5
Profit	5

With salaries so large a part of production costs, much attention was devoted to limiting, or at least controlling, their growth.[42] A major reason for the introduction of the continuity script was to better manage personnel resources, but competition for top talent continued to force these figures higher and higher.

Photoplay reported in 1916 that salaries of $1,000 per week had recently become common, while the highest figure for a single picture had reached $40,000 (Billie Burke's fee for Peggy). Leaving aside the well-known Chaplin and Pickford figures, they offered the following sampling of weekly star salaries:[43]

William Collier	$ 2,500	Keystone
Raymond Hitchcock	2,500	Keystone
Sam Bernard	2,500	Keystone
Eddie Foy	2,000	Keystone
Weber and Fields	3,000	Keystone
DeWolf Hopper	125,000/year ($60,000 guarantee)	Keystone
Henry B. Walthall	500	Essanay
Blanche Sweet	750	Lasky
Marguerite Clarke	1,250	Lasky
Fannie Ward	1,200	Lasky (one picture only)
Valeska Suratt	5,000	Fox
Victor Moore	500	Lasky
Frank Keenan	1,000	Ince (one picture)
William S. Hart	300	Ince
Francis X. Bushman	750 (plus a percentage of the profits)	_____
Beverly Bayne	350	_____

TABLE 4.3

Universal Film Manufacturing Co.

Pacific Coast Studios

DAILY MEMORANDUM PICTURE COSTS

DIRECTOR <u>Von Stroheim</u> PICTURE NO. <u>3322</u> EPISODE NO. _____ DATE <u>July 7, 1921</u>

	Estimate	Amount Today	Total Amount to Date	Amount UNDER Estimate	Amount OVER Estimate
Overhead	$	$	$ 57,761.74	$	$
Stock Talent					
Picture Talent					
Extra Talent, Story and Continuity			257,283.20		
Director and Staff		167.00	101,009.10		
Film Editing			2,299.60		
Negative			19,287.85		
Sample Print			10,066.66		
Wardrobe			20,258.79		
Props (Arsenal, Drops, Props)			46,226.62		
Scenery, Sets, Etc.		4.00	351,913.53		
Transportation (Automobile)			33,178.88		
Traveling			10,469.00		
Maintenance (Lunches and Hotels)			41,209.54		
Location Fees and Expenses			1,848.11		
Lighting and Labor			77,010.23		
Ranch and Zoo			9,347.97		
Special Automobiles			814.90		
Miscellaneous Supplies		6.00	13,305.08		
TOTAL	$	$ 177.00	$1,053,290.80	$	$
Net Amount Under or Over Estimate _____ $					

SOURCE: *Moving Picture Weekly*, 30 July 1921, p. 28.

These figures reflect a relatively brief period when Broadway headliners were able to command salaries five times those of reliable film favorites such as William S. Hart. More typical of the era were weekly salary statistics offered by theater owner William Brandt following the announcement of the Famous Players–Lasky shutdown in 1923. Brandt's concern was that the exhibitors would bear the brunt of carrying these stars at half-salary while they were between pictures.[44]

Norma Talmadge	$10,000	Conway Tearle	$2,750
Dorothy Dalton	7,500	Lewis Stone	2,500
Gloria Swanson	6,500	Milton Sills	2,500
Larry Semon	5,000	James Kirkwood	2,500
Constance Talmadge	5,000	Wallace Beery	2,500
Pauline Frederick	5,000	House Peters	2,500
Lillian Gish	5,000	Elaine Hammerstein	2,500
Tom Mix	4,000	Richard Barthelmess	2,500
Betty Compson	3,500	Betty Blythe	2,500
Barbara La Marr	3,500	Florence Vidor	2,000
May McAvoy	3,000	Elliott Dexter	2,000
Mabel Normand	3,000	Viola Dana	2,000
Priscilla Dean	3,000	Lon Chaney	1,750

Brandt's figures exclude United Artists' stars, and those, like William S. Hart and Harold Lloyd, whose incomes were tied to significant participation deals. By 1926 total earning figures to date for those stars had reached truly fabulous heights:

Harold Lloyd	$1.5 million per year
Charles Chaplin	1.25 million
Douglas Fairbanks	1 million
Mary Pickford	1 million
Gloria Swanson	Refused Famous Players–Lasky's offer of $1 million to sign with United Artists

The highest-paid star then on straight salary was Tom Mix, earning $15,000 per week at Fox.[45]

Studio overhead accounted for 20 percent of production budgets, and included such costs as preparation of illustrated title cards, seen here at the Ince studio in 1922.

Scenic Art

After salaries, the highest fixed costs were those related to set construction. Wilfred
Buckland, Ben Carré, and Anton Grot were already established as "art directors" by
1915, but most settings were still designed and constructed by carpenters. Cameraman Arthur Miller remembered Grot as "the first art director I ever worked with
who hadn't come up from the ranks of the construction department." Grot created
charcoal illustrations of the sets that displayed the scale and perspective of various
motion-picture lenses. This technique enabled him to build only those segments of
the set that would actually be used and resulted in substantial savings in construction
costs. (He taught this skill to William Cameron Menzies.) Grot had received his
training at the Akademie Sztuki in Cracow, Poland; Ben Carré came from the Paris
Opera; and Wilfred Buckland was long associated with David Belasco.[46]

In his very thorough 1918 study *How Motion Pictures Are Made*, Homer Croy was
still giving all of the credit for set design and construction to gangs of carpenters:

> With the scene locations determined upon, a list of the interior sets is
> handed the chief carpenter, who promptly starts building the necessary

*Shown with the tools of their trades, a scenic artist, director, and carpenter pose
before a newly completed East Coast set around 1918. The unbuilt upper portion
never showed onscreen. If a long shot was needed, a glass painting would complete
the illusion.*

This view of the Lasky lot in 1923 gives some idea of the tremendous quantities of lumber consumed in set construction during this period.

> woodwork. The list tells him in what order they will be wanted, with the date on which the first one will be needed impressed on his mind. He is held responsible for the finishing of the scene by the time specified. . . . From a bare wooden platform the carpenters, under the direction of their chief, may start to work (Homer Croy, *How Motion Pictures Are Made* [New York: Harper and Brothers, 1918], p. 110).

It should be remembered that, in this fashion, the master carpenter Huck Wortman constructed Griffith's Babylon in INTOLERANCE, albeit under the supervision of theatrical designer Walter Hall. These two traditions—that of the graphic artist or scene painter on the one hand, and the practical carpenter on the other—remained dominant in American studios during the early feature period. But they shared an identical goal, one well articulated by Austin Lescarboura in *Behind the Motion Picture Screen:*

> Realism is one of the main stocks in trade of the screen production. Compared with the speaking stage, with its highly artificial scenery which lacks correct perspective and general impressiveness, the motion picture

makes use of backgrounds both natural and artificial which have depth as well as height and breadth. . . . Realism has made the success of present photoplays; and the screen artisans have made film realism what it is (Austin Lescarboura, *Behind the Motion Picture Screen* [New York; Munn, 1922], p. 107).

Lescarboura wrote just as von Stroheim's FOOLISH WIVES appeared, with its full-scale reproduction of Monte Carlo's Casino, Hôtel de France, and Café de Paris, marking the apex of "realistic" set construction. Von Stroheim's *mise-en-scène* required such verisimilitude, but the vast majority of American films merely tried to stay one step ahead of the faultfinders. Scenic and technical accuracy became a fetish, and letters to the editors of various fan magazines prodded sloppy production teams.

But against this current, a feeble call for stylization defended that "highly artificial scenery which lacks correct perspective." As early as 1916 Edgar M. Kellar designed and produced THE YELLOW GIRL, a self-described "decorative playlet" in the style of Aubrey Beardsley. One critic casually characterized it as "Futurist," but Kellar insisted, "I see no reason why we can't have a romantic rather than a practical background." More significant yet were Maurice Tourneur's THE BLUE BIRD (1918) and PRUNELLA (1918), both designed by Ben Carré. Invoking Gordon Craig, Max Reinhardt, Konstantin Stanislavsky, and Harley Granville-Barker, Tourneur declared, "The time has come where we can no longer merely *photograph* moving and inanimate objects and call it art. . . . We must present the effect such a scene has upon the artist-director's mind, so that an audience will catch the mental reaction."[47]

Public rejection of these films was so severe that few remembered them in 1921, when THE CABINET OF DR. CALIGARI first reached the Capitol Theatre. Audiences identified the stylization in this film as "the world seen through a madman's eyes" and promptly forgot the stylistic lesson Tourneur had offered them three years earlier. Now spatial and temporal distortion became signals for lunacy and delirium (note the drug addict's visions in HUMAN WRECKAGE, 1923).[48] But even these hallucinatory exceptions were few, and three-dimensional realism ruled unchallenged.

This playground of graphic artists and carpenters lasted until around 1919, when producers began to turn to professional architects to create their settings. Robert M. Haas, who began designing for Famous Players–Lasky in New York in 1919, came to films after eight years as a practicing architect. His new position won two approving articles in the *American Architect*, which announced the fact that film design was now seen as "structural," not merely decorative, as in stage work. Haas was praised for the solidity of a town he had constructed in Elmhurst, New York, for THE COPPERHEAD (1920), where the details were aged to show the passage of time from 1846 to 1904. A rare full-card credit for the art direction on this film reads, "Robert M. Haas, Architecture; Charles O. Seesel, Decorations." His use of a ceiling "built to show" for ON WITH THE DANCE (1920) was also cited as an example of a new kind of structural realism unlike anything previously seen on the screen. Of course, this new approach to design only underscored the prevailing stylistic mode. "The men who design the 'sets' are constantly striving for the better effect of actuality," observed the *American Architect*.[49]

What Haas added to the Famous Players–Lasky art department was not just a new sense of creativity but a way of organizing the work flow that recalled the offices of top architectural firms rather than the workshops of fashionable graphic designers. In

Mr. and Mrs. William J. Burns pose incongruously on the expressionistic set of Thomas H. Ince's HUMAN WRECKAGE. *Burns, said to have been an adviser to the picture on "the crimes which result from dope," was head of the Justice Department's Bureau of Investigation.*

On location in Guadalupe, California, Cecil B. DeMille's construction crew begins work on the Avenue of the Sphinxes for THE TEN COMMANDMENTS (1923). *Horse-powered construction techniques seem to echo Egyptian models.*

the years that followed, teams of draftsmen, sketch artists, and model-makers would set a standard for studio efficiency at Paramount, MGM, and the other great Hollywood studios.

Behind the Camera

Unlike designers, cinematographers were not easily organized into hierarchical departments and in this period often contracted their services much as writers did. Some of the best were under contract to various studios on either a per-week or per-picture basis (for example, Joseph Ruttenberg with Fox from about 1915 to 1926). Some had long-term relationships, not always contractual, with the units of individual directors or stars (most notably G. W. Bitzer with D. W. Griffith from 1908 to 1928). But most drifted in and out of various jobs, hoping, especially before unionization began to offer a modicum of job security, for a decent run of steady employment.[50] Hal Mohr recalled that free-lance cameramen "used to haunt the studios" in the early 1920s, and groups of job-seekers would meet in the outer offices of production managers with work to offer. Often, the men would informally agree to demand the same salary, say $150 per week, in an effort to prevent a low bidder from depressing the wage scale. Unfortunately, someone always seemed to break the agreement, one reason for the considerable ill will and cliquishness that occasionally afflicted this particular craft.[51]

The diaries of Hal Sintzenich, a cameraman who struggled for work in the eastern studios during many production lulls, are filled with painful stories of missed paychecks and lost job opportunities. Erik Barnouw has analyzed the working records contained in these diaries:

> Most of these assignments are brief. They involve unlimited hours and intermittent pay. Two or more cameramen are often "cranking" side by side, but sometimes they work simultaneously on different scenes. A cameraman may supervise laboratory work, or edit, or even act; in one film Snitch is handed a robe and becomes a judge. His earnings rise to $175 a week but often fall much lower ("The Sintzenich Diaries," *Quarterly Journal of the Library of Congress* [Summer/Fall 1980], p. 310).

The American Society of Cinematographers (ASC), a professional organization designed to exchange useful information and promote the qualifications of its members, was chartered in Hollywood in 1919 (although earlier component organizations date from 1913). Most top cameramen quickly joined and as a group resisted the unionization they saw developing in the eastern studios. Dan Clark, ASC president in 1926, explained this anti-union position in terms of their perceived status as artists, not artisans, as well as a resistance to the fixed-wage scales they saw as detrimental to their own members. Or, as Hal Mohr remembered, "I made a pretty good reputation for myself by 1928 and I was pretty much in demand and considered a pretty fine cameraman, getting a high salary. I was getting around $350 a week then. So I figured, what the hell do I want with a union organization?" But Mohr did join, serving during a long career as president not only of the ASC but of the union local as well.[52]

ASC member Lewis Physioc *captured a feeling of cosmic boosterism in his cover design for* The American Cinematographer, *house organ of the American Society of Cinematographers.*

Largely because of the existence of the ASC and its house organ, the *American Cinematographer*, artistic and technical problems of cameramen were given relatively sophisticated discussion in a public forum, something that was not often the case for other film workers. During this period, these problems included the use of the close-up, "soft" versus "sharp" photography, the influence of German films and filmmakers, and the use of color.

While not necessarily a photographic issue, the close-up was a matter of some controversy throughout this period and of special concern to the cameramen because one of their prime responsibilities was the lighting of glamorous star portraits. Some historians argue that nickelodeon audiences resisted the introduction of the close-up, and patrons of early features in 1915 had their doubts as well. In reviewing DAVID HARUM (1915), the *New York Dramatic Mirror* commented on one sequence of Harum at dinner, which showed only his hands and the food he was eating. This "caused a spectator behind us to say at once that it was 'a poor picture because you cannot see his face.' "[53]

Audiences soon grew sufficiently sophisticated to accept the existence of offscreen space, but various stylistic complaints continued. Extreme close-ups were so rare as to be beyond general notice. The *American Cinematographer* defined the two forms of the close-up in 1923 as the waist-to-head two-shot and the chest-to-head single figure. Full-face was clearly too rare to consider, despite its dramatic use in INTOLERANCE and other Griffith films. Welford Beaton, an otherwise perspicacious critic, waged a lengthy war against the close-up. In a review entitled "Submerging the Production Under Senseless Close-Ups," he attacked Alexander Korda's THE YELLOW LILY (1928) as a "close-up orgy" and contended, "In this picture we have elaborate sets which flit across the screen to give place to an endless parade of utterly senseless close-ups. Ordinary business sense would dictate that the sets should be shown for a longer time to justify their cost." As for von Stroheim's THE WEDDING MARCH, Beaton told readers, "I would estimate that there are between seven and eight hundred close-ups in the entire picture, proving that von Stroheim treated Griffith's discovery as wildly as he did Pat's bankroll." (The "Pat" in Beaton's review is Pat Powers, producer of THE WEDDING MARCH.) Similarly, Frank Tuttle, director of a self-described "artistic" film production unit called the Film Guild, wrote in 1922, "The close-up mania is like the drug habit. It grows upon the afflicted company at a constantly accelerating pace until the whole studio is mortally ill of it."[54]

A wide array of diffusion effects suddenly became popular after 1919, when Henrik Sartov and G. W. Bitzer filmed close-ups of Lillian Gish that recalled Photo-Secessionist portraiture. The style soon spread even to war films. "In THE FOUR HORSEMEN I made all the exteriors I could on dull days in order to use an open lens and get a softer image," explained director Rex Ingram in 1921. "I wanted to get away from the hard, crisp effect of the photograph and get something of the mellow mezzotint of the painting; to get the fidelity of photography, but the softness of the old master; to picture not only the dramatic action, but to give it some of the merit of art."[55]

Some years later, cameraman Henry Sharp, then in New York filming THE CROWD (1928), found it useful to study Rembrandt's work in the Metropolitan Museum of Art. "Rembrandt's great strength was his use of one positive light scale. One central 'light perspective' was always used, rather than a multiplicity of attempted effects,

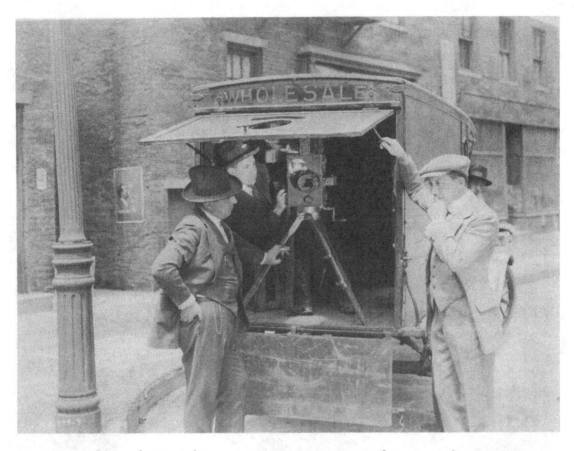

During the production of BOOMERANG BILL *in New York in 1922, director Tom Terriss and cinematographer Al Ligouri made use of this hidden camera for street shooting. The logo on the Pathé camera is that of the Motion Picture Photographers Association, a pre-unionization fraternal guild.*

and the results were contrasts in light and shade," he noted. The invocation of Rembrandt was used to cover a variety of pictorial effects, from Alvin Wyckoff's "smash of light from one side or the other" in DeMille's THE WARRENS OF VIRGINIA (1915) to Lee Garmes's celebrated "north light" effect. "Ever since I began, Rembrandt has been my favorite artist," Garmes told interviewer Charles Higham. "I've always used his technique of north light—of having my main source of light on a set always come from the north. . . . And of course I've always followed Rembrandt in my fondness for low key."[56]

By the close of the silent period, many of the cameramen most involved in the use of incandescent Mazda lighting, notably Lee Garmes and George Barnes, had eliminated much of the diffusion from their work, but Ernest Palmer, Karl Struss, and Oliver Marsh still continued to make heavy use of the more pictorial style.[57]

The most dramatic outside influence in silent Hollywood was certainly the importation, after 1925, of an entire generation of German filmmakers. Karl Struss, one of the American cameramen on F. W. Murnau's SUNRISE (1927), a film with a large number of Germans on the design team, saw the picture as "the fore-runner of a new type of picture-play in which thought is expressed pictorially instead of by titles."[58] Such cameramen as Gilbert Warrenton (THE CAT AND THE CANARY, 1927), Ernest

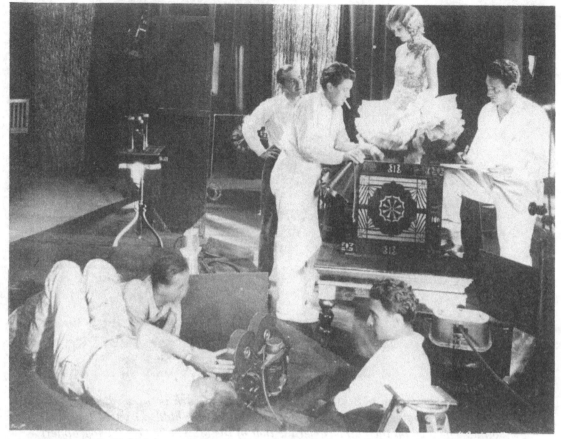

Cameraman Hal Mohr, noted at the time for his stylized photographic effects, lies on the floor to line up a shot of Mary Philbin for THE LAST PERFORMANCE *(filmed in 1928). Director Paul Fejos holds the megaphone.*

Palmer (THE FOUR DEVILS, 1928), and Hal Mohr (THE LAST WARNING, 1929) were especially involved in this style which featured complicated moving camera effects, frequent use of trick shots and superimposition, and stylized, low-key lighting schemes. But the death of the most important German technicians (notably Murnau and Leni), photographic problems attendant on the introduction of sound, and a general misuse of the techniques involved muted the impact of this movement after 1929. Looking back at the period, Hal Mohr, who photographed some exceptionally "Germanic" late silent films for Michael Curtiz, Paul Fejos, and Paul Leni, remembered it simply as "the era of the goofy ideas in film":

> I'll never forget one thing we did on BROADWAY [1929; an early talkie that proved to be one of the last great examples of the style]. We had this camera swinging around during one of the musical numbers, just rotating, swinging around the camera, photographing everyone on those sets all at one time like a big merry-go-round type of thing. If you make them dizzy enough they'll think it's a great scene, you know (quoted in Richard

Koszarski, "Moving Pictures," *Film Comment*, September-October 1974, p. 48).

Film Color

Until the introduction of Eastman Color multilayer negative and printing stock in 1949, color in film was largely a matter of craft. During the 1915–1928 period, color systems might be natural or artificial, with the latter by far the most commonly employed. Artificial-color systems date from the birth of cinema and involve a coloring of all or part of the image of each release print. Processes available were tinting, toning, hand-coloring, stenciling, and related variants, all of which were well established before the introduction of feature pictures.[59]

Tinting was defined by the Society of Motion Picture Engineers as "immersing the film in a solution of dye which colors the gelatine, causing the whole picture to have a uniform veil of color on the screen." Far from declining in popularity after the nickelodeon years, by 1920, according to the society's estimate, tinting was used for 80 to 90 percent of all films. Eastman Kodak began supplying pre-tinted release stock by 1921, eliminating the need for individual treatment of each release print. In toning, "a colored image [is] embedded in a layer of colorless gelatine, so that while the highlights are clear, the shadows are colored." This effect was achieved not by dying the prints but by causing a chemical change in the composition of the metallic salts that had created the black-and-white image, converting the original silver deposit into silver ferrocyanide, for example, to create a blue-and-white image. Laboratory costs were higher for toning than for tinting, and of course, no one could produce a release stock that was already toned.[60]

Combined tinting and toning allowed for complex color effects, such as "sunset and moonlight effects over water," but these were still more difficult and costly. King Vidor used a wide range of tinting and toning effects in THE SKY PILOT (1921), not only for decorative effect but as a significant element of the film's *mise-en-scène:*

> What I believe I have actually done is to "score" this photoplay for color. I have used a soft violet tint for scenes in which the earlier hours of the morning—the phantom dawn, as the orientals call the period just before sunrise—are represented. For the period after sunrise, I have used a pale yellow tint; for noon, a faint amber; for night, a blue green tone on all objects casting shadows, high lighted with a warm amber.
>
> I have tinted the moonlight scenes with carefully chosen deep blue tone, tinting the moon a faint, almost ethereal, amber, while I have used the conventional amber for interior night scenes. A delicate tint of green is used in all scenes of virgin nature where the day is supposed to be warm, while in the Canadian northwest snow scenes I have used a steel blue tint. To induce certain moods, I have scientifically played upon the varying degrees of happiness and sorrow with varying shades of pink and green. The heights of joy are enhanced with a delicate pink glow, while the depths of grief call for a ghastly gray green tone ("Brought into Focus," *New York Times*, 27 February 1921).

Another film of the period whose use of color is well documented is von Stroheim's THE DEVIL'S PASS KEY (1920), in which the various quick cuts of a dance sequence flash green, violet, red, rose, and amber. In *The Anatomy of Motion Picture Art* (1928) Eric Elliott credited this film with "introducing colour as a psychological influence on the film scene."[61]

Highly popular in earlier years, hand-coloring of individual frames was, after the arrival of feature films, usually limited to brief sequences in a few selected prints. Gustav Brock was one of the last to offer this specialty, advertising regularly in the annual *Film Daily Yearbook*. Brock labored over FOOLISH WIVES, THE WHITE SISTER (1923), THE NAVIGATOR (1924), and a number of Marion Davies pictures, including LITTLE OLD NEW YORK (1923). He did two sequences for this film: one in which Davies, disguised as a boy, overhears a risqué story and blushes; the other, a scene of the stars and stripes being raised on Robert Fulton's *Clermont*. The eight seconds of film required thirty hours of labor. Brock never colored more than a few prints of any title, so only the prime first-run houses were likely to screen his work.[62]

The stencil coloring system introduced by Pathé Frères had mechanized this hand-coloring process to a certain degree, using a mimeograph-like system to mass-produce release prints from an original master. Although continuing in France, stencil coloring was rarely seen here after Pathé stopped American production in 1914. Its place was taken by the Handschiegl process, developed by Max Handschiegl, an engraver who had perfected a means of dye-transfer coloring of release prints, otherwise known as imbibition. Using his knowledge of printing inks and engraving technology, Handschiegl prepared as many as three printing matrices to achieve a desired color effect. Beginning in 1917, he worked on such films as JOAN THE WOMAN (1917), GREED, THE PHANTOM OF THE OPERA, SALLY (1925), and THE BIG PARADE. [63]

Natural color films, "those photographed so that the colors are selected entirely by optical and mechanical means and reproduced again in a like manner," have a history almost as long as artificially colored films. In the silent-feature era, all those systems which achieved any commercial success initially separated each image into a pair of "color records" (*i.e.*, monochrome images, each recording the presence of a specific primary color), one frame generally carrying the blue-green record, another the red-orange. From these two primaries, shot on panchromatic negative stock, various methods were used to achieve a natural color screen image.[64]

Kinemacolor, the pioneer in this field, was effectively out of business by 1915. An additive system, it had projected its alternate frames through a revolving shutter that reintroduced the original colors. Commercially successful at first, it ultimately failed because of various technical liabilities and managerial problems.[65]

William Van Doren Kelley improved this system by devising a method of coloring the release prints. As a subtractive process, his Prizmacolor could be projected on standard equipment, which Kinemacolor could not. At first, Prizmacolor subtractive release prints had one frame toned red-orange, and the next toned blue-green, with the "natural color" image appearing only when the projected film was viewed on-screen. Kelley later began using duplitized stock (that is, stock with an emulsion on each side), printing the red-orange record on one side and the blue-green perfectly in register behind it. After toning each side the proper shade, he obtained a print in which every frame displayed "natural color" when viewed through transmitted light.

Director Victor Schertzinger and star Richard Dix begin their morning ritual of begging favor from the camera crew during the production of REDSKIN *(1928). At the left are two Mitchell cameras loaded with 400-foot film magazines for shooting black-and-white film. Harry Hallenberger and Edward Cronjager are the cameramen. At the right, two Mitchell cameras modified for Technicolor photography boast 1,000-foot magazines, since they record two frames for each image taken by the black-and-white cameras. Edward Estabrook and Ray Rennahan are the Technicolor cameramen.*

This double-coated system was the progenitor of Trucolor and other two-color processes later marketed by Consolidated Film Industries, which acquired the patent rights.[66]

Because each color record was still recorded sequentially (not simultaneously), there was a problem with color fringes around moving objects, and as a result, Prizma had its greatest impact in relatively static travelogue films. In 1922 Prizma made and released twenty-six shorts, the only all-color regular short-subject package on the market. The process was also used for occasional inserts in such features as WAY DOWN EAST (1920), THE GILDED LILY (1921), and BROADWAY ROSE (1922). In 1921 J. Stuart Blackton directed THE GLORIOUS ADVENTURE, an all-Prizmacolor feature filmed in England.[67]

Beyond its problems with fringing, Prizmacolor had two major liabilities: excessive graininess and poor quality control. To solve these problems, Kelley joined forces with Max Handschiegl in 1926 and began to use Handschiegl's imbibition process to produce single-coated release prints under the name Kelley Color. But by this time the color film market was already dominated by the Technicolor Corporation, a situation that would continue for nearly thirty years.[68]

After experimenting with an additive system on THE GULF BETWEEN (1917), Herbert T. Kalmus and Daniel Comstock introduced subtractive two-color Technicolor with THE TOLL OF THE SEA in 1922. A beam splitter inside the camera recorded the two color records simultaneously, foot-to-foot on the original negative, thus eliminating the fringing problems of earlier systems. Skip-printing every other frame made it possible to separate the blue-green record onto one filmstrip, the red-orange onto another. Prints from these strips were then toned the proper color and cemented back-to-back to form each release print.[69]

Despite the success of TOLL OF THE SEA (produced by Technicolor and distributed by Metro), there was considerable industry resistance to any color system. Rex Ingram agreed to have Technicolor film an exterior sequence for THE PRISONER OF ZENDA (1922), but "we thought the people looked like dark colored oranges, so we took it out of the picture and threw it away," recalled his editor, Grant Whytock, years later.[70] Successful insert work on THE TEN COMMANDMENTS (1923) and CYTHEREA (1924) led to the production of such all-Technicolor films as WANDERER OF THE WASTELAND (1924) and THE BLACK PIRATE (1926), but this "process two" had inherent difficulties of its own: the cemented film strips buckled under the heat of projection, throwing the picture out of focus.

Finally, Technicolor "process three" substituted a dye-transfer imbibition system for making release prints, one similar to that employed by Kelley and Handschiegl.[71] This produced a smooth, grainless image with far greater uniformity of color than any system based on chemical toning. KING OF KINGS (1927) and THE WEDDING MARCH (1928) made use of this system, which remained in general use until 1933.

When contracting with the Technicolor Corporation to use their process, producers acquired not only the Technicolor cameras but special cameramen to operate them, at first J. Arthur Ball and later Ray Rennahan. While generally open to new technologies, the ASC at first strongly resisted Technicolor since it meant subordinating their members to a group of color technicians. Phil Rosen, one of the founders of the ASC, felt that color in film was distracting and that "true art does not necessarily mean the exact reproduction of nature." Ray Rennahan, for example, was tolerated by ASC members as a slave to his light meter who always worked by the book, a technocrat rather than an artist. Not until 1938 was he invited to join this club.[72]

Performance

The studio machinery could deliver scripts, sets, and cinematographers in an impressive and efficient manner, but no studio manager or unit producer could guarantee what might happen after the doors closed and shooting began on the stages. Soviet director Lev Kuleshov had demonstrated that traditional acting was irrelevant in silent pictures, since the editing process imposed its own structure regardless of the intentions of the original performer. This idea would not have surprised the producers of the OUR GANG comedies or the many animal films starring Rin-Tin-Tin, Rex the Wonder Horse, or the Dippy Do-Dads (a group of monkeys). Given this situation, actors and actresses needed to work with their directors to create a new style of performance directly for the silent screen, a style that had no real precedent and would change dramatically with the coming of "talkies" after 1927.[73]

Nothing better illustrates the idiosyncratic nature of silent-film performance than the use of sideline musicians on the set to inspire the cast during filming, a practice that Kevin Brownlow dates to 1913.[74] As in a Victorian theater piece, this underscoring of drama with music enhanced the essentially melodramatic nature of the performance, but here it was for the benefit of the actors, not the audience. "During the making of a picture music has become essential," wrote one accompanist in 1923. "There was a time when the appearance of a violinist and a pianist on the set in a studio provoked laughter. Their presence elicited ridicule, but not now."[75]

Musicians needed to command a repertoire of sad, dramatic, and joyous arrangements and to be capable of flitting in an instant from the *Moonlight* Sonata to "Yes, We Have No Bananas." Gounod's "Ave Maria" and the intermezzo from *Cavalleria Rusticana* were judged most successful for tears, while dramatic action might call for Tchaikovsky's Fourth Symphony, the Massenet *Élégie*, or a Chopin prelude. According to the accompanist just cited, certain stars or directors would have their own favorite pieces, regardless of the action:

> Thomas Meighan likes "Macushla," possibly because he is Irish. Alice Brady prefers selections from *Madame Butterfly*, and Agnes Ayres has a penchant for "Kiss Me Again." D. W. Griffith sometimes chooses dreamy Hawaiian music ("Real Inspiration," *New York Times*, 24 June 1923).

An orchestra of seven musicians provides accompanying mood music during the filming of THE SPANISH DANCER (1923). *A "megaphonic booth" is used to amplify the sound.*

One special problem of silent-screen acting was the need to accommodate the over-speeding of projection, which was the inevitable fate of every projected "performance." Milton Sills acknowledged this in the entry on "Motion Picture Acting" he prepared for the fourteenth edition of the *Encyclopaedia Britannica*. Admitting that performances recorded at 60 feet per minute were typically projected at 90 feet per minute, Sills felt it "necessary for the actor to adopt a more deliberate *tempo* than that of the stage or real life. He must learn to time his actions in accordance with the requirements of the camera, making it neither too fast nor too slow."[76]

Controlling this tempo was ultimately the job of the director, who would elicit a performance in one of two very different ways. As Gloria Swanson put it:

> There's the director who allows the actor to give his own interpretation of a part, and becomes a conductor of an orchestra, moving it down or bringing it up. Then there's the other kind where the director is a thwarted actor, a ham as we call him, who wants to show the actor how to do it (quoted in Rui Nogueira, "I Am *Not* Going to Write My Memoirs," *Sight and Sound*, Spring 1969, p. 59).

Here, Swanson was praising her longtime collaborator Cecil B. DeMille, who would respond to actors' questions with an abrupt "I'm not running an acting school!" This approach was very much the opposite of another of Swanson's directors, Erich von Stroheim, who was notorious for indicating exactly how he wanted every gesture delivered. Von Stroheim would keep filming retakes until he saw the performance he had conceived in his mind's eye, a technique Swanson accuses Chaplin of employing as well (and with some justification, given the evidence provided in the Kevin Brownlow–David Gill Thames television series *The Unknown Chaplin*). As for D. W. Griffith, Swanson claimed:

> You could always tell when an actor had been working with Griffith, because they all had the same gestures. All of them. They'd cower like mice when they were frightened, they'd shut not their fingers but their fists, they'd turn down their mouths. . . . Lillian Gish, Dorothy Gish, all of them. Even the men had a stamp on them (Nogueira, p. 59).

The onscreen evidence indicates that von Stroheim, Chaplin, and Griffith were able to use this Svengali approach to good effect. Unfortunately, far less talented directors often employed equally intrusive techniques:

> Well do I remember watching J. Searle Dawley direct Pearl White in an intensely dramatic scene, in which he played all the parts before the rehearsal was over. . . . Mr. Dawley did everything. He reclined on the floor, as Miss White was to do, and leaned back in the villain's arms. He played the villain, and snatched her to him despite her struggles. And then, as the big red blooded hero, he burst into the room and hurled the villain back against the wall so forcibly that it shook (Inez and Helen Klumph, *Screen Acting: Its Requirements and Rewards* [New York: Falk, 1922], pp. 185–186).

Rowland V. Lee directing Florence Vidor in DOOMSDAY (1928).

By the late 1920s this technique had generally fallen out of favor, although some, including Ernst Lubitsch, continued to employ it successfully. Raoul Walsh, another of Swanson's directors, summed up the case for the DeMille approach:

> I should like to know how the silent drama is to develop great talent if the practice of curbing the players is adhered to. Granted the director must play an important part, he must supervise the players and see that they are getting the right stuff into the scene. There should, however, be a happy medium, as overdirection causes players to be self-conscious, mechanical and as colorless as dolls or marionettes on a string ("Spontaneity in Acting," *New York Times*, 27 April 1924).

Editing

As soon as filming had started, the director and editor would screen the footage processed each day ("the dailies"), make initial decisions on the best takes, and begin assembling the work print. This would be relatively easy for scenes where action was limited and only a few characters appeared, but complicated sequences presented far greater problems. Because editing was acknowledged as crucial by everyone from Griffith to Sennett, it was considered important for the director to establish an intimate working relationship with his cutter. Griffith worked for many years with Jimmy Smith, and Rex Ingram had his most successful pictures cut by Grant Whytock.

Ingram would film spectacular scenes for THE FOUR HORSEMEN OF THE APOCALYPSE with twelve or fourteen cameras grinding simultaneously. It was impossible for him to analyze so much footage each night, so he depended on Whytock to make an initial selection—something he did by ignoring all but two or three of the master cameras! The editor also assembled another original negative for foreign markets. Shots were recorded twice, either by adjacent cameras or through an additional take. Kodak duplicating stock was not available until 1926, and previous attempts at producing foreign negatives by duping the original resulted in such poor print quality that overseas audiences complained. For THE FOUR HORSEMEN OF THE APOCALYPSE, a third "original" negative was assembled by Whytock after heavy print demand wore out the primary domestic negative. Produced from third-best takes, this version lacked a few key shots and sequences, and Whytock considered himself lucky that "it all made sense."[77] (In 1971 FOOLISH WIVES was reconstructed by Arthur Lennig for the American Film Institute by wholesale interweaving of material from such foreign and domestic versions. Predictable problems with matching action resulted, especially given the film's long history of recutting and censorship.)[78]

When a film was completed, it was previewed at a local theater to gauge public reaction. Harold Lloyd, one of the most aggressive users of the preview system, remembered:

> Even back in the one-reel days, I would take a picture out to a theater when I knew the picture wasn't right. And the manager used to always have to come out and explain what was going on. When we were doing two-reelers, he came out in white tie and tails to do it, and it was quite an event for him and the audience would listen attentively ("The Serious Business of Being Funny," *Film Comment*, Fall 1969, p. 47).

By the time he moved to features, Lloyd would take "scientific" readings of audience laughter and plot them on large graphs, using the information to refine the way his comedies played.

Lloyd's rival Buster Keaton filmed a scene for THE NAVIGATOR in which, as an underwater traffic cop, he directed the movement of swarming schools of fish. Despite the fact that he was quite proud of this expensive gag, Keaton cut it from the picture when preview audiences proved too astonished to laugh.[79]

Occasionally, an already completed film would be drastically reshuffled following previews. Wrote critic Welford Beaton, months before the official premiere of THE WEDDING MARCH:

"I have seen *The Wedding March* twice, once at Anaheim and again at Long Beach. The Anaheim version had the weakness of characterizing von Stroheim as an all-good hero, a role that he has neither the appearance nor the personality to play convincingly. Nicki was made so spotless in that version that when the seduction scene was reached it gave the impression that Mitzi, his victim, had been the aggressor. In the final version Nicki is presented as the roue that he was drawn in the original story [*sic*], and all the scenes which developed that side of him were put back into the picture ("At Last One Fragment of Von's Opus Reaches Screen," *Film Spectator*, 17 March 1928, p. 7).

After the first preview of THE PHANTOM OF THE OPERA, a decision was made to put some comic relief into the film, and a considerable amount of footage with Chester Conklin was inserted. Later preview screenings led Universal to cut Conklin out of the picture entirely.[80] For modern audiences, Conklin is back in again, courtesy of a 1930 reissue and some questionable "film restoration."

Usually, of course, the preview process was far less traumatic, just another step in the production and polishing of any film. Henry King's rough cut of STELLA DALLAS (1925) was 26,000 feet, which he trimmed to 18,000 before previewing it in San Bernardino. Although nobody walked out on this 3½-hour cut, he trimmed another 3,000 feet before running it in Pasadena. At the screening of this fifteen-reel version, some 800 postcards were distributed asking for suggestions of which 420 were returned. It was discovered that Stella's dialogue titles were "resented by the public," so these were all done over. After this version was previewed in another small town, two weak sequences were excised, and the film went into general release at 10,157 feet.[81]

The director most taken with the preview idea was probably D. W. Griffith, who considered it an extension of the theatrical out-of-town tryout. Even the opening-night version was just another cut to Griffith, who continued refining his work well after the initial public showings. "As was his habit," Eileen Bowser tell us, "D. W. Griffith accompanied *Intolerance* on its first runs in the major cities, cutting the prints at the theater, striving to improve it. The result was that the print shown in Boston was not necessarily the same as that shown in New York, and it may be that neither was matched exactly by the original negative."[82]

Cameraman Hal Sintzenich's diaries show that Griffith not only recut his films after opening night but often continued shooting new footage as well. Notes Erik Barnouw:

On February 10, 1924, Snitch mentions a [preview] showing of *America* in South Norwalk, Connecticut. On the same day he is shooting scenes for its Valley Forge sequence in nearby Westchester, impelled by the arrival of ideal blizzard weather for "the men in bare feet in the snow trying to pull the big wagon" (2/10/24). The Battle of Princeton is shot the following day, in time to be included four days later in a showing in Danbury, Connecticut, when Snitch is shooting Washington's inauguration. Two days later they are remaking "the stockade scenes." On the day of the New York premiere, February 21, Snitch is still doing close-ups of Carol

Jane Loring cutting and assembling film prints at Paramount's West Coast studio, ca. 1928. Her workbench holds a Model C "Cutting Room" Moviola, several sets of rewinds, a film synchronizer, and an illuminated light table.

Dempster, and during the following week does retakes of "Miss Dempster & Hamilton" and new "stockade scenes with 30 extras" ("The Sintzenich Diaries," p. 326).

Years later, at the Museum of Modern Art, Griffith was still eager to recut his
pictures, running the now-antique prints in the Film Library's screening room,
never satisfied that he had achieved a definitive version.[83]

The implications of such behavior for film scholarship are considerable. What is the
authentic version of such a work? Griffith's incessant adding and subtracting of footage implies that he saw these films as essentially open texts, capable of showing one
face to Boston and another to New York. Yet he copyrighted the montage of THE
BIRTH OF A NATION and INTOLERANCE by submitting a frame from each shot to the
United States Copyright Office. Did he see those versions as definitive? And if so,
why the inevitable "improvements" that followed?

The problem goes beyond Griffith. By the late silent period, exhibitors could
choose alternate endings for a number of major films. Some audiences, viewing
Garbo as Anna Karenina in Clarence Brown's LOVE (1927), saw Anna throw herself
under a train. Other theaters showed Anna happily reunited with Count Vronsky.
King Vidor shot seven endings for THE CROWD and apparently issued it with two.
Griffith's DRUMS OF LOVE (1928) still exists with a pair of different endings, and
when it is screened by archives, audiences sometimes see them one after the other.
Why producers suddenly lost confidence in their ability to make such basic decisions
is unclear, but if they were moved to think twice about these films, later generations
should be at least as careful when asserting that any version of a silent film is
definitive.[84]

5

Technology

*T*he development of motion-picture technology during the silent-feature era was largely incremental. Increasing standardization and quality control brought film-makers' tools up to a professional level undreamed of in the short-film era. Yet this very standardization acted as a brake on the introduction of radical technical inno-vations. The intermittent surges of mechanical progress that mark the early cinema were hardly in evidence. The major exception to this trend, the development and introduction of the sound film, would eventually bring the silent cinema to an abrupt halt. But this work was carried on far from the silent stages and was of small conse-quence at the time to practitioners of silent filmmaking. Thus, in a 1926 paper for the American Academy of Political and Social Science, P. M. Abbott, vice-president of the Society of Motion Picture Engineers, divided motion-picture technology into five distinct process areas: manufacture of raw stock, studio machinery, laboratory equip-ment, material required for film exchange operations, and theater apparatus. Sound films had no place in his picture of cinema technology.[1]

Raw Stock

In Abbott's view, raw-film manufacture was a straightforward situation that could "be dismissed in one paragraph," since it essentially duplicated the process involved for still photography. It is true that the manufacture of stock had long been standardized and that the Eastman Kodak Company had dominated the American market for years. But 1926 marked the climax of a revolution that Abbott allowed to pass unnoticed: the triumph of panchromatic negative stock in the Hollywood studios.

In 1915 Eastman Kodak offered only one negative stock and one positive release-print stock. This negative stock was an orthochromatic variety sensitive only to blue, violet, and ultraviolet light. It bore no name other than "motion-picture negative film," but to differentiate it from stocks added later, it was eventually labeled Motion-Picture Negative Film Par Speed type 1201. Although it was not rated in terms of the current ASA scale, the speed of this film was approximately ASA 24 according to filmmaker and historian Kevin Brownlow. Super-speed negative film was introduced in August 1925, but this was also an orthochromatic stock.[2]

The fact that orthochromatic negative stock was insensitive to the red end of the spectrum created many photographic problems. With red and yellow registering as black, and blue as white, relative color values could not be properly reproduced. Such a negative was unable to distinguish a white cloud in a blue sky and had a great deal of trouble with blue-eyed actors and actresses. The use of filters and various lighting tricks could mask some of these problems, but the results were never completely satisfactory.[3]

Panchromatic stock, capable of reproducing proper tonal values across the entire visible spectrum, was first introduced for still photographic plates in 1906. That same year, George Albert Smith in England was able to sensitize motion-picture film to the red end of the spectrum for use in his Kinemacolor process, but his results were far from perfect. The Eastman Kodak Company introduced a panchromatic motion-picture stock in September 1913, also in connection with color work, but not until 1918 was this stock employed to solve the problems of monochrome photography. Sequences of Fox's QUEEN OF THE SEA (1918) were photographed on panchromatic negative that year, but the stock still had a shelf life of only two months and needed to be specially ordered in batches of at least 8,000 feet. In fact, laboratories would resist the introduction of panchromatic negative for some time, because its sensitivity to red prevented them from using their traditional red-light illumination during development.[4]

In 1922, Ned Van Buren successfully photographed THE HEADLESS HORSEMAN entirely on panchromatic stock, and the following year it became a regular Eastman product (later labeled type 1203). But laboratory resistance, lack of familiarity on the part of cinematographers, and an increased cost restricted its use to special occasions. For example, Robert Flaherty turned to panchromatic stock while filming MOANA in Samoa in 1923 only after rejecting the results obtained with orthochromatic. Despite the inherent processing difficulties, Flaherty was able to develop and print his footage deep inside a cave, using an underground spring as his water source.[5]

Gradually the use of panchromatic negative began to increase, especially when much exotic location work was involved. Henry King filmed ROMOLA entirely on panchromatic stock in Italy in 1923–1924, claiming that it was faster than he had expected. This unforeseen benefit arose because panchromatic's sensitivity to yellow and red permitted sufficient exposure under conditions unsuitable for par-speed film.[6]

In 1924 panchromatic stock was still 1½¢ per foot more expensive than par-speed film, but prices were equalized in 1926, with a resulting shift to panchromatic. OLD IRONSIDES (1926) was the first Famous Players–Lasky feature shot entirely on panchromatic stock, and George Barnes used it to film THE WINNING OF BARBARA WORTH and THE SON OF THE SHEIK that same year.[7]

For a time, as in ALOMA OF THE SOUTH SEAS and BEAU GESTE (both 1926), panchromatic location work was mixed with orthochromatic studio shots, but the results were unsatisfying. "After the visual grandeur of human faces in the desert," wrote John Grierson of BEAU GESTE, "one returned to the simpering lollipop studio faces of the final garden scenes." By the end of 1926, panchromatic negative was used more widely than par-speed film, a fact hailed by the SMPE as the year's "most prominent progressive step in connection with film and emulsions."[8]

By contrast, there was relatively little change in the stock provided for release prints. Kodak manufactured Eastman Cine Positive Film type 1301 throughout this

The Maximum Emotional Effect

THE GENERAL USE of Panchromatic Negative in motion picture production means much in the way of improvement in the art.

USED WITHOUT A FILTER it helps the picture—with a filter, the color corrections are positively sensational. As one user has put it: "The use of 'Pan' gives the maximum emotional effect on the screen."

EASTMAN PANCHROMATIC NEGATIVE is now the same price as ordinary negative. It keeps as well as ordinary negative and, except for the lighting in the darkroom, is developed in the same manner as ordinary negative.

Yet Eastman Panchromatic is an extraordinary product.

EASTMAN KODAK COMPANY
ROCHESTER, NEW YORK

period. Dupont release-print stock was introduced in 1918. In 1920 Eastman and Gaevert were the only firms advertising release-print stock for sale in the pages of the *Motion Picture News*. By the end of the silent era, Carl Louis Gregory listed Eastman Kodak, Dupont-Pathé, Zeiss-Ikon, Agfa, and Gaevert as the leading manufacturers, but he gave no indication of the relative importance of these brands in the American market.[9]

Eastman Duplicating Film, a low-contrast film with high resolving power, was in use by 1926 and was labeled type 1503. Prior to the introduction of this stock, any necessary duplicate negative was produced from an ordinary projection print through the use of par-speed negative, a process that resulted in significant graininess and noticeable halation surrounding dark objects in a light field ("Mackie line").[10]

Cellulose acetate film base ("safety stock") was available throughout this period but was generally restricted to non-theatrical use, as in release prints provided for schools and hospitals or for home movies. Theatrical filmmakers continued to use the flammable cellulose nitrate stock until 1950 because, despite the attendant fire hazard, it was far less prone to shrinkage and curling, which were especially severe problems in this period.[11]

Studio Machinery

Initially, motion-picture cameras were manufactured (or at least owned) by the producing companies. Biograph and Vitagraph, for example, had unique cameras dating from the industry's earliest period, and the movements of these cameras were founded on various key patents held by the corporations. But as these firms grew more interested in defending their patents than improving their camera design, European models of French, German, and English manufacture came to dominate the market. These machines were sold outright to any available customer, a list that soon included members of the Motion Picture Patents Company, independent firms, and ambitious individual cameramen. Since the cinematographer was held directly responsible for the optical quality of the film, these men had an interest in maintaining their own equipment and avoiding the "junk boxes" supplied by the studio camera department. They soon found that a new generation of American camera manufacturers, notably the Bell & Howell Corporation and the Mitchell Camera Company, were quite responsive to their needs and suggestions, and links were forged directly between these manufacturers and various individual cinematographers, with the studios playing a much less prominent role.[12]

Of course, the existence, side by side, of so many cameras of disparate manufacture led to significant standardization problems. Carl Louis Gregory wrote as late as 1917 that "no two cameras can be used in the same production at the present time without having the frame line adjusted to one another." Because various cameras presented a different relation of frame line to perforations, a sequence that intercut footage taken by different cameras would appear to go "out of frame" at every cut. Some firms tried to standardize all the cameras under their control, but those cinematographers who were suspicious of studio camera departments insisted on using their own equipment. These departments had improved greatly by the end of the silent period, when they were capable of providing the finest equipment for their permanent staff. By 1927 only the top cameramen could afford the investment of over

The Pathé camera, rugged and dependable, was still used by many major producers as late as 1923. Director Alfred E. Green and star Thomas Meighan pose with one while filming THE NE'ER DO WELL *(1923).*

$10,000 required for some complete outfits, but many free-lancers did continue to earn a good living, especially if they owned some unusual piece of apparatus not in the typical studio collection.[13]

In a 1915 ad in the *Moving Picture World*, the Motion Picture Apparatus Company of New York offered for sale "The Better Makes of Motion Picture Cameras," namely the Pathé, Moy, Prestwich, and Prevost. The Pathé studio model had been hailed as "the most popular camera world-wide . . . until after the First World War." A wooden camera encased in black leather, this rugged but inexpensive piece of equipment was noted for its curious, rear-positioned hand crank and external 400-foot film magazines. The film movement was the original Lumière harmonic cam, produced by Pathé under license after Lumière left the camera-manufacturing field. The camera came with a hooded Newtonian range finder and film footage counter. The Moy (or Moyer) was a British camera, whose film magazines were mounted internally, while the Prestwich was a very early British design capable of doubling as a printing machine. Designed specifically to circumvent American patents, the Prevost was assembled mainly from Pathé parts, but replaced the Pathé movement with a pear-

Eddie Lyndon and Jack Stevens crank Bell & Howell 2709 cameras, here equipped with complex matte boxes for producing irises and other trick effects.

shaped cam lobe of its own. These were typical of the cameras that would have been available from a general dealer.[14]

Not mentioned are two French cameras very commonly used at the Fort Lee studios, the Éclair and the Debrie, both of which had interior film magazines. The Éclair movement was similar to the Pathé, but the camera boasted a prismatic focusing unit, which eliminated the necessity for ground-glass focusing, common in most cameras of the day. The Debrie "Parvo" model had been introduced in 1908 and was highly regarded throughout the silent era for its precise workmanship and fine materials. Its unique reciprocating gear movement was highly accurate, and focusing was possible through a ruby window during cranking itself. Because it lacked a lens turret and a straight-line film feed, the Debrie never became a significant factor in the Hollywood studios but various models were favored by newsreel cameramen and European studio producers.[15]

The first camera to offer real competition to the Pathé studio model was the Bell & Howell 2709, introduced in 1911–1912, but not widely used until 1915. Now considered "one of the most important pieces of cinemachinery ever designed," this was the first high-precision, all-metal 35-mm motion-picture camera. The 2709 film movement had fixed non-moving registration pins and an intermittent motion mechanism so precise that many are still used for special-effects work today (the production line ran until 1958). Its turret lens allowed "making close-up views without budging the camera from its position," an interesting notion that prefigures one use for the modern zoom. Indeed, just about the only useful gadget missing from the 2709 was a cranking-speed indicator. The introduction of this camera changed cinematography from a tricky and inexact art to a science in which specific effects could be achieved with absolute predictability.[16]

But improvements were still possible, and in 1920 Charles Rosher demonstrated on THE LOVE LIGHT the prototype of the Mitchell camera that would soon force the Bell & Howell from the studios. The key feature of this camera was its unique focusing device, a rackover system invented by John Leonard that allowed the cameraman to frame and compose directly through the lens without moving either lens or aperture. This rackover was accomplished by turning a handle that shifted the entire camera body to the right, placing the finder immediately behind the taking lens. A similar operation with the Bell & Howell not only was time-consuming but risked misaligning the taking lens in the process.[17]

George Mitchell, who had acquired Leonard's patent, devised a three-cam movement of great accuracy, one that would prove easier to silence than the Bell & Howell when talking pictures arrived. He also incorporated masks, irises, and mattes directly

Cameramen Hal Mohr and Stanley Cortez use a motorized Mitchell camera to film a close-up for BROADWAY (1929).

into the camera body, a substantial increase in convenience. These special qualities made the Mitchell's dominance in the American studios inevitable, but the fact that its designer was a cameraman, and its factory was in Los Angeles, did not hurt matters. The gossip columns of the *American Cinematographer* often noted with pride that this or that cameraman had invested in a Mitchell: it was a local product that made good. Bell & Howell eventually introduced a less efficient "shiftover" of its own, but the general convenience of the Mitchell had already won the market.[18]

Various other cameras were used throughout this period for special applications. According to Carl Louis Gregory (1927), the Universal was "the first moderate priced camera to stand the test of time." Solidly constructed of wood and metal, it was widely used by the government during the First World War and became a favorite of industrial filmmakers and explorers. Far superior was the Akeley, an all-metal camera designed by Carl Akeley of the American Museum of Natural History for use on his field expeditions. In order to better follow moving objects at a distance, Akeley replaced the usual pan and tilt cranks with a single handle. His viewfinder was paired with the taking lens and so mounted that it adjusted comfortably to the eye no matter how the camera was tilted. A focal-plane shutter maximized the light for exposure. Robert Flaherty used an Akeley on NANOOK OF THE NORTH, but "Akeley specialists" soon appeared in the studios as well, to film aerial dogfights and cowboy chases. These men were so specialized in the use of their equipment that they were listed separately on ASC rosters, like stills cameramen.[19]

In 1925 Bell & Howell introduced the 35-mm Eyemo, a spring-wound, hand-held camera patterned after the 16-mm Filmo, which they had marketed since 1923. Initially presented only as a news camera, it was quickly taken up by cameramen like Dan Clark "to get to difficult places" on Tom Mix films. Soon Bell & Howell began promoting this use in Hollywood with advertisements like that in the January 1927 *American Cinematographer*, showing Cecil B. DeMille using an Eyemo during the filming of KING OF KINGS.[20]

Experiments in the hand-held use of a motorized Debrie Parvo and a Moy Aerial Camera (which contained a gyroscopic stabilizer) were conducted at the Paramount Astoria studio in 1925–1926, but these systems were too clumsy for general use. The Debrie Sept and the Zeiss-Ikon Kinamo also failed to find a market in America, essentially because of their limited film capacity. The Devry, introduced in 1925, did find some acceptance among newsreel cameramen and wealthy amateurs, but the Eyemo remained the only practical hand-held professional motion-picture camera throughout the silent period and continued to be successfully marketed until 1970.[21]

A major reason for the success of the Bell & Howell and Mitchell cameras was the superiority of their turreted lens system to the threaded lens mount of the Pathé or even the Debrie's bayonet mount. Lenses were often marketed separately from camera bodies and by 1925 were commonly supplied at speeds of $f/2.3$, $f/2.7$, or $f/3.5$. Interior views of the Scopes trial were successfully filmed that year with an $f/2.7$ lens. By 1926, a lens of $f/1.6$ was considered "quite common" by the SMPE, and the following year an $f/1.5$ lens was claimed to be the fastest available. By the end of the silent period there was a great demand for fast lenses of $f/1.5$ to $f/2.5$, which allowed savings in lighting costs, better results in bad weather, and a greater range of artistic effects. Of the various specialty lenses, one of the most important was the Struss Pictorial Lens, originally developed by Karl Struss as a still-camera lens capable of producing a Photo Secessionist effect without the bother of negative manipulation.

September, 1925   AMERICAN CINEMATOGRAPHER   Five

Bell & Howell Introduce New Automatic Camera

Details *of* New Model Are
Given *for* First Time.   Big
Improvements Announced

Specifications Revealed.
Diversified Use *in* Many
Fields Is Foreseen

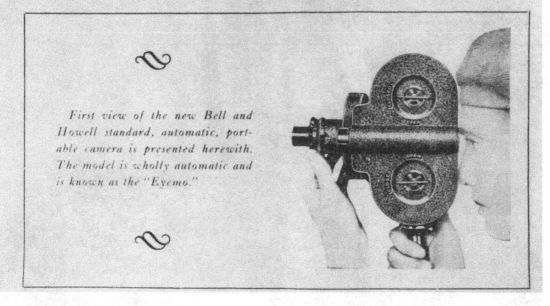

First view of the new Bell and Howell standard, automatic, portable camera is presented herewith. The model is wholly automatic and is known as the "Eyemo."

The first announcement of the Bell & Howell Eyemo camera (American Cinematographer, *September 1925, p. 5*).

John Leezer was the first to use it in motion-picture work, on THE MARRIAGE OF MOLLY O (1916).[22]

By the late 1920s, cinematographers were quite fond of the "softly diffused pictures" they could obtain with the aid of the Struss Pictorial Lens and similar devices, but the rest of the industry did not share their feelings. When Joseph Dubray of the ASC praised such techniques before a Hollywood meeting of the Society of Motion Picture Engineers, he was attacked by various members who claimed that "fuzzy pictures are annoying to look at" and that "the ordinary man on the street wants his pictures clear." Indeed, when the negative of STREET ANGEL was sent to the Fox lab in New York in 1928, it was originally returned as unprintable, although Hollywood cinematographers saw fit to honor Ernest Palmer's heavy use of fog filters here with an Academy Award nomination.[23]

The development of motion-picture camera lenses affected the work of the stills photographer as well. Despite the fact that these images have always been crucial in promoting current films or recalling past releases, little has been written about the significance of the motion-picture still. Stills were needed for advertising, marketing, production reference work, and trick photography. The first photographers employed to shoot scene stills posed the cast specially at the end of each action. Since

B. Reaves Eason, directing with pistol and megaphone, films location scenes "at the edge of the Los Angeles underworld" for HUMAN WRECKAGE (1923). *The still camera at left is positioned to record almost the same view as the Bell & Howell motion picture camera.*

this practice was costly in terms of time and money, photographers were told to shoot during action. But the eight-by-ten-view cameras then in use required a twenty-inch lens to duplicate the field of a 35-mm motion-picture camera with a two-inch lens. An f/6 lens of nineteen-inch focal length was the best available for still work, and by using fast film, a focal plane shutter, and exposures of one-fifth of a second, "fairly good results" could be obtained if the cinematographer was shooting around f/4.5.[24] But when motion-picture lenses began to increase in speed, the stills men could not keep up, and scene stills once again required posing. Glamour photography done in portrait studios for advertising and publicity purposes was modeled on the work of the most fashionable society photographers. After the war, it was not unusual to see Baron de Meyer, Arnold Genthe, or Edward Steichen handling a portrait sitting for a top star, and their style was carried on for many years by George Hurrell, Clarence Sinclair Bull, Ruth Harriet Louise, and many other Hollywood studio photographers.

Cinematographers generally calculated their exposures by eye, on the basis of their previous experience. A short strip of test film could immediately be developed if necessary; a sign posted in the Universal camera department offered the sage advice, "If in doubt, shoot at 5.6." It was a matter of professional pride to be able to produce a negative of uniform density entirely without recourse to meters, but several were available. The Harvey Calculator was little more than an exposure table operated like a slide rule. The Watkins Actinometer measured overall actinic power with the aid of a sensitive paper that darkened on exposure to light. Most satisfactory was the Cinophot, a visual extinction meter that measured reflected light. Unfortunately, reading an extinction meter is a largely subjective task, and various users could report different results. "Because of this, the old school photographers refer to exposure meters as 'Guessometers,' " noted Carl Louis Gregory in 1927.[25]

Three main varieties of artificial lighting were employed in the studios during this period: mercury vapor tubes, arc lamps, and incandescent units. A 1915 survey found that fifty American studios employed some form of artificial lighting, forty-three of them using mercury vapor tubes alone or in combination with other units. Known as

At the opening of the Fox studio in New York on 24 May 1920, visitors were able to observe Charles Brabin directing Estelle Taylor in BLIND WIVES. *Banks of Cooper-Hewitt lamps hang from the rafters, while smaller arc lamps are rolled directly onto the set.*

Cooper-Hewitts, the mercury tubes were introduced as early as 1905. Each assemblage contained a bank of eight tubes capable of throwing "a mass of light upon the scene similar to that from a fair size window or skylight." Arranged in rows directly overhead, or angled slightly for front lighting, these units produced a flat, undifferentiated flow of light. Since the units were originally introduced to assist (and later supplant) sunlight diffused by muslin scrims, this was exactly what the filmmakers required. An added benefit was that the light given off by the Cooper-Hewitts was very rich at the blue and ultraviolet end of the spectrum, and almost absent at the red end. This dovetailed remarkably with the photosensitive properties of orthochromatic negative. "A scene which has been photographed with mercury vapor light invariably shows better modeling and tone relationships than subjects which have been made with other light sources," reported the head of the Ansco Research Laboratories in 1922.[26]

White-flame carbon arcs, adapted from theatrical lighting units and capable of concentrating a volume of light in a limited area, were introduced in 1912 and marketed widely by M. J. Wohl and Company and the Kliegl Brothers. Cecil B.

This small set, constructed on the New Bedford location of DOWN TO THE SEA IN SHIPS (1922), *is lit entirely by Wohlites. Note the amount of heavy electrical cable needed to supply even the small number of lights seen here.*

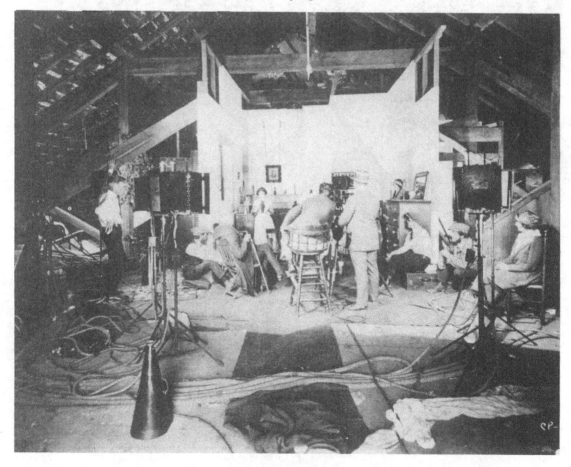

Sun-arcs are used to illuminate a massive village set constructed inside New York's Cosmopolitan studio for UNDER THE RED ROBE *(1923).*

DeMille recalled borrowing such a lamp from a downtown Los Angeles theater to produce a dramatic effect in THE WARRENS OF VIRGINIA (1915), which was his eighth film but purportedly his first to use artificial light. By 1916–1917 Sun-Arcs (similar to naval searchlights) and twin-arc broadsides were being used to illuminate large sets and create more sculptural lighting effects. According to the *New York Times,* cameraman Harry Fischbeck developed "a new system of lighting, in which a preponderance of spotlights are used. He obtains his effects of highlights and shadows by employing spotlights as an artist uses a brush and colors on the canvas. The basic idea is to make each picture scene look like a painting, with the characters standing out in bold relief." Fischbeck used this system quite conspicuously on MONSIEUR BEAUCAIRE (1924).[27]

But compared to Cooper-Hewitts, arcs were dirty (hot ash floating through the air was a real problem), tremendously hot, and so labor-intensive that each unit required its own electrician. In addition, the problem of "Klieg eyes," a painful redness and swelling that could incapacitate the performers, was eventually traced to the powerful ultraviolet rays given off by the arcs. The use of thirty-seven Sun-Arcs to light the cathedral set for THE HUNCHBACK OF NOTRE DAME (1923) may have been spectacular, but something else was required for more practical studio shooting.[28]

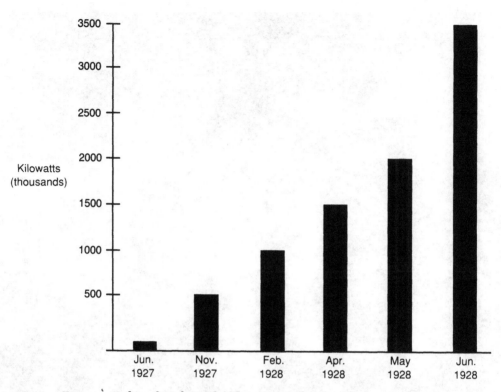

Fig. 5.1. Sales of Mole-Richardson Incandescent Units, 1927–1928

By the late teens, incandescent tungsten lamps were being used for close-ups and other special purposes by Lee Garmes and a few others, but existing units were not available in suitably high wattages. Even worse, their actinic quality was so heavily weighted to the red end of the spectrum that they were relatively inefficient when used with orthochromatic negative. Serious development of incandescent lamps for motion-picture work did not begin until 1920, when the actress Maude Adams, who was promoting a color-film system, appealed to General Electric for a new type of lighting unit. This eventually resulted in the 10K and 30K tungsten Mazda lamps, later known more generically as "inkies." As early as 1922, Victor Milner had hoped that incandescent lamps might soon replace arcs, which he found "glary," but little real progress was made until 1927.[29]

That year, a tremendous surge in the use of incandescent lamps was fueled by the dramatic rise in the use of panchromatic stock. This move knocked the Cooper-Hewitts out of the market and temporarily made arcs the dominant studio lighting units. But in addition to their previously mentioned problems, arcs were too directional and difficult to diffuse to be used as the sole unit in the cameraman's lighting kit. They would also prove unsuitable for early talkies, since their operation produced a crackling on soundtracks that engineers had not yet learned to eliminate. In 1927 the Mole-Richardson Company was formed in Hollywood to market incandescent units with a wide range of motion-picture applications, and existing production conditions caused their sales to balloon immediately (see fig. 5.1).[30]

Even without the sound-film problem that restricted the use of arcs, Mazda lamps dominated the last days of the silent picture, and films such as THE LITTLE SHEP-

HERD OF KINGDOM COME, TWO LOVERS, SHOW BOAT, SINS OF THE FATHERS, MASKS OF THE DEVIL (all 1928–1929), and the original silent version of HELL'S ANGELS were shot entirely or mainly with Mazda lights. Not only did the system have innate mechanical advantages, but operational costs were far lower. The number of men required to handle the lighting equipment on an average set dropped from twenty or thirty to as low as eight or twelve, while electric bills were reduced by one-third to one-half.[31]

It should be remembered that the studio itself also functioned as a kind of lighting unit. Greenhouse construction was characteristic of the Fort Lee studios in the mid teens, with glass roof and walls maximizing the available New Jersey sunlight. Overhead scrims served to diffuse this light, and if it began to fail, Cooper-Hewitts could be called in as a supplement. Glass studios were less frequently seen in California, where better weather conditions allowed large open-air stages, such as the one at Universal City, to operate well into the teens. Enclosed studios entirely dependent on artificial lighting had been known in the East for many years, but with the

Cinematographer Bert Glennon stands at the center of an interior set for JAVA HEAD *(1923). Most of the light on the set is provided by Cooper-Hewitt lamps, but electricians Ken Styles and Gus Anderson will supply backlighting and apparent window illumination with the help of arc lamps mounted at the rear of the set.*

introduction of Klieg and Wohl arcs, this curse suddenly became a blessing: cinematographers could ignore the vagaries of sunshine and could paint with their own light. By the late teens, many of the greenhouse studios were feverishly being painted over.[32]

The proliferation of arc lighting in this period turned the average stage floor into a jungle of electric cables. Studio wiring followed the "wall pocket" system, with 100-amp pockets of two or three lines placed every twenty or thirty feet around the stage perimeter. Lighting for a stage would be centrally controlled from one master switchboard, no matter how many companies were working simultaneously. Each would have to shout or otherwise signal its orders to the main board. In 1920 remote-control systems were introduced in New York at Famous Players–Lasky's Amsterdam Opera House and Hearst's International studio. In this scheme the master switchboard was replaced by a conductor box capable of being operated remotely by each company. Power was carried overhead on runways, clearing the floors of cable. A small push-button unit controlling some six contactors was dropped from the runway near the director and cameraman, who could now act independently of the main board. Derivatives of this system soon appeared in the Famous Players–Lasky Astoria studio, the Fox New York studio, and the Metro Hollywood studio.[33]

The use of overhead electrical runways to supply power to the stages is apparent in this photograph of the Famous Players–Lasky Astoria studio. Previously, all these cables would have been on the ground. Note the contactor box on the floor at right.

The editing process was the studio worker's final contact with the film, although for most of the silent period little of the apparatus involved here was worthy of the name "technology." A light table, a pair of rewinds, and a splicing block were all the specialized equipment needed to edit INTOLERANCE or GREED. Off-the-shelf supplies included a pair of scissors to cut the film, a razor blade to scrape the emulsion, and a bottle of film cement. Miniaturized viewing machines to aid novices in admiring their work had been available for years, but professional pride kept most film cutters away from such devices. A good film editor could judge pacing and rhythm simply by pulling the film through his or her fingers, but the Moviola, a device that could achieve this effect far more accurately, began to force a change around 1924. This machine, developed by Ivan Serrurier, was essentially a motorized version of the earlier viewers, capable of running at variable speeds in either direction. It also had the benefit of proper illumination. Originally it was used only with open spools of film, but by 1928 the Model D, or "Director's Model" Moviola, boasted 1,000 foot take-up and feed reels. Still resisted during the silent era by many traditional film editors, the Moviola would prove invaluable with the introduction of talking pictures.[34]

The Laboratory

Laboratory handling of motion-picture negatives and positives underwent significant changes during this period, as procedures advanced from the nearly handcrafted methods of earlier days to the fully automated systems that would be required by talkies.

The rack-and-tank system dominated laboratory practice for many years. In the dark room, exposed negative would be wound in spiral fashion onto wooden frames or racks, emulsion side out, each rack being about 4½ feet square and capable of holding about 200 feet of film. A pair of racks would be dipped into a deep, narrow tank containing about 110 gallons of developing solution (generally Eastman 16, or some other member of the methol-hydroquinone group) until the handler judged it to have achieved the proper density. He would do this by periodically withdrawing the rack and examining the film against a ruby light. After a session in a washing tank, the rack of film was transferred to a fixing bath of sodium hyposulphite until all the active silver salts had dissolved out. Eight to twelve racks at a time were then placed in a very large washing bath, often located outdoors, and thoroughly rinsed with running water. Finally, each rack was attached to a wooden frame, or "horse," and the film was unrolled onto huge revolving wooden drying drums (an intermediate step sometimes used in the early days added a glycerine bath before drying to guard against excessive moisture loss).[35]

The potential for mechanical or chemical failure, or human error, was quite high. "It is," wrote one lab man in 1923, "an impossibility to preserve an exceedingly careful attitude in a number of workmen who are by nature of their work wet and uncomfortable." As the film became soaked in developer, it would expand, thus requiring the technicians to tighten thumb screws on the rack to keep it from slipping off. Conversely, as it dried, it began to shrink, and the screws all needed to be reset again. So much handling caused scratching and tearing problems. There were difficulties with non-uniformity of development, especially since the racks held such

A laboratory technician demonstrates the development of motion-picture negative by the rack-and-tank method.

short lengths of film. Frequent exposure to air created dust problems and air-bell marks (spots caused by evaporating droplets of water that kept developer from the film). Rack marks—dark bands on the film where it had been wrapped over the top or bottom of a rack—caused rhythmic flashing onscreen. Laboratory specialists as late as 1925 felt that "much of the film shown in the present day theatre" suffered from such visible defects.[36]

Kodak had installed Gaumont equipment for automatic processing of positive film as early as 1913, but not until 1920 did the Spoor-Thompson machine (which had the capacity to correct for shrinkage during processing) begin to make an impact on general laboratory practice. The Erbograph, in use soon after, was a horizontal-feed machine that could even perform messy tinting and toning operations. Its manpower savings were also considerable. Not until the end of the silent era, however, would filmmakers trust the development of motion-picture negatives to any automated system. Old-time laboratory men, who were leery of machines damaging irreplaceable camera negatives, also felt that "hand-developing" gave them an opportunity to correct exposure problems that might have occurred during photography. In 1925 Alfred B. Hitchens, technical director of the Duplex Motion Picture Laboratories, argued that it was the cinematographer's responsibility to provide a properly exposed negative and that the greatest contribution a laboratory could make was to guarantee consistency of development. Criticized by those who felt that every negative needed uniform density throughout (so-called "one-light" negatives), he answered that negatives could be timed, with varying densities compensated for by automatic light changes during printing. Nevertheless, such a system was slow to catch on in Hollywood, where most negative was processed. Not until 1927 did Universal install an improved Spoor-Thompson machine for automatic negative developing. Capable of processing 4,000 feet of film per hour, it was first used on THE MAN WHO LAUGHS and resolved most of the problems associated with the rack-and-tank method. Negative timing, of course, continued to be done by eye.[37]

Little change occurred during these years in the actual printing of release positives. The most commonly used machines were the Duplex, a step printer, and the Bell & Howell Model D, a continuous printer introduced as part of the Bell & Howell system in 1911. The Duplex featured a complicated intermittent movement in which each frame was stopped and printed individually. It was especially suited to an age when perforations and frame lines were not yet completely uniform. The Bell & Howell was a continuous-contact printer in which both positive and negative traveled in unison around a printing sprocket. Its speed of 60 feet per minute was triple that of most step printers. Still fairly labor-intensive, the machines were fed by women who worked all day in the weak glow of a ruby light. A range of printing densities could be selected and automatically programmed for each reel, with the changes triggered by notches cut in the side of the negative. The Duplex, for example, could provide a range of eighteen different densities and change these densities eighteen times per sitting.[38]

Film Exchanges

P. M. Abbott, in his 1926 report to the Academy of Political and Social Science, stated that "relatively little equipment was used in film exchanges," the business being for the most part devoted to distributing, inspecting, repairing, and storing circulating prints. Exchanges shared much of what apparatus they did use with laboratories and theaters, notably the rewinds used for inspecting the film and the reels it was wound onto. It was traditional, however, for exchanges to mount their films on the worst available reels. "I myself stood beside the manager of an exchange supplying dozens of theaters," reported F. H. Richardson, "and we have both watched the winding of a new roll of film just received from the producer on a flimsy, rickety, bent up, decrepit reel, which in the process of a single winding of the film would cause more damage to the same than would cover the cost of a fairly good new reel." Projectionists would remove the film from these "exchange reels" whenever possible, but the damage might well be done already, as Richardson suggests.[39]

Most exchanges were equipped with the Bell & Howell Standard Film Splicing Machine soon after it was introduced in the mid 1920s, but their employees were often antagonistic to any such mechanical splicing device. The Vidaver Film Inspection Machine was available in 1924, but theaters seemed more interested in this first non-manual examining device than were the exchanges. Properly equipped or not, the performance of exchange workers seems to have left much to be desired. Richardson reports "reels loaded with film taken from the shipping case by exchange employees and literally thrown, or tossed, a distance of fully six feet to a board-top

Photograph No. 7. Correct way of handling film.

Photograph No. 8. Clean gloves.

The studios tried to instruct employees of exchanges and theaters in the correct method of handling film by issuing training manuals such as this (from "Proper Inspection, Splicing, and Care of Films," by Earl J. Denison, published by the Famous Players–Lasky Company, January 1923).

table." Exchange workers may have had to deal with only a few kinds of technical apparatus, but the way they used, or abused, these items could easily result in the "tangled mass in the shipping case" that not infrequently arrived at local theaters.[40]

Theaters

Theater equipment included most of the same film-handling devices used by exchanges, namely splicers, rewinds, and various examining machines. Some projectionists would supply themselves with a foot-candle meter to measure screen-illumination intensity. All booths would have some form of magic lantern to project slides for various purposes, and atmospheric theaters would use the Brenograph, which could project everything from song slides to the Aurora Borealis. Ben Hall supplies the quintessential Brenograph tag line: "Please Do Not Turn On the Clouds Until the Show Starts. Be Sure the Stars Are Turned Off When Leaving."[41]

But, of course, projecting the film remained the theater's most crucial mechanical task, the final technological link between filmmaker and audience. Because of a burst of new projector designs in the years just prior to 1915, only a few new machines were introduced into the American market during the period under discussion. While the Motiograph, Powers Cameragraph, and Simplex projectors dominated the field, it should be remembered that many theaters chose less elaborate machines, such as the American Standard or the Baird, or continued to make do with surviving models from the early days of cinema. David Hulfish's *Motion Picture Work*, a 1913 manual that had wide circulation in the late teens, still contained detailed descriptions of such antique apparatus as the Selig Polyscope, Edengraph, and Lubin projectors. The same 1915 issue of the *Moving Picture World* that carried the camera ads referred to earlier included an announcement from the Amusement Supply Company, which identified the major brands of projectors as Powers, Motiograph, Simplex, and Edison. On another page, the same firm offered the following rebuilt machines for sale: a 1908 model Motiograph for $60, an Edison Exhibition model for $65, a Powers No. 5 for $75, a Powers No. 6 for $115, and a 1911 Motiograph for $125. A rival firm, the Stern Manufacturing Company, offered floor samples of the Simplex or Powers 6A for $185. The Powers was also available from them with motor drive at $230.[42]

The Motiograph was introduced in 1908, a development of A. C. Roebuck's Optigraph, which had been one of the earliest American projectors to be widely distributed (via the Sears, Roebuck Company). The Motiograph No. 1 was the first projector having all gears enclosed, as well as the first in which the movement could be easily removed for cleaning or repairs. This Geneva-type movement operated an intermittent sprocket wheel known as the "star and cam," and the entire movement assembly slid up and down for framing. While the earliest models seem unusually slight, the Motiograph was constantly under development throughout this period. The addition of cylindrical rear shutters in 1928 gave the Motiograph a decided advantage over its competition when sound-on-film arrived by increasing the amount of available light. Although Don Malkames could write in 1957 that the Motiograph "is still considered one of the finest projectors manufactured today," it was relatively ignored during the 1920s. James Cameron neglects to mention the Motiograph in his encyclopedic *Motion Picture Projection* (perhaps because the manufacturer failed to buy a display ad in the book), but T. O'Connor Sloane leaves the machine out of his book as well.[43]

A trade-paper ad for the Simplex projector. Note the option of a hand-powered crank or motor drive (located below the take-up magazine).

The machines that do merit detailed description in such manuals are invariably the Simplex and the Powers Cameragraph. The most significant of the Cameragraphs in use during this period were No. 5 and No. 6, both on the market by 1909. The Powers Cameragraph No. 5 incorporated a traditional Geneva movement with a four-slot star and a one-pin cam, kept in balance by a heavy flywheel mounted directly on the drive shaft. It was available with two styles of safety shutter and boasted fireproof feed and takeup magazines. The No. 6 introduced a remarkable new movement called the "pin cross." A four-armed cross mounted on the drive shaft carried four pins that engaged a revolving cam ring, thus effecting movement of the sprocket shaft. This system afforded a longer exposure without added strain on the mechanism. Before the Cameragraph No. 7 could be placed on the market, the Nicholas Power Company merged with the International Projector Company, and the trademark disappeared. Nonetheless, the Powers name was extremely respected throughout the silent period. The company constantly upgraded the basic equipment by offering devices such as the Nupower motor (a universal motor capable of running on either AC or DC), the Powers speed indicator, which gave projector speed in feet per minute and minutes per reel, a film-footage recorder, and a remote instrument panel that could provide readings on current and voltage regulation of the arc, as well as projector speed. When Grauman's Chinese Theatre opened in 1927, there were three Powers Cameragraphs in the booth.[44]

The Simplex projector was introduced by the Precision Machine Company in 1911 and eventually, with the demise of the Nicholas Power Company, came to dominate the market. "It was the first completely enclosed mechanism with center frame bearings. It had means for adjusting the revolving shutter during operation, a new style of sliding gate instead of the former hinged types, a new type of fire shutter and governor, and a precision-focusing and lens-mount attachment," wrote Malkames. The Simplex Model S employed the standard arc lamp, while the Model B was adapted for Mazda projection. As with the Powers, a motorized variable-speed control was also available. The intermittent used was the traditional Geneva cross. By the end of the silent era, the Simplex was the projector of choice in theaters such as the Roxy. The introduction of the Simplex marked the arrival of the modern motion-picture projector, and although it reached the market several years before the period under discussion, no major improvements were seen in American projection design until the introduction of the rear shutter by Motiograph in 1928 (a feat matched by the Super Simplex of 1930).[45]

6

The Show

The Balanced Program

*T*he burst of picture-palace construction that followed the opening of the Strand in 1914 may have heralded the primacy of the feature, but one should not assume that short films conveniently left the scene at the same time. The palaces demanded a continuing stream of shorts to fill out their programs and supply the variety they felt necessary to attract audiences.

Initially, those established industry forces that were doing well with short films tried to hold the line against features; the result was a "generation gap" among producers so strong that it even forced old enemies to make common cause. Universal's Carl Laemmle, one of the leading independents, carried on a vehement campaign on behalf of shorts well into 1917.[1] Over at the Motion Picture Patents Company, Edison's production manager, Horace Plimpton, declared to the *New York Dramatic Mirror*:

> Almost every one of my friends that I talk to—friends not in the business—tell me that he prefers the short subjects and the varied programme. He does not mind a good two or three reel, but he does object to sitting through a film that takes an hour and a half or two hours to show, and he particularly objects to the latter if he happens to come in during its running so that he is forced to sit through some thousand feet of film which cannot interest him because he does not understand it. And yet the theatres, generally speaking, have got the "feature craze" pretty badly. They advertize them liberally and generally get good houses—besides which we shall have to admit—they attract a class of patrons formerly absent from picture theatres. Generally speaking, I suppose that the theatres in residential sections are more likely to do better with long films because families are able, or more apt, to make an evening's entertainment out of their visit, whereas those catering to more transient trade are better off with more and shorter subjects ("How Long Should Films Be?" *New York Dramatic Mirror*, 24 February 1915, p. 22).

Plimpton obviously had his eye on the transient trade, but a week later Samuel Goldfish, a leading promoter of features, told the same paper that short-film programs were finished. The *Dramatic Mirror*, showing its age, chose to differ with him in a strong editorial placed on the same page. What eventually happened, of course, is that silent theaters carefully walked the line, by presenting both feature-length pictures *and* a "varied programme" of shorts.[2]

The 1922 *Motion Picture News* survey revealed that comedy, news, and novelties dominated the short-film market, but one house in seven still offered a dramatic short, generally a Western. Between 1925 and 1927, for example, Universal alone produced 135 two-reel "Mustang" Westerns, 21 of them directed by William Wyler. Only two of these Wyler-directed shorts appear to survive at present, indicating the problems that historians face even in locating such material, much less in dealing with it adequately.[3]

Equally problematic are the "scenics"—proto-documentaries that appeared as frequently as animated cartoons on 1922 theater screens. The fact that Prizmacolor scenics were the only regularly available program of color films that year may have temporarily inflated the popularity of this genre, but Burton Holmes and Robert Bruce were doing well with black-and-white reels of their own. Little was written about these films at the time, and next to nothing is known of them today. Yet their influence in shaping audiences' perceptions of nonfiction material may have been significant.[4]

The Serial

Serials, newsreels, animation, and short comedies are, by comparison, much more accessible today, although few general histories attempt to integrate them into their overall picture of the silent-film scene. Anthony Slide's *Early American Cinema* includes a chapter on serials, for example, but despite the fact that 35 percent of theaters were running them in 1922, the form is ignored by most other writers on this period. Hard information on silent serials comes from a handful of genre specialists, while John Hampton's Silent Movie Theatre in Los Angeles provided the only regular public screenings of such films in recent decades.[5]

Serials were among the first attempts to develop very long and complex screen narratives, and they served as a useful bridge between the short film and the feature during the crucial 1913–1915 period. Edison's WHAT HAPPENED TO MARY? (1912) numbered a dozen one-reel episodes, although it lacked any necessary connection between the segments and is better classed as a series production. But unlike earlier series such as Essanay's "Broncho Billy" pictures, WHAT HAPPENED TO MARY? did have a unifying narrative line, with a beginning, middle, and ending, and employed many of the "thriller" devices common to later serials. Produced in cooperation with the *Ladies World*, which serialized the episodes in printed form, it established the direct link between these two media that would ignite the growth of film serials in 1914.

THE ADVENTURES OF KATHLYN (the first episode was released on 29 December 1913) is usually considered the first true motion picture serial, with a narrative thread continuing directly from one episode to the next, week after week. The *Chicago Tribune* serialized this Selig production as a circulation-builder, an idea soon picked up by William Randolph Hearst. THE PERILS OF PAULINE (Pathé, 1914), the first

Jack Mulhall struggles to keep from being thrown off the Brooklyn Bridge during the shooting of Pathé's INTO THE NET *(1924). Top serial directors George B. Seitz and Spencer Bennet (holding script) flank their co-star, Edna Murphy. The camera is a Wilart, an American-made all-metal copy of the Pathé.*

serial produced for Hearst, became the most famous of early "chapter plays," defining the genre and establishing its greatest star, Pearl White. Not well reviewed at the time (except in the Hearst press), the film is derided by Anthony Slide as "badly written and badly directed" and attacked by another historian as "appalling beyond belief . . . crude and inept." The magic that burned this film into the national consciousness was clearly not just coming from the screen but was part of a larger cultural phenomenon, quite possibly created by the massive Hearst press campaign.[6]

The heroines of these early serials—Pearl White, Ruth Roland, and Helen Holmes in particular—were spectacularly active characters always at the dramatic center of their films and often executing the most difficult and dangerous stunts themselves. The characterization grew directly from earlier one-reel melodramas such as Biograph's THE GIRL AND HER TRUST (1912) or Kalem's GRIT OF THE GIRL TELEGRAPHER (1913), but the serials outperformed these models in stuntwork and villainy. These women were a match for their opponents not only mentally but physically. However, this aggressive, even threatening, posture softened by 1916. For example,

Grace Cunard, who wrote her own films, had previously appeared as a traditional, active heroine in serials such as THE BROKEN COIN (1915). By 1916 such "unladylike" behavior was out of fashion and needed considerable dramatic justification. For her last serial, THE PURPLE MASK (1916), she concocted a script that apparently had her on the other side of the law, as the leader of a criminal gang. The situation offered an excuse for an aggressive matching of wits with the hero, a ploy Cunard had not previously needed.[7]

An alternative was to emphasize the male figure, which led to the rise of serial heroes such as Eddie Polo and Joe Bonomo at Universal and Charles Hutchison at Pathé. While Ruth Roland's career lasted throughout the silent era, and she was joined after 1924 by Allene Ray, the character of most successful serials shifted after the war to emphasize male heroics.

The market value of serials was simultaneously downgraded as their production was abandoned by the more prestigious producers and left in the hands of Pathé, Universal, and an assortment of small independents. In 1915 Pathé and Universal already dominated the serial market, releasing four titles apiece, but Vitagraph, American, Mutual, Lubin, Reliance, and Kalem also released one or two.[8] Five years later, Pathé released seven serials, Universal six, and Vitagraph four. But seventeen more serials came from fourteen other producers, generally minor outfits, including Burston (THE HAWK'S TRAIL), Hallmark (THE SCREAMING SHADOW), and Canyon (VANISHING TRAILS). By 1925 many of these small companies had left the field, leaving most production to Pathé (five serials) and Universal (four) and contributing only four other titles.

None of these firms were in the business of supplying the major downtown palaces; instead, their products went to small urban houses, country theaters, and other unaffiliated venues. Because children made up a large portion of the audience in these theaters, the serial came to be known as a children's genre, and censorship groups began to direct more attention to the problem of serials and youth. Ellis Paxson Oberholtzer, head of the Pennsylvania board, wrote in 1922:

> The "crime serial" is perhaps the most astounding development in the
> history of the motion picture. . . . It is meant for the most ignorant classes
> of the population with the grossest tastes, and it principally flourishes in
> the picture halls in mill villages and in the thickly settled tenement house
> and low foreign-speaking neighborhoods in the big cities. . . . The crim-
> inologist would find the picture serial a fruitful field of study (*The Morals
> of the Movie* [Philadelphia: Penn, 1922], pp. 55–56).

But while Oberholtzer could produce prison wardens to testify that "criminals are made in the picture houses," by the 1920s few others were taking the form so seriously.

In 1917 William Randolph Hearst sought to mold public opinion with the release of PATRIA, a "preparedness" serial in which Mexico and Japan were identified as fomenting a secret fifth-column insurrection in America. All Hearst gained for his trouble was a presidential rebuff, but it is significant that he made the attempt. Only a few years later, the once-glamorous serial would be trapped forever in a world of circuses, cowboys, and jungle adventures.[9]

Newsreels

> "Did you boys ever see a moving picture newspaper?" the photographer went on.
>
> "Do you mean one telling the business, and giving news and printing advertisements of shows?" inquired Joe.
>
> "Not exactly. I mean a series of moving picture films, taken daily, weekly, or perhaps monthly, showing current events, such as coronations, inaugurations, and all sorts of events of interest. Just as an ordinary newspaper prints the news of what happens, the moving picture newspaper shows pictures of the same thing."
>
> "I think I have read something about that," said Blake (Victor Appleton, *The Moving Picture Boys; or, The Perils of a Great City Depicted* [New York: Grosset and Dunlap, 1913], p. 68).

The newsreel itself was something new to Victor Appleton's young chums in *The Moving Picture Boys; or, The Perils of a Great City Depicted*. THE PATHÉ WEEKLY had been introduced domestically in 1911, but only in 1913–1914 did a stream of popular news weeklies reach American screens.[10] Some were connected with the major national producer-distributors, such as THE UNIVERSAL ANIMATED WEEKLY, which first appeared the same year as Appleton's book. Others were regional productions, such as San Francisco's GOLDEN GATE WEEKLY, distributed by Sol Lesser in 1914. Eventually, the early picture palaces, including New York's Strand, Rivoli, and Capitol, began assembling their own news programs, cannibalizing these existing services and shooting extra material of their own to order. The character of these newsreels was established at a very early date, and it soon became apparent that coronations and inaugurations could not be depended on to keep the public's interest week after week. Even Appleton's young news-cameramen soon came to question the bulk of the material in their weekly reel:

> "I hope there aren't any harrowing scenes," murmured Joe.
>
> "One thing I don't like about this business is that we have to show so much of the sad side of life."
>
> "Well, it's there—every one knows it, and we're like a newspaper—obliged to give all the news we can get," replied his chum. "Look out!" (p. 123).

A near car collision turns our heroes away from such reflection and back into another round of tenement fires, harbor catastrophes, and rapid-transit accidents, those perils of a great city which were the true meat of the news cameraman.

Emmanuel Cohen, editor of THE PATHÉ WEEKLY, divided his newsreel subjects into three categories: "sudden events" like the Japanese earthquake or the *Shenandoah* dirigible disaster; "impending events" whose occurrence might be predicted from existing situations, such as the burning of Smyrna during the 1922 war between the Greeks and the Turks; and "scheduled events" such as ballgames, coronations, and inaugurations.[11]

Cohen realized, as did Appleton's heroes, that it was the sudden event which gave the newsreel its essential dynamism. Yet newsworthy accidents were scarce, and the

A full-page ad promoting another "scoop" for Universal's weekly newsreel, "the world war's most astounding event," the Russian Revolution (Moving Picture Weekly, 21 July 1917, p. 35).

reel needed to appear on schedule every week (or twice weekly by the end of the silent period). Newsreel editors met this problem by keeping a core group of cameramen on staff in various cities for regular assignments—beauty pageants, parades, road races—and supplementing their footage with material supplied by as many as 1,500 "stringers," free-lance cameramen scattered across the country. For capturing newsworthy tornadoes or air crashes, these men could be paid from thirty-five cents to one dollar per foot of negative, possibly more for choice material.[12]

Competition among free-lance cameramen was fierce because an editor could use only so much footage of a given event. The ability to maneuver one's seventy-five-pound load of camera, tripod, and extra film magazines into the most advantageous position soon built up an aura of machismo around the newsreel cameraman that was unique in the industry. "No weakling's game is this," boasted one prominent Pathé newsman.[13]

On a more organized level, competition among the various newsreel producers was equally fierce. When Pathé acquired exclusive rights to a major 1923 horse race, it attempted to blind "pirate" cameramen through the use of smoke pots and a crop-dusting plane. Because these actions obscured the race for everyone, less intrusive tactics were usually employed. Austin Lescarboura describes a battle at Ebbets Field between the "official" camera crew and some pirates atop a nearby apartment building. The weapons were pocket mirrors, used to flash sunlight into the opponent's lens.[14]

In general, audiences were well served by this competition, since newsreel editors felt compelled to "scoop" their rivals by rushing stories onto local screens in record

Newsreels often featured very little hard news, instead padding their length with human interest stories, comical vignettes, or outright hoaxes.

TABLE 6.1   NEWSREEL MARKET, 1925–1928

	Newsreel Companies	Weekly Cost	Weekly Income
1925	4	$ 75,000	$115,000
1928	6	$125,000	$110,000

SOURCE: Howard T. Lewis, *The Motion Picture Industry* (New York: Van Nostrand, 1933), p. 133.

time. Jack Cohn had footage taken of a New York City subway explosion at 8:30 A.M. developed and printed during the morning and onscreen at Broadway houses by noon.[15] But some felt that this situation fostered inefficient duplication of staffs and services and created a strong inducement to fabrication and fraud. Howard Lewis indicates that the four existing newsreels in 1925 were able to turn a healthy profit, but after Universal, Fox, Pathé, and Kinograms were joined by Paramount and MGM in 1927, the market became oversaturated (table 6.1).

Nonetheless, with newsreels considered an obligatory part of the balanced theater program, producer-distributors hoping to supply a theater's complete show felt obliged to offer a newsreel of their own. By the time Fox introduced its talking MOVIETONE NEWS in 1927, it was estimated that 90 percent of American theaters regularly programmed one or another of the existing newsreels.[16]

Animation

Newsreel production was centered in the East not simply because most newsworthy events were best covered there but because the newsreels were closely tied to various press syndicates. For much the same reason, silent animation studios were also headquartered in New York and, to a lesser extent, Chicago.[17] Just as newspaper comic strips arose as adjuncts of expanding urban broadsheets, so animated cartoons would be taken up by newsreel distributors and the press lords who often sponsored them. While J. Stuart Blackton and Winsor McCay had earlier demonstrated the potential of cartoon animation as a curiosity, it was J. R. Bray and Earl Hurd who made the medium economically feasible by their separate development, in 1914, of what became the Bray-Hurd process.[18]

When he created GERTIE THE DINOSAUR (1914), Winsor McCay drew each frame separately and completely—a labor-intensive process that challenged even his prodigious drafting abilities. But producing such films in large numbers was impossible without dividing the work and automating the non-creative aspects. Bray took the first step by conceiving of the background as a separate plane, offset-printing it in quantity, and animating only the necessary foreground elements. While Bray mentioned the use of celluloid overlays in one of his patent applications, its modern use was developed by Earl Hurd, whose own application was filed later in 1914. Through the use of transparent plastic "cels," various layers of action could be sandwiched and only the necessary "moving" elements, such as an arm or a mouth, animated. When combined with Raoul Barré's introduction that same year of the peg system for registering the various overlays, all the key elements of animation technology had been established by 1915.

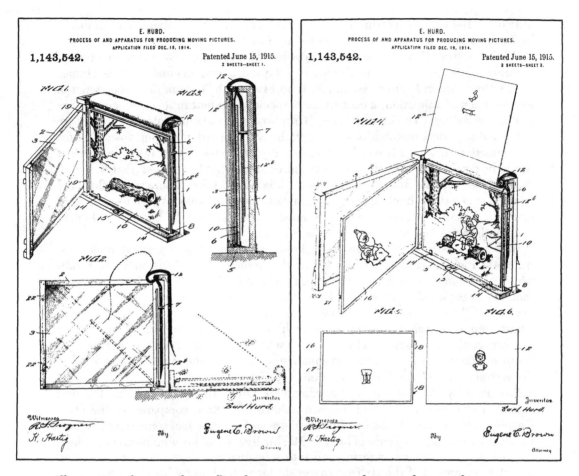

Illustrations from Earl Hurd's cel animation patent, showing the use of transparent overlays to carry distinct motion elements.

Bray and Hurd were able to effect a patent monopoly on the strength of their pooled patents, ironic at a time when the original Motion Picture Patents Company was being dissolved by the courts. Studios either took out a license for the use of cel animation or restricted themselves to animating on paper. Surprisingly, many important animators in this period stayed with paper, not only because they wished to avoid the license fee but because they preferred that medium to celluloid.[19] Felix the Cat, the most popular of silent cartoon characters, was animated on paper by the talented Otto Mesmer, whose spare compositions made a virtue of this necessity.

Bray produced a series of COL. HEEZA LIAR cartoons beginning in 1913, and Raoul Barré's ANIMATED GROUCH CHASER appeared on the Edison program in 1915. The third significant animation studio in this early period was the International Film Service (IFS), organized to highlight characters appearing in the Hearst newspapers' comic pages. George Herrimann's KRAZY KAT, Frederick Opper's HAPPY HOOLI-GAN, and George McManus' BRINGING UP FATHER were three of the more important IFS series that Hearst appended to his newsreel.[20] The original artists had nothing to do with the creation of these films, which were under the direction of Gregory La Cava (later a noted director of live-action comedies). Bud Fisher's MUTT

AND JEFF, the most successful of the recruits from the funny papers, was produced by Fisher's own company and distributed by Fox.

While the Bray-Hurd process made possible this rapid expansion of production, it severely diluted the quality of the work. A typical period manual, such as Homer Croy's *How Motion Pictures Are Made*, is obsessed with "bottom line" economics in its discussion of animation, a concern not especially evident in its coverage of other industry activities. "The constant aim," Croy writes, "is to eliminate all unnecessary detail and to perfect methods of shortening the work, in order to bring down the cost of production to where it will be commercially profitable." Any available shortcut would be taken. Croy says that most exposures are doubled or tripled (that is, two or three frames are shot from each drawing), while Austin Lescarboura insists that only one object at a time should be shown in motion. Where "balloons" are used to show dialogue, Lescarboura notes, all action must cease, purportedly because audiences would otherwise become distracted and confused.[21]

In fact, it was such threadbare assembly-line methods that dismayed audiences. Animator Richard Huemer, who entered the industry with Barré in 1916, recalls widespread audience antipathy to cartoons, which he felt survived only because of their status as part of a program package. They were able to maintain a position here because of their low cost and the occasional use of popular comic-strip characters whose names had value. "Funny as a crutch" is the way he describes them.[22] After the war, Paul Terry carried on this tradition with his tedious AESOP'S FABLES series, featuring Farmer Al Falfa. Truly imaginative work within the studio system awaited the arrival of Ko-Ko the Clown and Felix the Cat.

Produced by Pat Sullivan and animated by Otto Mesmer, Felix was the first animated character to develop his own following.[23] Often compared to the early Chaplin in his resourcefulness and physical grace, Felix also had something of Chaplin's worldview and wry sense of humor. Making free use of his ubiquitous tail, which might serve as a ladder or form itself into a floating question mark, Felix was in complete command of the stylized spaces designed for him by his creators.

Time and space came under even broader attack in Max Fleischer's OUT OF THE INKWELL series, in which Ko-Ko the Clown was the nominal lead. Although his clown may not have had much personality, Fleischer more then compensated with a bizarre assortment of self-referential gags, usually involving the relationship between the animator and his troublesome creation. KO-KO'S CARTOON FACTORY (1925), a surreal masterwork, has Ko-Ko turn the tables and mass-produce scores of animated Max Fleischers, who then proceed to harass *their* creator. Fleischer's development of the rotoscoping technique, in which previously filmed live-action material was traced by the animator, not only gave his films an uneasy suggestion of human motion but helped make him an expert in the combining of live action and animation.[24]

Austin Lescarboura's *Behind the Motion Picture Screen* (1922) devotes most of its animation section to live-action animation, but today this significant work is largely neglected, with only Willis O'Brien's model animation for THE LOST WORLD (1925) noted in the general histories. Lescarboura spends considerable time on an (unnamed) Chicago puppet animator and the five-reel animated feature he had just completed, possibly Howard Moss and his little-known Essanay feature, THE DREAM DOLL (1917).[25]

Certainly the most extravagant live-action animator of the period was Charles Bowers, who had once been a partner of Raoul Barré. While O'Brien gradually

The first international animation star, Felix the Cat, on the cover of the British fan magazine Picture Show, *5 April 1924.*

mastered the ability to give his tiny creatures the illusion of life, Bowers animated things like eggs and automobiles. In a highly imaginative series of shorts produced at his Astoria, New York, studio, Bowers brought to live-action animation the physical, and metaphysical, freedom of action that Mesmer and Fleischer had given to their cartoons. Neglected even in its time, Bowers' work exists today only because the curator of the Toulouse Cinémathèque discovered a cache of reels once owned by a traveling Gypsy exhibitor.[26]

During the pre-1927 period, most animation studios were very modest affairs, the kind of operation that might be located above a tailor shop.[27] A few key animators and their support teams went from one small outfit to another, with releasing arrangements changing so frequently, even for a successful producer like Fleischer, that little could be taken for granted. Walt Disney, who drifted to Los Angeles in 1923 after failing in Kansas City, would begin to change the face of this industry again by the end of the decade. But until the advent of Mickey Mouse, he and his studio were victims of this same turmoil and had nothing very impressive of their own to show for it.

Comedy

While dramatic subjects essentially abandoned shorts for features after 1915, the same route was not followed by comedies. Relatively few feature-length comedies were produced before 1920, and even in 1925, the year of THE GOLD RUSH, THE FRESHMAN, and SEVEN CHANCES, almost one thousand reels of short comedies were released. It was nearly impossible to avoid catching a one- or two-reel comedy, or sometimes both, in the average silent-movie house. History remembers the great character comedians who moved into features, but with a few key exceptions, the army of two-reel comics who created the bulk of silent comedy has been forgotten.[28]

Large "fun factories" like Keystone were not in the lead in producing feature-length comedies. They continued to develop the short-film form, while producers such as Lasky or Vitagraph added long comedies to their release schedules with varying degrees of success. Mack Sennett produced the six-reel TILLIE'S PUNCTURED ROMANCE in 1914 but refused to follow up on it. When Triangle presented him with Weber and Fields, a vaudeville team who seemed ready-made for features, he put them into two-reelers.[29]

When comedy features did appear, they tended to be adaptations of popular stage successes, often with the original stars. Cecil B. DeMille directed Victor Moore in CHIMMIE FADDEN (1915), which was popular enough for a sequel but did not immediately impel DeMille to produce more comedies. His vision of cinema, like D. W. Griffith's, was far more sober than that, at least in 1915. At Vitagraph, Mr. and Mrs. Sidney Drew moved from shorts to features with the rest of the company, but the extended length seems to have changed their status very little.

In terms of audience appeal, it is clear that shorts surpassed features on the pre-1920 comedy scene, with one notable exception. Douglas Fairbanks, working almost entirely in features, was generally considered "one of film land's most popular comedians" for his work in such breezy light comedies as WILD AND WOOLLY (1917) and WHEN THE CLOUDS ROLL BY (1920).[30] Fairbanks had come from the theater and began in films doing the usual theatrical adaptations. Gradually his production unit began to craft new scripts to suit the jaunty screen persona he had established, and his career flourished. But Fairbanks was one man against an army of Chaplins, Arbuckles, and Lloyds then working entirely in shorts. His comedy positioned a realistic character in situations that took time to develop; their comedy, while more than simple slapstick, was certainly gag-based and far more dependent on stereotypes and conventions.

Audiences now began to see two distinct types of comedy. The more "high-class" comedy descended from Broadway adaptations and portrayed recognizable characters in believable situations. It was generally to be seen only in features. Short films were the province of "low comedy," a continuation of the slapstick tradition of nickelodeon days. Low comedy had its intellectual champions, especially Gilbert Seldes, but was constantly under attack by moralists for its vulgarity, disrespect, and inducement to lawlessness. Sennett and the early Chaplin became lightning rods for both these forces.[31]

These brief films made use of a visual shorthand well suited to the capabilities of early screen narrative. Stereotyped characters represented familiar figures developed on the stages of British music halls and American vaudeville theaters. Racial and ethnic stereotyping, with its attendant "humor," was an integral part of this scheme. Its physical aspects drew on the same primal impulses tapped in the *com-*

Production of short comedies continued to be big business throughout the silent period. Here Harold Beaudine directs Neal Burns and Doris Dawson in a Christie comedy for Paramount, about 1927.

media dell'arte; indeed, the word "slapstick" itself originally described Harlequin's wooden paddle. As Mack Sennett put it in the argot of 1918, "Explanations must be Hooverized to as great an extent as possible in the movies. By custom side-whiskers and stove-pipe hats have come to be recognized as the badge of the official goat of the comedy. Just as a white lawn dress and curls are the sign of the heroine in drama."[32]

When Chaplin began adding a note of pathos to his short comedies, as early as THE TRAMP (1915), critics took notice. "A moving episode like this must be seen to be appreciated," wrote one otherwise skeptical reviewer, referring to Chaplin's first lonely trudge up a dusty road.[33] Chaplin continued this tentative exploration but refused to abandon either his stylized comic costume (developed at Keystone to suit the demands of Sennett's comedy) or—until the 1920s—the short-film form itself. His chief rival, Fatty Arbuckle, occasionally inserted a sentimental note into his raucous comedies, but Arbuckle was not very interested in character comedy as such.

Much more important was the change in comic persona affected by Harold Lloyd in 1917–1918. Abandoning his clownish "Lonesome Luke" character, Lloyd suddenly appeared as a middle-class white-collar worker whose only comic prop was a pair of eyeglasses. Still working within the tight format of the one-reeler, Lloyd began to merge the physical comedy of the slapstick tradition with the believable situations and characters successfully employed by Fairbanks. This proved to be crucial to the great age of silent feature comedy to follow.

There is still some controversy as to who was responsible for this change, Lloyd or his producer, Hal Roach.[34] Whatever the truth of the matter, Roach immediately began to investigate the possibility of other realistic characters in believable situa-

Harold Lloyd as "Lonesome Luke" in a 1915 trade advertisement.

"Nothing Succeeds Like SUCCESS"

"COMEDIES THAT ARE"

This is

HAROLD C. LLOYD

Our Double-Jointed Rubber Comedian with Two of the Many

See Him Fall and Get Tossed in

PHUNPHILMS

Released Through Pathe Exchange, Inc.

Hal Roach Is Directing
Some Company

ROLIN FILM COMPANY
Los Angeles

D. Whiting, Gen. Mgr.   907 Brockman Bldg.

HAROLD LLOYD

presented by

THE HAROLD LLOYD CORPORATION

IN HIS OWN PRODUCTIONS

A decade later, a very different trade ad shows Lloyd as head of his own corporation
(Film Daily Yearbook of Motion Pictures [1925], p. 6).

tions. Roach and Sennett were in direct competition for supremacy in short-comedy production, and this new angle would enable Roach to differentiate his product from Sennett's by bringing in some of the elements of "high-class" comedy involving character and situation. His use of this approach can be seen not only in the Lloyd films, but in later Roach comedies featuring Charlie Chase, Will Rogers, Laurel and Hardy, and even Our Gang. Sennett continued to work in the earlier tradition throughout the silent era, relying on such baggy-pants comedians as Ford Sterling, Billy Bevan, and Ben Turpin—clowns whose appeal was primarily based on funny costumes and makeup. While he continued to discover future stars such as Harry Langdon, Sennett's "fun factory" was unable to accommodate their comic style, and the importance of his studio declined.

Adolph Zukor saw the potential of placing an important slapstick comedian in a feature-picture framework and in 1920 signed Fatty Arbuckle to a $2 million contract. The first Arbuckle feature, THE ROUND UP, appeared on 10 October 1920, and a total of seven features were released before a notorious scandal destroyed the comedian's career less than a year later (two more completed films were shelved).[35] To get full value for his money, Zukor used the most high-pressure assembly-line methods, at one point running Arbuckle from a Joseph Henabery film on one stage to a James Cruze film on another.

Arbuckle seems to have been removed from any creative control, and the scripts, taken from stage plays or magazine stories, have no feeling for his particular comic strengths. One film, canceled during production because of the scandal, was successfully repackaged for Will Rogers. Seen today, the surviving Arbuckle features have nothing to recommend them over the shorts. A comedian noted for movement and energy in his films, Arbuckle was slowed to a halt, reduced to exchanging humorous dialogue titles with his supporting cast. Audiences at the time were apparently satisfied by small bits of pantomime or an occasional appearance in drag, but how long such indulgence would have lasted is an open question. Zukor's decision to mass-produce Arbuckle films was clearly the problem. In 1919 Arbuckle released only seven two-reel comedies, each a small masterpiece of timing and invention. During the same amount of time on his Paramount contract, Zukor squeezed nine features out of the man, more than triple the amount of screen time. The results were obvious and served as an object lesson to other short-film comedians moving to features.

The same fate almost befell Arbuckle's protégé Buster Keaton, whose first feature picture, THE SAPHEAD, appeared only a week after the initial Arbuckle feature. Cast arbitrarily in this adaptation of a familiar stage farce, Keaton struggled to assert some of his own style but accomplished little more than a few pratfalls. Fortunately, this was only a one-shot affair, and Keaton was able to develop his style in two-reelers until 1923.

Chaplin's THE KID, released on 6 February 1921, was the first really successful example of the move to features by an established short-film comedian. In complete control of the production, Chaplin polished the film until he had everything exactly the way he wanted it. THE KID was a revelation, and the posters produced for its original release tell why. "This is the great picture upon which the famous comedian has worked a whole year," they boasted.[36] None but Chaplin could afford to spend that kind of time refining a comedy, but time was what was required to get things right. It would be 1923 before Chaplin released a feature again and 1925 before he would issue another feature-length comedy.

Harold Lloyd, last of the big four to enter features, was the first, however, to do so successfully on a regular basis. Following the release of A SAILOR-MADE MAN on 25 December 1921, Lloyd never returned to shorts; he produced a steady flow of one or two features per year for the rest of the silent period. With Chaplin appearing on screen so infrequently in the twenties, Arbuckle gone, and Keaton's films often losing money, Lloyd became not only the most popular comedian but the greatest box-office attraction of the period.[37]

There is scarcely space here to mention, much less discuss, the remainder of the vast number of comics starring in shorts and/or features in the silent era. Larry Semon, Raymond Griffith, Harry Langdon, Reginald Denny, Mabel Normand, Will Rogers, and W. C. Fields all produced work of high quality. A few had as much control over their work as Chaplin or Lloyd, and several were making more money than Keaton. But their contributions to silent comedy clearly are more limited than those of the big four: less original, less imaginative, or simply less able to survive the decades.[38]

The great silent comedians may dominate history's image of this era, but it could be argued that a revolution in the crafting of situation comedies was of greater significance in the overall development of film comedy. Chaplin and Keaton were inimitable, after all. The key problem with such comedies was dependence on a preexisting literary text. Adaptations of dramatic successes might be opened up a bit onscreen, but the purchaser of a witty Broadway farce wanted to see the original jokes and gag-lines in the filmscript, which meant a profusion of title cards. Unlike dramas, few comedies achieved success onstage because of an underlying story idea (CHARLEY'S AUNT would be one exception). Instead, audiences were attracted to the dialogue, the songs, or an especially engaging performance. But because only the narrative line was essentially transferrable to the silent screen, these other values were meaningless. Pre-1920 adaptations of light comedies are among the most static films of their era and offer a strong explanation for the concurrent popularity of short gag comedies.

The Fairbanks films, as scripted by Anita Loos, indicated an effective new model: attractive young characters, a fresh comedy concept, and minimal reliance on title-card repartee. "Whenever possible build your story about a theme and make your climax the outcome of some great universal truth," Loos counseled. "The old truths, of course, are pretty well worn, but every day our civilization finds a new truth born."[39]

Cecil B. DeMille was keenly aware of the "new truth" of the postwar world and lightened his society melodramas with stylish directorial touches and attractive per-formances from Gloria Swanson and other fashionable young leads. His methods were not lost on Ernst Lubitsch, who built on them to create a new comedy of manners that would revolutionize late silent-screen comedy. In addition to DeMille, Lubitsch also drew on Chaplin's A WOMAN OF PARIS (1923), especially for its use of visual symbols and telling details of characterization. His first American comedy, THE MARRIAGE CIRCLE (1924), already demonstrated that purely cinematic devices—editing, the close-up, camera movement—could be used to communicate a high degree of visual wit: the "Lubitsch touch." Spread by such disciples as Mal St. Clair, Monta Bell, and Harry D'Arrast, the new style was an indigenous high-comedy silent-screen form, distinct from literary antecedents on Broadway as well as from the antics of the great character comedians. In place of *bons mots* or pratfalls, Lubitsch created comedy through the shot of a door closing or Adolphe Menjou raising an

Very much in the Lubitsch tradition, Mal St. Clair directs GENTLEMEN PREFER BLONDES *at Paramount in 1927 (released 1928).*

eyebrow. By the time he directed LADY WINDERMERE'S FAN (1925), Lubitsch was able to eliminate all Wildean epigrams, substituting visual analogues instead. This was no mere stunt but the culmination of several years of increasingly sophisticated work in silent comedy by a number of writers and directors. While Lubitsch may have been the first to synthesize these elements successfully, the eventual demonstration was probably inevitable.[40]

By 1925 screen comedy had achieved a happy balance of verbal and visual elements, something apparent even in the work of otherwise minor performers and directors. A Reginald Denny comedy for Universal, SKINNER'S DRESS SUIT, for example, confidently displays a sophisticated style unknown only two years earlier. A star like Marion Davies was able to take advantage of this and change the shape of her career from period-picture heroine to bright young comedienne (SHOW PEOPLE [1928]). As William K. Everson points out, many of the situation comedies of the late silent era hang on conventionalized plots hardly different from those of television sitcoms. But while the television approach is almost entirely verbal, these silent films were able to mine the same situations in terms of visual comedy, a far more difficult achievement.[41]

Drama and Melodrama: The Genre Film

For the most part, silent dramatic features failed to take advantage of their added length in any but the most peripheral ways. Continuing to operate in the melodramatic tradition that had worked so well during the nickelodeon era, they simply added larger quantities of information on plot, locale, and characterization. The world thus created was far more dense than that suggested by the one- and two-reelers: the illusionistic power of the narrative was increased without altering the main ingredients of plot and characterization, which remained highly conventionalized.

There were good reasons for melodrama to take hold so firmly in the pre-1914 cinema. As a dramatic style, it dominated the American stage at a time when Ibsen, Shaw, and even Pinero were considered too radical for the mass audience. Less sophisticated filmgoers could hardly be expected to patronize more subtle entertainments at their local nickelodeon. In addition, the limited narrative capabilities of the silent short film severely restricted what might be accomplished in terms of characterization or thematic development. Early filmmakers inevitably turned to the melodramatic tradition for instant characterization of heroes and villains, simple dramatic confrontations that could be powerfully sketched in visual terms, and familiar thematic structures invoking traditional nineteenth-century ideals.[42]

A film such as THE LONELY VILLA, directed by D. W. Griffith in 1909, makes effective use of all these elements. Only 750 feet in length, it plays on the audience's familiarity with stock villains and heroes, the theme of the family endangered, and the ultimate victory of good over evil. The effective use of crosscutting in the final "race to the rescue" demonstrates Griffith's ability to adapt or invent cinematic devices capable of increasing the emotional impact of such conventions.

THE BIRTH OF A NATION, released in 1915, was twelve reels long, or sixteen times the length of THE LONELY VILLA. Nonetheless, the film could hardly be described as anything more than a super-melodrama, offering the same heroes and villains, the same image of the family endangered, and the same inevitable victory of good over evil, all driven by the filmmaker's growing command of his medium. What Griffith did gain from this added length is a richness of detail that allows his narrative an almost Dickensian texture. We learn how his characters walk and talk, what their streets and houses look like, what they wear, and what they eat (the historical accuracy of the film is another matter). While Henry B. Walthall, Lillian Gish, and George Siegmann still play the conventionalized hero, heroine, and villain of a Biograph one-reeler, Griffith's skilled assemblage of milieu detail provides their characters with great richness and resonance. The famous homecoming scene, in which "The Little Colonel" suddenly realizes how the war has devastated the culture of the South, depends on our knowledge and understanding of that culture, not on our recognition of this character as in any way emotionally or psychologically "real."

Instead of psychological realism, what this film offers are characters who are true to type. Over twelve reels, Walthall's character experiences a host of traumatic episodes, but the effect of these episodes is seen in his face, not his spirit. He does not and cannot change. The nobility of his character is a fixed point, like Siegmann's duplicity or Gish's innocence. Yet this accomplishment on Griffith's part is a major achievement because he demonstrated that the most powerful effects of the short narrative form could successfully be amplified in a feature-length work. Many other

D. W. Griffith imported a squad of Civil War veterans to "advise" on the filming of THE BIRTH OF A NATION, *and made sure a stills photographer was on hand to record the event.*

early filmmakers, both before and after THE BIRTH OF A NATION, failed completely in their efforts to deal with the expanded form, losing plots and characters in a meaningless welter of extra footage.

Melodrama continued to represent the dominant stylistic mode in Hollywood all through the silent period. Only a few directors—King Vidor, Erich von Stroheim, and William deMille among them—attempted to offer a vision of life more complex and multidimensional than that to be found in UNCLE TOM'S CABIN (1918), BLUE JEANS (1918), or WAY DOWN EAST (1920).

The dominance of melodrama can be seen in the high percentage of genre films produced in this period. These films utilized recurrent situations, locales, and characters and were perfectly suited to an age that saw most of its dramatic conflicts in highly conventionalized terms. The most popular of silent genres was unquestionably the Western, which flourished throughout the period in shorts as well as features, in low-budget films as well as spectacles, and created some of the era's greatest stars.[43] Cecil B. DeMille's first film, THE SQUAW MAN (1914), was the screen version of a popular stage Western, and DeMille soon followed it with THE VIRGINIAN (1914), THE ROSE OF THE RANCHO (1914), and THE GIRL OF THE GOLDEN WEST (1914). William S. Hart, who had appeared in some of these shows onstage, made a career of presenting the screen westerner in what he considered a more accurate and realistic light. When Hart first appeared in films, in 1914, Gilbert M. "Broncho Billy"

Anderson, an eastern "dude" obviously uncomfortable on a horse, was still the screen's best-known cowboy. But Tom Mix had also preceded Hart onscreen and by the 1920s would eclipse Hart's own popularity by substituting a circus rider's bag of tricks for the dour realism offered by Hart. The change in public taste was predictable, because Westerns had moved from the serious plateau of the early DeMille pictures to a genre clearly intended for children. The form ultimately became so degraded that Westerns were the only genre segregated from the balance of a studio's product line (as in ". . . and eight Westerns"). The surprising success of THE COVERED WAGON in 1923 initiated a small flurry of Western epics whose appeal was somewhat more adult, but no silent Western ever approached the maturity of the best examples produced in the 1940s and 1950s. The low status of most silent Westerns made them useful entry points for a number of young directors, most notably John Ford and William Wyler, both of whom began their careers at the studio most heavily involved in such productions, Universal.

The more traditional family melodrama also flourished on the silent screen, often as the direct adaptation of some tent-show classic. UNCLE TOM'S CABIN was filmed

Crew shot for a Jack Hoxie Universal Western, directed by Al Rogell, probably THE WESTERN WHIRLWIND *(1927). This five-reel feature was made for $15,935.44 and grossed five times that amount. Note the Akeley camera at the right, used for telephoto action scenes, which supplements the traditional Bell & Howell 2709 at the left.*

eight times in the silent period, and despite the derision of some critics, WAY DOWN EAST proved to be Griffith's second-biggest moneymaker. Scorned for trying to "develop 'The Old Oaken Bucket' into grand opera," Griffith not only opened up his elaborate adaptation of this warhorse with a set-piece ice-floe sequence, but successfully updated the show's moral posture as well. BLUE JEANS, UNDER THE GASLIGHT (1914), LENA RIVERS (1914), and KATHLEEN MAVOURNEEN (1919) were also filmed, although with less overall success. Their concern with false marriage and illegitimacy was no longer so compelling to audiences, although the filial-ingratitude plot proved a crowd-pleaser throughout the 1920s. HUMORESQUE, OVER THE HILL, and STELLA DALLAS, clever screen adaptations of sentimental novels or poems on this theme, were sensational box-office hits. The key to bringing the family melodrama to the screen in this era lay in understanding the rapid changes buffeting the American family, especially in the years following World War I. By exploiting such painful new issues as the growing gap between the generations, this genre was able to maintain its prominent position with its traditional audience.[44]

An offshoot of the family melodrama, especially evident after 1920, was the society melodrama. These films typically dealt with tribulations in the lives of the rich and famous and served as showcases for glamorous costumes and settings. Often a working-class character, usually female, would be introduced into upper-class society by some twist of the plot. This allowed the filmmakers to demonstrate the moral superiority of the working class while lavishing attention on the glamorous life-styles of the wealthy. Gloria Swanson made a career of such films: she appeared as both an upper-class heroine (WHY CHANGE YOUR WIFE?, 1920) and a working-class girl thrust into gilded society (MANHANDLED, 1924). Society melodramas were a fixture at the Paramount Astoria studio, where their production often necessitated lengthy wintertime junkets to Palm Beach and other millionaires' playgrounds.[45]

The 1935 *Variety* headline "Sticks Nix Hick Pix" marked the collapse of the once-popular subgenre of rural melodrama. Especially successful in the small-town and country theaters, which constituted the bulk of American cinemas, this subgenre celebrated the fast-vanishing world of small-town America and the endangered value system it represented. A few stars, notably Charles Ray, worked almost exclusively in rural melodrama, but the majority of these films lacked either big names or big budgets. King Vidor's early independent studio, Vidor Village, produced films like THE JACK KNIFE MAN (1920), in the spirit of James Whitcomb Riley, but it closed when audiences began to tire of such pictures.[46] After the early 1920s, rural melodramas were generally relegated to unsophisticated venues, but they continued to be produced by studios like Universal that could sell them to the same houses that bought their serials and two-reel Westerns. At their best, as in Griffith's A ROMANCE OF HAPPY VALLEY (1919) and TRUE HEART SUSIE (1919), these films were gentle, unpretentious, and not always nostalgic efforts to capture on film an already disappearing way of life (helped on its way, in part, by the proliferation of movie theaters). Once almost as common as Westerns, rural melodramas essentially expired with a few valedictory pieces in the 1940s and 1950s by such silent-era directors as Henry King and Clarence Brown.

There was no horror or science-fiction genre in films of this period, although pulp fiction of this kind was already prevalent. Instead, a generalized "thriller" genre included mysteries, crime and detective pictures, and occasional "dark house" films in which the secrets were never supernatural. "Crook films" such as ALIAS JIMMY

One of the few science fiction fantasies of the era was THE MYSTERIOUS ISLAND, in which Jules Verne's submariners encounter a race of undersea aliens. Unusually complicated special effects shots such as these were one of the reasons production dragged on at the MGM studio from 1926 until the film's release in 1929. The director in the top photo is Lucien Hubbard.

VALENTINE (filmed in 1915, 1920, and 1929) or RAFFLES, THE AMATEUR CRACKS-MAN (1917, 1925, and 1930) often had a touch of society melodrama about them, especially after the Hays Office began to frown on crime as a theme after 1922. Detective heroes were not uncommon, and Sherlock Holmes made several appearances (most notably in 1916 with William Gillette and in 1922 with John Barrymore), while Charlie Chan reached the screen in a 1926 serial. Following a wave of Broadway successes, THE BAT (1926) and THE CAT AND THE CANARY (1927) introduced clutching hands and mock supernaturalism, and made good use of the growing influence of German film style.[47] Considering the decade's obsession with mysticism and the occult, it is puzzling that the supernatural had almost no part in American films of the 1920s. Tod Browning's LONDON AFTER MIDNIGHT (1927) featured a vampire ultimately revealed as a hoax, while the German NOSFERATU did not even reach American art theaters until the end of 1929. Universal's decision to film DRACULA (1931) marked a significant departure from established thriller conventions of the silent period.

In a sense, THE BIRTH OF A NATION was the culmination of a vogue for Civil War military melodrama that ran back to the early nickelodeon days, but World War I soon offered a more topical replacement. While the conflict raged, American producers handled it in strictly propagandistic terms, first with preparedness sagas like THE BATTLE CRY OF PEACE (1915), then with full-scale battle-action films like THE HEART OF HUMANITY (1918). Immediately after the war, some films already in the production pipeline appeared as "vengeance pictures," but audiences soon lost interest in such diatribes. Serious views of the war, notably THE FOUR HORSEMEN OF THE APOCALYPSE (1921), THE BIG PARADE (1925), WHAT PRICE GLORY? (1926), and WINGS (1927), were among the top-grossing films of the 1920s. These occasionally attempted to humanize the enemy and even to question the value of the crusade itself, a stark change from the earlier wartime efforts. THE BIG PARADE, while establishing such war-film conventions as the variegated platoon (with its assorted character types), actually moved away from melodrama in its realistic characterization of the film's hero.[48]

Films looking back at the war after five or ten years were, in fact, period, even costume, pictures. As such, they could say things about contemporary society in the guise of a discussion of the past. Costume pictures were very much a part of the early feature scene and provided an excuse for lavish scenic displays in films such as INTOLERANCE and A DAUGHTER OF THE GODS (1916). Griffith's use of related historical narratives to comment on contemporary life was sometimes directly copied, as in Maurice Tourneur's WOMAN (1918) or Cecil B. DeMille's THE TEN COMMANDMENTS (1923), but more often the parallels were less explicit. The general popularity of costume pictures wavered considerably during the 1915–1928 era, and when asked, audiences usually expressed no enthusiasm for such films. Nonetheless, many of the most popular films of the era were costume pictures, including all of Fairbanks' films after THE THREE MUSKETEERS (1921). Mary Pickford, Norma Talmadge, Marion Davies, and even Buster Keaton frequently appeared in costume films, but available box-office figures indicate that they were often better received in contemporary stories. Marion Davies' problems with costume films are well known, but history has forgotten the sad story of Charles Ray. In an attempt to move away from rural melodrama, Ray financed and starred in an extravagant version of THE

COURTSHIP OF MILES STANDISH (1923). He invested his entire fortune in the film, and its failure destroyed him personally as well as professionally. He was never again able to recapture his position as a major star.[49] Nor was Ray the only star to lose money on costume films. It is unclear whether the drive to produce such films was entirely the result of Fairbanks' success with the genre or simply a desire on the part of a few big stars to create lavishly appointed dream environments for themselves.

One final genre that should be mentioned is the social-problem film. Most prominent as a major force during the Progressive era, such films had gradually been pushed to the periphery of the industry by the late teens. Lois Weber, the director most associated with these films, had an active social agenda that she sought to promote through the medium of screen melodrama. For birth control and against abortion, against capital punishment and for child labor laws, she was surprisingly silent on the issue of women's suffrage. Here, the void was filled by films sponsored by various lobbying organizations that also cast their agenda in the most effective film style available, melodrama. The demise of this genre as a potent force in the market (Weber's WHERE ARE MY CHILDREN? [1916] had been a great box-office success) resulted from the unhappy conjunction of two forces: growing censor pressure to avoid topics of controversy, and the public's eventual distaste for direct sermonizing. By the end of the war, if a filmmaker had a message to send, he or she generally took Sam Goldwyn's advice and used Western Union.[50]

The above categories refer to the product of major film producers operating within the purview of the Motion Picture Producers and Distributors of America. But apart from this world were parallel cinemas, sharing the technology, the audience, and the narrative impulse of the Hollywood cinema but little else. Al Di Lauro and Gerald Rabkin, in their study of the American stag film, indicate that this form had become conventionalized as early as 1915. Unlike the pornographic loops that developed much later, stag films of this era employed a traditional narrative format and even attempted to offer some dramatic motivation for the graphic hard-core couplings that followed. Men-only smokers and stag parties were the typical venues for such material, which was even available in animated cartoon form. While it is impossible to ascertain the exact quantity of such films produced, the surviving footage at the Institute for Sex Research (the Kinsey Institute) indicates an increase in production during the mid 1920s coinciding with the introduction of 16-mm film. While industrial, advertising, and other varieties of nonfiction film were also making use of 16-mm, it seems probable that pornographic films were the first fictional "genre" to use this new technology for both production and distribution.[51]

Such producers built their operations completely outside the established industry framework. It was possible, however, for some filmmakers to try their best to copy Hollywood models and still find themselves locked out of the established system. Thomas Cripps shows that black filmmakers, beginning with Noble Johnson's Lincoln Film Company in 1915, tried to operate by the same rules that governed other small independents. Lincoln, and other producers that followed, aimed their products at the large number of theaters across the country that served black audiences. But their efforts faltered because of a lack of access to capital and distribution. The most successful black filmmaker of the era, Oscar Micheaux, managed to circumvent this problem to a degree by raising money door to door and distributing his films in a laborious road-show fashion. An independent spirit even within the black film

The WAGES of SIN Is DEATH!

HOW true is that old adage—"The Wages of Sin Is Death," and how awful was the poor girl's punishment who at heart was in no way at fault. "The wages of sin is death"—an unchangeable law of Nature that ofttimes strikes down the blameless. The young girl in that remarkable picture "Where Are My Children" who died because of her folly was not so much to be censured as to be pitied. Thousands of young girls fall by the way every year thru the same causes. This cause and it's effect plainly told in this gripping picture,

is told in such a way as to remain in highest dignity, yet withal powerfully gripping and sensational. Endorsed by the New York Newspapers, by the Rev. Dr. Parkhurst, Superior Paulist Father John J. Hughes and thousands of citizens. Played by a brilliant cast of Universal players, headed by that great artist,

TYRONE POWER

This is the picture that set all New York City agog. That created the sensation of sensations. This is the subject that will impress every living soul who sees it. It is remarkable, in that it deals with the premeditated slaughter of innocent lives by those who claim to be of the higher social standing in communities. This is the picture you will never forget. It is true to life, human, sensational yet dignified. A subject that every man and woman should see. Now playing at—

[This space for Theatre name, date, address, etc., etc.]

SCENARIO AND STORY BY
LOIS WEBER
Produced by
Lois Weber and Phillips Smalley

community, Micheaux may have copied the prevalent Hollywood genres, but he always gave them a decidedly black twist. Not afraid to deal with such sensitive topics as lynching or charismatic religion, Micheaux was also the only American filmmaker of the silent era, black or white, to use the noted black star Paul Robeson (BODY AND SOUL, 1924).[52]

The discussion of all these films in terms of their adherence to melodramatic convention does not imply that all silent narratives were melodramas or that this tradition could not be used in a highly sophisticated manner. SUNRISE (1927), voted the most important American silent film in an international critics' poll of the 1970s, uses so many melodramatic devices that it almost seems a conscious recapitulation of the style, elegantly sculpted by director F. W. Murnau and scenarist Carl Mayer.[53] In fact, some of the most interesting silent American features begin as melodramas, whose conventionalized heroes and heroines face predictable crises, but evolve before our eyes into rich explorations of modern characters in crisis. As might be expected, the changing status of women in American society provided a focus for many of the more thoughtful filmmakers. Eugene O'Neill's *Anna Christie*, sanitized but essentially intact, reached the screen in 1923. Hollywood was behind O'Neill in this case, but not by much. It could be argued that William deMille's MISS LULU BETT adapted from the Zona Gale novel, in 1921, had already raised previously unasked questions about the nature of marriage and the value of women in American society, and before O'Neill's play was even written.

As a small number of women began to gain a measure of real authority within the previously all-male power structure, at least two courageous films dealt with this change in terms of sexual politics. Clarence Brown's SMOULDERING FIRES (1924) showed a middle-aged female business magnate marrying her boyish private secretary. As was inevitable in the 1920s, the film insists that "May–December" romances are ill starred, and the businesswoman frees her young man to marry a woman his own age. What is interesting here is not just the admission of sexual longing in a woman over forty, but the fact that this character has the power to make all the decisions that impel the drama.

More radical still was Universal's THE HOME MAKER (1925), in which a husband and wife must change roles after his failed suicide confines him to a wheelchair. She soon proves to be better at business than he, while the husband demonstrates superior skills in child-rearing and housekeeping. Just as both begin to realize true satisfaction in their new roles, the husband regains the use of his legs. THE HOME MAKER is one of the few dramatic works of the 1920s to argue unequivocally for the abandonment of stereotyped sex roles and to criticize the structure that prescribes such behavior.[54]

In DANCING MOTHERS (1926), Alice Joyce (also the star of THE HOME MAKER) is expected to adhere to traditional family values while her husband and her flapper daughter, played by Clara Bow, enjoy the liberated atmosphere of the day. The mother attempts to prevent her daughter's unsuitable association with an older playboy and falls in love with the man herself. Challenged by husband and daughter to behave properly, she abandons them and leaves for Paris. Herbert Brenon directed the film, which was adapted from a play by Edgar Selwyn and Edmund Goulding, a Jazz Age version of *A Doll's House* (itself filmed three times between 1917 and 1922).

Few such films had major stars or budgets, and a number clearly did not even earn back their negative cost. There were more, of course, on these and other themes, but audiences had little interest in films that raised serious questions about contemporary issues. The idea that the motion picture was essentially an escapist medium was not only accepted but celebrated. A few classic works such as GREED or THE CROWD are well known for their daring critique of the American dream, issued in the midst of Coolidge-era prosperity, and their artistic success and commercial reception have become familiar landmarks of the silent-picture era.[55]

7

Watching the Screen

Newspapers

*T*he feature film was born during the heroic age of American journalism, when even an average-size town might offer its citizens a wide selection of morning and afternoon papers. As noted elsewhere, various newspapers and their publishers involved themselves in motion pictures very early on, specifically in the production of newsreels, animated cartoons, and serials. William Randolph Hearst's Cosmopolitan studio even used short fiction from the Hearst press as a source for features.

Film as a subject for newspaper coverage was another matter, one that proved especially attractive to the more aggressive papers of the day. In this regard, it is an unfortunate accident of history that the one newspaper whose film reviews are most easily accessible, the *New York Times*, was never very interested in motion pictures and gave them extremely low priority throughout the silent period. Not only is the entire run of *Times* film reviews reprinted, but there is also a volume of highlights and a multivolume selection of *Times* feature articles on film, which generally are of far greater value than the reviews. The level of criticism in the *Times* was so shallow that many historians, looking here first and assuming that it represented the current journalistic standard, dismiss newspaper reviews of the period out of hand. Myron Lounsbury, for example, in an otherwise comprehensive analysis of early American film criticism, manages to ignore newspaper reviewing altogether. But the broad market penetration of American newspapers during the first decades of this century suggests that their coverage of film was of real significance in shaping the way their readers approached the phenomenon of motion pictures.[1]

While film might be covered on the same arts page that dealt with the legitimate stage, the cinema's relatively recent arrival put it in a very different category from music or theater. The first newspaper coverage of motion pictures presented them as a technological phenomenon ("Edison's marvel"), then as a social problem ("nickel madness"), and ultimately as an economic statistic ("the nation's fourth largest industry"). The movies were news before they were art, and so the earliest film reviews in American newspapers were straightforward accounts of news events.

Not yet worthy of a by-line, the generally anonymous reviewers of the era tell us what happened when they went to the picture show. They report not only on the film but on the theater, the audience, the stage performance, even the weather. It should be remembered that the film was not always the most significant element of this mix anyway, and that critical commentary was usually extracted from the sum of these parts. "Judging from the comments of the auditors who were a unit in declaring it to be one of the greatest pictures they had ever seen, this picture promises to be the most talked about film ever seen in Paterson," wrote one small-town critic, reviewing BLIND HUSBANDS (1919) by reporting on the audience response.[2] Often, owing to a lack of press screenings and the short duration of many runs, some "reviews" would be simple announcements, pasted together from press handouts, trade papers, or out-of-town notices.

Pressure to use editorial space as a reward for advertising was traditional in the newspaper industry and was certainly reflected in reviews and feature articles. To what extent this occurred varied from paper to paper, with some critics purportedly quite independent (Richard Watts, Jr., on the *New York Herald Tribune*, for example), others simply reprinting distributors' press handouts under their own bylines.

By the 1920s many more writers were signing their reviews, but the ultimate goal was still more journalistic than critical. Instead of developing an aesthetic of cinema, these men and women used their columns as literary sounding boards for pontificating, amusing, cajoling, or otherwise entertaining their growing readership. Ward Marsh of the *Cleveland Plain Dealer*, Harriette Underhill of the *New York Tribune*, and Kitty Kelly of the *Chicago Examiner* are all worth reading for these period insights, but perhaps the most interesting was the reviewer of the *Chicago Daily News*, poet Carl Sandburg.[3] From 1920 to 1927 Sandburg discussed films and film stars, interviewed visiting celebrities, and generally enjoyed the opportunity to speak his mind regarding this powerful new cultural force. Like most reviewers, he reviewed the show as much as the film, and the best of his columns deal with the larger social phenomenon involved as much as with any particular picture. His thoughts on UNDERWORLD are an example:

> The scene is yesterday at noon. The doors of the Roosevelt Theater swing open and crowds wander out. A "spill" has come—a "spill" being the departure of large groups of customers at the end of the picture.
>
> Those faces look exhausted, eyes turn up and down State Street as in a daze. *Underworld* has left them limp, these Chicagoans who have come to see the gunmen and gangsters of their city brought at last to the screen.
>
> Within the theater packed rows of faces are staring as the picture starts again on its endlessly circling path of savagery. Faces have been rapt and nerves have dangled in suspense here before, but never like this (*Chicago Daily News*, 14 November 1927, reprinted in *Carl Sandburg at the Movies*, p. 189).

Such reportage assumed that going to the movies meant more than just watching a film, and like a good newpaperman, Sandburg was able to use his column to comment on something beyond the immediate issue at hand. Few daily reviewers were able to accomplish this very consistently, but the fact that the attempt was being made is one of the critical hallmarks of the period.

Fan Magazines

The earliest fan magazines, *Motion Picture Story* and *Photoplay*, were founded in 1911, essentially as short-fiction magazines trading on the increasing popularity of films and film stars. Most of their pages were filled with plot synopses of one- and two-reelers, while star portraits, letters to the editor, popularity contests, and rambling editorial columns made up the rest. In January 1915 James R. Quirk became vice-president of *Photoplay* and, substantially revising its editorial policy, first appointed Julian Johnson editor, then took full editorial control himself in 1920. Quirk strove to eliminate the synopses and increase the magazine's critical and informational content, bringing in as reviewer the respected legitimate critic Burns Mantle, editor of the annual *Best Plays*. Occasionally Quirk himself fired an editorial salvo, most notoriously his 1922 blast at FOOLISH WIVES as "an insult to every American."[4]

That Quirk could be so inflamed only underscores the high regard in which he held film, as well as his notion of film criticism as an active method of improving the field by educating filmmakers and audiences alike. His own standards were too idiosyncratic for any reader to fully comprehend, but more important than the reviews in Quirk's *Photoplay* were the feature pieces. Adela Rogers St. Johns contributed a witty series of profiles and interviews, and it was for *Photoplay* that Terry Ramsaye originally composed his massive industry history, *A Million and One Nights*. Quirk's main competition was provided by Eugene V. Brewster, co-founder of *Motion Picture Story* (after 1914 simply *Motion Picture*) as well as *Motion Picture Classic* (1915–1931) and *Shadowland* (1919–1923). *Motion Picture* proclaimed itself "the oldest, largest, and best movie magazine in the world," but while it did antedate *Photoplay* by several months and exceeded it in circulation, its editorial policy (and layout) was largely derivative of Quirk's magazine (table 7.1). With much of *Motion Picture*'s editorial space still devoted to plot summaries as late as 1919, there was correspondingly less space available for interviews and features, and in any case, Hazel Simpson Naylor was no Adela Rogers St. Johns. When *Motion Picture* did find some room for a serious piece, the tone was often more adventurous than what could be found in *Photoplay*, however. Katherine Anne Porter interviewed boyish film star

TABLE 7.1 CIRCULATION PER ISSUE OF MOTION-PICTURE MAGAZINES, 1918–1919

	1918	*1919*
Photoplay	204,434	no record
Motion Picture Magazine	248,845	400,000
Motion Picture Classic	140,000	275,000
Picture Play	127,721	200,000
Photoplay Journal	100,000	no record
Shadowland	———	75,000

SOURCE: *American Newspaper Annual and Directory*, reproduced in Bordwell, Thompson, and Staiger, *The Classical Hollywood Cinema*, p. 99.

Fan-magazine czar Eugene V. Brewster promotes his editorial staff in a two-page trade advertisement (Film Daily Yearbook of Motion Pictures [1926], pp. 144–145).

Charles Ray in the October 1920 issue, and Harry Carr's continuing series on Hollywood directors set an agenda for decades of *auteur* criticism to follow.

Brewster's *Motion Picture Classic* was an upscale version of *Motion Picture*, with occasional feature pieces by Matthew Josephson or Jim Tully, the celebrated "tramp author" whose biographical sketches of film personalities also appeared in *Vanity Fair*. Laurence Reid handled the film reviews. *Shadowland* was the most elaborate of Brewster's journals, although, belying its title, it usually included only a single film article per issue. Covering the entire art scene, *Shadowland* featured highbrow prose and artistic photography, with a liberal sprinkling of nude studies. Its discussion of movies on the same plane as poetry, photography, or modern dance marked a major step in the acceptance of film as serious business by the more fashionable elements of eastern society. Other journals were far less ambitious, as in the case of Bernarr MacFadden's *Movie Weekly* (1921–1925), which, as Anthony Slide notes, operated more like a modern fan magazine, eliminating serious criticism and concentrating on sensational scandals and exposés.[5]

For the most part, fan magazines in this period served a highly educative function, rather than simply providing readers with data on the latest releases or the private lives of movie stars. While critical standards were generally diffuse, these magazines did suggest various aesthetic bases for differentiating "good" from "bad" and supplied their readers with enough technical, social, and economic background to help inform their decisions. The interviews and features were often quite detailed and contain material of considerable value to scholars and historians. Unfortunately, even the best of these magazines are only sporadically indexed today.

Trade Papers

For those within the industry, information and opinion were shaped by a number of aggressive trade papers, each competing for the same limited number of subscribers. The film business had first been discussed in general entertainment-industry papers such as the *New York Clipper* or *Variety*, which began covering short films as acts in 1907. Most important was the *New York Dramatic Mirror*, whose film reviewer, Frank Woods, is often cited as the first significant American film critic. But by 1915 Woods was writing for D. W. Griffith, the *Dramatic Mirror*'s film section was in decline, and even *Variety* had been surpassed by newer papers devoted solely to the motion-picture industry.[6]

Chief among these was the *Moving Picture World* (1907–1927), which, setting a standard for the broadest possible coverage, reviewed current releases and published news, features, and interviews relating to all aspects of the industry. The vast quantity of advertisements published each week was by itself enough to make the *World* a veritable industry encyclopedia. An exhibitor-oriented paper whose genesis coincided with the original nickelodeon boom, it also carried regular columns on projection, advertising, and theater music. At its height in 1915, when the annual pagination reached 8,930, the *World* was a significant industry force and remains of great value to this day, although more for the raw data it provides than for its reviews.[7]

Very similar in format was the *Motion Picture News*, edited by William A. Johnston (1913–1929), which supplanted the *World* in importance after about 1920. The appeal to the theater owner was even stronger here, with extensive exploitation tips

Vol. 25, No. 2   July 10, 1915   Price 10 Cents

MOVING PICTURE WORLD

THE FILM INDEX   EXHIBITORS' GUIDE

Scene from "Under Two Flags" (Biograph)

Post Office Box 226   NEW YORK   17 Madison Avenue
Madison Square Station   Telephone Madison Square 3510

PACIFIC COAST NUMBER

Moving Picture World (*10 July 1915*), *the dominant industry trade paper in the pre-1920 period.*

appended to reviews (often by the perceptive Peter Milne), much coverage of theater design and operation, and a continuing "Check Up" column in which the box-office performance of every feature in release could be tracked via exhibitors' reports.

The same general format was also employed by the *Exhibitor's Trade Review* (1916–1926) and the *Exhibitor's Herald* (founded in 1915); the *Herald* contained the classic "What the Picture Did for Me" column, where theater owners from across the country described with relish their experiences with every release. For example, there was this warning, submitted by W. S. Feezor of Badin, North Carolina:

> If there ever was a flop this is the climax. What is Famous Players trying to do? It seems as if they are trying to discourage the exhibitors and trying to keep them from using their product. *Wet Paint* was sold to me for a comedy, and there was not a laugh in it. I am still looking for the laugh. Brother Exhibitors, beware of *Wet Paint*, as it is the third piece of cheese from Raymond Griffith (*Exhibitor's Herald*, 28 August 1926, pp. 67–68).

The *Exhibitor's Herald* combined with the *Moving Picture World* in 1927, then merged with the *Motion Picture News* in 1931 to create the *Motion Picture Herald*, which united all the major weeklies under the editorship of *Exhibitor's Herald* publisher Martin Quigley.[8]

Less encyclopedic (if more idiosyncratic) were a variety of smaller papers intended to fill gaps in the big weeklies' coverage. In 1915 Wid Gunning published *Wid's Films and Film Folks*, which became *Wid's Daily* in 1918. Carrying no advertising, the paper sold itself on the strength of Gunning's enthusiastic and purportedly unbiased reviews. "Tell 'em this is Bill's latest and oil up the ticket machine" was Wid's characteristic way of approving the latest William S. Hart release.[9] The paper took on a more sober air under the editorship of Joe Dannenberg, who changed its name to the *Film Daily* in 1922. From 1918 it published the standard industry reference annual, *Wid's Yearbook* (later the *Film Daily Yearbook of Motion Pictures*).

Harrison's Reports, published from 1919 by P. S. Harrison, was a slim tip sheet that combined extremely opinionated (and cold-blooded) reviews with insider information on "real" picture grosses and distributor-exhibitor relations. *Harrison's Reports* had the most contentious producer relations of all the trades and was capable of calling a film like GREED "the filthiest, vilest, most putrid picture in the history of the motion picture business."[10]

Similiar to *Harrison's Reports* in their personal approach, but far more thoughtful in their critical policies, were the *Film Mercury* (1924–1933), edited by Tamar Lane, and the *Hollywood Spectator* (1926–1931), edited by Welford Beaton. Both men were interested enough in the art of the film to have written serious books on the subject, and they tried to infuse this feeling into their analyses of the weekly releases. What Stanley Kaufmann has said about Beaton's work might just as well be applied to the best writing in the other trades: "There was a great consciousness that the trade critic's best way to help the industry was to write the most vigorous, informed criticism that he could, emphasizing expertness about films and studios and picture people without slavishness to business criteria." The late silent period would prove the heyday of such papers, as industry economics in the early Depression years forced many journals to merge and drove the more personal publications out of business.[11]

The National Board of Censorship

Trade-press coverage was quite comprehensive in providing assessments of the economic value of particular releases and background information on industry activities. But the first critics seriously to regard the motion picture as a cultural force were not inside the industry, nor were they enlightened tastemakers seeking a place for film within the larger realm of the arts. Rather, the first serious consideration of motion pictures as a medium of unique expressive power came from social reformers of the nickelodeon era, who sought to control or suppress it (as did Canon William Chase of the Society for the Prevention of Crime) or to guide and liberate its positive energies (as did Charles Sprague Smith and the People's Institute).[12]

In 1909 the National Board of Censorship was established as "the first formal attempt by the film industry to ward off legal film censorship through quasi self-regulation." Responding to the storm surrounding Mayor McClellan's abortive closing of New York's nickelodeons in December 1908, industry figures turned to the People's Institute, which earlier that year had produced a lengthy study of motion-picture-theater conditions in New York, not entirely unfavorable to the industry. The Institute took the lead in establishing a Board of Censorship of Motion Picture Shows, whose members represented such groups as the Women's Municipal League, the Public Education Association, the Federation of Churches, and the League for Political Education, as well as representatives of the Association of Motion Picture Exhibitors of New York State.[13]

The Board would view films, recommending cuts or possibly suppressing entire subjects. The New York exhibitors agreed to abide by its decisions, and since they represented so large a percentage of the domestic market, the Board's influence was soon being felt by producers nationwide. Within a few months, the Board became a national organization, operating out of offices in New York, with a bureaucracy funded by per-reel charges for each subject reviewed.

For several years the industry was able to use the Board to help ward off calls for legalized censorship in most jurisdictions, although Pennsylvania (1911), Ohio (1913), and Kansas (1913) had already established official state censorship boards before a nationwide storm over film censorship broke in 1914–1915. On 18 March 1914 Senator Hoke Smith of Georgia introduced national legislation calling for the establishment of a federal motion picture commission. Its commissioners would have licensing powers over all films in interstate commerce, with the ability to suppress prizefight and bullfight films, and other films of an indecent, immoral, or obscene character.[14] Increasing agitation over fight films, as well as a recent cycle of white-slavery and birth-control films, enabled Canon William Chase and the Reverend Wilbur Crafts of the International Reform Association to generate considerable public support for the bill.

Their real target was not the motion-picture industry but the National Board of Censorship itself, which Chase thought a corrupt tool of the film interests. In the hearings that followed, Chase and his allies attacked the Board for failing to deal with all films in distribution (submission was voluntary), for being in the pay of the industry, and for applying relatively liberal New York standards to films that were being exhibited nationwide.

The Board and its supporters testified against the bill, which they saw as a violation of First Amendment guarantees of free expression. They defended the notion of voluntary censorship (or "review," as they now began to call it) and insisted that

The approval seal of the National Board of Review, ca. 1916, which appeared at the head of all subjects passed for exhibition by the Board.

members of their reviewing committees were unpaid volunteers whose decisions were financially insulated from any film-industry contributions. In addition, they attacked the idea of a federal motion-picture commission as a potential hotbed of nepotism and graft, an argument also taken up by the industry.[15]

On 16 February 1915, the U.S. House of Representatives Committee on Education voted unanimously in favor of the bill, a serious blow but one that was overshadowed a week later by the Supreme Court's decision in the case of *Mutual Film Corporation* v. *Ohio Industrial Commission*.[16] This landmark decision, involving the prior restraint of D. W. Griffith's film THE BIRTH OF A NATION in the state of Ohio, would ground all federal policy on motion-picture censorship until the 1950s. Speaking for a unanimous court, Justice McKenna completely undercut the Board's main argument in opposition to film censorship:

> The exhibition of motion pictures is a business pure and simple, organized and conducted for profit, . . . not to be regarded, nor intended to be

A Winsor McCay editorial cartoon attacking the prospect of federal film censorship, originally drawn for Hearst's New York American, *as reproduced in* Moving Picture Weekly, *4 March 1916.*

regarded by the Ohio Constitution, we think, as part of the press of the country or as organs of public opinion. They are mere representations of events, of ideas and sentiments published or known; vivid, useful, and entertaining no doubt, but . . . capable of evil, having power for it, the greater because of their attractiveness and manner of exhibition (236 U.S. 230 [1915], quoted in Richard Randall, *Censorship of the Movies*, p. 19).

As Richard Randall points out, the logic of this decision overstated the differences between film and print, even in 1915. Books and newspapers were also published for profit, after all, and no conclusive evidence of the film's special power for evil had been submitted.[17] The notion that film was a mere show or spectacle not conducive to the play of ideas was an outdated concept clearly belied by the controversy surrounding the film in question.

At this point the industry moved to disassociate itself from the Board, which had become a lightning rod for Chase, Craft, and all the other pro-censorship forces. Despite the Supreme Court's decision in the Mutual case, the Board continued to base its anti-censorship campaign on First Amendment grounds. The industry saw this as a dead issue, and, with their product now firmly categorized as interstate baggage, hoped to develop some other form of defense, perhaps along the line of property rights. Assessing their options, some in the industry felt that national censorship would be preferable to a spate of state and local boards scattered across the country, each demanding registration fees, and each applying a different set of standards.[18]

Soon after the Mutual decision, the *New York Dramatic Mirror* admitted that the industry was badly in need of strong and effective censorship:

We place before the eyes of our children comedies made of ingredients that composed the burlesque of a decade ago; we give our daughters in their teens the harrowing *Nigger*; we turn half-baked directors loose upon erotic themes that have spelled failure for genius. And then we tell the world we do not need censorship (24 March 1915, p. 22).[19]

But the *Dramatic Mirror* muted its call by supporting restraint, good taste, and the same sort of unofficial censorship already being dispensed by the Board.

The State Censorship Boards

Only an additional three states established their own censorship boards in the years following the Mutual decision, namely Maryland (1916), New York (1921), and Virginia (1922). The vast majority of such proposals never made it out of the state legislatures or were vetoed in the governors' offices. This situation did not mean that films in those other states were uncensored, since local authorities could simply agree to accept the cuts demanded by a neighboring state. Deletions made for Pennsylvania could be expected to recur in West Virginia, while Kansas set the tone for Missouri.[20]

After viewing a film, a local board would specify deletions or title changes for each reel. For example, New York ordered the following "eliminations" in GREED:

Reel 2: Elim. view of administering ether.
Reel 3: Elim. underlined words from title: "I've got her. *By God,* I've got her."
Reel 4: Eliminate title: "Damn his soul."
Reel 7: Elim. all scenes of McTeague biting Trina's fingers.
Reel 10: Elim. last view of horse kicking in agony on ground after it had been shot.

According to a formalized list of reasons employed by the New York Board, the above material was condemned as "inhuman" and "sacrilegious."[21]

Ellis Paxson Oberholtzer, chief of the Pennsylvania Board, boasted in a 1922 volume that his "suggestions" were often needed to polish a film's dramatic values and add literacy to its titles. For the 1917 release ONE HOUR he suggested:

Subtitles can be inserted in Reel 4 changing the theme of fornication to one of love and valor. The *One Hour* should be changed to indicate the hour in which the army officer shows his chivalry by promising to love and protect the young girl, and at the earliest opportunity marry her. He will go through any hardship and make any sacrifice to prevent Opal's marriage with King Otto (*The Morals of the Movie*, p. 128).

Oberholtzer then offers a detailed plan by which to accomplish this change in theme. His extensive revisions of HARRIETT AND THE PIPER (1920), WHISPERING DEVILS (1920), and THE DISCARDED WOMAN (1920) are equally ingenious.[22]

It should be remembered that local audiences—and reviewers—did not see these films until the required cuts had been made. When Richard Watts, Jr., called GREED "the most important picture yet produced in America," he was speaking of the version passed for exhibition in New York.[23] Audiences today, if they are lucky enough to see such films at all, occasionally see "uncut" versions descended from the master printing negative. Since the New York cuts described above were local, only the prints exhibited in that state were so mutilated. Producers would not cut the negative to suit the dictates of any one state, since the other boards all had their own "suggestions" as well. Consequently, in modern screenings of the film, McTeague is allowed to bite Trina's fingers, something Watts and the other first-nighters were not permitted to see. On the other hand, the integrity of a film that descends from a single print discovered in a midwestern barn may have been compromised to an unknown degree by any number of censors or exhibitors.

In a 1930 study of American film censorship, Pare Lorentz and Morris Ernst were able to characterize each state board according to its unique standards and methods of operation. Virginia was the "most lenient," but was especially concerned with sexual matters; "indecent kicking" seems to have been a frequent complaint of the Virginia board. In Ohio, a more stringent board concerned itself with small gestures and close-ups of facial expressions, often reducing the core of an Emil Jannings performance, for example, to a series of brief flashes. The chief of the Kansas board,

Emma Viets, is quoted as justifying her censoring of one picture with the explanation, "The film was long anyway and could stand cutting." The display of bootleg liquor was strictly forbidden in Kansas, as was the act of nose-thumbing. Maryland freely passed those activities but stopped all scenes of neck-kissing. Pennsylvania was seen as "the most arbitrary and severe" of all the boards. Acting in the Oberholtzer tradition, its changes often reconstructed the entire shape of a film. (Example: "Insert newspaper notice of marriage before showing bedroom scene" in FAZIL [1928].) Intimations of political corruption especially worried the New York board. "Political job-holders themselves, the New York board very logically refuses to allow any ugly remarks to be passed about politicians in general."[24]

While the characterizations provided by Lorentz and Ernst are somewhat glib, they are supported by numerous references to specific deletion orders and interviews with board members. Elsewhere in their book, they publish a very useful chart listing all the cuts demanded by the various boards in 1928 (table 7.2). Of 572 films submitted that year, only 42 passed review unscathed. Sex and crime provided the dominant reasons for the cuts, while references to narcotics, a problem only a few years earlier, had completely disappeared. Nose-thumbing remained a minor nuisance, especially with MGM, Paramount, and Universal releases.[25]

It did not take long for filmmakers to predict many of the actions of these boards and take preemptive countermeasures. Cecil B. DeMille was the first master of this technique. Debauched orgies seen in films such as MANSLAUGHTER (1922) and THE TEN COMMANDMENTS were able to justify themselves through the inevitable scenes of retribution that followed. More witty solutions, often considered the creation of Ernst Lubitsch, actually developed quite early. In Charles Maigne's THE FIRING LINE (1919), a startled deer signifies an offscreen suicide. The *New York Times* felt that existing censor inhibitions were the reason for this artful circumlocution, with a far more poetic image the result.[26]

Still, not all such changes and eliminations were accepted with equanimity. In Chicago, which had instituted police licensing of motion pictures as early as 1907, film censorship was under the control of the notorious Major M. L. C. Funkhouser, "nationally known as the extreme type of police censor," according to *Photoplay*. Since Chicago was the largest domestic market after New York, it was a matter of some industry concern when Funkhouser continually suppressed material that had been passed by the National Board in New York. These situations might include "shots of a ballerina puffing on a cigarette [or] a policeman standing in his underwear." Funkhouser finally went too far in 1918, when he cut two atrocity sequences from Griffith's war-propaganda film HEARTS OF THE WORLD. Morris Gest, who was handling the film in Chicago, accused Funkhouser of pro-German sympathies (a serious and not uncommon slur at the time) and filed formal complaints with the State Council of Defense, the Department of Justice, and President Woodrow Wilson.[27]

The MPPDA

The industry's problems with censorship reached a peak in 1921. The proliferation of state and local censor boards, each with its own set of standards, created an unmanageable problem for the expanding producer-distributor-exhibitor combines. The

**TABLE 7.2   CENSOR CUTS OF 1928
INCLUDING CLASSIFICATIONS AND LEADING COMPANIES**

Censors' classifications	Educational	Fox	Metro-Goldwyn-Mayer	Paramount	Pathé	United Artists	Universal	Warner Brothers	First National	Totals
1—Portrayal of Crime	1	180	55	56	59	—	106	28	14	499
1A—Suicide—Reference to	—	—	—	—	—	—	—	—	17	17
2—Display of Dangerous Weapons	3	91	162	48	135	12	52	13	12	528
3—Cruelty—Brutality	2	19	53	56	52	16	52	16	10	276
4—Reference to Cruelty	3	20	15	18	46	23	15	5	5	150
5—Mean or Mischievous	3	16	24	8	25	3	16	3	6	104
6—Capital Punishment— Reference to	—	—	4	3	—	2	2	—	—	11
7—Gambling	—	3	10	—	3	3	14	—	3	36
8—Profanity—Lip or Title	—	10	13	6	6	3	16	3	7	64
9—Drinking or Reference to	—	3	8	7	9	2	16	6	2	53
9A—Narcotics	—	—	—	—	—	—	—	—	—	—
10—Sex—Suggestive	—	13	90	163	117	89	8	30	99	509
11—Over-Passionate Love- Making	1	6	40	12	13	20	3	10	10	115
12—Nudity—Indecent Exposure	6	15	28	31	16	13	22	8	16	155
13—Vulgar Dancing	1	2	10	16	3	6	14	4	4	60
14—Improper Reference to Women	—	5	3	8	6	2	3	3	3	33
15—Derogatory Reference to Countries	3	2	18	6	3	3	11	—	4	50
15A—Derogatory Reference to Religion	—	3	2	4	—	—	5	2	—	16
16—Vulgarity	29	20	18	40	47	77	10	—	8	249
16A—Nose-Thumbing	1	3	10	7	2	—	7	3	2	35
17—Unclassified	—	—	—	—	—	—	—	—	—	—
TOTAL	53	411	563	389	542	274	372	134	222	2960

SOURCE: Lorentz and Ernst, *Censored: The Private Life of the Movie*, pp. 82–83.

recent burst of theater construction had been torpedoed by the postwar recession, and box-office receipts were down. Fierce competition for the remaining customers forced producers to resort to a reliable theatrical remedy: releases for the 1920–1921 season included such titles as THE AFFAIRS OF ANATOLE, BLIND WIVES, THE BLUSH-ING BRIDE, THE BRANDED WOMAN, THE CHILD THOU GAVEST ME, DISCONTENTED WIVES, A DIVORCE OF CONVENIENCE, DON'T CHANGE YOUR HUSBAND, EVER SINCE EVE, FORBIDDEN FRUIT, GODLESS MEN, THE GOOD BAD WIFE, THE INFA-

MOUS MISS REVELLE, THE LEOPARD WOMAN, LURING LIPS, NO MAN'S WOMAN, PASSION'S PLAYGROUND, THE PLAYTHING OF BROADWAY, THE RESTLESS SEX, SHAME, SHORT SKIRTS, SILK HOSIERY, THE SINS OF ROSANNE, SQUANDERED LIVES, THE TRUTH ABOUT HUSBANDS, WHAT'S YOUR REPUTATION WORTH?, WHY GIRLS LEAVE HOME, and WITHOUT BENEFIT OF CLERGY.[28]

There was also a growing connection in the public mind between the content of films like these and the life-styles of the men and women who created them. In the spring of 1920 a brief press flurry surrounded the Reno divorce of Mary Pickford, and her husband Owen Moore's charges of fraud, collusion, and "insufficient residence" in the state of Nevada. Pickford had married Douglas Fairbanks only four weeks after her initial decree had been granted, but the Nevada courts ultimately ruled against Moore.[29]

Support for the National Board of Censorship had all but evaporated. Since 1919 the major producers, operating through the National Association of the Motion Picture Industry (NAMPI), had begun organizing for self-regulation, calling for a boycott of noncomplying exhibitors and avoiding the Board altogether. In a series of muckraking exposés early in 1921, the *Brooklyn Eagle* showed how industry money was used to pay the salaries of Board commissioners, who would then steer troublesome films to the more lenient of the "volunteer" reviewing committees. It also revealed specific financial interests in the motion-picture business on the part of several Board members. Hearings in the Albany legislature that followed quickly led to the passage of the Clayton-Lusk Bill, which established a state censorship board in the nation's most important market. Virginia would establish its board the following year.[30]

Pressure for federal censorship was mounting, led once again by Dr. Wilbur Crafts. At a meeting with NAMPI representatives in March 1921, he forced the industry to admit the need for censorship and, rejecting their plea for internal controls, insisted on an official federal body instead. On 2 August, Senator Myers of Montana, focusing on NAMPI's avowed lobbying activities and its public support of various state and local candidates, called for an investigation of the motion-picture industry by the Senate judiciary committee.[31]

The industry tried to coopt these efforts in several ways. Straightforward political pressure was the most direct method, but Carl Laemmle's invitation for all censors to meet with filmmakers at Universal City was perhaps the most imaginative. The reason given was for the censors to view a rough cut of Universal's million-dollar production FOOLISH WIVES, to offer their advice on refinements of the editing, and to learn something of filmmaking from the producers' perspective. Members of the Pennsylvania, Maryland, Kansas, Chicago, and Boston boards took advantage of the junket, as did several Canadian censors and a representative of the National Board. They were shown a lengthy cut of FOOLISH WIVES (variously given as 24 reels or 17,000 feet) and issued a statement that allowed Laemmle to headline, months before the film's official release, "Censors Approve 'Foolish Wives.' " But as the studio house organ indicated, the group had little time in their schedule for such official duties: "Surf bathing in the opalescent spray of the Pacific, meeting with other producers at elaborate luncheons, intimate contact with Universal stars at work and at play, a day on Harry Carey's ranch, a magnificent banquet at the famous Sunset Inn, and a week-end at Catalina Island" left them exhausted as they checked out of their Beverly Hills Hotel suites a week later.[32] The members were back in their offices by Labor Day, just in time to read all about the worst Hollywood scandal of the decade.

Roscoe "Fatty" Arbuckle, one of the most popular and highly paid of all Hollywood stars, was being held in San Francisco on murder charges. At a wild party thrown by Arbuckle at the St. Francis Hotel, a would-be starlet, Virginia Rappe, was taken violently ill and died soon after in a local sanatorium. Her associates brought charges against Arbuckle for the death. The evidence against Arbuckle was clearly suspect, but the ambitious San Francisco district attorney, Matthew Brady, decided to pursue the Hollywood star in the courts with a case based on sensationalism and innuendo.[33]

The press went wild. Fed by rumors, lies, and half-truths, they condemned Arbuckle as a rapist and murderer. While most of Arbuckle's friends and employers had originally supported him, the tide began to turn when his first trial (on manslaughter charges) resulted in a hung jury. By the time Arbuckle's second trial began, on 11 January 1922, industry leaders had already announced that Will Hays, President Harding's postmaster general, was leaving the cabinet to supervise the cleanup of Hollywood.[34]

Hays's vehicle for this campaign would be a new organization, the Motion Picture Producers and Distributors of America (MPPDA). Far from limiting his powers to the scandal and to censorship problems, Hays would serve as front man for the industry on a range of issues. But he needed to quell these disturbances before he could deal with matters of industry finance, competition, and antitrust investigation. On 2 February 1922 director William Desmond Taylor was found shot to death in his Los Angeles home; rumors of sex and drugs reached the press, and both Mary Miles Minter and Mabel Normand were implicated. The following day, the second Arbuckle jury reported itself hopelessly deadlocked.[35] By this time FOOLISH WIVES had finally opened, and the state censors did a double take. After first approving the film, the New York board ordered it withdrawn from exhibition for further cutting. Universal hastily complied.[36]

Not until 12 August was there a final verdict in the Arbuckle case: an acquittal, complete with an apology to Arbuckle on the part of the jurors. Unfortunately, it had come too late. Women's groups across the country, stirred by the press campaign, had been agitating for months to remove Arbuckle's films from the theaters. To his employers at Paramount, their one-time star was now a significant liability. Hays exercised his new authority for the first time, six days after the acquittal, and banned Arbuckle from the screen. This unconscionable act succeeded in making Arbuckle the scapegoat for all the industry's moral shortcomings. Hays established his *bona fides* by taking action against Arbuckle, a move that lent credibility to the informal industry censorship he was about to establish. Whereas reformers had previously rejected all industry pleas for self-regulation, they now accepted the notion from Hays. After 1922 no more states established censorship boards, and the MPPDA successfully lobbied against all bills for federal regulation.

To complete his cleanup, Hays promoted a "gentlemen's agreement" within the industry involving the so-called thirteen points, which were intended to eliminate pictures that:

1. dealt with sex in an improper manner
2. were based on white slavery
3. made vice attractive

4. exhibited nakedness
5. had prolonged passionate love scenes
6. were predominantly concerned with the underworld
7. made gambling and drunkenness attractive
8. might instruct the weak in methods of committing crime
9. ridiculed public officials
10. offended religious beliefs
11. emphasized violence
12. portrayed vulgar postures and gestures, and
13. used salacious subtitles or advertising

This agreement lacked any means of interpretation or enforcement, and in February 1924 the MPPDA adopted a "formula" that gave the thirteen points some organizational credibility. Story departments were requested to submit to the MPPDA office readers' reports on all preexisting story material under consideration (original scripts were excepted), along with readers' opinions on any "questionable theme or treatment." That year, sixty-seven stories were rejected by the MPPDA, but submission of reports and adherence to MPPDA judgments was still voluntary.[37]

Hays's lobbying skills succeeded in fending off new legislation, but the existing state boards were not mollified by this lenient form of self-regulation, and reformist agitation continued. In 1927 the "formula" was considerably strengthened by the adoption of a series of "Don'ts and Be Carefuls" based on the original thirteen points.

Cecil B. DeMille and Jesse L. Lasky greet Will Hays (center) as he visits the Paramount lot on his arrival in Hollywood.

Members now specifically agreed to avoid eleven objectionable topics and to treat twenty-six others with care and good taste. There was still no penalty for failing to abide by these restrictions, but for the first time, producers had agreed among themselves on a codified set of standards. It would be the basis of the Production Code, which followed in 1930.[38]

The Better Films Movement

Creation of the MPPDA marked the end of the National Board of Review as a formal censoring body, but it continued to review films and bestow its seal as a form of endorsement. A certain amount of quasi-official power remained with the Board, however, since Florida, by statute, still agreed to accept any film that it passed. But after 1922 the Board concentrated its activities on the promotion of worthy films rather than the suppression of objectionable ones. [39]

The Board had begun to emphasize the positive side of its reviewing operation as far back as 1914, when it formed the National Committee for Better Films. This group was initially concerned with identifying films especially suitable for young audiences, what today might be called "family pictures." The Better Films Movement grew out of this body in 1917. According to the Board's executive secretary, Wilton A. Barrett, this was "a conscious effort to encourage the production and exhibition of a high type of films [sic] by discriminating patronage of the best." Better Films activities were ambitious, well organized, and certainly the earliest national effort to promote film as a medium of social and artistic importance.[40]

Across the country, various community groups fostered the Better Films idea on a local level. Some of these were formed independently, others were instigated directly by the National Board. Among the earliest were the Cleveland Cinema Club (organized in 1915), the Cincinnati Council of Motion Pictures, the Woman's Civic Club of Duquesne, and the Indiana Indorsers of Photoplays. Certain critics of censorship were not happy about this "woman's club" aspect of the Board, which they saw as coming under the sway of the Daughters of the American Revolution, the International Federation of Catholic Alumnae, the Parent-Teacher Association, and the General Federation of Women's Clubs. "The biggest woman's club machine in the country" is how Ernst and Lorentz characterized the Board in this period, suggesting that the social and political agenda of these groups might be used to channel and control the media.[41]

After the formation of the MPPDA, the Board turned its full attention to the Better Films Movement. Dues-paying membership in the National Committee for Better Films was established in 1923, and members received subscriptions to three Board publications: the *Photoplay Guide*, which listed approved films suitable for various audiences; *Film Progress*, a monthly paper carrying national news of the Better Films Movement and reviews of films listed in *Photoplay Guide*; and *Exceptional Photoplays*, which offered "critical appraisal of films adjudged to have unusual merit or significance in the development of motion picture art," the first journal of serious film criticism in the United States.[42]

The Committee also involved itself in the 1923 Russell Sage survey (see page 28), sponsored such activities as Motion Picture Week at local libraries, and in 1923 held a series of screenings of "exceptional photoplays" at New York's Town Hall, which included Charles Brabin's DRIVEN, Thomas H. Ince's production of ANNA CHRISTIE, and Robert Boudrioz's TILLERS OF THE SOIL. This set of screenings eventually grew into the "little photoplay theater" idea, modeled directly on the "little theater" movement in postwar drama. Such theaters would appeal to a select audience by screening revivals, imports, experimental films, and noteworthy commercial releases that had not found an audience. The Cameo Theatre in New York was the first to put this idea into practice on a commercial level, followed by the Fifth Avenue Cinema. By 1926 Better Films groups around the country had promoted similar screenings in Jacksonville, Florida; Akron, Ohio; Rutherford, New Jersey; and Atlanta, Georgia. In 1927 the Board produced a compilation film, THE MARCH OF THE MOVIES, "showing the progressive steps and influence in the growth of pictures," probably the first serious effort at a film-on-film history of the cinema. With university study limited to a handful of "photoplay analysis" courses, it is clear that the activities of the Board, and its associated Better Films Committees, set the national agenda for serious film study during this period.[43]

By 1927 an incipient film culture had developed in the United States, not centralized, as with the Film Society in London (founded 1925), but spread democratically across the country and involving various ages, social groups, and levels of interest and activity. From this largely amateur tradition came the nation's first generation of cinéastes, men like Theodore Huff, Harry Alan Potamkin, Seymour Stern, Dwight MacDonald, Herman G. Weinberg, and Lewis Jacobs, who created a school of American film scholarship that would flourish over the next three decades. Before them, serious writing on film occupied a very small shelf. Technical studies and instructional manuals were common, but few had attempted to deal with film as a medium of unique expressive power. Vachel Lindsay's visionary analysis *The Art of the Moving Picture* was the first such work of any stature. The original 1915 edition hailed the cinema as a new democratic spectacle that embraced the classical arts of painting, sculpture, and architecture and was especially linked to various ancient ideographic traditions. When Lindsay reissued the book in 1922, he found that he could dedicate it to "the new art museums springing up all over the country," where the motion picture was to find its proper home. Writing from the Denver Art Museum, he even offered programming suggestions for such museums—Griffith's THE AVENGING CONSCIENCE (1914) on a double bill with THE CABINET OF DR. CALIGARI, for example.[44]

Hugo Munsterberg of Harvard produced a very different work in 1916, *The Photoplay: A Psychological Study*, which attempted to describe the ways in which the viewer invests movement, depth, and emotion in the flickering projected image. Munsterberg had discovered films only in 1915 but embraced them with the passion of a convert, hobnobbing with film stars and even editing a short reel for Paramount. His death later in 1916, as well as the growing criticism he was receiving for his alleged pro-German sympathies, combined to limit the effect of his work. By the time social scientists again turned seriously to film in the late 1920s, his writing was largely forgotten.[45] Gilbert Seldes saw film as a major part of the popular-culture scene in *The Seven Lively Arts*, placing Chaplin and Sennett on the same plane as Ring Lardner, Florenz Ziegfeld, and Krazy Kat. Where Munsterberg hoped that film would bridge the highbrow and lowbrow elements of American culture, Seldes celebrated the middlebrow.[46] Robert E. Sherwood, then film critic for the old comedy magazine *Life*, published *The Best Moving Pictures of 1922–23*, a compendium of reviews packaged with an industry yearbook and a "who's who." Its value lay in the clear connection Sherwood made between motion-picture art and economics, a dose of reality often lacking in the writings of Lindsay or Seldes.[47]

Industry critics Tamar Lane, Peter Milne, and Welford Beaton have been mentioned earlier, as have Columbia University academics Victor Freeburg and Frances Taylor Patterson. Beyond these works there was very little of value on cinema shelves in American bookstores before 1928. In terms of film study, it was an era of preparation, with the first tentative steps being taken in everything from film festivals to film magazines. Ironically, the silent film, which had generated this enthusiasm, would not survive to enjoy the fruits of its popularity.

8

The Filmmakers

*I*n SUNSET BOULEVARD (1950), Billy Wilder's poisoned love letter to the silent cinema, Erich von Stroheim gives William Holden a little lesson in film history. "There were three young directors who showed promise in those days," he says. "D. W. Griffith, Cecil B. DeMille, and Max von Mayerling." This judgment is not proto-auteurism, nor a self-serving application of the great-man theory of film history. Instead, it reflects the realization, common in the days of silent pictures, that directors were generally the people who made things happen, at least as far as the art of cinema was concerned.[1]

Today, industry analysts tell us that such power is spread among a small group of stars, directors, agents, and creative production heads.[2] While a number of silent stars certainly developed the same authority, they were essentially seeking to control their own vehicles. Agents had no such power, and most producers were little more than glorified production managers. A few studio production chiefs did manage to put their imprint on a season's output, and an even smaller number of key screenwriters or "literary editors" could wield similar power. With producers exercising little authority, studio chiefs preoccupied with business and contractual matters, and the value of a screenplay not yet established at the level talkies would allow, much creative power was concentrated in the hands of a relatively small group of filmmakers capable of conceiving, orchestrating, and executing specific projects.

A look at the careers of some of these men and women reveals several ways in which this power was acquired and executed. The following pages are not intended as comprehensive career surveys but do seek to indicate how some of the main creative issues of the day were addressed by a number of the industry's most prominent figures.

Most of these examples are drawn from the ranks of directors, and it is useful to understand what comparative value their employers placed on their services. In November 1926, Paul Kohner, then a producer at Universal, prepared a confidential memorandum for the company's president, Carl Laemmle. Kohner had been asked to compile a listing of "the most important directors and the salaries they are getting." He used whatever confidential sources were available to him within the industry in producing the accompanying list, which leaves blanks for those figures of which he was uncertain. Note that the list does not consider such directors as Griffith or DeMille who worked for their own companies, or Murnau and von Sternberg who were not yet established in Hollywood. The fact that some directors had profit-sharing arrangements is also not taken into consideration. Misspellings have been corrected.

DATE NOVEMBER 8, 1926
TO MR. LAEMMLE   FROM MR. KOHNER

PLEASE KEEP CONFIDENTIAL

As per your request, please find below a list of the most important directors and the salaries they are getting. I am not quite correct in every point but I have tried to check up as closely as I could, and you will find that the figures in most cases are correct and in some cases approximately as they are now. Where I was not sure of the salary I have left a blank space.

George Archainbaud	$ 1250.	weekly
Clarence Badger	1500.	weekly
Wm. Beaudine	1750.	weekly
Harry Beaumont	1250.	weekly
Monta Bell	25000.	per picture
Frank Borzage	1500.	weekly
Charles Brabin	25000.	per picture
Herbert Brenon	2500.	weekly
Clarence Brown		
Tod Browning	1500.	weekly
Dimitri Buchowetzki	35000.	per picture
W. Christy Cabanne	1000.	weekly
Eddie Cline	1000.	weekly
Jack Conway	1000.	weekly
Donald Crisp		
Alan Crosland	20000.	per picture
James Cruze	50000.	per picture
Irving Cummings	1000.	weekly
John Francis Dillon	25000.	per picture
Alan Dwan	50000.	per picture
George Fitzmaurice	50000.	per picture
Victor Fleming	1500.	weekly
Emmett Flynn	1250.	weekly
John Ford	1750.	weekly

Sidney Franklin	2000.	weekly
Edmund Goulding	1500.	weekly
Alfred Green	25000.	per picture
Victor Heerman	10000.	per picture
Hobart Henley	2000.	weekly
Howard Higgins	15000.	per picture
Lambert Hillyer	10000.	per picture
George W. Hill	1250.	weekly
E. Mason Hopper	12500.	per picture
James Horne	1250.	weekly
William K. Howard	1250.	weekly
Ralph Ince	1000.	weekly
Rupert Julian		
Erle Kenton	1000.	weekly
Henry King	50000.	per picture
Rowland Lee	1500.	weekly
Robert Z. Leonard	20000.	per picture
Ernst Lubitsch	175000.	per picture
Harry Millarde	1250.	weekly
R. Wm. Neill		
Marshall Neilan	35000.	per picture
Fred Newmeyer	1000.	weekly
Fred Niblo	2500.	weekly
Sidney Olcott	30000.	per picture
John Robertson	25000.	per picture
Victor Schertzinger	2000.	weekly
Victor Seastrom	2500.	weekly
Edward Sedgwick	1250.	weekly
George B. Seitz	1000.	weekly
Malcolm St. Clair	2000.	weekly
John Stahl	40000.	per picture
Sam Taylor	1750.	weekly
Maurice Tourneur		
King Vidor	40000.	per picture
Robert Vignola		
Von Stroheim	100,000.	per picture
Raoul Walsh	1500.	weekly
Millard Webb		
Roland West	45,000.	per picture
Irvin Willat	1000.	weekly
Sam Wood		

D. W. Griffith

On his death in 1948, D. W. Griffith was eulogized by James Agee as the one irreplaceable creator of film art: "He achieved what no other known man has ever achieved. To watch his work is like being witness to the beginning of melody or the first conscious use of the lever or the wheel, the emergence, coordination, and first eloquence of language, the birth of an art: and to realize that this is all the work of one man."[3]

All the work of one man! When Griffith died (and for many years after) this was one of the two key themes of Griffith criticism, the other being the even more romantic "he lived too long" (also a note sounded by Agee). Griffith directed films until 1931, but as Agee suggests, he had long since ceased to function as a force in the industry. The period covered in this volume contains the years of his fall from power, but it is not true that, as at least one critic believes, Griffith made no contributions of lasting significance in these years and all his work of value is contained in the pre-1914 Biograph films.[4] Even leaving aside the tremendous significance of THE BIRTH OF A NATION to the cinema's social, cultural, and economic development, Griffith and his films continued to hold a dominant position on the American film scene through 1922 at least. While it could be argued that we see few additions to Griffith's technical bag of tricks in these years, it is a mistake to reduce the man's art to a handful of optical or mechanical innovations such as the close-up, trucking shot, or parallel editing— none of which he "invented" in any case.

Griffith's reputation continued to develop in these years on the strength of a series of masterworks—INTOLERANCE (1916), HEARTS OF THE WORLD (1918), BROKEN BLOSSOMS (1919), WAY DOWN EAST (1920), and ORPHANS OF THE STORM (1922). What filmmaker has been able to match so varied and powerful an output over so short a span of time? Griffith's stature alone invited imitators (Allan Dwan and John Ford, for example), while his former assistants (Erich von Stroheim and Raoul Walsh) spread firsthand knowledge of "the master's " philosophy and method of work. These major films demonstrated that the struggles of individual characters, which could only be sketched in the best of the Biographs, might be significantly illuminated when placed against a broad, novelistic background. Griffith was not the first filmmaker to make this attempt, as a viewing of Pastrone's CABIRIA (1914) will illustrate. But Cabiria's struggles and the events of the Punic Wars seem only coincidentally connected. One does not inform the other.

Griffith's works, on the other hand, demonstrate how human lives are inextricably bound up with the larger forces of culture and history. Eisenstein and others made much of Griffith's debt to Dickens in his ability to characterize through carefully developed imagery, but what Griffith really took from Dickens was the ability to balance the intimate and the epic within the span of his broad narrative canvas.[5] To execute this possibility, he needed the increased scale his longer features allowed. It is for this reason that he inflated the production values of a film like WAY DOWN EAST. By emphasizing the social milieu that produced an Anna Moore, and by calling up the forces of nature for his climax, Griffith underscored his distance from the vision of Lottie Blair Parker, author of the original play.

Recent criticism, it might be noted, has added to Griffith's reputation several of the inexpensive pastorals he directed between these more elaborate works, notably A ROMANCE OF HAPPY VALLEY and TRUE HEART SUSIE (both 1919). Though ob-

D. W. Griffith directing THE BIRTH OF A NATION (*1915*).

scured at the time by the attention given his more costly films, these modest works show Griffith to have been just as comfortable without major budgets and masses of extras.[6]

In terms of his position within the industry, Griffith is also significant as one of the first major filmmakers to reject the growing power of the Hollywood establishment and to attempt to operate in a quasi-autonomous fashion. He quit Biograph when his first employer began to question his policies and established fruitful relationships with Mutual (1914–1915), Triangle (1915–1917), Paramount-Artcraft (1917–1919), First National (1919–1920), and United Artists (1920–1924). These arrangements allowed him a more or less free hand, but while the artist in Griffith flourished, the inept businessman drove the operation to disaster.

The Griffith papers collected at the Museum of Modern Art in New York demonstrate how the vast grosses of films such as ORPHANS OF THE STORM or even ONE EXCITING NIGHT (1922) were not enough to offset Griffith's expenses, caused largely by his inefficient distribution system and the high overhead of the Mamaroneck studio he built for himself in 1919–1920. The loss of his studio compelled him to sign with Paramount as a costly contract director, but Griffith had no ability to function on this level. He could be seen late at night, talking to himself as he wandered around Paramount's cavernous Astoria studio. His energy went into a string of complaints to Paramount executives and a doomed attempt to promote Carol Dempster. His last silent films are his weakest. By 1926 he had already lived too long.[7]

Thomas H. Ince

By 1915 Thomas H. Ince was already established as one of the leading American producers. Once a small-time stage actor, he appeared in one of Griffith's Biograph films in 1910, then won a contract with the IMP Company, for which he directed Mary Pickford throughout 1911. On the strength of these films, he was hired by the New York Motion Picture Company to take charge of their Edendale studio later that year.

In a lengthy series of one- and two-reel films, Ince took advantage of the spectacular California landscapes and the services of the Miller Brothers 101 Wild West Show to breathe new life into the traditional Western and Civil War action genres. More important, he was one of the first to systematize film-studio production in a practical and efficient manner. While the Vitagraph studio had employed an effective division of labor before this time, little is known about its day-to-day operations, and it is unclear just how the various production units were organized under J. Stuart Blackton's executive control. Enough data does exist on the Ince studio, however, to demonstrate that by 1913 he was employing a carefully diagrammed continuity script to extend his control over a number of directors and production units operating simultaneously away from his personal supervision.[8]

Soon after arriving in California, Ince split his forces into two units, maintaining personal control of one and assigning the other to Francis Ford, an experienced actor-director who already specialized in outdoor action pictures. Instead of using the relatively open scenario form common in 1911, Ince provided Ford with highly detailed shooting outlines. Over the years, these outlines evolved into formal blueprints (perhaps a better allusion would be to a musical score) that the director was expected to film without change. George Pratt reprints one of these, the scenario for SATAN McALLISTER'S HEIR, a two-reel production filmed in one week at the close of 1914. The script material includes a 154-scene shooting script detailing the use of close-ups, iris openings, lighting effects, and stage directions. In addition, a scene plot groups all interiors and exteriors, indicating that all shots at "mouth of rocky cave" are to be done at one time. A cost sheet, prepared after production, indicates

Thomas H. Ince on the set of CIVILIZATION (*1916*).

to the penny the payroll and material expenses ($815.09 total) and the final amount of negative used (3,579 feet).[9]

As his operation expanded, Ince learned to delegate more and more authority to his staff and ultimately retreated from the specific writing, directing, and even editing functions, although he maintained careful supervision of each of these procedures. It is unlikely that he could have drawn on his own business expertise to establish such an organization. Kalton Lahue has suggested that George W. Stout, the studio's fiscal supervisor, created the "Ince system" in 1913, and then replicated it at the Sennett studio.[10]

In 1915 Ince joined Griffith and Sennett in the Triangle Film Corporation and moved completely into the production of feature pictures.[11] Their greater length allowed his chief writer, C. Gardner Sullivan, to develop more fully the internal conflicts sketched in some of the two-reelers. These "soul fights" had been significant in moving the early releases away from the stylization of melodramatic convention. Now, in films such as THE COWARD (1915) and THE ARYAN (1916), true psychological development appeared.

While Ince's films were highly successful domestically, in Europe he was hailed as an artist "infinitely superior either to Griffith or to Cecil B. DeMille," at least according to the French film historians Maurice Bardèche and Robert Brasillach:

> By the end of the war Ince was more famous than Griffith. Delluc compared him to Rodin, to Debussy and Dumas, even to Aeschylus. "He is the first," he wrote, "to synthesize the confused but brilliant impulses of this art as it emerges from the matrix." . . . Thanks to him the film discovered several basic truths, above all the fact that in a dramatic film the actors are only part of the *mise-en-scène*, and that inanimate objects, trees, roads, and winds, can once more assume their ancient and proper role (*History of the Film*, pp. 109–11).

Of all Ince's stars, the French were especially taken with William S. Hart (whom they knew as Rio Jim). While Louis Delluc and others automatically attributed the qualities of these films to Ince, we know today that his supervision of them was perfunctory at best, and that by 1917 his credit on the Hart films was purely contractual.

That year, Ince began distributing through Paramount-Artcraft. He now supervised fewer releases each year, but somehow the mechanical qualities of his productions began to overwhelm the creative elements. Peter Milne defended Ince and his method in a 1922 study of motion-picture directing, but even Milne admitted that little flexibility was allowed the director on the Ince lot. "When a director works for Mr. Ince he does what Mr. Ince tells him to do," Milne reported approvingly.[12] A look at the roster of Ince contract directors reveals Fred Niblo and Reginald Barker as the best-remembered of the group, which is hardly an indication of excessive creativity on the stages.[13]

In fact, Ince's vaunted system was merely an extension of his personal taste and style. A mature production line, such as the one Irving Thalberg developed at MGM, can function effectively despite changes in top management. But when Thomas Ince died suddenly in 1924, operations at the Ince plant shut down completely. His system failed to survive him.

Mack Sennett

The most important events in the career of Mack Sennett—his days with Griffith at Biograph, his formation of Keystone, and his development of Chaplin, Arbuckle, and Mabel Normand as major stars—were already history by 1915. In January of that year alone, he released seventeen reels on the Mutual program, including five reels of Arbuckle–Normand comedies, a pair of half-reel educational subjects, and a scattering of slapstick shorts of one reel or less, featuring Chester Conklin, Sydney Chaplin, Charlie Chase, Mack Swain, and Charlie Murray.[14]

Keystone, which began as a comedy producer in 1912, had long since passed the days when its product could be assembled more or less off the cuff. Gilbert Seldes and other supporters of the early Keystone films might have prized Sennett's air of improvisation above all else, but by 1915 the requirements of a heavy release schedule had turned his studio into a "fun factory" in the fullest sense of that term. While Ince has been given credit for organizing production at his studio, Mack Sennett's achievement at Keystone was no less remarkable. In fact, Sennett devised a method of delegating production authority that not only maintained the quality standard of his releases but transmitted their characteristic style and subject matter as well, to create Hollywood's most consistent studio look. Clarence Badger, a writer and director for Sennett at that time, recalled that this studio "slant" was constantly kept in mind, especially when hiring new talent.[15]

In 1915 the journalist Harry Carr visited the Sennett lot and observed this system in action. According to Carr, Sennett started with a rough scenario, hardly more than an idea, which he had thrashed out in committee with his writers. Kalton Lahue, the author of several volumes on Sennett and Keystone, reproduces one of these documents, called "Aeroplane Elopement Story," which begins as follows: "Roscoe leaves aeroplane near clump of bushes and goes to girl. Establish a love affair in opening scene between Roscoe and the girl—get over that her father is trying to marry her off owing to her ferocious temper or something."[16]

Using such a document as a guide, Sennett gathered together actors and crew and began breaking down the action and indicating, with chalk marks on the floor of the

Mack Sennett on the set of A SMALL TOWN IDOL (1921).

studio, where players, cameras, and props should be positioned. A stenographer followed, taking down every word of his instructions. The next day these notes would be handed to a "subdirector" on location, who would do his best to execute the plan. "By this singular method Sennett is able to direct the whole thing in miniature in a few hours," marveled Harry Carr. Sennett was thus able to "personally direct the scenarios" of his ten or twelve companies and maintain a high degree of individual control.[17]

In the cutting room, Sennett studied incoming footage intently, twitching in his chair or spitting if anything displeased him. He told Harry Carr that only about 25 percent of the material shot would eventually be used, a figure that had shrunk to 20 percent by the end of 1916, according to figures provided by Lahue. The numbers indicate that considerable leeway was being allowed for polishing material and thus undercut tales of offhand production methods in this period.[18]

"Mack Sennett supervised his pictures all along the way," his editor William Hornbeck told Kevin Brownlow. "But he couldn't afford to reject any; good or bad, the pictures had to go."[19] The success of his operation, and the pressure to continue the stream of new product, ultimately began to take its toll. Brownlow notes an instance where Mabel Normand was directing Chaplin in one of his earliest films, made in 1914:

> Mabel asked him to stand with a hose and to spray the street so that the villain's car would skid. Chaplin remembered the old Lumière film in which a boy steps on a gardener's hose and when the gardener peers down the nozzle to see what's wrong, he gets a jet of water in the face; he suggested this gag to Mabel, who knew how fast the Sennett comedies had to be ground out. "We have no time," she said. Chaplin refused to play the scene, and sat on the kerb in a sulk (*Hollywood: The Pioneers*, p. 143).

Sennett took her side when they returned to the studio, and Chaplin considered quitting. Changes of pace and characterization had no place in Sennett's scheme, so Chaplin went elsewhere to develop his talents. Over the years, he was followed by a string of others—Fatty Arbuckle, Harry Langdon, gagman Frank Capra—because Sennett had no interest in their efforts to craft comedy to character, and either fired them or allowed them to leave. When running a fun factory, what was needed were interchangeable parts. A fat man, a baggy pants comic with a cane, a baby-faced innocent—to Sennett these were types, clowns who needed only to remember where he had put the chalk marks.

Hal Roach would be the man to profit from these lessons. Working with Harold Lloyd, Charlie Chase, and Stan Laurel and Oliver Hardy, it was Roach who would perfect situation comedy based on realistic characters and storylines. By the end of the silent era, Mack Sennett's fun factory was mired in its own rust belt.

Herbert Brenon

The postwar period marked a watershed in silent-feature production, and few successful directors operated in the twenties who had been equally prominent in the early days of feature films. One of the most important was Herbert Brenon, a director originally noted as a pioneer of overseas location shooting and lavish spectacle who successfully adapted his style to the requirements of the postwar era. He developed a new reputation for his handling of actresses and adaptations of literary properties, and he closed out the silent era as one of its most popular and best-paid directors.

There was never a personality cult centered around Brenon and his work, however, and while the production of some of his films did make good copy, the man himself was too ordinary to capture the imagination of critics or acolytes. When he gradually stopped making films, he seems not to have been missed, and with so much of his key work gone, there is little possibility of reviving his reputation. Nevertheless, Brenon's career is crucial to understanding the development of the American studio system in this period.

Brenon was born in Dublin in 1880. He came to the United States in 1896 and looked for work in the theater, eventually finding a job directing a stock company in Minneapolis. With his wife, Helen Downing, he formed a vaudeville act, but they abandoned the stage to run a nickelodeon in Johnstown, Pennsylvania.[20] He left this business a few years later and went to work as a scenario editor for the IMP studio.

Herbert Brenon and his longtime cinematographer James Wong Howe, ca. *1924.*

After five months behind a desk, Brenon was given the chance to direct his first film, ALL FOR HER (1912), which quickly established him as a director.

He made the first IMP three-reeler, LEAH THE FORSAKEN (1913), and later that year was sent to Europe, where he made important films in Britain, France, and Germany. The most significant of these films was the four-reel IVANHOE (1914), filmed at Chepstow Castle.[21] Unlike the Ince–Pickford unit sent by IMP to Cuba the previous year, this was no ill-conceived excursion but a serious effort to take advantage of European locales and produce work of scope and significance. In addition, the trip marked one of the few important attempts by American filmmakers to challenge the dominance of European producers by sending a complete crew right into their own backyard. Brenon's ABSINTHE (1913) appears to have been the first American film made in France, although French companies at the time were deeply involved in American production.

On his return to the United States, Brenon produced the seven-reel epic NEPTUNE'S DAUGHTER (1914), an aquatic fantasy starring Annette Kellerman, which was a tremendous success. It ran at the Globe Theatre on Broadway for twenty-six weeks, a record not matched until the arrival of THE BIRTH OF A NATION.[22]

Moving to Fox, Brenon worked with Theda Bara for a time, then set out to top his success with the Kellerman picture through a kind of sequel, A DAUGHTER OF THE GODS (1915–1916). Taking over an entire corner of the island of Jamaica for eight months, he used 2,000,000 feet of lumber and 2,500 barrels of plaster to create vast, fantastic settings, and put 20,000 extras on the payroll. Far from Fox's supervision, Brenon shot 220,000 feet of negative and completely outstripped his budget. Worse, he began a war with William Fox over the personal publicity he was accruing (at Fox's expense), and when the company returned to New York, the film was taken from him and edited by the studio. When he heard that Fox intended to remove his name from the credits and advertising, Brenon went to court, but his motion was dismissed. Fox eventually restored the credit, but this battle between studio head and director nonetheless seems an eerie foreshadowing of Erich von Stroheim's later troubles. Decorated with nude tableaux and precocious tracking shots, the film was a considerable topic of conversation in 1916 but does not appear to have been completely successful.[23]

Brenon subsequently eschewed such spectacle, and THE FALL OF THE ROMANOFFS (1917) was staged in his Hudson Heights studio. Becoming associated with more restrained dramatic vehicles, he directed some of the best films of Alla Nazimova, Norma Talmadge, and Pola Negri. Between 1923 and 1928 he was one of the key Paramount directors, and surviving films from this period, including the proto-feminist DANCING MOTHERS and the James M. Barrie adaptations PETER PAN (1925) and A KISS FOR CINDERELLA (1926), reveal an exceptionally assured style. He closed out the silent era at the top of his form with BEAU GESTE (1926) and SORRELL AND SON (1927) and was named the best director of 1927–1928 in a massive *Film Daily* critics' poll, quite a compliment considering the competition that season.[24]

But Brenon was unhappy with the talkies and as late as November 1928 labeled them a fad that would stand in the way of the film's perfection as a graphic art.[25] An individualist in an increasingly producer-oriented system, Brenon found it harder to work in the manner in which he was accustomed and eventually returned to England, where he directed his last film in 1940.

Lois Weber

The most remarkable thing about women directors in the silent period is not that there were so many of them but that their contributions should have been so thoroughly effaced in all later histories of the period. At Universal alone, in 1916–1917, one could have observed Ruth Ann Baldwin, Grace Cunard, Cleo Madison, Ruth Stonehouse, Ida May Park, Elsie Jane Wilson, and Lois Weber directing every sort of picture on Carl Laemmle's release schedule. Most of these women soon dropped out, presumably for lack of talent, interest, or the ability to cope with Hollywood politics, but Lois Weber flourished. During the war years, she achieved tremendous success by combining a canny commercial sense with a rare vision of cinema as a moral tool. For a time, Weber made a fortune trying to improve the human race through movies.

As a young woman, Weber worked for a time as a street-corner missionary in Pittsburgh, but later dropped this vocation and followed the advice of an uncle in Chicago to try the stage. The transition was not as radical as it might seem, since she had had previous experience as a touring concert pianist. "As I was convinced that the theatrical profession needed a missionary, he suggested that the best way to reach them was to become one of them, so I went on the stage filled with a great desire to convert my fellowman."[26]

Soon after joining a road company of *Why Girls Leave Home*, she married the troupe's actor-manager, Phillips Smalley, but the constant separation involved in the touring life proved difficult, and Weber settled in New York to establish a home. In 1908 she discovered that motion pictures required little road work and signed with the Gaumont studio in Flushing, New York. Here, she would have observed the screen's first woman director, Alice Guy Blaché, who had come to the United States with her husband, Herbert Blaché, to take charge of Gaumont's American interests.

Weber grew comfortable with the film form—writing, directing, and starring in Gaumont's one-reelers—and Smalley soon joined her. As a team, they eventually moved to the Reliance studio, then to Edwin S. Porter's Rex Company, which they took over when Porter left in 1912 and Rex became part of the new Universal. Their films from this period were signed by "The Smalleys," although Weber typically received sole writing credit. How the directorial chores were divided is not clear, but by 1917 Weber was putting her own name on the productions, and Smalley gradually faded in importance.

Few early Weber films survive, and the most remarkable, SUSPENSE (1913), is uncharacteristic in its flashy cutting, photographic effects, and lack of a direct moral statement. The following year, the Smalleys produced for the Bosworth Company their first great success, HYPOCRITES! (1914). This four-reel feature was cast in the form of an allegory, with "the mirror of truth" being held up to various tableaux representing politics, family life, and other areas of moral concern. Weber's use of a (double-exposed) nude actress to represent Truth caused a considerable stir at the time.

Returning to Universal, Weber increased her production of such morality plays, culminating in the notorious WHERE ARE MY CHILDREN? (1916), self-described in its publicity as "a five-part argument advocating birth control and against race suicide." Her films were often attacked by censorship groups as simple exploitations of

Lois Weber on the steps of her office, talking to representatives of the Motion Picture News, *1917. Men standing are part of her staff.*

taboo subject matter, but Weber sincerely believed in her position as artist and evangelist. "In moving pictures I have found my life's work," she declared in a 1914 interview. "I find at once an outlet for my emotions and my ideals. I can preach to my heart's content, and with the opportunity to write the play, act the leading role, and direct the entire production, if my message fails to reach someone, I can blame only myself."[27]

She continued dealing with such "women's issues" as divorce, poverty, child abuse, capital punishment, and birth control, although women's suffrage does not seem to have been one of her prime concerns. In 1917 she starred in a fictionalized account of the imprisonment of Margaret Sanger, originally called Is A WOMAN A PERSON?, which was recut and retitled THE HAND THAT ROCKS THE CRADLE after still more trouble from pressure groups.[28] After this film, she began to play down the blatant sermonizing in her work, as in THE BLOT (1921), which substitutes a nuanced analysis of the effects of poverty on a poor minister's family.

Despite these changes, Weber seems to have abruptly lost her public after 1920. A four-picture deal with Paramount, which would pay her $50,000 per picture and 50 percent of the profits, was dropped after the poor reception of the first two films. The new audience of the 1920s had even less use for Weber's analysis of their moral shortcomings than they had for Griffith's. She directed a few films after 1921, was divorced and remarried, and seems to have suffered some form of nervous breakdown. Poor management of her real-estate holdings depleted her fortune in the early 1930s, and when she died in 1939 her funeral expenses were paid by friends who remembered her devotion to an impossibly high ideal of screen art.

Maurice Tourneur

The ranks of early film directors were drawn from a startling array of occupations, with engineers, sailors, stuntmen, vaudevillians, and explorers all represented. A few successful Broadway figures did work behind the cameras, but in general, the men and women responsible for producing early films were far less noted than those hired to act in them. Adolph Zukor's slogan may have been "Famous Players in Famous Plays," but to direct, he hired the great mechanic Edwin S. Porter.

One notable exception to this rule was Maurice Tourneur, who came from Éclair's Paris studio to Fort Lee, New Jersey, in 1914. Tourneur was born in Paris in 1876, and after studying at the Lycée Condorcet he worked as an interior decorator, an illustrator, and a designer of posters and textiles. He was an assistant to Auguste Rodin and Puvis de Chavannes and, for Puvis, he designed sketches for the Boston Public Library staircase mural. After three years of military service he turned his attention to the theater and toured the world with the great actress Réjane. While working with André Antoine at the Théâtre de l'Odéon, he married an actress in Antoine's company; their son Jacques (later a film director of note) was born in 1904.[29]

Tourneur began directing for Éclair in 1912; he was brought into films by Émile Chautard, with whom he had worked on stage (Chautard, who later joined Tourneur in America, would also be the mentor of Josef von Sternberg). In America, Tourneur first worked for the World Film Corporation, a company managed by Lewis J. Selznick and generally devoted to filming theatrical successes. In the hands of a less inventive director these films might have been straightforward transcriptions of the Broadway originals, but Tourneur was able to take advantage of the opportunities for stylization opened up by the camera. In fact, he often connected his goals to those of Edward Gordon Craig, Max Reinhardt, and Konstantin Stanislavsky.[30]

His earliest extant American film, THE WISHING RING (1914), displays a sophisticated handling of deep space, with an ingenious use of foreground and background action. A brooding squire sulks in his dark sitting room, while his sunlit garden, whose roses he never picks, is always visible through the French doors in the distance. The use of sunlight to light interiors in this period brought such effects within every director's grasp, but relatively few were able to avoid the visual chaos it could easily bring on. Fewer still were able consistently to employ patterns of deep space to achieve effects that were considered rare when von Stroheim employed them a decade later.

Tourneur's command of editing, even in this early work, is equally good. While he avoids the pulse-pounding tempo of directors like Griffith, he carefully uses cutting to establish a three-dimensional playing area and to enhance, when desired, the feeling of offscreen space.[31]

Perhaps most interesting to modern eyes is Tourneur's use of formal distancing devices. Especially when dealing with period or fantasy subjects, Tourneur consistently filmed through a proscenium-shaped mask, "theatricalizing" even events that were filmed outdoors. THE WISHING RING, subtitled "An Idyll of Old England," is introduced by three graces reminiscent of a Julia Margaret Cameron photograph. In addition to opening and closing a curtain, which "frames" the narrative, they appear

Maurice Tourneur celebrates the completion of filming on THE CHRISTIAN *(1921):*
Charles Van Enger at the camera, Mae Busch and Richard Dix the performers.

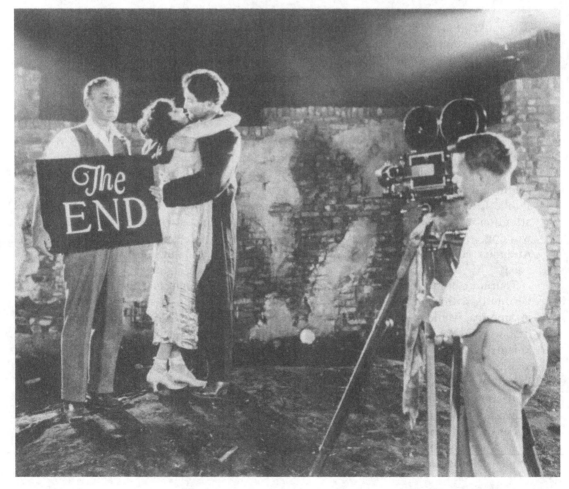

at intervals during the film as well and thus participate in the action they are framing.[32]

Like other successful directors of the period, Tourneur was too busy to labor over his work, which averaged six features per year between 1914 and 1920. He made two of Mary Pickford's finest pictures, THE PRIDE OF THE CLAN and POOR LITTLE RICH GIRL (both 1917), and also directed several notable successes of Olga Petrova and Elsie Ferguson. But in 1918 his avant-garde productions of THE BLUE BIRD and PRUNELLA were resounding box-office failures. Tourneur felt betrayed by his audience. In an article bluntly entitled "Meeting the Public Demands," he wrote, "I would rather starve and make good pictures, if I knew they were going to be shown, but to starve and make pictures which are thrown in the ashcan is above anybody's strength."[33]

Once heralded as "the poet of the screen," Tourneur grew bitter over increasing commercial pressures. TREASURE ISLAND and THE LAST OF THE MOHICANS (both 1920) were among his last satisfactory efforts. That year, he dissolved a highly successful relationship with Jules Brulatour, the financier and agent for Eastman raw stock, and joined five other noted directors in forming Associated Producers, Inc. The move only snarled him in red tape, however, and the combine soon dissolved.[34]

While always gainfully employed afterward, Tourneur had good cause to complain about the weak scripts he was given to direct. The increasingly departmentalized routine of Hollywood production was unable to sustain the creative atmosphere he craved. In 1926 he was directing MGM's first Technicolor feature, THE MYSTERIOUS ISLAND, when Irving Thalberg assigned him a producer. Two weeks after the man walked onto his set, Tourneur quit the picture and left Hollywood to continue his career in Europe.

Cecil B. DeMille

Cecil B. DeMille arrived in Los Angeles on 20 December 1913. He was the newly appointed director general of the Jesse L. Lasky Feature Play Company and was traveling with the firm's entire production unit. The journey had been undertaken in order to film Edwin Milton Royle's Western play, *The Squaw Man*, in surroundings of greater authenticity than those available in New Jersey. DeMille had with him Dustin Farnum, star of the stage production, and Oscar Apfel, an experienced motion-picture director who would co-direct the picture (DeMille was fresh from the theater and had no knowledge of film or film technique). The company soon acquired a lease on the property at 6284 Selma Avenue, a renovated barn and adjacent grounds in the suburbs of Hollywood. They were not the first filmmakers in Hollywood (the Nestor Company had been operating out of Blondeau's Tavern on Sunset Boulevard since 1911), but they were the first company there to specialize in feature pictures, the dramatic form that would soon dominate the industry and make the name "Hollywood" internationally famous.[35]

DeMille constructed an open-air stage on the lot and here managed to film the studio scenes of THE SQUAW MAN (not inside the barn, as some would have it, since he had no lights). Despite a series of misadventures, including a problem with variant framelines (still visible in existing prints of the film), the picture was successfully sold on the states rights market, and DeMille's screen career was launched.[36]

Over the next three years, DeMille directed the twenty-nine features on which his early reputation was based. Made for the Lasky Company, and later Famous Players–Lasky, these films were closely tied to their theatrical sources and the performances of their Broadway stars. James Card has noted:

> Not until his eighth film did he entrust a lead to an actress primarily of the cinema, when he cast Blanche Sweet. Not until his fourth year of production did he discover, with Gloria Swanson, that an actress with no stage experience whatsoever, could prove to be more popular and more successful under his direction than were any of his stage-trained leading ladies ("The Silent Films of Cecil B. DeMille," in *"Image": On the Art and Evolution of the Film,* edited by Marshall Deutelbaum, p. 119).

But Swanson came later. His early stars were legitimate troopers, including Theodore Roberts, House Peters, Raymond Hatton, and even Geraldine Farrar—all contract talent signed by Lasky to help convince exhibitors of the proven theatrical underpinnings of the company's product.

DeMille was able to distance himself from rival producers of canned theater by an arresting visual style and a true genius for self-promotion. Benjamin Hampton felt that DeMille and Griffith were the only directors of the period whose names meant anything at the box office, and DeMille took steps to ensure his popularity throughout a career much longer than Griffith's.[37]

DeMille was never very successful at articulating screen space through the use of such devices as editing or camera movement, but from the beginning he was quite concerned with pictorial composition and won immediate attention for his lighting effects. Working with cameraman Alvin Wyckoff, DeMille pioneered a style of illumination soon known as "Lasky lighting" or (when DeMille was speaking) "Rembrandt lighting." His concern with visual style was relatively advanced at a time when most companies were satisfied to record a clean, detailed image. In a 1917 article titled "Photodrama a New Art," he wrote, "No longer does every detail in the set where action takes place have to be absolutely distinct. Much is being done in following out the Rinehart [sic] idea of suggestive settings. The audience is made to feel the background rather than see it." Such mastery of light and shadow can be seen at its best in DeMille's The Cheat (1915), one of the most widely acclaimed films of the era.[38]

This self-conscious artistry reached its peak in The Whispering Chorus (1918), which DeMille considered the first film to deal with internal psychological conflicts.[39] Although relatively successful at the box office, it marked the end of his early period of artistic experimentation. He followed it with Old Wives for New (1918), the first in a series of titillating melodramas designed to capture postwar audiences. "Accurately appraising the new civilization that was emerging, DeMille decided that the majority of theatre patrons were fundamentally curious about only money and sex," wrote one contemporary observer.[40]

This series, especially Male and Female (1919) and Why Change Your Wife? (1920), inspired a flock of screen imitations, reflecting Hollywood's vision of postwar American social mores. As Lewis Jacobs, who lacks enthusiasm for even the early DeMille, acknowledged, "If, in the artistic perspective of American film history, Cecil Blount DeMille is valueless, in the social history of films it is impossible

Cecil B. DeMille on the Paramount lot, 1921.

to ignore him."[41] The postwar films became those on which his later reputation was to build (especially his first version of THE TEN COMMANDMENTS [1923], with its portents of later spectacles), and the early years of innovation were soon forgotten. When he began to film Gloria Swanson in golden beds and golden bathtubs, DeMille moved permanently from artistic pioneer to cultural phenomenon.

Marshall Neilan

The legend of the great silent-film director who dissipates his own success in a welter of fast parties and bootleg liquor has at least some basis in reality: the crippled career of Marshall Neilan.

As early as 1918 *Motion Picture* magazine was calling Neilan "the youngest Big director in the motion picture industry." He had just directed four of Mary Pickford's finest and most popular films, including the powerful STELLA MARIS (1918), which both Peter Milne (in 1922) and Edward Wagenknecht (in 1962) thought contained her best work. He was twenty-six years old when he made the Pickford films and earned $125,000 per picture for directing them. By the time he was thirty, his career was already showing signs of strain; by the time he was forty, he was reduced to directing slapstick two-reelers and hillbilly musicals.[42]

Neilan did leave considerable evidence of his talents, especially in the features he directed in the late teens. But by 1923 even his supporters were paying more

Marshall Neilan and his wife, actress Blanche Sweet.

attention to his life-style than to his films. Tamar Lane, who spoke of him in the same breath with Griffith and von Stroheim, accused him of not taking his work seriously and of leaving too many key scenes in the hands of various assistants. Later historians dubbed him "the last of the shoot-from-the-cuff directors" and "an incorrigible play-boy [who] never applied himself to his craft with any seriousness."[43]

What seems to have been lost over the years, however, is the tremendous sense of respect (and affection) that Neilan engendered among his critics and colleagues, a feeling based not only on his engaging personality but on the fine performances and strong dramatic values evident in the best of his work.

Neilan began his career in films in 1911 as an actor for the Kalem Company. Handsome and personable, he was soon signed by Allan Dwan to play opposite J. Warren Kerrigan at the Flying A studio, and when Dwan left for Universal, Neilan came with him. Gradually he began directing the films he appeared in, and on returning to Kalem in 1913 he found himself acting, directing, and generally running the studio. But after a few months at the reins of Kalem's bizarre HAM AND BUD comedy series (DON'T MONKEY WITH THE BUZZ SAW was a typical title), Neilan was ready to return to acting and joined Allan Dwan's Lasky unit in New York.[44]

The Lasky pictures were Neilan's first important films, giving him the chance to play opposite such stars as Marguerite Clark and Mary Pickford (he was Pinkerton to Pickford's MADAME BUTTERFLY in 1915). After a brief season directing for Selig, Neilan returned to Lasky and directed a series of features with Blanche Sweet (whom he later married), Sessue Hayakawa, and Mary Pickford. These were the pictures on which his reputation was based.

Not surprisingly, Neilan felt that all directors needed a certain amount of acting ability, and he preferred to mime each part for his players, then watch quietly during shooting as they joined their conception to his own. He was especially good with child actors and developed the successful career of Wesley Barry, who starred in Neilan's DINTY (1920) and PENROD (1922). In the silent film, such performances could be shaped completely by a director with a firm grasp of editing, dramatic construction, and proper use of the camera. Neilan once listed the essential requirements of screen acting as beauty, personality, charm, temperament, style, and the ability to wear clothes. In other words, all that was required was that a performer be a suitable mannequin; talent was unnecessary because the director was expected to provide that component.[45]

Neilan's wife, Blanche Sweet, whom he later directed in such films as TESS OF THE D'URBERVILLES (1925), once gave an extraordinary interview "explaining" Neilan's undisciplined working habits:

> They are all wrong about Mickie. Everybody around the studio thinks that Mickie is a careless, happy-go-lucky idler who drifts in late to the studio and just sort of makes the thing up as he goes along. I used to think so myself until we were married. The fact is that Mickie is doing his hardest work when he appears to be playing. I can always tell at home when Mickie is working out a big scene in his mind. Our home life straightway takes on an atmosphere of jazz and excitement. Mickie whirls me around to jazz emporiums at loud and unusual hours of the night. We dance at road houses and Mickie gives prizes to the best fox-trotters, and we whirl thru a round of pleasure until I am positively dazed and dizzy.

I have learned from experience to know that at these times, Mickie is working some big situation in a big story (*Motion Picture Classic*, February 1924, p. 18).[46]

By the mid 1920s the partying seemed almost continuous. Neilan's biographer Jack Spears characterizes him as living out an F. Scott Fitzgerald fantasy and tells of increasing bouts of drunkenness and absenteeism. Neilan was off the set so frequently that one of his films was credited as "Directed by Marshall Neilan and Staff." In addition, although the center of an admiring group of supporters and drinking buddies, Neilan alienated several key Hollywood figures with his wicked sense of humor. "An empty taxi cab drove up and Louis B. Mayer got out," he once quipped— a line that did not help him find work around MGM.[47]

Unlike Griffith or von Stroheim (or, to cite a later example, Orson Welles), Marshall Neilan's tragedy had little to do with the cost, style, or box-office success of his pictures. His story cannot be read as a failure of the system but only as the inability of one talented, undisciplined, and self-destructive individual to adjust to the success he had wrested from the system itself.

King Vidor

Much work remains to be done on the small regional film centers that grew up within the United States in the teens and early twenties. Far from the main production centers in New York and Hollywood, or even Chicago, movie-struck amateurs with access to such simple cameras as the Universal or the Institute Standard (both widely available by the late teens) made actualities, short comedies, and even occasional features. Kathleen Karr locates some of these companies in Wilkes-Barre, Pennsylvania, Providence, Rhode Island, and even Saranac Lake, New York.[48] If regional centers had been able to flourish, the character of the American cinema in this period might have been significantly different. But the ultimate dominance of Hollywood and New York led to standardization of product. This homogenized perspective might have been economically efficient, but it eliminated most nonconforming approaches.

These centers did produce a few individuals who successfully carried on their careers in Hollywood however. The most notable was King Vidor, a director who was able to play the Hollywood studio game while maintaining an independence of style and subject matter seldom found in the mature American film industry.

Vidor was born in Galveston, Texas, in 1894, and writes in his autobiography of falling under the spell of a vaudeville projection of Georges Méliès' VOYAGE À LA LUNE. In 1914–1915 he worked with friends filming short comedies and industrials, and acted as a stringer for THE MUTUAL WEEKLY before leaving for California, where the real movies were made.[49]

His wife, Florence Vidor, an aspiring actress who had worked with him on the Texas films, soon signed with the Ince studio and began a steady rise to stardom (her later films included THE MARRIAGE CIRCLE [1924] and THE PATRIOT [1928]), but director Vidor could land only odd jobs. His writing credit appears on a few Universal comedy shorts, but it was not until 1918 that he was again able to work as a director. Significantly, he achieved this not through the established studio structure but by

King Vidor and cameraman John Boyle observe the problems of an assistant director on the WILD ORANGES *location, 1924.*

convincing a group of doctors and dentists to back him in the production of a Christian Science subject called THE TURN IN THE ROAD (1919). Its moral agenda recalls the sermonizing of a director like Lois Weber, and Vidor's seriousness of purpose was immediately clear (as was his popular touch—the film was quite profitable). A little later, Vidor published in the trade papers a "Creed and Pledge" outlining his intentions. He announced that the motion picture should serve humanity and help free it from the shackles of fear and suffering. He rejected evil subjects and embraced pictures that were "absolutely true to human nature."[50]

He was able to establish his own studio, Vidor Village, where he produced films for distribution through First National. The studio specialized in Americana subjects, and Vidor sought to duplicate a mood he found in the writings of Mark Twain, Booth Tarkington, and James Whitcomb Riley. Owning and operating one's own studio was a goal of most independent directors of the day, among them Griffith, Neilan, and again, Weber. With THE JACK KNIFE MAN (1920) Vidor proved himself true to his ideals, creating one of the most affecting of American pastorals. The film is the story of a folk artist, a woodcarver, living as an itinerant boatman on the Mississippi. Vidor may, in fact, have seen himself as such an artist, pursuing his own ideals just outside the Hollywood community. In any case, he was soon forced out of this paradise, lost his studio, and began free-lancing, eventually joining the new Metro-Goldwyn-Mayer.[51]

His long and fruitful relationship with MGM (twenty films over the next twenty years) provides a model for the accommodation of a strong-willed director to the requisites of big-studio production. Vidor soon made himself indispensable by helping develop John Gilbert into a major star and directing THE BIG PARADE (1925), one of the highest-grossing pictures of the silent era. Establishing a close relationship with Irving Thalberg, Vidor would trade off projects by agreeing to two of the studio's projects as long as he could direct one of his own. The most spectacular example during this period was THE CROWD (1928), a drab urban poem largely shot on location in New York and admittedly influenced by E. A. Dupont's VARIETY (1925) and Fritz Lang's METROPOLIS (1926).[52]

While directors such as Clarence Brown and John Ford found America in the countryside, Vidor was capable of seeing the nation in its cities as well. Later, in THE FOUNTAINHEAD (1949), he would show a superman asserting his will over such a city, but THE CROWD is one of Vidor's films of ordinary life, and the resolution is far less operatic.

A director who was able to maintain his own ideals while remaining flexible enough to serve the interests of his employers, Vidor duplicated his silent success in the talkie era, while his less adaptable compatriots, including Brenon, Neilan, and von Stroheim, soon found themselves unemployed.

Erich von Stroheim

Erich von Stroheim's first biographer dubbed him "the Hollywood scapegoat," the victim chosen to suffer ignominy and expulsion for the sins of the many.[53] He was not the only director to go far over budget, behave outrageously on the set, or inflame the nation's various pressure groups. But he was the only one to do so while flouting the authority of his studio superiors and failing (for the most part) to bring in adequate box-office returns.

Between 1919 and 1932 von Stroheim began the direction of nine films, all but the last of which were silent. Of this number, one was never released, two were completed by others, one was halted during production and released in truncated form, two were taken from him after shooting and savagely cut, two more suffered minor studio-inflicted cuts, and one was released essentially intact. In terms of a body of work, this collection of footage might hardly seem worth evaluating. Von Stroheim himself once referred to the released version of one of his films as "the skeleton of my dead child." Yet throughout the 1920s he remained one of the most respected, and best paid, of all Hollywood directors.[54]

This esteem has continued over the years. In the 1976 Belgian Royal Film Archive poll von Stroheim was still seen as being among the ten most important American directors, despite the fact that not one film from his hand survives intact. His best-known film, GREED (1924), notorious for being slashed to one-quarter its intended length, was cited in this poll as the third most important American film of all time. Clearly, such judgments are not being made on aesthetic grounds alone, and it is largely in terms of their symbolic value that von Stroheim and his films continue to hold such a position of prominence.[55]

Von Stroheim, the son of a Jewish dry-goods merchant, was born in Vienna in 1885. A failure in both the business world and a brief military career, he emigrated to the United States in 1908 and worked at a series of odd jobs. He tried his hand at the stage as early as 1912, writing a short play, called *In the Morning*, which contained, in rough outline, many of the themes he would later develop in such films as THE WEDDING MARCH (1928). His first Hollywood experience came with the Griffith company, although it is impossible to substantiate his claim to have worked as an extra in THE BIRTH OF A NATION. He did act in a number of Griffith-produced

Erich von Stroheim during the editing of FOOLISH WIVES (*released in 1922*).

subjects for Mutual, however, and often assisted the prominent stage director John Emerson. Griffith's method of working soon became von Stroheim's model, and under "the master" he worked on INTOLERANCE and HEARTS OF THE WORLD. Von Stroheim began to have some success as an actor, specializing in the portrayal of fiendish Huns in war-propaganda films, but such roles disappeared with the Armistice.

At that moment he was able to convince Universal's Carl Laemmle to allow him to star in and direct an original script of his own. By giving Universal the script for nothing, taking no salary as director, and accepting only $200 per week for playing the leading role, von Stroheim made the tight-fisted Laemmle an irresistible offer. He also seems to have appealed to "Uncle Carl's" gambler's instinct and his penchant for hiring relatives and other German-speaking emigrés from the old country. Von Stroheim far exceeded the budget, but the results justified the gamble. This first film, BLIND HUSBANDS (1919), earned some $328,000 during its initial year of release, approximately six times the take of an average Universal feature.[56] Critics were also suitably impressed, and the result of this acclaim was to increase von Stroheim's leverage with Laemmle, an advantage he stretched to its breaking point on FOOLISH WIVES (1922), touted as "the first million-dollar picture." But the financial failure of FOOLISH WIVES, and increasing production problems on his next film, MERRY-GO-ROUND (1923), moved Universal's new production head, Irving Thalberg, to fire von Stroheim midway through production.

That a studio should remove a director of this caliber from "his own" picture was unprecedented, but it was nothing personal. Thalberg was able to use the firing of von Stroheim to intimidate every director in Hollywood, and it was largely von Stroheim's visibility that caused him to be used as the lightning rod in this demonstration. Von Stroheim's career went downhill from there. His next film, GREED, was taken away from him in a further storm of publicity and was virtually cut to ribbons. Now at MGM, he ran afoul of the powerful Louis B. Mayer, who threatened to blacklist him in the industry.[57] A financial success with THE MERRY WIDOW temporarily reestablished him in Hollywood, but cost overruns on THE WEDDING MARCH and incessant squabbling during production of the never-completed QUEEN KELLY ultimately destroyed his credibility.

Von Stroheim, a student of Griffith, felt that the cinema was an art form, the writer-director an artist, and the studio head, at best, a patron. Postwar Hollywood reality destroyed this fiction. After the first blush of success, he soon learned that the relationship was more accurately that of employer and employee.

Rex Ingram

If there was one director who gave Louis B. Mayer almost as much trouble as Erich von Stroheim, it was certainly Rex Ingram. The problems these two had with Mayer quickly became a major part of early Hollywood lore, but such stories have more than merely anecdotal value. When Mayer positioned himself against this pair (and, to a lesser extent, Marshall Neilan), he was asserting not just his personal authority but the authority of MGM's entire production system. Ingram and von Stroheim championed the position of freewheeling directors operating within a supportive industrial framework. Mayer (and his associates Irving Thalberg and Harry Rapf) felt the need

Rex Ingram on the set of THE ARAB, *filmed in North Africa in 1924.*

to establish a hierarchical power structure, with authority flowing down from key studio executives. There is no question as to who won this battle, but how it was waged reveals much about the position of key Hollywood filmmakers in the early and mid 1920s.

Volumes have been written about von Stroheim's troubles, but the details of Rex Ingram's career are not nearly so familiar. Like von Stroheim, Ingram was a European who arrived in America during the nickelodeon era and dabbled in other media before entering films as an actor, changing his name, and eventually directing his first film at Universal. He was born Reginald Hitchcock in Dublin in 1893, and he arrived in the United States in 1911 to study art at Yale. As Rex Hitchcock, he began acting for Edison in 1913, transferred to Vitagraph the following year, and by 1915 was working on scripts for Fox, at which point he adopted his mother's maiden name, Ingram.[58]

Unlike von Stroheim, Ingram began directing before America's entry into World War I and completed his first feature for Universal in 1916. He enlisted in the Royal Canadian Flying Corps as an aviation instructor, saw no action, but was severely injured in a crash. Making his way back to Hollywood, he was appalled to see Erich von Stroheim occupying "his" spot as a director on the Universal lot. Years later, von Stroheim remembered how uncomfortable it made him feel to have "yesterday's wonder boy," now an injured veteran in uniform, glaring at him from the sidelines the first day they met. But the pair soon became friends and found that their attitudes toward film, and the process of directing, were remarkably similar. Within a short time they were competing for the industry's accolades, with von Stroheim's FOOLISH WIVES winning the sort of attention for Universal that Ingram's THE FOUR HORSE-MEN OF THE APOCALYPSE (1921) had garnered for Metro the previous season (although the Ingram film was vastly more profitable). In 1923 the critic Tamar Lane found only four real leaders in the motion-picture industry—D. W. Griffith, Cecil B. DeMille, Marshall Neilan, and Rex Ingram.[59]

Neither Ingram nor von Stroheim was shy regarding his opinion on the nature of film art, but for Ingram, the key was always his experience at Yale. In a 1922 essay, he repeatedly compares film to painting and sculpture, refers to his days at the Yale School of Fine Arts, exalts his teacher Lee Lawrie, compares the scenario to a sculpture's armature, and equates actors with paint or clay.[60]

This vision of a director gradually shaping a film, with the contributions of other collaborators being reduced to the merely technical, is in the direct tradition of Griffith and von Stroheim. Like both of these men, Ingram preferred to avoid professionally trained actors and actresses, convinced that he could "discover" a personality and then shape it to fit. He made a star of Valentino (although who actually did the discovering is open to question), and when Valentino left him, he set out to do the same with Ramon Novarro. His wife, the actress Alice Terry, was another of his discoveries, and her passive blond beauty glides through most of Ingram's greatest films. In fact, his affection for nonprofessional actors was so great that he once listed Nanook's performance in Flaherty's film as the finest piece of screen acting he had seen.[61]

Ingram also shared with von Stroheim an obsession with atmosphere, believing that a convincing mood on the set could affect actors and audience alike. To help achieve this mood, he might ask his principals to speak to one another in French if the silent film they were making was set in France. Like von Stroheim, he would film many takes of the same scene, hoping to achieve one magical synthesis of all the elements he sought to bring out. Grant Whytock, an editor who worked for both men, says that Ingram rivaled von Stroheim in the amount of film shot and would often lose track of the vast amounts of footage. But the effect on screen was appreciated. Wrote one critic of Ingram in 1922, "He *suggests* scenes in his pictures and refuses to *label* them. In this respect he is farther advanced than most any director in the art today."[62]

Von Stroheim had to deal with Louis B. Mayer in Hollywood, but when the Metro-Goldwyn merger occurred Rex Ingram was in North Africa filming THE ARAB (1924). Thus he was able to negotiate a new contract directly with Nicholas Schenck in the New York office of the parent company, Loew's, Inc. This contract allowed him to acquire the Victorine studio in the south of France and base his operations there. More surprisingly, his films were not to carry Louis B. Mayer's name on the credits, a unique concession that infuriated the Hollywood mogul.

Working away from the studio and away from Mayer, Ingram was able to make his films according to his own standards, although there were some difficulties regarding the length of MARE NOSTRUM (1926). According to Whytock, the films were generally inexpensive enough to remain profitable, but as Mayer gradually increased his authority, MGM decided that it had little use for such working arrangements, and the contract was not renewed. Again like von Stroheim, Ingram made only one talking picture, which was scarcely distributed and soon forgotten. Failing health and a lack of interest in necessary studio politics kept him from directing again. The Victorine solution offered only a temporary answer to the creative struggles of 1920s Hollywood.

June Mathis

Many silent scenarists exercised a degree of power that extended far beyond the drafts emerging from their typewriters. Frances Marion had the ear of Mary Pickford, and the prolific C. Gardner Sullivan skewed the character of Ince releases by the sheer quantity of his own output. But the most influential screenwriter of the day was undoubtedly June Mathis, the dynamic, mystic "editorial director" whom *Photoplay* magazine called "the million dollar girl."[63]

She was born in Leadville, Colorado, in 1890 and was onstage from the age of eleven. Well known on the touring circuits in various ingenue roles, she was with the Julian Eltinge company in 1912–1913 as the only woman in the cast of *The Fascinating Widow*. When road-company business declined, she turned to writing and soon settled in New York with a place on the staff of the Metro studio. Few film writers had been able to exercise any degree of creative control in this period, when most significant producers and directors were either drafting their own scripts or isolating their writing staffs behind a bureaucratic curtain. But Mathis won the attention of Metro president Richard Rowland and soon began shaping the course of Metro releases. She had a flair for the romantic and the exotic, and frequently emphasized elements of mysticism and spiritualism in her films. In a 1917 *Moving Picture World* article, she advised prospective authors not to think about their works too long before setting them down on paper in order to prevent the ideas from being stolen by those with conscious or unconscious telepathic powers. "It all depends upon the voltage of the brain," she claimed. Mathis would never write without wearing her magical opal ring, which she claimed had brought disaster on its previous royal owners but which, democratically, was good magic for her.[64]

Inevitably, Mathis joined forces with Metro's mysterious Russian star Alla Nazimova, mistress of her own occult circle. Together they made such films as OUT OF THE FOG (1919) and THE RED LANTERN (1919), which proved too exotic for general tastes, although Mathis maintained her own commercial standing with a series of successful potboilers. Her most important film was THE FOUR HORSEMEN OF THE APOCALYPSE (1921), which she convinced Metro to produce on an elaborate and spectacular scale. Not only did she adapt the Ibáñez novel, but she also selected director Rex Ingram and was responsible for casting the relatively unknown actor Rudolph Valentino in the main role.

Benjamin Hampton notes that Mathis had "full authority" on the film and with her own staff devised a careful plan to control all aspects of production. "Efficiency

Scenario editor June Mathis in a publicity portrait taken by the Hoover Art Studios in Los Angeles.

engineering applied to films," he called it. Her contributions to the film were widely acknowledged, and a few critics took pains to note the characteristic elements of mysticism that had crept into the adaptation.[65]

Mathis, Ingram, and Valentino then made THE CONQUERING POWER, an adaptation of Balzac's *Eugénie Grandet*, but Valentino soon quarreled with his director and aligned himself with Mathis, with whom he shared an interest in the occult. She would be the most significant creative figure in his career. He appeared in the CAMILLE she wrote for Nazimova, then signed with Famous Players–Lasky. Mathis, too, had outgrown Metro. For a time she followed Valentino to Famous Players–Lasky, where she scripted BLOOD AND SAND (1922), one of his greatest successes. But THE YOUNG RAJAH (1922), a steamy travesty of Hindu mysticism, was ridiculed by critics and damaged Valentino's career.

Mathis was now signed by the desperate Joe Godsol, who appointed her editorial director of Goldwyn Pictures. She was to set studio production policy, pass on contracts, and involve herself personally with the most important films. Soon the Goldwyn studio was populated by such directors as King Vidor, Victor Seastrom,

Marshall Neilan, and Erich von Stroheim, but its financial status only grew less secure. Mathis did take a hand in cutting von Stroheim's GREED, which she had personally approved for production, but her suggestions were bypassed in the final version.[66]

What occupied most of her time was the protracted filming of BEN-HUR (1926). Kevin Brownlow, who calls Mathis "one of the most important figures in the industry," has detailed the production of BEN-HUR, with emphasis on her responsibility for launching it on the wrong foot. She ordered the entire production to be shot in Italy, but this time adequate preparations were never executed. Her director of choice, Charles Brabin, shot reels of useless footage and refused the suggestions she made when she journeyed to Rome to oversee production. Ultimately the Goldwyn company was absorbed in the Metro-Goldwyn-Mayer merger, and the new executives fired Brabin, Mathis, and George Walsh (her choice to play Ben-Hur), scrapped all the footage, and returned the production to Hollywood.[67]

Mathis emerged from this debacle relatively unscathed and became editorial director at First National. Here she concentrated on stories for Colleen Moore and Corinne Griffith, comedies and melodramas such as WE MODERNS (1926), THE MARRIAGE WHIRL (1925), and IRENE (1926). Although none of these films had the impact of the best of her early work, Mathis was able to demonstrate her successful supervision of a major studio's entire output, personally handling some of the most important titles. Perhaps Frances Marion's filmography is more impressive, but June Mathis was the only screenwriter ever to achieve this degree of control.

On 26 July 1927 Mathis was in New York with her mother, attending a performance of *The Squall*. Near the end of the final act, she suddenly began screaming, "Oh mother, I'm dying, I'm dying!" and was rushed out of the theater to an adjacent alley. A doctor immediately pronounced her dead, but her disbelieving mother tried for an hour to revive her, massaging her wrists and begging her to speak as she lay in the street outside the Forty-fourth Street Theatre. In 1926 her friend and discovery Rudolph Valentino had also died on a visit to New York. He was interred in June Mathis' vault in Los Angeles, where she would join him less than a year later.[68]

Robert Flaherty

Robert Flaherty completed only two nonfiction features in this period, hardly a prolific output. But these two films, NANOOK OF THE NORTH (1922) and MOANA (1926), were the most significant works of their kind yet produced by an American filmmaker. With NANOOK, Flaherty succeeded for the first time in winning public support and critical accolades for what eventually came to be called "documentary cinema." The term itself did not yet exist. When Robert E. Sherwood heaped praise on the film in *The Best Moving Pictures of 1922–23*, he grouped it by necessity with "travel pictures" and "scenics."[69]

In fact, it was not until MOANA appeared in 1926 that the word "documentary" was first applied to such films, when John Grierson, writing anonymously in the *New York Sun*, referred offhandedly to the film's "documentary value." The following year Flaherty's wife, Frances, a significant collaborator in all of his film work, wrote that "pictures of life, of the drama inherent in life, are documentary and philosophic,"

Robert Flaherty in Samoa during the filming of MOANA *(released 1926). The camera is an Akeley.*

thus neatly identifying this style with Robert Flaherty's own highly interpretive approach to it. One could argue that the very word "documentary" was coined to describe the cinema of Robert Flaherty.[70]

Legend has it that none of this might have happened if not for the dangerously flammable qualities of nitrate film. According to this story, Flaherty had returned from the Arctic in 1916 with twenty-five thousand feet of exposed negative, the raw material for a film on Eskimo life, which was assembled in the traditional travelogue manner. A work print was struck and shown to limited audiences, but the negative was accidentally destroyed when Flaherty carelessly dropped a cigarette on it. He was thus forced to begin all over again on another expedition but this time with the lessons of the first experiment behind him.[71]

The audiences on which Flaherty had tested his first Eskimo film were attuned to the usual Burton Holmes travelogue, a home-movie style ramble in which the Western adventurer situates himself in exotic climes. "People were polite, but I could see that what interest they took in the film was the friendly one of wanting to see where *I* had been and what *I* had done. That wasn't what I wanted at all. I wanted to show the Innuit," Flaherty wrote in his diary while at work on the new version of the film.[72]

To the industry's great surprise, this personalizing of a nonfiction subject proved innovative and exciting, especially when combined with the stark drama of the Northern landscape. NANOOK OF THE NORTH was irresistible, and Robert E. Sherwood immediately recognized why:

> Nanook was the center of all the action, and on him was the camera focussed. In this way Mr. Flaherty achieved the personal touch. Another producer, attempting to do the same thing, would have been content to photograph, "A Native Spearing Fish" or "Another Native Building His Igloo." Moreover, he would have kept himself in the foreground, as is the way of all travelogue rollers. Mr. Flaherty makes Nanook his hero (*The Best Moving Pictures of 1922–23*, p. 4).

While foregrounding his hero, however, Flaherty opened himself to charges of ethnographic manipulation. It soon became clear that he had altered the cultural and historical context to suit his dramatic purposes. He reconstructed certain events and occasionally fabricated others entirely. Flaherty's biographer Arthur Calder-Marshall goes so far as to call NANOOK "a costume picture."[73] Flaherty worked this way in order to capture what he felt was the essence of a culture, trying to reveal it to film audiences in its "unspoiled" state. On the other hand, Hugh Gray, in a thoughtful defense of Flaherty's methods years later, supported the filmmaker's conclusion that "one often has to distort a thing in order to catch its true spirit."[74]

Flaherty's methods were remarkably similar to those of the photographer Edward S. Curtis, whose twenty-volume series *The North American Indian* was published from 1907 to 1930. Both men felt the obligation to record on film images of indigenous North American cultures already "corrupted" by contact with European society and both employed a certain amount of dramatic license to achieve their ends. In fact, Curtis' proto-ethnographic film about the Kwakiutl Indians, IN THE LAND OF THE HEAD HUNTERS (1914), is said to have been a direct influence on Flaherty and NANOOK.[75] Both men would be attacked by traditional ethnographers for this same reason, but it is important to remember that Flaherty and Curtis were poets, not scientists. The truth they reveal lies not in the inviolability of their details but in the creative interpretation of the material that they present to their viewers. As Paul Rotha said of NANOOK:

> It brought alive the fundamental issue of life in the sub-arctic—the struggle for food—with such imaginatively chosen shots and with such a sin-

cere feeling for the community interests of these people, that it suggested far greater powers of observation than the plain description offered by other naturalistic photographers (*Documentary Film*, p. 82).

Samuel Goldwyn

In a neglected 1956 monograph, Richard Griffith, then curator of the Museum of Modern Art Film Library, laid out the case for Samuel Goldwyn as an overlooked auteur. Griffith argued that Goldwyn's hand was clearly visible in each of his films and that, between 1922 and 1956, he had been the most prominent and successful of independent Hollywood producers. Operating without investors and without partners ("When you have a partner you don't need an enemy," Goldwyn once said), he exercised complete control over the handful of features issued by his studio each year.[76] Avoiding the system of mass production employed by Thomas H. Ince, Goldwyn retained the principle of direct producer involvement that he had observed when he first entered motion pictures in 1913. This approach, which allowed both flexibility and eccentricity, was later developed by David O. Selznick and, in a different context, Walt Disney. But it was Goldwyn who demonstrated that it was possible to break with the big-studio method of production, maintain a personal vision, and still operate in an efficient and profitable manner.

Goldwyn was born Schmuel Gelbfisz in Warsaw in 1879, and anglicized the family name to Goldfish when he arrived in Birmingham, England, a dozen years later. He came to America in 1896, eventually amassing a tidy fortune in the glove business. In 1913 he became one of the original partners in the Jesse L. Lasky Feature Play Company. Goldfish was in charge of the financial end of the new concern, which soon became one of the most successful early feature producers. When it merged with Adolph Zukor's Famous Players Film Company in 1916, Goldfish became the new board chairman and Zukor the president. But Goldfish was unable to share authority with Zukor, and at the latter's instigation he was voted out of the company three months later, netting some $900,000 for his interest.[77]

Later the same year he entered into a partnership with Edgar Selwyn, and their two names yielded the corporate name Goldwyn Pictures (according to Terry Ramsaye, industry wags suggested the name "Selfish Pictures" instead). Operating out of East Coast studios, the Goldwyn Company invested heavily in theater and opera stars such as Maxine Elliott, Geraldine Farrar, and Mary Garden, a move that earned it the nickname "Goldwyn's old maids' home" when audiences rejected these transplanted stars. By this time Goldfish had legally appropriated the Goldwyn name for himself to become Samuel Goldwyn.[78]

The company prospered on the strength of some Mabel Normand and Will Rogers pictures but was unable to survive Goldwyn's "Eminent Authors" project, an attempt to inject literary values into the studio's output by signing a number of popular novelists and short-story writers. Goldwyn never seemed to give up on this idea and later expended a considerable sum in bringing the Belgian symbolist Maurice Maeterlinck to Hollywood, with equally dismal results. "That Morrie. I trusted him, and he wrote me a story about bees," Goldwyn is reported to have said.[79]

These steps may have been taken for publicity purposes, but probably Goldwyn sincerely felt that his films could benefit from the work of serious writers. As he told a pier reporter in 1925, upon leaving for a European trip (where one of his goals was to sign Sigmund Freud to a Hollywood contract), "Professor Freud will inject into pictures truth and reality, where now we have only tinsel and shadows."[80]

In 1919 one of Goldwyn's partners, Joe Godsol, induced the Du Pont interests to invest heavily in the Goldwyn Company. Combined with backing from the Chase Bank and the Central Union Trust, this created a pool of $7 million for corporate expansion, which was used to purchase and overhaul the Triangle studio in Culver City, California. This lot would later become the longtime home of MGM. Unfortunately, a coup engineered by the same interests ultimately bounced Goldwyn from the company in 1922. He retired briefly to Great Neck, Long Island, where he issued a rather fatuous "autobiography" consisting of a series of vignettes praising everyone in the industry except Joe Godsol.[81]

In 1923 he began fully independent production, free of partners and investors. He made a few ethnic comedies (the POTASH AND PERLMUTTER series, 1923–1926), a lengthy string of Ronald Colman vehicles, often co-starring Vilma Banky, and at least

Samuel Goldwyn flanked by stars Mabel Normand and Geraldine Farrar, with members of the Eminent Authors and other notables at the Goldwyn studio, 1920.

two highly regarded adaptations, STELLA DALLAS (1925) and THE WINNING OF BARBARA WORTH (1926). Although George Bernard Shaw once quipped that he wouldn't sign with Goldwyn because Goldwyn cared only about art, whereas Shaw cared only about money, Goldwyn's twenties productions in fact seldom attained the artistic. He took care to hire the most talented workers in the industry, including directors George Fitzmaurice and Henry King, screenwriter Frances Marion, and cinematographers Arthur Miller and George Barnes. From each, he extracted work of uniformly high caliber, often through outrageous exertions on his own part. But all too often, everyone seemed to be straining, working entirely too hard to achieve the effects Goldwyn hoped to see on screen. Goldwyn made films "like a man shaking a slot machine," said Ben Hecht, who worked with him often enough to know.[82]

It was during the sound period that Goldwyn produced the bulk of the films that confirmed his reputation and were most responsible for his being awarded the Presidential Medal of Freedom in 1971.[83] But his decision to turn his back on big-studio production methods and operate as an independent for the balance of a long and successful career must stand as his most significant contribution to the industry itself.

James Cruze

James Cruze was one of the highest-salaried directors of silent pictures, and many of his films were among the most popular of the postwar decade. Writing in 1926, Terry Ramsaye casually grouped him with D. W. Griffith as one of only two "major directors" at Famous Players–Lasky. But within a few years, all such acclaim began to sour. Cruze soon lost not only his lucrative contract but his critical standing as well. By 1939, Lewis Jacobs, in a lengthy discussion of Cruze and his films, announced that he was "a minor figure whose talents were unrealized" and a director who had been "unable to make any valuable contribution to American film."[84]

Meteoric reputations are not uncommon among silent-era directors, but few have fallen with such finality as that of James Cruze. Is this a career in need of rediscovery, or did an inflated reputation simply achieve its inevitable collapse?

At the present moment, Cruze's reputation is largely bound up with that of his best-known film, THE COVERED WAGON (1923). During the twenties, however, he was initially applauded for a series of lively and unpretentious Wallace Reid and Fatty Arbuckle films made between 1918 and 1921. In commercial terms, these pictures capped Reid's career as a matinee idol and helped Arbuckle move successfully from shorts to features. But the rise of both stars ended abruptly, and in revamping the script of a proposed Arbuckle vehicle to suit Will Rogers, Cruze hit upon a new style of satirical comedy, one that he would continue to develop over the next several years. ONE GLORIOUS DAY (1922) was the story of a mild-mannered professor temporarily possessed by a mischievous spirit sent from Valhalla. What might have been a straightforward situation comedy was shaped by Cruze into a canny satire of politics and spiritualism, replete with expressionistic touches influenced by THE CABINET OF DR. CALIGARI.[85] Audiences resisted the film, but critical support moved Cruze further in the direction of satirical comedy. His RUGGLES OF RED GAP (1923) and MERTON OF THE MOVIES (1924) established him as a master of this form before it was taken over by the Lubitsch school. Cruze adopted the expressionistic theater staging of BEGGAR ON HORSEBACK (1923) for his film version

James Cruze during the filming of THE COVERED WAGON (1923).

and continued with this style in HOLLYWOOD (1923), a much-praised satire of life in the young movie colony. Cruze's current reputation might be different if he were more identified with films like these, but when Lubitsch's work captured the public's imagination, Cruze's efforts were forgotten. Today, nearly all these films have disappeared, and it is impossible to judge Cruze's real contribution to the genre.

With the Reid and Arbuckle films also out of sight, Cruze's reputation rested on a handful of outdoor epics that followed the success of THE COVERED WAGON, namely

THE PONY EXPRESS (1925), OLD IRONSIDES (1926), and the talkie SUTTER'S GOLD (1935).

THE PONY EXPRESS and SUTTER'S GOLD have had few defenders, and their occasional screenings do little to help Cruze's image. OLD IRONSIDES, considered a costly flop on release, was still being damned a decade later as "a dismal failure" which made it clear that "his success with THE COVERED WAGON was a flash in the pan." Lewis Jacobs may have been reflecting here the hostility of the moment, but his harsh assessment of OLD IRONSIDES seems hard to justify in light of recent screenings.[86]

This leaves us with THE COVERED WAGON, a film whose value, even at the time of its initial release, was the subject of some debate. Jesse Lasky had acquired the rights to Emerson Hough's *Saturday Evening Post* serial and felt that he could revive the Western genre by shifting the emphasis from stars (like William S. Hart) to scenery and situations. Accordingly, he authorized Cruze to take a large unit on location and to expend considerable sums in capturing a degree of physical authenticity previously unknown in Westerns. Largely thanks to the camerawork of Karl Brown, who photographed most of Cruze's silent films, THE COVERED WAGON set a visual standard for Western epics to come and was the dominant critical and commercial success of the season. Victor Freeburg's *Pictorial Beauty on the Screen*, perhaps the most sophisticated analysis of film aesthetics until then published in America, was dedicated to Cruze that year, and a still from THE COVERED WAGON served as the frontispiece. Many were impressed by the palpable authenticity of props and locations in this pageant of American history, but details of the action were criticized by a knowledgeable few, while others found the casting of J. Warren Kerrigan and Lois Wilson in the leads a serious mistake. But the film's very success in launching a cycle of epic Westerns soon began to cut into its reputation. John Ford's THREE BAD MEN (1926), for example, seems far more satisfactory by any possible standard, especially when compared with the truncated prints of THE COVERED WAGON available today. Although Kevin Brownlow defends the film for its documentary value, George Fenin and William K. Everson in *The Western* more accurately reflect current opinion when they berate it for being "slow and pedestrian, often crudely faked," and "of negligible creative value."[87]

When Cruze was unable to repeat its success, his standing at the studio began to fall, and he especially bore the brunt of the costly failure of OLD IRONSIDES. In addition, he was the sort of director who preferred to work with a small unit, loyal primarily to himself. As in the case of von Stroheim and Marshall Neilan, this approach did not suit the developing production practices of the studios. When Cruze's contract was dropped in 1928, Paramount production chief B. P. Schulberg issued the following terse explanation: "The day of the individual in pictures is over." [88]

Ernst Lubitsch

Before 1914 America had been the world's most important film market, but by the close of World War I it was the most important film producer as well. The French and the Italians were no longer viable as international competitors, but even before the Armistice, a potential new rival had arisen. Backed by the Alfred Hugenberg

Ernst Lubitsch (in well) and Mary Pickford are visited on the set of ROSITA *(1923) by her United Artists partners Charles Chaplin and Douglas Fairbanks.*

fortune and masterminded by impresario Paul Davidson, the German film industry had pulled itself out of the cultural wreckage that hung over Berlin in 1918. In a dramatic turnaround, German films were sent off to conquer foreign capitals so recently denied to German troops.

It was not until 1920 that this wave was allowed to break on American shores. But when the presentation of MADAME DUBARRY (renamed PASSION) at New York's giant Capitol Theatre successfully overcame the firmly entrenched anti-German hysteria among American audiences, the domestic market once more seemed vulnerable to foreign infiltration. This was an intolerable and utterly surprising development for Hollywood. Reporting on the vast crowds being turned away from the theater by extra policemen summoned for the occasion, the *New York Times* marveled that "none of the hostility that has greeted attempts to revive German opera and drama" was still in evidence. The success of DUBARRY was matched a few months later by that of DECEPTION (ANNA BOLEYN) and one or two others. But not all German films were greeted so warmly. THE GOLEM (1920) flopped with American audiences, while THE CABINET OF DR. CALIGARI (1919) inspired picket lines of disgruntled war veterans. Only those films directed by Ernst Lubitsch seemed surefire successes, and a race to lock up Lubitsch, his films, and his star, Pola Negri, soon became the obsession of Hollywood dealmakers.[89]

Lubitsch's first American employer was Mary Pickford, for whom he directed a Spanish costume romance called ROSITA (1923). Warmly received by critics but generally ignored by audiences, it was later suppressed by Pickford, who hated the film, hated Lubitsch, and hated the whole experience of working with the man. Pickford had expected to be well served by Europe's greatest director and was unwilling and unable to bend herself to his wishes. She, after all, was producing this picture. "He was very self-assertive, but then all little men are," Pickford told Kevin Brownlow decades later.[90]

Lubitsch had been trying to get himself to America for years. "'Hollywood by Christmas' is his banner cry," reported an interviewer who observed him on the set in Berlin in 1922.[91] Now he appeared to have ruined his big opportunity, antagonized one of the world's most powerful stars, and sullied his box-office reputation. But Lubitsch was a survivor. In a dazzling change of pace, he dropped the large historical canvas that had brought him his greatest success since his days with Max Reinhardt and turned to the comedy of manners.

On his first visit to America, in 1922, Lubitsch confided to Peter Milne his "amazement" over Cecil B. DeMille's handling of minute details of characterization, hardly more than touches, in FORBIDDEN FRUIT (1922). Milne, who felt that the acclaim for Lubitsch's German films was somewhat excessive, noted in his book *Motion Picture Directing* that the strength of Lubitsch's films, at the time, lay in their handling of mass action and that Lubitsch's concern with DeMille's "touches," while a step in the right direction, seemed quite out of character. In fact, the remark was prescient.[92]

Moving from Pickford to the small Warner Bros. studio, Lubitsch quickly produced a series of films, including THE MARRIAGE CIRCLE (1924), KISS ME AGAIN (1925), and LADY WINDERMERE'S FAN (1925), which redefined sophisticated American screen comedy. Early efforts in this genre by James Cruze and others were forgotten, and for many critics, DeMille himself was "swept aside" by a man with more style and better taste.[93]

The films were characterized by clever bits of business, soon referred to as "Lubitsch touches," which illuminated character or situation and cast ironic (never sentimental) reflection on the action. Threatened with a palace revolt, Adolphe Menjou in FORBIDDEN PARADISE (1924) reaches for his hip—and draws out a checkbook to quell the disturbance. In the same film, Pola Negri surreptitiously moves a footstool into position so as to better plant a kiss on handsome Rod La Rocque. That these touches were often associated with aggressive female sexuality only added to their mild titillation. While many critics and historians to this day insist that Lubitsch's new style had its roots in Chaplin's A WOMAN OF PARIS (1923), anyone seeing that heavy, German-influenced exercise will find such a claim difficult to credit.[94]

It should be noted that Lubitsch was not an easy director to work for. He planned out every shot, every gesture, far in advance of shooting, and set a pattern for Alfred Hitchcock in his subjugation of actors. No one ever won an Oscar for acting in a Lubitsch picture. All the performances were his own, and when the time came to edit his films, they could be assembled in a matter of days, a feat that astounded contemporary critics.[95]

At the end of the silent period, Lubitsch returned to the historical spectacle. United with Emil Jannings for the first time since their Berlin days, he made THE PATRIOT, a tale of Czar Paul, which proved a failure with audiences but was nonetheless cited as the best picture of 1928 in the broadly based *Film Daily* critics' poll.[96] With talkies on the horizon, Lubitsch did not need to change. Sound held no terror, and the microphone only provided opportunities for more Lubitsch touches.

Irving Thalberg

Allene Talmey, in her 1927 volume of film industry profiles, says nothing about Louis B. Mayer but offers the following about his second in command, Irving Thalberg: "Out of the dulness of middle class complacency there has come an unnatural phenomenon, known in Hollywood as 'Irving Thalberg, the boy producer.' "[97] What was dull and unnatural to Talmey was Thalberg's unspectacular background, a comfortable middle-class upbringing, some education, and a professional life that left little time for personal foibles. Talmey complained that ambitious pants-pressers, junkmen, and steerage passengers all made better copy but that Thalberg knew better than any of them how to make successful pictures.

Talmey credits Thalberg with the success of THE BIG PARADE (1925), THE MERRY WIDOW (1925), and FLESH AND THE DEVIL (1927), and tries to explain how his supervision of production acted to shape these hits, working sometimes with, and sometimes against, Metro-Goldwyn-Mayer's noted writers, directors, and stars. Thalberg himself never took a credit. The general public in the 1920s knew of him largely through uncertain fan-magazine profiles that emphasized his shy charm and youth.[98] Without the traditional rags-to-riches story to cling to, they were at a loss to understand exactly what he did around the studio or how his function differed from that of his associates at MGM, Harry Rapf and Louis B. Mayer.

But those within the industry were not uncertain. They knew that Thalberg had whipped the untidy Universal lot into shape when he arrived there in 1920 and that he had masterminded the string of hits that placed the newly assembled MGM among the most profitable of Hollywood studios. In addition, he had done this by "breaking eggs": seizing authority and exerting it against procedural inertia and executive paralysis.

His most significant steps were taken at Universal. As Carl Laemmle's private secretary, the twenty-year-old Thalberg had been deposited at the West Coast studio and assigned to supervise production in concert with three other executives, Tarkington Baker, Maurice Fleckles, and Isidore Bernstein (the last two were Laemmle relatives). Since the opening of Universal City five years earlier, there had been no clear authority on the lot and no clear chain of command to Laemmle in New York. Managers and supervisors were appointed at frequent intervals, their orders undercut by cables from the East. The various production units at Universal City had once operated almost as independent outfits and had never quite been brought under unified command. Soon Thalberg had rid himself of his three associates and turned his attention to the most powerful of the lot's independent spirits, Erich von Stroheim.[99]

FOOLISH WIVES was already in production when Thalberg arrived, so there was little he could do but watch von Stroheim run the budget far over the original projections. When the time came to launch the next von Stroheim picture, MERRY-GO-ROUND, Thalberg kept the director from also acting in it, thus implicitly threatening to remove him from the picture if things went awry. He also sent spies to report on daily progress and kept a careful eye on rising expenditures and censorable rushes.[100] After $220,000 had been spent and only a small fraction of the film com-

Irving Thalberg in his office at Universal City, 1922.

pleted, Thalberg removed von Stroheim, brought in another director, and quickly completed the project.

There are two items of significance here. First, despite the fact that von Stroheim personally appealed to Laemmle in New York, his attempt to circumvent the studio production head failed. Laemmle threw his support behind Thalberg, thereby asserting the primacy of a central executive over any of the individual talents on the Universal lot. What has been forgotten over the years is that MERRY-GO-ROUND, as revamped under Thalberg, became a huge commercial success that validated his judgment in the eyes of the industry. If one producer could succeed in this, so could another. "The age of the director was over," remembered one startled director.[101]

In 1923 Thalberg was stolen away from Laemmle by Louis B. Mayer, who gave him a similar position at his studio on Mission Road. Within a year the MGM merger had taken place, and the "boy producer" found himself with a tremendous and somewhat nightmarish responsibility—supervising the efforts of all the merged companies. There was no guarantee that anyone could hold these disparate egos together. Professional and personal rivalries, and the problems of fusing the merged organizations, were all laid at Thalberg's door. He had to contend with such willful figures as Neilan, Seastrom, Vidor, and von Stroheim, establish a central authority, stay out of Mayer's way, and not miss a beat in the release schedule.

Backed when necessary by Mayer's strong-arm tactics, Thalberg accomplished all this within a single season. He learned to accommodate Vidor, fired Neilan and von Stroheim, and seemingly charmed the rest into submission. This last element is hard to quantify, but those who worked with Thalberg still seem in awe of his taste, intelligence, and personal magnetism. The section on Thalberg in Kevin Brownlow's *The Parade's Gone By . . .* consists mainly of a series of tributes from his old employees so lavish as to approach hagiography.[102]

Thalberg was not infallible. He fired Mauritz Stiller while he was directing Greta Garbo in THE TEMPTRESS (1926), and the result was the only Garbo picture of the period to lose money. He dragged his feet on the introduction of sound for so long that despite MGM's eventual success with the medium, rival studios had already seized a large share of the market. But the legend remained. Thalberg died in 1936, and the following year the Academy of Motion Picture Arts and Sciences named a special award after him, "given each year for the most consistent high level of production achievement by an individual producer, based on pictures he has personally produced during the preceding year." Some years, they just cannot bring themselves to award one.[103]

F. W. Murnau

"The camera is the director's sketching pencil," F. W. Murnau wrote in 1928. "It should be as mobile as possible to catch every passing mood, and it is important that the mechanics of the cinema should not be interposed between the spectator and the picture." Long before Alexandre Astruc, Murnau was aware of the principle of the *caméra stylo*. He articulated the doctrine of the long take, and seemed to recoil from the lavish studio fabrications that marked the early days of the German expressionist film. While other directors working in Hollywood, even von Stroheim or Lubitsch, built their work around scenarios of substance, Murnau approached his art from

F. W. Murnau in a Paramount publicity portrait issued before the release of TABU
(1931).

another direction. With the camera as his pencil, he wrote the essential elements of
his films directly on the screen.[104]

Murnau was brought to America by William Fox in 1926. He made three films for
the Fox Company, none of which was commercially successful. Yet the impact of his
method of working changed the entire direction of the American cinema in this
period. Hollywood had absorbed and Americanized such talents as Lubitsch, Seastrom, and Benjamin Christensen, but Murnau proved to be the one European
filmmaker of the era who succeeded in changing Hollywood.

Murnau's THE LAST LAUGH (1924) had been a great critical success in America,
though a box-office catastrophe ("The last laugh was on me" for having distributed
the film, quipped Universal's Carl Laemmle). William Fox, eager to enhance his
industry position and be seen as the peer of Adolph Zukor, signed Murnau to a
luxurious four-year, four-picture contract. The salary began at $125,000 and rose in
annual increments to $200,000. Fox had acquired a German director as costly as
Lubitsch, although without that earlier import's box-office record.[105]

But in signing Murnau, Fox had not just bought himself a German director; he had
acquired a substantial segment of the German film industry as well. For the first film,

SUNRISE (1927), a script came in from Carl Mayer, scriptwriter of THE CABINET OF DR. CALIGARI and THE LAST LAUGH. To build the sets, designer Rochus Gliese was imported, and so were Herman Bing and Edgar G. Ulmer, who acted as Murnau's assistants and intermediaries. Even one of the film's American cinematographers, Charles Rosher, had just spent a year with Murnau in Germany.

A vast city set was constructed in diminishing perspective on the Fox lot. Inside the stages was built a great marsh, with the camera suspended from tracks in the studio ceiling. As it moved with actor George O'Brien through the bullrushes, Karl Struss, Rosher's associate, had to hang from the ceiling with one eye glued to the inverted image in his Bell & Howell viewfinder. Most elaborate of all was the village set, constructed at Lake Arrowhead. "I crawled over it for a day and a half," remembered director Clarence Brown. "It was wonderful."[106] Brown did not even work for the Fox Company. Directors, designers, and cameramen from all over the industry trooped through Murnau's sets and stages. SUNRISE became a demonstration project of German film techniques applied with Hollywood budgetary resources.

Soon even those directors most closely associated with cozy Americana subjects, men like Brown, Frank Borzage, and John Ford, had absorbed the lessons of Murnau and his style. Ford actually shot much of FOUR SONS (1928) right on the old SUNRISE village sets. Too costly to be profitable, too arty to be popular, SUNRISE made no money but left a deep mark on the final few years of silent film in Hollywood. Shadows, camera movements, artfully stylized settings and gestures, all became the mark of true film art in Hollywood during 1927 and 1928. The studios had flirted with, and rejected, the hard-edged expressionism of the CALIGARI tradition a few years earlier, but from Murnau they learned that it was possible to style and design "the real world," and to match their own predilection for plastic realism with European notions of gestural and architectural stylization.[107] Only when sound changed the rules did Hollywood filmmakers begin to let go of this new style.

Murnau failed to benefit from the impact of his work. His next film, THE FOUR DEVILS (1928), caused little stir, and his final effort for Fox, OUR DAILY BREAD, shot largely on a farm outside Pendleton, Oregon, in 1928, was not even released in the form he left it. Remarkable mainly for its sensuous tracking shots sweeping through fields of wheat, CITY GIRL (as it was called on its release in 1930) at least moved Murnau off the back lot again. When he broke with Fox, he teamed with Robert Flaherty, a pairing that some critics damned as a mismatch of documentarist and expressionist.[108] But the Murnau-dominated film that emerged, TABU (1931), remains the last great achievement of the silent cinema.

Josef von Sternberg

In one sense, the achievements of Josef von Sternberg should properly be discussed in a later volume of this series. His films with Marlene Dietrich, his stylized use of dialogue, and his ultimate fall from favor all postdate the silent era. Yet von Sternberg occupies a significant place in the history of this period as well, insofar as his career reflects the primary contradictions built into the developing studio system: how to balance the requisites of an essentially personal style with the demands of industrial mass production.

Von Sternberg was the most self-consciously artistic of all Hollywood's silent directors, one who sneered at stars and producers and affected eccentric habits of dress and decorum. Apparently a large part of this was mere posing. According to one often-quoted source, he first grew his moustache because it made him look more "terrible," and therefore more noticeable. The first film he directed, THE SALVATION HUNTERS (1925), was a grim exposition of life on a dredge, clearly intended to outrage its viewers by exceeding even GREED in ashcan realism. In later years the director was often uneasy about acknowledging this heavy, graceless exercise, and when asked to speak before a screening in New York in 1954 he said, "I don't know why I should introduce this film since I made it to introduce me."[109]

Produced for $5,000, THE SALVATION HUNTERS succeeded in catching the attention of Chaplin and Pickford and won for itself a place on the United Artists release schedule. According to von Sternberg, the film had reached the screen of Chaplin's private projection room following the bribing of his household staff.[110] Critical response to the picture was wildly mixed, but it did lead directly to a contract at Metro-Goldwyn-Mayer. Von Sternberg began the direction of two films there, but the first was completely redone by another director, while von Sternberg walked off the second after only a few days of shooting.

Since the studio system was not adapting very well to Chaplin's discovery, the comedian offered a project of his own. Von Sternberg would direct Edna Purviance in a story of life among the fisherfolk, THE WOMAN OF THE SEA (1926). But after one preview, Chaplin shelved the picture, and it was never seen again. Mary Pickford then set von Sternberg to work on a story for her, but when he returned with the outline for BACKWASH, the tale of a poor blind girl living in the slums of industrial Pittsburgh, that project also dissolved.

Von Sternberg had been able to attract attention with a personal film of "horrible" distinction but had not been able to turn this success into the basis of a future career. Not only had he failed at MGM, but his friends at United Artists had proven less than reliable. Finally, he was reduced to working at Paramount in a vaguely defined capacity, submitting story ideas and directing bits and pieces of other people's films. Then, one fortunate day, the direction of a new gangster film, UNDERWORLD (1927), was taken away from Arthur Rosson and handed to von Sternberg. This time he was prepared.[111]

In the four silent films he directed for Paramount in 1927 and 1928, von Sternberg was finally able to resolve the tensions between his own demands and those of his employer. Von Sternberg was happy to tackle a commercial subject like this because he was prepared to ignore those elements of plot and locale which made it valuable to Paramount. What interested him was happening elsewhere: mood, theme, and characterization. "I'm sort of a poet," he announced later, an uncharacteristically blunt admission.[112]

UNDERWORLD created a vogue for gangster films that lasted well into the sound era, and it achieved a financial success that assured von Sternberg's ability to work with relative freedom on the pictures that followed. A completely romanticized view of crime and criminals, the film was attacked by some for its technical inaccuracies and amoral perspective, a type of criticism that would increase over the next decade. But UNDERWORLD set the pattern for later von Sternberg essays into exotic worlds, foreign and domestic. Later, with Dietrich, he would channel this approach through the personality of one star, but the roots of his sensuous, ambiguous screen style lie here—along with the seeds of later critical problems.

Josef von Sternberg with Mae Murray (center) while he was still directing THE
MASKED BRIDE *at MGM, 1925.*

In the 1930s many critics, especially those on the left, felt that von Sternberg's
work suffered from "bad montage and an amazing ignorance of the moving forces
behind human behavior and social reality."[113] To which he might have replied, as he
did many years later to Kevin Brownlow:

> When I made UNDERWORLD I was not a gangster, nor did I know any-
> thing about gangsters. I knew nothing about China when I made *Shang-
> hai Express* [1932]. These are not authentic. I do not value the fetish for
> authenticity. I have no regard for it. On the contrary, the illusion of
> reality is what I look for, not reality itself. There is nothing authentic
> about my pictures. Nothing at all. There isn't a single authentic thing (*The
> Parade's Gone By* . . . , p. 202).

In an especially notorious attack, the critic-filmmaker John Grierson announced,
"When a director dies he becomes a photographer."[114] But perhaps it was to be
expected that the director of DRIFTERS (1929) would hardly be in sympathy with the
man who made THE DOCKS OF NEW YORK (1928).

9

The Stars

During the nickelodeon era, the star system had rapidly established itself in the American motion-picture industry. After watching the growing popularity of Florence Lawrence and Mary Pickford, Carl Laemmle lured them to his IMP Company with greater salaries and the promise of wide publicity. He was not alone. Soon other producers had entered the star search, working actively through fan magazines and other promotional media to familiarize audiences with their players. Favorite actors and actresses, firmly identified with their employers' corporate trademarks, were used to help establish product loyalty. Thus, a fan-magazine popularity poll published in October 1914 was careful to list the appropriate studio along with each star:

1. Earle Williams (Vitagraph)
2. Clara Kimball Young (Vitagraph)
3. Mary Pickford (Famous Players)
4. J. Warren Kerrigan (Universal)
5. Mary Fuller (Universal)
6. Marguerite Clayton (Essanay)
7. Arthur Johnson (Lubin)
8. Alice Joyce (Kalem)
9. Carlyle Blackwell (Alco)
10. Francis X. Bushman (Essanay)[1]

At the very beginning of the feature-picture era nearly the entire roster of top stars had been developed from within the industry, basically holdovers from the one- and two-reelers of nickelodeon days. In 1915 Harry Aitken tried to supplant this group by signing top theatrical talent for the new Triangle Film Corporation. The experiment failed, but Aitken did establish extremely high salary levels for top performers, figures that Adolph Zukor had to match when he began assembling a new collection of stars at Famous Players.[2]

Zukor's experience with Mary Pickford had taught him that one top star could carry an entire season's output of mediocre releases. By signing most of the stars in

Earle Williams, according to one survey the most popular star in films at the beginning of the feature picture era, in an advertisement for Arrow Collars (Motion Picture Magazine, April 1917, inside back cover).

Hollywood, Zukor could drive his competitors out of business and dictate terms to the nation's exhibitors. The result of even his partial success was to frighten theater owners into forming the First National Exhibitors Circuit in 1917, which outbid him for such stars as Chaplin and Pickford. By this time, the entire industry was "thoroughly obsessed by star frenzy," and even moderately priced performers could win highly advantageous contracts. Benjamin Hampton claims that only 5 percent of American features that year were without the protection of a star name.[3]

Another fan-magazine poll, in December 1918, showed a dramatic shift in the ranks of the most popular stars[4]:

1. Mary Pickford
2. Marguerite Clark
3. Douglas Fairbanks
4. Harold Lockwood
5. William S. Hart
6. Wallace Reid
7. Pearl White
8. Anita Stewart
9. Theda Bara
10. Francis X. Bushman

After four years, only two top stars had maintained their popularity, indicating the uncertainty of public response and the lightning changes in the industry over this period. Of course, the accuracy and impartiality of these polls are also open to question: votes could be purchased with magazine subscriptions, for example. But taken as a whole they do reflect something of the stars' changing status in the public eye. If manufacturing stars was part of the business of early cinema, managing popularity polls was a necessary business skill. All references to such polls in this chapter should be understood with this caveat firmly in mind.

To counter the increasing power of the stars, Cecil B. DeMille produced, in 1918, an "all-star" remake of THE SQUAW MAN, which in fact featured no top stars and was promoted on the strength of its story and director. He followed its success with OLD WIVES FOR NEW (1918), for which he signed a minor Triangle castoff, Gloria Swanson. The success of these films, and the phenomenal popularity of THE MIRACLE MAN (1919), another "all-star" production, damaged the notion of star supremacy and added power to certain key directors who seemed to be able to create stars or at least to do without them.

With the major studios experimenting with the "all-star" policy, and a threatened merger between Famous Players–Lasky and First National in the offing, Chaplin, Pickford, and Fairbanks decided to protect their interests by forming United Artists, while Norma Talmadge, Harold Lloyd, and a few others arranged lucrative releasing deals with other distributors. Stars below the first rank began to feel the squeeze of a saturated market.

More conservative business practices adopted during the twenties acted to freeze many stars into repeated variations of familiar routines. Performers who a decade earlier had constantly developed and expanded their roles were now content to exploit their audience-tested images. A few critics noticed and complained. "The Čapek Brothers' mechanical Robots have nothing on the creatures who are inhabiting our photoplays," carped Tamar Lane in 1923. "Heroes, heroines, vampires and villains, they are all ground out of the camera like so many frankfurters out of a butcher shop; each one of exactly the same peculiarities and consistencies as the others, each one striving his utmost to remain true to type."[5]

In 1924, *Photoplay* magazine again polled fans on their favorites, while the *Film Daily* polled exhibitors on their top box-office attractions. The results show an interesting discrepancy between stated preferences and actual support:[6]

Photoplay	*Film Daily*
1. Mary Pickford	1. Harold Lloyd
2. Douglas Fairbanks	2. Gloria Swanson
3. Gloria Swanson	3. Tom Mix
4. Pola Negri	4. Thomas Meighan
5. Thomas Meighan	5. Norma Talmadge
6. Norma Talmadge	6. Corinne Griffith
7. Harold Lloyd	Rudolph Valentino
8. Tom Mix	7. Douglas Fairbanks
	8. Colleen Moore
	Mary Pickford
	Reginald Denny

While such surveys are not directly comparable, they do indicate that some stars, such as Pola Negri, were honored more in theory than in practice. One also observes the tendency of fans in this period to rank comedy stars far lower than their box-office pull would suggest. Chaplin had not released a film for some time when these polls were taken, but even when this was not the case he typically ranks very low on such lists. Comedy stars were somehow separated from other movie actors in the minds of many fans. Note how Harold Lloyd, the industry's top box-office attraction throughout the late silent period, places lower than Thomas Meighan or Pola Negri on the *Photoplay* list. The drawing power of such low-profile favorites as Corinne Griffith and Reginald Denny is also revealing.[7]

By the end of the silent era, Wall Street analysts had quantified the value of a star and could rank this value along with any other corporate asset. In their 1927 analysis of the motion-picture industry, Halsey, Stuart and Company observed:

> Whatever change of emphasis from actor to play which the future may hold, the "stars" are today an economic necessity to the motion picture industry. In the "star" your producer gets not only a "production" value in the making of his picture, but a "trademark" value and an "insurance" value, which are very real and very potent in guaranteeing the sale of this product to the cash customers at a profit. It has been amply demonstrated that the actual salaries (not the mythical exaggeration) paid to motion picture actors, however famous, are determined by the law of supply and demand in exactly the same way as are the rewards of executives in the business world ("The Motion Picture Industry as a Basis for Bond Financing," 27 May 1927 prospectus, reprinted in Balio, *The American Film Industry*, pp. 179–180).

Charlie Chaplin

Dominating this period as both a creative force within the industry and a cultural icon of unparalleled visibility, Charlie Chaplin remains the most significant figure in the history of the silent film. The Chaplin bibliography is vast, an almost continuous stream of publications dating from his first weeks at the Mack Sennett studio and ranging across the entire critical and cultural spectrum. Chaplin and his image were appropriated by e. e. cummings, Darius Milhaud, and Fernand Léger—artists whose attention wove Chaplin into the fabric of twentieth-century culture. "The little tramp" ultimately pulled the rest of the cinema along with him, going far to legitimize a medium that even Griffith's efforts had not made entirely acceptable. There is no competitor for this mantle.[8]

Arguments as to the superiority of Chaplin's art to those of his main competitors—Keaton, for example—are outside the scope of this study and, in any case, are thoroughly developed elsewhere. But Chaplin's function as an engine, as a force powering the expansion of film as an artistic vehicle and an economic force, can never be overstated.

Born in London in 1889, Chaplin suffered a Dickensian boyhood, and this background clearly informs the search for food, shelter, and affection pictured so vividly in his films. He was onstage from the age of ten and while still a young man was a leading star of Fred Karno's company, a touring British music-hall group that brought him to America in 1913. At the end of that year he left Karno and signed a year's contract with Mack Sennett's Keystone studio for $150 per week.

Chaplin appeared in thirty-five pictures for Sennett, all released in 1914, and this so-called Keystone period remains his most controversial. Was Chaplin discovered and developed by Sennett and his Keystone "fun factory," or did he succeed despite their inability to grasp the nature of his comedy? Lewis Jacobs points to the hostility that greeted Chaplin on his arrival and "the inconsistency between his pantomimic style and Sennett's demand for slapdash, whirlwind action pictures." It is possible, as Jacobs suggests, that Sennett and his staff attempted to "alter Chaplin's delivery to conform to their standard," but if so, they gave up rather quickly, since Chaplin was allowed to direct his own pictures after the twelfth of this series, an honor not lightly bestowed.[9]

Conversely, Gilbert Seldes, in his remarkable study of popular culture *The Seven Lively Arts*, defends the Keystone period within the context of his general support for slapstick comedy. He says of Chaplin:

> That he exists at all is due to the camera and the selective genius of Mack Sennett. It is impossible to disassociate him entirely from the Keystone comedy where he began and worked wonders and learned so much. The injustice of forgetting Sennett and the Keystone when thinking of Chaplin has undermined most of the intellectual appreciation of his work, for although he was the greatest of the Keystone comedians and passed far beyond them, the first *and decisive* phase of his popularity came while he was with them, and the Keystone touch remains in all his later work, often as its most precious element (p. 42).

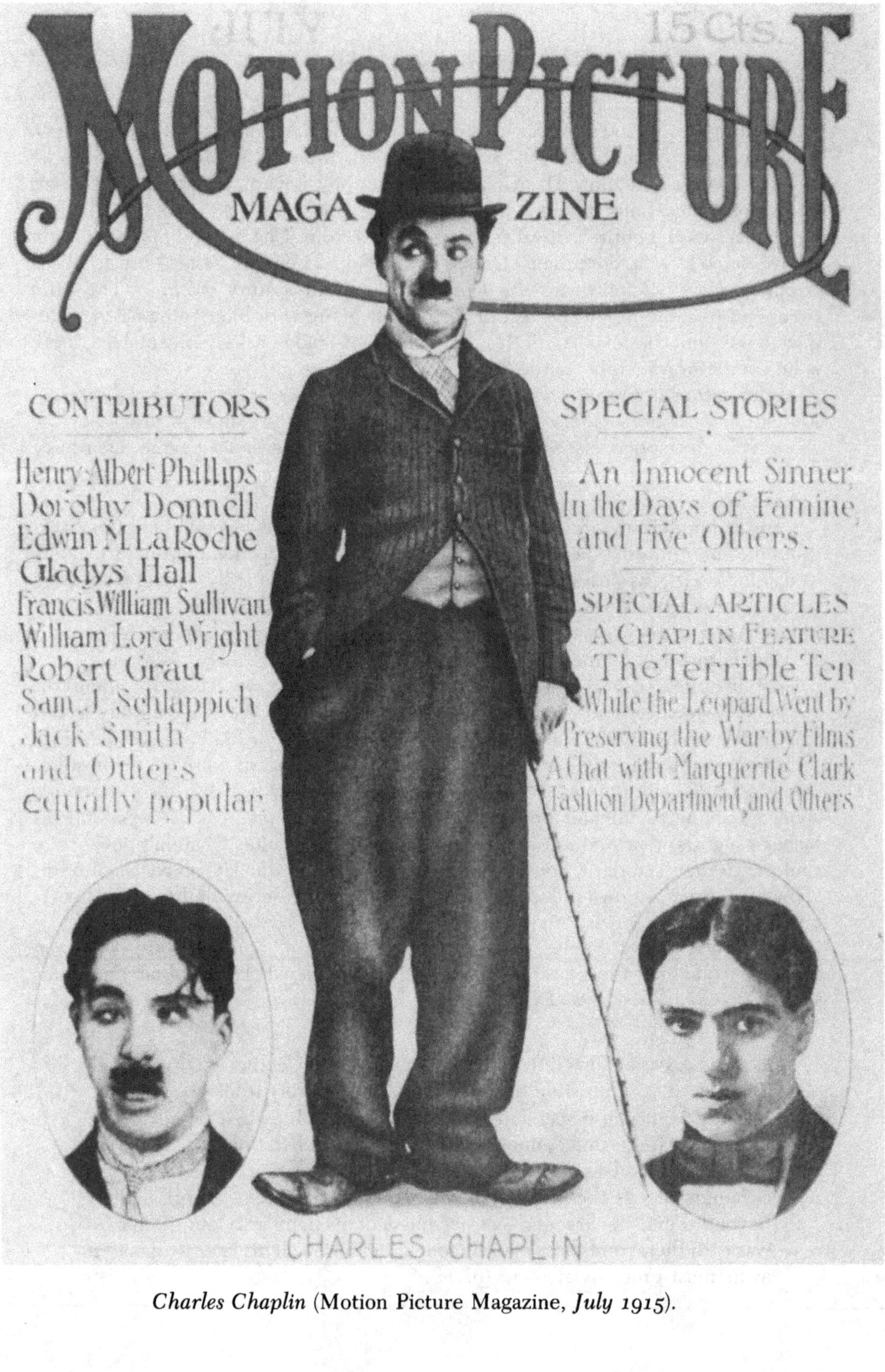

Charles Chaplin (Motion Picture Magazine, *July 1915*).

Seldes is correct in singling out the Keystone films for launching Chaplin's world-wide popularity, but his own affection for the Sennett knockabout style, wistfully compared to the *commedia dell'arte* throughout his essay, seems to blind him to the greater resonance of Chaplin's more mature films. From Keystone, Chaplin moved to the Essanay Company, with a salary of $1,250 per week, and in 1916 to Mutual, where his salary soared to $10,000 per week—figures that have traditionally been used to illustrate Chaplin's impact on the rise of star salaries in general over this period.

In these later short films, Chaplin can be seen at his finest and most characteristic. The character of "the little tramp" is fully developed, his pantomimic gestures are displayed with elegance and ease, and the working-class milieu is forcefully presented. Classic Chaplin began to appear in the bittersweet climax of THE TRAMP (1915), the gritty streetscapes of EASY STREET (1917), and the stark undertones of social criticism in THE IMMIGRANT (1917). Calling Chaplin "the man who made comedy and pathos out of working class people's lives and dreams," Robert Sklar suggests that it was a difference in class, not style, that separated Chaplin's art from that of Mack Sennett. According to this argument, the main thrust of Keystone violence was middle-class frustration, while Chaplin, picturing extremes of wealth and poverty more traditional in British culture, ultimately acts to subvert the established order tacitly accepted by Mack Sennett.[10]

As Chaplin moved into longer films, first three- and four-reel subjects, then full-length features, he began to ration his onscreen appearances. Between release of THE GOLD RUSH (1925) and THE CIRCUS (1928), he was off the screen for two and a half years (except for reissues), a gap that would further increase as his career developed. The amount of time and attention devoted to each sequence was unprecedented; even von Stroheim's working habits pale by comparison.[11]

But Chaplin was working only for himself. The drawing power of "the little tramp" was still so strong that he could afford to work at his own pace, a luxury unavailable to other filmmakers of the period. Chaplin may have been the era's most visible creative force, but he left no tradition, no disciples, and a body of work that was essentially inimitable (which is not to say that he lacked imitators). In the final sequence of THE CIRCUS the show moves on, and the character, Charlie, is left alone. His creator liked it that way.

Mary Pickford

Of the three greatest stars of the early cinema—Pickford, Fairbanks, and Chaplin—Mary Pickford remains the most elusive for modern audiences. Not only are her films generally difficult to see, but what image remains of Pickford in the public imagination is far from correct. There seems to be a vague confusion with Shirley Temple and a fixation on REBECCA OF SUNNYBROOK FARM (1917), partially the result of the film's poster art having been widely reprinted in the 1970s.[12]

James Card, Edward Wagenknecht, and other Pickford fanciers have spent much time countering this image, arguing that "the composite Pickford character was considerably less simple than she is generally supposed to have been."[13] In tracing the image of women in the American cinema, Molly Haskell, who took the trouble to view Pickford's films, saw her as not just a figure of sweetness and light but an active, aggressive young woman not unsuitable as a role model for the period:

> Even at her most arch-angelic, Pickford was no American Cinderella or Snow White whose only claim to consequence was a tiny foot or a pretty face. She was a rebel who, in the somewhat sentimental spirit of the prize pup as underdog, championed the poor against the rich, the scruffy orphans against the prissy rich kids. She was a little girl with gumption and self-reliance who could get herself out of trouble as easily as into it (*From Reverence to Rape*, p. 60).

While most of the writing on Pickford remains impressionistic and appreciative, other critics have brought out her key economic role in the development of the motion-picture industry, Benjamin Hampton being the earliest and most explicit. Hampton, who was a key figure in the 1915 negotiations among Zukor, Hodkinson, and Pickford, devotes an entire chapter of *A History of the Movies* to "The Pickford Revolution." He argues that the increasing salary demands of Pickford (and her mother) not only raised the level of star salaries and production costs but "created the precedent that soon altered the entire industry."[14]

Pickford had been working for Adolph Zukor since 1913, and as her popularity grew it became apparent that the exhibitors' desire for her films was carrying the entire Famous Players product line. In January 1915 her contract had been renegotiated to offer her $2,000 per week (double the previous salary) and 50 percent of the profits on ten films each year. But in order to meet her escalating salary demands, the following year Zukor had to set Pickford up as her own producer, creating the Artcraft label to handle her films separately from the general Paramount line. Exhibitors would pay extra for these Artcrafts, and with good reason: their star earned $10,000 per week, swallowed 50 percent of the profits, and, in effect, was Adolph Zukor's partner.[15]

Pickford's Artcraft films cost some $165,000 to $170,000 to produce, of which $125,000 represented Pickford's salary.[16] This still left enough of a budget to lavish special care on the entire series, which employed only the finest directors, writers, cameramen, and designers. Maurice Tourneur, Cecil B. DeMille, and Marshall Neilan directed most of the Artcraft films, often from scripts by Frances Marion or Jeanie Macpherson. Walter Stradling and Charles Rosher were Pickford's cameramen, and in a period when few films employed credited art directors, she used two of the finest in Hollywood, Ben Carré (for the Tourneur films) and Wilfred Buckland.

Today these seem her most accomplished works, entirely lacking in the self-importance that began to affect her later releases. While THE PRIDE OF THE CLAN (1917) and THE POOR LITTLE RICH GIRL (1917) may be better read as Tourneur pictures, her own performing abilities are stressed in the Neilan films, notably the sophisticated STELLA MARIS (1918).[17]

Late in 1918 Pickford followed Chaplin's lead in moving to First National, where she was granted even more creative control and a salary of $675,000 to make three films. With her 50 percent of the profits this would net her over a million dollars per year. Chaplin had reached this plateau already, although not because of any superior business acumen. It was Pickford who was the acknowledged fiscal expert of the group that, in 1919, would form United Artists. Wrote Chaplin, "She knew all the nomenclature:

MOTION PICTURE

THE QUALITY MAGAZINE OF THE SCREEN

JUNE

MAGAZINE
25 CTS

Mary Pickford

Hollywood
Has
Married
and
Settled
Down

The Business
of
Fan Mail

Mary Pickford (Motion Picture Magazine, *June 1924*).

the amortizations and the deferred stocks, etc. She understood all the articles of incorporation, the legal discrepancy on Page 7, Paragraph A, Article 27, and coolly referred to the overlap and contradiction in Paragraph D, Article 24." Before she died,
the *New York Times* would characterize Pickford as "one of the richest women in
America."[18]

After her marriage to Douglas Fairbanks in 1920, Pickford slowed her output,
relishing her regal position as mistress of Pickfair and vying with Fairbanks in the
care and attention that might be devoted to each film. She released only one film a
year after 1921, and while some, such as SPARROWS (1926), were popular hits,
attempts at more mature parts in ROSITA (1923) and DOROTHY VERNON OF HADDON
HALL (1924) were less successful. Pickford had not been limited to children's roles
when she began at Biograph and did not play a child throughout an entire feature
until THE POOR LITTLE RICH GIRL, her twenty-fourth such film. But audiences
insisted on seeing her in this characterization, and as she grew older the women she
found herself playing grew younger. The popularity of any star is subject to natural
limits. Pickford reached hers when she bobbed her hair in 1929. She always regret-
ted it.[19]

Douglas Fairbanks

> There is one thing in this good old world that is positively sure—happiness
> is for *all* who *strive* to *be* happy—and those who laugh *are* happy (Douglas
> Fairbanks, *Laugh and Live*, p. 9).

In 1917 there were no melancholy thoughts of death and taxes from Douglas
Fairbanks. In the first of a series of volumes of popular philosophy, Fairbanks outlined a credo of American optimism that was one part Émile Coué and one part
Teddy Roosevelt. Fairbanks' buoyant, optimistic cinema effortlessly captured this
public image, but he lived that way offscreen as well. What other star would have
published those eight inspirational volumes for the edification of his young audiences, books with titles such as *Initiative and Self-Reliance* and *Profiting by Experience* that tried to set the tone for an American century?

One of the most popular American stars throughout the period of silent features,
Fairbanks was idolized overseas as well and mobbed by thousands in London, Paris,
and Moscow. His subject was always the American Everyman, and even when this
was masked behind the veil of a costume picture, the source of his character's energy
and optimism was unmistakable.

Fairbanks was a stage actor of minor reputation when he was brought into films in
1915 by Triangle's Harry Aitken, who offered him a starting salary of $2,000 per
week. Aitken had been assembling a stable of Broadway celebrities to appear in
Triangle features under the supervision of D. W. Griffith, but when such high-
salaried performers as Weber and Fields or Sir Herbert Beerbohm-Tree failed to
register with film audiences, the entire project began to seem hopeless and ill advised. By the time Fairbanks arrived on the lot, Griffith's people were so opposed to
the Broadway imports that they actively tried to sabotage his debut.[20]

Douglas Fairbanks (Motion Picture Magazine, *August 1918*).

Griffith himself had no sympathy for "the jumping jack" or his style and foisted him off on Christy Cabanne, one of the least-imaginative directors on the lot. Aitken nervously slipped the first Fairbanks picture, THE LAMB, onto the premiere Triangle program, which opened with considerable attention at New York's Knickerbocker Theatre on 23 September 1919. Billed with an Ince picture and a short Sennett film, THE LAMB captured critical attention and proved to be Triangle's first real hit. Frank Woods, the head of Triangle's scenario department, had a better grasp of Fairbanks' potential than did Griffith and teamed him with writer Anita Loos and director John Emerson. Over the next two years, this group would fashion a series of popular light comedies that defined the early Fairbanks persona. Their hero was a bright young representative of the moneyed classes who realizes his dreams through a witty application of initiative and physical agility. At a time when many films still featured working-class heroes, Fairbanks often appeared as a young broker or businessman, a fact which made the realization of these dreams that much easier. Audiences approved. By the end of 1916 Fairbanks had raised his salary to $10,000 per week and was ready to set up his own production company, taking Emerson and Loos with him.[21]

History records the daring and acrobatic skill of Fairbanks in his prime, but the star was no mere stuntman. Alistair Cooke, in a study of Fairbanks' career published by the Museum of Modern Art in 1940, saw his greatness in the apparent effortlessness of his achievements and the harmony of his movements with their environment, "a virtuoso use of the landscape as a natural gymnasium whose equipment is invisible to the ordinary man."[22]

In 1919, in an effort to gain complete control over the financing and distribution of his pictures, then in the hands of Adolph Zukor, Fairbanks became one of the founders of United Artists. Within a year he had dropped the character of the American Everyman and reappeared in the guise of Zorro, beginning a series of costume adventures that lasted throughout the twenties. What might have been a wrenching change of image for a lesser star only served to increase Fairbanks' popularity, for his new Don Diego character was simply Doug's old American aristocrat dressed up for a costume party. Behind Zorro's mask was the Fairbanks his fans had come to adore, now fully liberated through the simple expedient of the period setting. THE THREE MUSKETEERS (1921) and ROBIN HOOD (1922) were more of the same, and even when Fairbanks played a rogue, as in THE THIEF OF BAGDAD (1924) or THE BLACK PIRATE (1926) he was building on the old prewar virtues of self-reliance, initiative, and responsibility.

These films were among the most commercially successful of the silent era. Fairbanks' popularity grew throughout the twenties, and the care he lavished on his productions bespoke his position as true Hollywood nobility. The vast settings of ROBIN HOOD, the expressionist magnificence of THE THIEF OF BAGDAD, or the costly and experimental use of Technicolor in THE BLACK PIRATE, were production exercises unmatched by his few rivals.[23]

As Fairbanks aged, he realized that the ability to continue in this genre was finite. In THE IRON MASK (1929) he bade a formal farewell to the swashbuckler, and to the silent drama that had nurtured and developed it. In one of the most elegantly mounted of costume epics, a film that labors over the correctness of every setting and costume design, he kills off D'Artagnan and the Three Musketeers, annihilating his ageless screen persona. Fairbanks, who had once brought new vigor and imagination to silent films, became the first to offer the medium a melancholy elegy.

Pearl White

While many American stars had wide international followings (especially Chaplin, Pickford, Fairbanks, and Hart), Pearl White was most clearly the product of a pre-1920 international film community. Not only did she achieve stardom with a French company (Pathé) and a French director (Louis Gasnier), but the serial genre with which she became identified was much more highly regarded in Europe than America, and her greatest admirers were certainly the French.

"I like Pearl White very much," wrote Louis Delluc in 1919. He found her energy a better tonic during the dark war years than even the exploits of Chaplin or Fairbanks. Decades later, René Jeanne and Charles Ford claimed that her "perfect image of the athletic, good-natured young American girl" was a key factor in the eventual dominance of French screens by American films.[24] If so, there is considerable irony here, for Pearl White became a celebrity of international renown only after she was signed by Gasnier to appear in the most famous of the early serials, THE PERILS OF PAULINE (1914).

Pearl White was one of the first film stars to publish an autobiography, *Just Me*, which appeared at the height of her fame in 1919. Setting a pattern for similar works to follow, the information provided is hardly reliable, with large portions of her career ignored or distorted. Recent scholarship indicates, for example, that the picture of her impoverished childhood is a considerable exaggeration. But her name really was Pearl White, the result of a parental quirk that had already christened her older sister Opal.[25]

Originally a stage actress, Pearl White entered films in 1910. *Just Me* does have a flavorful account of her first efforts to land a job in the New York studios, where she pounded the pavements of the strange city and couldn't find the Edison studio because she could not tell uptown from downtown on the elevated train. She worked for Powers, Lubin, and Pathé in a standard assortment of shorts between 1910 and 1912, then moved to the Crystal Film Company in the Bronx.[26] These Crystal productions were very simply made, primitive split-reel subjects imposing a crude slapstick treatment on traditional situation-comedy plots. The few that survive, such as PEARL AS DETECTIVE (1913) and THE RING (1914), offer little of interest save the personality of Pearl White herself. Attractive and athletic, she transcended with her wholesome good looks the mugging and eye-rolling called for by the Crystal directors. Within a few months of her arrival the studio was naming the films after her.[27]

In 1914 she was approached by Theodore Wharton to appear in a serialized film that he and his brother Leopold were to produce for Pathé. Intended to coincide with a weekly print version in the Hearst press, THE PERILS OF PAULINE was conceived largely as a device to increase newspaper circulation, a standard practice of the day.[28] But director Louis Gasnier and his new star suddenly tapped a level of audience response not previously evoked by earlier serial films. THE PERILS OF PAULINE quickly became the archetype of the silent American serial and found a permanent place in twentieth-century popular culture.

Pearl White (Motion Picture Magazine, *January 1918*).

Realizing the value of their new property, Pathé and Gasnier immediately followed up with THE EXPLOITS OF ELAINE (1914–1915) co-directed by George Seitz, who would work on all of White's later American serials. Altogether, she appeared in nine serials for Pathé from 1914 to 1920, thus dominating the genre in its most significant period.[29] In running popularity polls taken between 1916 and 1918 by *Motion Picture* magazine, she ranked as the third most popular female star, behind Mary Pickford and Marguerite Clark. But her following was not limited to readers of American fan magazines.

A reporter visiting Pearl White's home in Bayside, New York, was struck by the peculiar character of her mail:

> I had never seen such an enormous, worldwide representation of atten-
> tion. My first thought was that a stamp collector would have paid her a
> hat-checker's privilege price merely for a secretaryship. There were let-
> ters bearing the stamps of countries I had never heard of—
> commonwealths given birth by the Peace Commission in Paris. . . .
> Mostly from women. There were few mash notes (Julian Johnson, "The
> Girl on the Cover," *Photoplay*, April 1920, p. 57).

Granted this somewhat unscientific survey of Pearl White's fan mail, what is it that explains her appeal to foreign audiences and to women? If Europeans were fascinated by her exotic American athleticism, American women must have seen something else. Lewis Jacobs offered one explanation in a 1939 discussion of silent-serial her-oines:

> All were renowned for their stunts, physical powers, and daring. Their
> exploits paralleled, in a sense, the real rise of women to a new status in
> society—a rise that became especially marked on America's entrance into
> the war, when women were offered participation in nearly every phase of
> industrial activity (*The Rise of the American Film*, p. 280).

What Jacobs does not add is that when this offer was retracted after the war, the popularity of serials suffered a coincidental change, falling almost entirely into the hands of second-rate producing companies that pitched their appeal much more strongly to children. Pearl White moved into features in 1920, but without success; the aggressive heroine she portrayed had passed from popularity in the postwar era, at least in America. The creator of this image would spend most of her later years in France, spending her time at casinos and breeding horses. She died in 1938 and was buried in Paris.

Theda Bara

In the nickelodeon era, showman Carl Laemmle demonstrated that an already pop-ular player like Florence Lawrence could be built into a stellar attraction and that tickets, and many of them, could be sold on her name alone. Other stars of the era worked their way up through the ranks (even Pickford started at five dollars a day) or were brought from the legitimate stage. Not until the age of fan magazines and feature pictures were conditions ripe for the creation of stars out of whole cloth, and the first great fabricated star, Theda Bara, reached the screen in January 1915.

She was born Theodosia Goodman, the daughter of a Jewish tailor who had emigrated from Poland to Cincinnati. Her mother's family was Swiss, of French descent, and when the future star first tried the stage around 1908, she used her mother's family name, appearing as Theodosia de Coppet.

Theda, the diminutive by which her family traditionally addressed her, spent several years in New York attempting to gain a foothold in the theater. Her stage career never seems to have amounted to more than a handful of roles, but in 1914 she was spotted by Frank Powell, who decided to cast her as the seductress in A FOOL THERE WAS (1915), an important feature he was about to direct for William Fox. Powell and Fox had been considering a number of potential temptresses to play opposite Broadway star Edward José, but Robert Hilliard, who had produced the stage version, suggested signing an unknown. He claimed that the part would make an overnight success of anyone who appeared in it, and that by signing this actress to a long-term contract Fox could acquire a potential star at little cost. In fact, the initial contract was for $75 per week, a sum that grew to $4,000 weekly by the time Theda left the company.[30]

The film version of A FOOL THERE WAS traced its genesis to a stage version that had appeared at New York's Liberty Theatre in 1909. This, in turn, was inspired by the Burne-Jones painting *The Vampire*, first exhibited in 1897, and the Rudyard Kipling poem of the same name:

> *A fool there was and he made his prayer*
> *(Even as you and I!)*
> *To a rag and a bone and a hank of hair*
> *(We called her the woman who did not care)*
> *But the fool he called her his lady fair—*
> *(Even as you and I!)*

Painting, poem, play (and subsequent novelization) had already established a powerful image in the public's mind of the vampire-enchantress. Employing a sex lure on any male within striking distance, this amoral adventuress drained her victim of wealth, position, pride, even life itself. Onscreen, she appeared at least as early as 1913 in Kalem's THE VAMPIRE, so the Fox film was building on a strong foundation of public awareness.[31]

What was needed was an angle, and after studying the performance Theodosia de Coppet delivered under Powell's direction, Fox put press agents Johnny Goldfrap and Al Selig on the job. They created the name Theda Bara, an anagram, they claimed, for "Arab Death." (Some historians believe that "Bara" derives from the name of Theda's maternal grandfather, François Baranger de Coppet.) The Fox publicity mill launched a bizarre campaign generating a detailed fantasy background for their new star: she was born in the shadow of the Sphinx, played leads at the Théâtre Antoine, distilled exotic perfumes as a hobby, and was well versed in black magic. They informed readers that Theda Bara offscreen was identical to the character she played in A FOOL THERE WAS, destroying males and turning a cold shoulder to the pleadings of abandoned wives and children. The press agents' achievement was not that they succeeded in launching this campaign but that they successfully

Theda Bara (Motion Picture Magazine, *October 1916*).

kept it up for the full four years of Bara's stay at Fox, a period in which she ground out forty feature pictures.[32]

Bara did not always play the vamp; she appeared in ROMEO AND JULIET (1916), THE TWO ORPHANS (1915), UNDER TWO FLAGS (1916), and KATHLEEN MAVOURNEEN (1919) as well. But it was with this character that Fox's publicity identified her, and on which her career rose and fell. As late as December 1918 Bara was listed ninth in a popularity contest conducted by *Motion Picture* magazine, but the following year she parted company with Fox, and although she made several attempts, she never effectively revived her career. How are we to explain this sudden fall from public favor?

Some critics see the Bara character simply as one pole of a standard male fantasy running from virgin to vamp, but this analysis fails to recognize the character's real popularity with women of the pre-flapper generation. In 1917 Victor Freeburg almost put his finger on the source of her appeal: "Few are either daring enough or desirous enough of leading a vampire existence, but thru the medium of Theda Bara they can do her deeds and live her life." What Freeburg could not see was that this character was one of the only females on screen who consistently demonstrated real power over men and who did not always have to pay the price for it. Or, in the words of Theda Bara, "The vampire that I play is the vengeance of my sex upon its exploiters. You see, I have the face of a vampire, but the heart of a *féministe*."[33]

Wallace Reid

Wallace Reid was the final heir to the "Arrow Collar" tradition of motion-picture stardom, which from the earliest years of features had dominated the American screen. The *Motion Picture* magazine's 1914 popularity poll found Earle Williams the nation's most popular screen star, with J. Warren Kerrigan, Arthur Johnson, Carlyle Blackwell, and Francis X. Bushman his nearest male rivals. These strong-jawed, all-American figures exuded stability, friendliness, optimism, and reliability. They were at home in overalls or evening clothes and did very nicely in a uniform when the occasion arose. Their imitators were legion and, to modern eyes, indistinguishable. Few silent-film historians spend much time on these men or their films, but occasional lip service is paid to the last and greatest of them, Wallace Reid.[34]

Unfortunately, the attention directed to Reid nearly always centers on his tragic death in January 1923, while he was attempting a cure for his morphine habit. Few discuss his long and successful career, and received opinion notes his brand of stardom only to highlight the Valentino and Gilbert tradition that supplanted it.[35]

Reid was born into a theatrical family in 1891. His father, Hal Reid, was an actor and playwright of some success who began writing scenarios for the Selig Company in Chicago in 1910. He would later work as a writer and director for firms such as Vitagraph and Universal, and his son Wally generally came along as part of the package. By 1912 Wallace Reid was a popular leading man in short action melodramas produced by a variety of nickelodeon-era studios, eventually becoming a fixture on the Universal lot. Historian DeWitt Bodeen was able to identify over one hundred Reid films prior to his brief appearance as Jeff the blacksmith in Griffith's THE BIRTH OF A NATION.[36]

Wallace Reid (Motion Picture Classic, *December 1922*).

Here, Reid was spotted by Jesse L. Lasky, who immediately cast him in Famous Players–Lasky features opposite some of that firm's most notable stars, including Cleo Ridgely and Geraldine Farrar.[37] Lasky's use of Reid was similar to William Fox's treatment of Theda Bara. Even after the 1916 merger, Famous Players–Lasky was still heavily committed to established stars brought from the theater at great expense, and it was economically imperative that some newcomers with potential drawing power be put under long-term contracts and developed into credible screen stars on their own. They could then be controlled more readily, and worked harder, while their salary demands could be kept within reason, at least until they had proven their screen appeal.

Lasky struck gold with Wallace Reid. Within a few months he was established as one of the nation's most popular stars, a position he would maintain throughout his career. Reid seemed to capture the all-American spirit offscreen as well, at least according to the fan magazines. One 1917 article found Reid and his wife such a model of domestic bliss that they put the lie to all those tall tales about Hollywood life. "There is strong verification in the life of Wallace Reid and Dorothy Davenport which condemns the oft-repeated aspersions against the members of the Hollywood film colony," the reporter wrote with unknowing irony.[38]

Reid was especially effective in such Cecil B. DeMille productions as CARMEN (1915), JOAN THE WOMAN (1917), and THE AFFAIRS OF ANATOLE (1921). Later, his films were directed by James Cruze and Sam Wood. Famous Players–Lasky made sure to get value for their money. In 1916 the first full year of his contract, Reid appeared in six features. The following year he was seen in ten. The pace continued without letup, and during 1922, when most stars of his caliber were appearing in two films per year, Reid made nine. Over a seven-year period, Reid was seen in a new feature picture every seven weeks, eclipsing Theda Bara's pace at Fox. Amazingly, he seems not to have suffered overexposure at the box office and was still at the height of his popularity when he collapsed during production of his final film.

Reid had been taking morphine tablets for several years and recently had begun drinking heavily. He committed himself to a cold-turkey "cure" at a local sanatorium. Once he had been an athlete and dancer of considerable renown, but his body was now hopelessly debilitated. He lapsed into a coma after a bout of influenza and died on 18 January 1923.

Reid's wife made a public issue of his commitment and took pains to put the truth of Reid's condition before the public. But even she drew back from revealing all the facts. By the time of his death, newspapers were editorializing in support of Reid ("he died game," wrote the *Los Angeles Examiner*), but in the end the affair only provided more ammunition to those attacking Hollywood immorality, and early supporters soon began to keep their distance. The studio's complicity in Reid's addiction and death was hinted at, but sensational stories of an underground dope ring gained wider currency. In fact, Reid had been introduced to morphine by a studio physician eager to keep the star working after he suffered an injury during location filming on VALLEY OF THE GIANTS (1919). In light of this revelation, the exhausting schedule imposed on Reid over the next three years seems especially unconscionable.[39]

Those inside the industry who knew the truth collectively repressed the whole affair. Within a few years, it was as if Wallace Reid had hardly existed. Terry Ramsaye's extensive and influential insider history, published in 1926, barely mentions Wallace Reid—and then mainly in connection with his father, Hal Reid.[40]

William S. Hart

Eastern folks called it a tragedy story,
An' tragedy—it rides herd on me;
Fer I know'd Ben, that cow-pony,
An' that pink-nosed Pinto know'd me.
(William S. Hart and Mary Hart,
Pinto Ben, p. 23)

William S. Hart's poem "Pinto Ben," of which this is the opening stanza, mirrors Hart's respect for the simple virtues of western life, as well as his identification with his beloved pinto pony. Ben and his master, the boss rider who narrates the tale, travel to the Chicago stockyards with a thousand head of range-bred cattle. Careless urban stockhands accidentally stampede the herd, which heads straight for man and horse. After a mad dash to outrun the herd, Ben vaults a high stockyard gate, saving his master but losing his own life. Cradling the pony's head as it dies, the boss rider reflects that some of the blood they lie in must have come "out o' my heart," the mingled essence of two kindred spirits.

This tale of self-sacrifice and betrayal by crass easterners certainly haunted the author.[41] Not only was his career shadowed by misunderstanding and recrimination, but the conscious identification of man and beast was directly carried over into his films and into the offscreen persona that Hart developed during his years of fame.

The vehicle for this was Hart's own pinto pony, Fritz, whom he acquired soon after he joined Thomas H. Ince and the New York Motion Picture Company in 1914. Hart was an established legitimate actor, a man who had been acclaimed on Broadway for his novel interpretations of Western characters in *The Squaw Man* and *The Virginian*. With some justification, Ince had told him that Western films were a glut on the market, and Hart had accepted the low salary of $125 per week. But Hart's own films soon began to reshape Western pictures in a more realistic fashion. In his first feature, THE BARGAIN (1914), he offered the public an emotionally complex figure whose personality was neither good nor evil but a prototypical "good bad man" who would reappear in subsequent films.[42]

Hart felt a personal responsibility to move Western drama, on the stage or screen, away from the dime-novel conventions it had descended to by the turn of the century. Although born in Newburgh, New York, and (despite his later claims) lacking any significant firsthand experience of the West, Hart gradually became part of that celebration of frontier culture which grew up in the age of Theodore Roosevelt. He came to interpret the West with the same dramatic flair as his friends the painters Charles Russell and Frederic Remington, and with the same concern for the region's legendary moral code.

He believed that the bond of friendship between himself and Ince meant more than a simple business arrangement and was sincerely shocked when he came to realize that Ince had been trading on his loyalty by keeping his salary at scandalously low levels. In 1916, for example, Hart appeared in one of his most famous films, THE RETURN OF DRAW EGAN (which he also directed) for just $875. The picture took three and a half weeks to film, and the day after it was finished Ince had Hart and his unit at work on their next picture. This, at a time when untested Broadway stars like Douglas Fairbanks were being signed at $2,000 per week by the same company, Triangle, that was making the Hart–Ince pictures.[43]

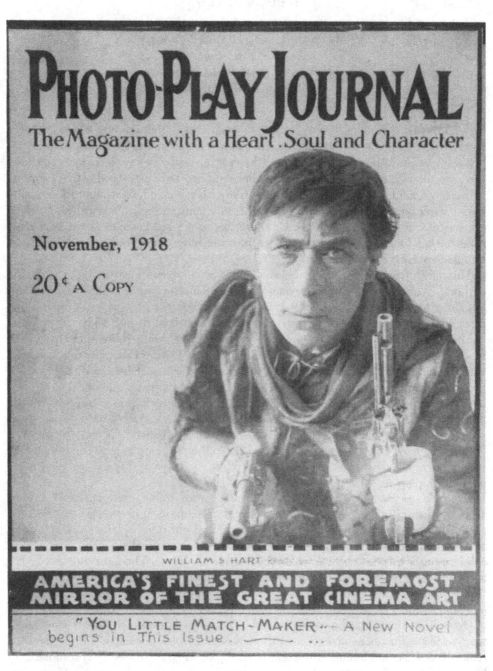

William S. Hart (Photo-Play Journal, *November 1918*).

When Triangle collapsed, Ince moved to Artcraft and was able to bring Hart with him. Here, Hart was finally paid a salary commensurate with his true status, $150,000 per picture. But he had to split with Ince the promised 35 percent of the profits, despite the fact that Ince no longer had any creative connection with Hart's pictures. Now entirely soured on their relationship, Hart resented the enforced partnership and schemed to find a way around it. His solution was ingenious and highly characteristic. After their first Artcraft picture, THE NARROW TRAIL (1917), Fritz publicly "announced" his retirement from the screen. Ince might be making money from the sweat of Bill Hart's brow, but he would not make another penny from the pinto pony.[44]

Hart would have other problems, with Paramount's Jesse L. Lasky, who failed to understand his choice of subject matter, and with the executives of United Artists, whom he successfully sued for shoddy distribution of his last picture, TUMBLEWEEDS (1925). By the time talkies arrived, Hart and Fritz had retired to their ranch in Newhall, California.

A 1930 inscription to King Vidor, in a copy of Hart's autobiography, *My Life East and West*, tells the story. In the "handwriting" of Fritz, we read:

> *Humans have voices to help 'em,*
> *Animals have only their eyes.*
> *That's why I ain't workin' in "talkies."*
> > *So long*
> > Fritz

To which Bill Hart adds, "Now you can understand my handicap—being hitched up with a horse."[45]

Norma Talmadge

Of all the silent stars whose reputations collapsed with the coming of sound, Norma Talmadge was certainly the most important. Guided by her husband, the powerful film-industry executive Joseph Schenck, she formed her own production company in 1917 and operated it until her last film in 1930, one of the few stars to maintain popularity during this entire period. In a list of salaried stars given in the 1924 *Film Daily Yearbook*, her $10,000 per week far outstrips the nearest competition. The acerbic critic Tamar Lane felt that she was, after Pickford, the screen's finest actress, while Adela Rogers St. Johns called her "our one and only great actress."[46]

Norma Talmadge was born in Jersey City in 1897. With her sisters Constance and Natalie, she was raised by her strong-willed mother, Margaret, one of the great stage mothers of Hollywood history.[47] Norma began posing for stereopticon slides in 1910 and made a fitting transition to the Vitagraph Company that same year. Over the next five seasons, she appeared in some 250 films for Vitagraph before striking out on her own and eventually landing a contract with Triangle–Fine Arts. But not until she returned to New York in 1917 and opened her own studio on East Forty-eighth Street did she emerge as a major star.

Norma Talmadge (Balaban & Katz Magazine, *1 May 1926*).

Throughout the era of silent features, Norma Talmadge maintained a remarkably consistent screen persona. Swanson or Pickford would alternate melodramas, comedies, and costume romances, but Talmadge steadfastly offered the one image her audiences seemed to demand: "a brave, tragic, and sacrificing heroine, lavish settings and beautiful clothes, and buckets of tears before the eventual redemption at the fadeout."[48] Her one real attempt to break this mold, an appearance as the Parisian *gamine* in Clarence Brown's KIKI (1926), seems to have been a serious commercial failure.

The demand for the familiar Talmadge persona was so strong that even supportive critics began to despair. Robert E. Sherwood wrote as early as 1923:

> Miss Talmadge is a good actress. She has power, she has poise, and she possesses a delicate subtlety of expression. But her undeniable talent had been guided into false channels; she had become a box-office star, devoting herself to standard, stereotyped "emotional" roles which permitted her to wear a given number of fashionable gowns, and to occupy a given number of close-ups. She had become terribly monotonous (*The Best Moving Pictures of 1922–23*, p. 25).

Gloria Swanson nearly broke with Paramount the same year, complaining of monotony in the roles she was asked to play. But Talmadge made her own choices and decided to keep on giving the public what it wanted. The decision may have been wise in the short term, but when the vogue for this particular brand of screen heroine faded, she and her films were violently rejected. In 1930 Paul Rotha was busy attacking the Hollywood system and promoting various continental approaches to screen art. His attack on American film acting (which, by the way, includes everyone from Pauline Frederick to the Gish sisters) focuses most directly on Norma Talmadge:

> The ideal type for the film star was the blank-minded, non-temperamental player, steeped in sex and sheathed in satin, who was admirably suited to movie "acting," which called for no display of deep emotions, no subtlety, no sensitivity, no delicacy, no guile. All through her career Norma Talmadge achieved success by looking slightly perplexed and muzzy about the eyes (*The Film Till Now*, p. 131).

Rotha and Sherwood certainly saw the same films, but the change in critical taste over only a few years effectively wrote Norma Talmadge out of the history books. As luck would have it, there seems no way to write her back in. Even such diligent chroniclers as Kevin Brownlow, Anthony Slide, and William K. Everson have little to say about Talmadge or her work. Nearly all of her most important films have remained unseen for decades. Among the top-grossing films of the 1920s, critically well received and often directed by such major figures as Herbert Brenon, Sidney Franklin, and Frank Borzage, the Talmadge films are one of the last major secrets of the silent cinema. Whether the judgment of history will vindicate Sherwood or Rotha remains to be seen.

Marion Davies

The screen career of Marion Davies is of course inextricably bound up with the name of William Randolph Hearst. While this fact has always been recognized, the critical treatment of this particular partnership has shifted considerably over the years. When Hearst and Davies were still actively producing films, none dared mention the personal side of their relationship. Benjamin Hampton, writing in 1930, summarized Hearst's film activities by noting, "few producers have derived more enjoyment from the game." More recently, the "Citizen Kane" school of film history sees nothing but the awkward relationship of the patriarchal magnate and his hand-fashioned "discovery."[49]

The emphasis in all periods has been to suggest that Davies' screen career was manufactured, then foisted on unwilling audiences and exhibitors. Reassessments of her late silent comedies such as SHOW PEOPLE and THE PATSY (both 1928) usually compare these films favorably to earlier costume pictures in which Hearst somehow "forced" Davies to appear.[50] But the current high regard for Davies as a comedienne is largely a modern fashion, and her accomplishments in the bulk of her silent features are much more varied than is generally admitted.

Hearst's interest in film predated his encounter with Davies. He operated the International Newsreel, an animation studio, and produced several of the most important early serials, including THE EXPLOITS OF ELAINE (1915). He spotted Marion Davies in the 1916 Ziegfeld Follies and after seeing her performance in a cheaply made feature called RUNAWAY ROMANY (1917) decided to fold her into his own motion-picture empire. Under the Cosmopolitan banner, Hearst was already producing a series of features with Alma Rubens, but because of his special interest in Davies, he now became involved on a much more personal level.

The bulk of Davies' Cosmopolitan productions, which were made in New York until Hearst shifted his center of operations to California in 1924, are light romantic melodramas. Some are more tearful than others, but one finds a wartime spy plot (THE BURDEN OF PROOF, 1918), a comedy (GETTING MARY MARRIED, 1919), and a flapper-era morality tale (THE RESTLESS SEX, 1920). These films do not seem to have been especially successful, and Hearst was already being chided in print for his string of Davies features. After discussing the early serials and newsreels Robert E. Sherwood concluded:

> Up to this point Hearst had probably made money from pictures, but then he founded Cosmopolitan Pictures Corporation and started losing on a triumphant scale. He made picture after picture in which Marion Davies was featured, and on which he lavished incredible sums, and one after another flopped dismally. Miss Davies did not prove to be a stalwart box office attraction, and an irreverent wag in the movie industry remarked that Mr. Hearst had to bribe the exhibitors to rent his pictures (*The Best Moving Pictures of 1922–23*, p. 50).

Why these films failed is not at all clear. Perhaps the use of second-rate directors like Julius Steger or George D. Baker had something to do with it. One of the few films to survive from the period, BEAUTY'S WORTH (1922), suggests that Davies'

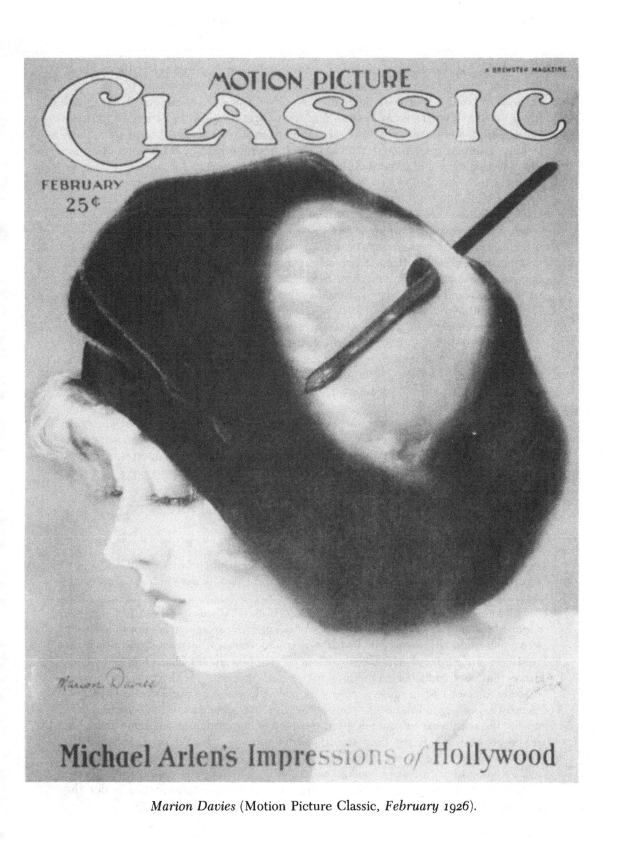

Marion Davies (Motion Picture Classic, *February 1926*).

screen persona was not a problem. Yet the public did not respond to these films. Only when Hearst began production of costume spectacles in the wake of the 1921–1922 revival of this genre was he finally able to sell Davies to audiences. Their initial effort, WHEN KNIGHTHOOD WAS IN FLOWER (1922), proved to be one of the season's big hits, although seen today it suffers from its overstuffed period detail and lackluster direction by Robert Vignola. The film did utilize the full resources of the vast International studio, an old Harlem beer garden that had been taken over by Hearst when Prohibition arrived. It was followed by the equally successful (and similarly dull) LITTLE OLD NEW YORK (1923). This featured even more lavish settings, including an entire neighborhood of nineteenth-century Manhattan rebuilt inside a vast Brooklyn armory. But the spectacles that followed reverted to the original run of bad luck. YOLANDA (1924), a still more elaborate medieval pageant, gorgeously designed by Hearst's house art director, Joseph Urban, was a complete failure. So was the lavish American Revolutionary War melodrama JANICE MEREDITH (1924) and the Hollywood-produced LIGHTS OF OLD BROADWAY (1925). Hearst could hardly be blamed for trying to duplicate the success of his earlier hits, but he did cease production of these costume epics after 1925.

Davies' late silents, produced on the MGM lot, are as varied as those of any silent star. They include a large group of comedies, among them the still underrated THE FAIR COED (1927), and such literary adaptations as QUALITY STREET (1927) and THE RED MILL (1927). Her transition to sound was relatively painless, but she never recaptured her former status.[51]

Marion Davies was no Susan Alexander Kane. In viewing her films today one finds a bright, engaging performance style so often lacking among silent-screen actresses. While Hearst's backing certainly provided the wherewithal to get Davies onscreen and keep her there during periods of public apathy, the performances we see today are quite capable of standing on their own.

Lon Chaney

Few silent-screen players passed directly into the popular idiom, but historians assure us that one could always raise a smile in the 1920s by exclaiming, "Don't step on it—it might be Lon Chaney!"[52]

Still known today as "the man of a thousand faces," Chaney seemed to many the silent-film actor *par excellence.* He was a performer whose appeal lay not in his good looks, offscreen adventures, or lavishly mounted vehicles but in his traditional recourse to makeup and pantomime. Chaney whipped up his characters out of his makeup kit and applied his emotions with similar panache. At the time, much was made of Chaney's birth to deaf-mute parents, with whom he was forced to communicate through sign language.[53] But while this experience may have helped him during the early years of cinema, by the period of his stardom the movies no longer relied on pantomimic representation in order to make themselves understood. In fact, Chaney's acting style was largely molded by his barnstorming years in stock and vaudeville, and his films are weakest when he is called upon to express any degree of subtlety. To understand this, compare Conrad Veidt's performance under the makeup of THE MAN WHO LAUGHS (1928) to anything of Chaney's.

Lon Chaney (Universal Weekly, *6 June 1925*).

Chaney certainly was at home, however, in the stylized world of the *Grand Guignol*. After 1919, and his great success in THE MIRACLE MAN, Chaney came to specialize in twisted minds and twisted bodies, objective correlatives of evil unmatched onscreen before or since. In THE PENALTY (1920) a careless surgeon leaves the young Chaney a legless cripple who grows up to revenge himself on society. In WEST OF ZANZIBAR (1928) the target is Lionel Barrymore, who has not only stolen Chaney's wife but left him paralyzed after a brutal struggle. THE BLACKBIRD (1926) reverses this formula, with Chaney playing the role of a suave criminal who masquerades as a kindly but twisted Limehouse clergyman. The quick changes eventually catch up with him, and the evil Chaney finds he can no longer "take off" the crippled guise of the good Chaney.[54]

Irony and sacrifice are the punch lines of these films, typically played with all stops out. In WEST OF ZANZIBAR, Chaney realizes too late that Barrymore's daughter, on whom he is extracting fiendish revenge, is in fact his own daughter. Time and again he makes great sacrifices for his leading lady, only to see her wind up in the arms of a handsome rival. The most baroque of these sacrificial ironies occurs in Tod Browning's THE UNKNOWN (1927), where Chaney has his arms amputated in fruitless pursuit of Joan Crawford, who has expressed an aversion to the romantic embrace. Browning proved to be the most sympathetic of Chaney's collaborators, although his most famous films were made for other directors.

Near the end of his career, Chaney starred, inevitably, in an adaptation of *Pagliacci* (LAUGH, CLOWN, LAUGH, 1928), thus capping a recurrent strain in his work that marked even his famous Quasimodo in THE HUNCHBACK OF NOTRE DAME (1923). When Chaney allowed this sort of pathos to get out of hand, as he did in NOMADS OF THE NORTH (1920) or MOCKERY (1927), the result was an embarrassing display of silent-movie clichés, all broad gestures and eye-rolling. Any number of lesser actors could have demonstrated the restraint that these roles called for, but restraint was not a major element in Chaney's performing vocabulary.

His most famous film, THE PHANTOM OF THE OPERA (1925), does show Chaney at his best. Completely hidden behind a brilliant death's-head makeup, Chaney stalks the passages of an elegantly designed Paris Opera—largely the creation of Opera veteran Ben Carré. Despite the efforts of two mediocre directors, Rupert Julian and Edward Sedgwick, the film manages to express much of the eerie texture of the original Gaston Leroux novel. With the chandelier sequence thrown away, and an unsatisfying chase at the end, only the authority of Chaney's performance holds the production together. Furiously pounding his pipe organ, or staring madly at Mary Philbin with eyes of fire, Chaney becomes a gargoyle unmatched in twenties cinema.

Tom Mix

Adult audiences began deserting the Western genre after 1915. It was abandoned by serious filmmakers like DeMille and Ince (apart from his Hart releases), and trade-paper criticism grew increasingly condescending. But an underclass of Western films, and the popularity of a few individual Western stars, did continue to grow. During the late teens, William S. Hart dominated the Western market, but by the close of the war he was being eclipsed by Tom Mix, a rival who actually predated him in the motion-picture business.

Tom Mix (Wid's Yearbook, *1921, p. 18*).

Some have argued that it was Mix's heavy use of stunts, comedy, and outlandish Western garb that somehow stole away the Hart audience, an explanation that implies an increasing frivolity among postwar filmgoers. But it was not the individual moviegoers who changed. The adult audience who had supported the gravity of a Hart film like THE DARKENING TRAIL (1915) had long since abandoned the genre. Children now made up the bulk of the Western audience, and the relatively mature themes of the Hart films had little interest for them. Tom Mix, who offered "action and excitement spiced with a boyish sense of fun," captured this young audience, and with it the Western market. The pattern held true in Europe as well. Mix's films were "just the stuff for children," wrote French film historians Maurice Bardèche and Robert Brasillach, who saw them drawing larger audiences than Hart even before the war ended.[55]

Whatever his audience, Mix was highly successful in appealing to it throughout the mid 1920s. Benjamin Hampton claims grosses of as much as $600,000 to $800,000 for the peak Mix films, and since he was releasing seven or eight of them a year, his annual earnings must have compared quite favorably with those of even the most prominent dramatic or comedy stars. Hampton claims that Mix made more money for his studio than any other star, which would certainly justify the $17,000 weekly salary claimed for him by Fenin and Everson.[56]

The appeal of a Mix film was straightforward and direct. In 1920 the *Photoplay Plot Encyclopedia*, which analyzed the story lines of one hundred recent features, said about THE CYCLONE (1920), in which Mix played a Canadian mountie:

> The value of this production as an entertaining photoplay does not depend upon the plot of the story, which is basically trite, but upon the unusual treatment and especially the development of thrilling stunts of horsemanship for the star to perform. It is a simple and convenient plot upon which to build Tom Mix's usual tricks. . . . One forgets the simplicity and triteness of the plot in marvelling at the star's agility (*Photoplay Plot Encyclopedia*, pp. 78–79).

This analysis notes the film's simplicity only as a limiting factor that is somehow overcome by Mix's athletic ability. The powerful appeal of an uncomplicated narrative (and uncomplicated hero) is hardly considered. But it is precisely this quality that separated Mix from William S. Hart, and on which much of his appeal to unsophisticated audiences was based. While Hart offered the ambiguity of a "good bad man," and emotionally wrenching "soul fights" from the pen of C. Gardner Sullivan, Mix avoided such dramatics. George Pratt reminds us that Mix knew his limitations as an actor and that he emphasized those roping and riding tricks that could show him off to best advantage.[57] Uncomplicated characterizations and simple narratives put no strain on his histrionic abilities and made his films much more accessible to young audiences.

Such behavior laid the foundation for the B-Western genre, a category identified not merely by budgetary limitations but by an entire Mix-inspired, "code of the West." B-Western heroes inhabited a world without ambiguities, avoided romantic entanglements, lived clean American lives, and would rather rope a rustler than shoot him full of holes.[58] Like Tom Mix, they often sported outrageous dude-ranch versions of Western garb, fantasies of cowboy life that drew their inspiration from circuses and Wild West shows.

For Mix, it all led inevitably back to the circus (he toured with his own for several years before his death) and to life as a media cowboy in vaudeville, comic books, and radio. On the air, his "Ralston Straight Shooter Pledge" summed things up neatly: "I promise to shoot straight with Tom Mix by regularly eating good old Hot Ralston, the official Straight Shooter's cereal, because I know Hot Ralston is just the kind of cereal that will help build a stronger America."[59]

Lillian Gish

To one observer, Lillian Gish was "a white fingered maiden with the fragility of a Fragonard." To another, "She seems to float on the screen like a remembered vision of Botticelli's women." Lillian Gish has long inspired her admirers to flights of romantic metaphor, with visions of pale blossoms and fluttering doves recurring over the decades as new audiences discover the rare delicacy and spirit in her performances.[60]

But those who worked with her tend to remember another Gish: a committed artist so intensely wrapped up in her work that her very life might ebb before the cameras if the scene required it. King Vidor, who directed Gish in LA BOHÈME (1926), recalls with trepidation her ability to stop breathing while she played the death of Mimi. Arriving on the set parched and gray, she announced that "she had succeeded in removing all saliva from her mouth by not drinking any liquids for three days, and by keeping cotton pads between her teeth and gums even in her sleep." When she breathed her last in the scene, Vidor could only think, "What will the headlines say?"[61]

Gish was, of course, a disciple, some say a creation, of D. W. Griffith. From the time she and her sister, Dorothy, first appeared at the Biograph studio in 1912 (to visit their friend Mary Pickford) Lillian Gish was Griffith's most important performing tool. From short films like THE MUSKETEERS OF PIG ALLEY (1912), through nearly all of his great features, Gish delivered the needed balance of strength and fragility. The heroines Griffith offered might have appeared helpless in the face of melodramatic onslaught, but they were not about to whimper and collapse. Sustained by an inner strength, they justified Griffith's vision of a world in which spiritual values always overcame the forces that threatened them. The vision found its greatest exponent in Lillian Gish.

This notion was writ large in THE BIRTH OF A NATION (1915), HEARTS OF THE WORLD (1918), and ORPHANS OF THE STORM (1922). But consider Gish's work in TRUE HEART SUSIE (1919), a nostalgic pastoral where her sacrifices go unnoticed and her opponent is only an uncaring city vamp. The same strength of character serves her here, and without the distractions of rides to the rescue, the clarity and sophistication of her performance are all the more evident.

Gish had remained with Griffith through the production of ORPHANS OF THE STORM, but he sent her out on her own when her fame began to exceed his financial resources. For Inspiration Pictures she made two lavish costume romances in Italy THE WHITE SISTER (1923) and ROMOLA (1925). Then, in 1925, she signed with Metro-Goldwyn-Mayer for two years at $8,000 per week. From Griffith she had learned the importance of personally supervising each detail of her films, and the attention she lavished on her MGM pictures was soon the talk of Hollywood. She had left the West Coast five years earlier to work with Griffith in New York and had

Lillian and Dorothy Gish (Photoplay, *December 1914*).

continued her career in Europe. Returning to Hollywood, she was shocked at the rigidity of studio production; the few films she supervised were made with such personal care and conviction that even then they seemed handcrafted and pre-industrial.[62]

Her contract gave her not only the right to choose stories and directors but the ability to rehearse the entire film in advance, as Griffith did, and to employ such technicians as Henrik Sartov, the cinematographer whose gauze work enhanced her ethereal screen presence.[63] Such working methods were far from standard at MGM, and Mayer and Thalberg seemed unhappy, especially when the returns on her pictures proved disappointing.

Griffith had created for her an image of virginal purity, but at MGM Gish began to explore more mature characterizations. While her conception of the love scenes in LA BOHÈME (1926) was based on keeping the lovers always apart (playing on what she called their "suppressed emotion"), the next subject she selected was THE SCARLET LETTER (1926). Gish notes in her autobiography how this novel had found its way onto a censorial blacklist, and only her personal reputation silenced the pressure groups opposing the filming.[64]

Choosing a Swedish director, Victor Seastrom, and a Swedish co-star, Lars Hanson, Gish succeeded in giving the picture the aura of the early Swedish cinema classics. Time and place became powerful characters, compensating for the necessarily delicate handling of the adultery theme. Gish continued with Seastrom and Hanson on THE WIND, now considered one of the finest of silent features but barely released in 1928 during the transition to sound.[65] By then MGM was actively trying to rid itself of Gish's contract.

In a controversial discussion of MGM's handling of Greta Garbo and Gish, Louise Brooks suggests that MGM tried to build up the Swedish actress (over whom they had more effective control) in an effort to damage Gish's position in the industry. Not only was Gish earning a fabulous salary, but she was exercising the sort of control over her pictures that the studio preferred to reserve for itself. At one point, Louis B. Mayer asked her to sign, without legal consultation, a release that would take her off salary until the studio found a suitable vehicle for her. When she demurred, Mayer threatened, "If you don't do as I say, I can ruin you." Gish made one last, ineffective film for MGM, then signed with United Artists for $50,000 a picture, a small fraction of her previous salary.[66]

She returned to the stage, and to a social circle that included Joseph Hergesheimer, George Jean Nathan, F. Scott Fitzgerald, and Carl Van Vechten. Although her later film appearances were few, she continued working into the 1990s as the last great survivor of her generation. Most remarkable of all, Lillian Gish became a roving ambassador for the silent cinema, traveling to distant campuses and film festivals with only one purpose—to bear witness to the "universal language" of film, so powerfully developed by her great director and friend, D. W. Griffith.[67]

Gloria Swanson

Unlike the screen careers of Chaplin, Wallace Reid, and Theda Bara, that of Gloria Swanson does not display a conventional arc of achievement. Her stardom was not manufactured and presented to the public as a *fait accompli*, nor did she strive to perfect one particular image and cling to it for as long as popular taste allowed.

Gloria Swanson (Motion Picture Magazine, *November 1926*).

Instead, Swanson's career progressed in a series of plateaus, as her image in 1915, 1918, and 1923 shifted from comedienne to ingenue to (occasional) tragedienne. But the evolution of her screen image was not the only extraordinary development in her career. In 1926 Swanson walked away from her $7,000 weekly salary and set up her own production company. She was not the only female star to attempt this, but Pickford and Talmadge could call on their husbands as business partners. Swanson was alone at the top.[68]

Gloria Swanson began in films at the Essanay studio in Chicago in 1914. Signed as a stock player at $13.25 per week, the fifteen-year-old schoolgirl soon became a steady member of the company, making up each morning to play sophisticated characters twice her age. Chaplin was then at Essanay, and Swanson made a brief appearance in HIS NEW JOB (1915), but the comedian who really impressed her was Wallace Beery, who was starring in the SWEEDIE comedy series, transvestite slapstick in which he appeared as a Swedish housemaid. They were married after Swanson transferred to Essanay's Niles studio in California. The marriage was a disaster, but Swanson did follow Beery to the Sennett lot, where she won some success in a series of eight two-reelers for director Clarence Badger. Swanson, however, resisted being developed by Sennett as "a second Mabel Normand." She broke with Sennett and abandoned the comedies on which her small reputation was entirely based.[69]

In 1918 a reporter for the *Motion Picture* magazine caught up with her on the Triangle lot, where she had been appearing in melodramas for Frank Borzage and Jack Conway. Already Swanson referred to her comedies as mere "stepping stones"— useful preparation for dramatic vehicles to follow. She acknowledged the best of them but made it clear where she believed her future lay. Swanson appeared in eight of these Triangle features, most of which she denigrates in her autobiography. Many were simple exploitations of the current war hysteria, uncomfortably jingoistic and laced with absurd espionage plots. But her Triangle films did demonstrate that the public would accept Swanson in dramatic high-society roles, and they allowed her to build on the comic timing she had developed in her films with Badger. Cecil B. DeMille recognized this, and when Triangle collapsed he cast her in DON'T CHANGE YOUR HUSBAND (1919), the first of his sex-obsessed postwar melodramas.[70]

DeMille realized that he had found an average American girl who could wear clothes. He understood that the fashion in heroines was about to change and that options were now available other than the traditional virgin or vamp. Swanson would be his vehicle in fusing these two characters.

The six films they made together over the next two years, including MALE AND FEMALE (1919) and WHY CHANGE YOUR WIFE? (1920), offered a new female role model for postwar America, what Alexander Walker has called "the playmate wife," a tantalizing figure who never really breaks the old taboos.[71] Swanson proved to be the one actress, even more than Bebe Daniels, whom DeMille could cloak in worldliness without obscuring the homelier American virtues underneath.

The team broke up when they became too expensive for each other, and Swanson began a long series of films for Sam Wood that seemed to endlessly repeat the formulas established by DeMille. Fleeing to Paramount's East Coast studio in Astoria, New York, and working with Allan Dwan, she took over creative control of her pictures for the first time. She did her share of costume romances, notably ZAZA (1923), but brought new life to her career by tapping her experience in comedy for MANHANDLED (1924) and STAGE STRUCK (1925).

By 1926 she had been luxuriating in her East Coast isolation for three years and had come to see Hollywood as simply a factory town where the key decisions involving her career were being made by unsympathetic executives. That year, she broke with Paramount, rejecting a salary offer that, she later claimed, topped $1 million.[72]

The establishment of Gloria Swanson Productions proved to be an organizational nightmare. Without adequate fiscal or technical advice, she needed to construct an entire corporate infrastructure, and production on her first film, THE LOVE OF SUNYA (1927), lagged far behind schedule. A move to Hollywood eased some of these problems, and she was able to restore much of her position with her next film, SADIE THOMPSON (1928). Unfortunately, a distracting affair with her business partner, Joseph P. Kennedy, combined with the painful production of QUEEN KELLY (1928–1929), an $800,000 exercise that was never domestically released, brought the era of her greatest popularity to an end.[73]

In the decades that followed, Swanson was able to keep recasting her public image as businesswoman, artist, inventor, stage actress, food faddist, and occasional film star. In SUNSET BOULEVARD (1950) she played the actress Norma Desmond, frozen into her silent-star image and surrounded by a set of "waxworks" equally trapped in their old roles—if somewhat less secure financially. But Swanson's success at keeping herself in the public eye proved that she was no waxwork. As a teenager, she once told an interviewer, "I intend to work until I drop dead." Sixty years later she was the last of the silent-screen stars still playing the part.[74]

Pola Negri

In the wake of the formation of United Artists, Adolph Zukor faced a sudden shortage of star material. He had managed to hold onto William S. Hart, but the loss of Douglas Fairbanks, following the departure of Mary Pickford, made a decided impact on the top of the Paramount line. In addition to these key defectors, stars such as Norma Talmadge and Lillian Gish were also unavailable on the open market. A dangerous trend was brewing, and Zukor reacted in two ways. First, he orchestrated a publicity campaign announcing the decline of the importance of stars and began the production of so-called all-star pictures (in fact, these were no-star pictures). When this failed, he imported Pola Negri.[75]

The Polish actress was the rage of the Continent following her appearance in a series of dramatic productions directed by Ernst Lubitsch, especially CARMEN (1918), MADAME DUBARRY (1919), and SUMURUN (1920). When DUBARRY (renamed PASSION) opened at New York's giant Capitol Theatre, record crowds marveled at Lubitsch's control of mass action and were electrified by the fiery performance of Negri. Here was an actress who took risks, who threw herself into a role with terrifying enthusiasm, oblivious to the need for posing and primping so common to American screen actresses. American producers competed for Negri's services throughout 1921, but when she arrived in New York the following year it was Zukor who held her contract.[76]

Negri's place in American film history has never been adequately evaluated. If mentioned at all, she is seen as a foil for Gloria Swanson, and the concocted "feud" between them (generated by the Paramount publicity office) is either taken at face

Pola Negri (Motion Picture Classic, *August 1923*).

value or treated as an example of period press-agentry. Negri is pictured as exotic and aloof, not in the acceptable Garbo manner, but as some Slavic version of Theda Bara. The impact of her presence in Hollywood is never seriously discussed.[77]

How much of the Negri phenomenon was real and how much was purely manufactured? The exact financial returns on Negri's pictures, as with most silent Paramount releases, are unavailable. While modern critics praise such films as FORBIDDEN PARADISE (1924), A WOMAN OF THE WORLD (1925), and BARBED WIRE (1927), most of her films were poorly reviewed, and gossip columnists periodically dropped hints that the public was tiring of her. But in 1926, after four years in Hollywood, she far out-polled her nearest rivals in a *Motion Picture Classic* popularity contest. Her contract had been renewed in 1925, when she signed for $7,500 per week, and in the following years it rose to $8,000 and then $10,000 per week.[78] Failed German imports Camilla Horn and Lya de Putti did not merit such treatment, and one can only conclude that Negri's films generated adequate profits. Her problems lay elsewhere.

Negri was a product of the fervid Berlin theater and film scene in the late teens and early twenties, when she worked with Reinhardt, Lubitsch, and Jannings. She was the first of this group to go to Hollywood and probably the most self-consciously "artistic" of the lot. She was appalled at Hollywood's backwater culture and frank in discussing her feelings with the American press, which suspiciously characterized her as "an intellectual" and "a reader of books." Visiting British columnist Alice Williamson reported, "Pola is an exotic flower, transplanted to America, yet never completely rooted."[79]

Negri's complaints about the poor quality of the roles she was offered were lost in the press coverage of her private life, especially her well-publicized romances with Chaplin and Valentino. A diva in the grand tradition, Negri rushed to Valentino's New York funeral in a cascade of publicity and sent "$2,000 worth of blood-red roses woven into an eleven-foot-long by six-foot-wide carpet with 'Pola' picked out in white buds." Her public collapse at the bier, the press hinted, was a pure media event, staged on cue for the newsreel cameras.[80]

Despite such murmurs, Negri's career continued to flourish, and HOTEL IMPERIAL (1927), released a few months after the funeral, was a tremendous hit. But less than a year after Valentino's death, she married Prince Serge Mdivani. "My fan mail, formerly requiring a staff of secretaries to answer it, fell off to a series of abusive letters," she wrote in her autobiography. "The American Valentino cult was determined to ruin me for daring to live a life that was not completely dedicated to the memory of Rudy."[81] Whatever the reason (and the real situation in Hollywood was considerably more complex than Negri allows in her error-ridden book), her contract expired when talkies arrived in 1928 and was not renewed.

More than anyone else, Pola Negri lived the life of a silent-movie queen. Draped in emeralds and chinchilla, she rode through Hollywood in a white Rolls-Royce trimmed with ivory and upholstered in white velvet (the color scheme set off her dark eyes and hair). Other stars could match the opulence, but none could handle the style. Twenty years later, Billy Wilder offered her the role of Norma Desmond, the silent-screen star living with her memories in a decaying Sunset Boulevard palazzo. Negri threw him out. To burlesque her former triumphs would be irredeemably vulgar, and even the suggestion was insulting. Gloria Swanson was less particular. She had better judgment, of course, but Swanson never did have the real Negri style.[82]

Rudolph Valentino

Rudolph Valentino has become the cultural historians' most popular icon of silent-screen stardom, and with good reason. More than sixty years after his death, when the face of Norma Talmadge has been forgotten and few can name the title of a single Mary Pickford film, Valentino's recognition factor remains surprisingly high. It does not seem to matter that the accuracy of this Valentino image is considerably askew, battered by a series of inept screen biographies, and not very well served by a string of more traditional literary works. That Irving Shulman should be acclaimed the most accurate of his many biographers is a telling revelation.[83]

Valentino died at a peak in his popularity. Stories of the riot at the Frank Campbell Funeral Home and newsreels of the endless procession of black limousines have become a standard reference point in any cultural history of the twenties.[84] Far outlasting the fan clubs of his contemporaries, Valentino Memorial Societies have operated continuously for decades.

But there is a strange dichotomy between Valentino's place in American culture and his standing among silent-film specialists. Kevin Brownlow, for example, admits that Valentino made more bad films than good and that only the force of his personality transcended the "romantic *kitsch*" of his material. Anthony Slide, meanwhile, derides the screen personality as well as the filmed material, at least the largest portion of it.[85] How can this situation be explained?

The posthumous passion for James Dean was fueled by a small group of highly successful films periodically reissued to new converts, but Valentino's body of work died with silent pictures. To the average modern viewer, his acting style is incomprehensible. "Today scenes from *The Sheik* make us laugh," writes David Carroll, author of a popular survey entitled *The Matinee Idols*. "We watch as Valentino bulges his eyes at Agnes Ayres, walks around her like a dog circling a veal cutlet, and pulls her headfirst into his tent."[86]

Although a few of his films have their supporters, Valentino's ongoing recognition does not draw its strength from this direction. Nor is the death cult entirely responsible. Rather, we need to consider how the image of Valentino changed the way America looked at its heroes, both on and off the screen. It is this offscreen dimension that keeps the Valentino legend alive, even when his own pictures are scorned and derided.

When the *Motion Picture* magazine published the final results of the "Motion Picture Hall of Fame" popularity contest in December 1918, there were five male stars listed in the top ten: Douglas Fairbanks, Harold Lockwood, William S. Hart, Wallace Reid, and Francis X. Bushman. It would be hard to find a more clean-living group of all-Americans (at least onscreen). William S. Hart might occasionally play an outlaw, but only to demonstrate the fine, essentially American virtues underneath.[87]

The same year, the *Motion Picture Studio Directory*, a trade annual, carried a professional advertisement for "Rodolfo Di Valentina—Playing a New Style Heavy." The new style referred to the sophisticated rotter played by Valentino in THE MARRIED VIRGIN (1918), his first major role. As Count Roberto di San Fraccini, he is a blackmailing adventurer romancing both mother and step-daughter. This foreigner who cloaks his designs behind a charming facade is not unrelated to von Stroheim's "man you love to hate" of the same period. The following year, in A ROGUE'S ROMANCE, Valentino (previously a professional dancer) played the small role of a sinister *apache* dancer. The cliché of the Parisian underworld *apache*, drenched in

Rudolph Valentino (Movie Weekly, *11 August 1923*).

treat-'em-rough machismo, fitted Valentino like a glove. When the powerful screen-writer June Mathis saw him take roles like these and transform stock villains or seducers into attractive figures of raw sexual energy, she cast him in the leading role of her latest and most important project.[88]

The American cultural scene was changing rapidly by 1921. That year the new-style heavy electrified a nation as the new-style hero of THE FOUR HORSEMEN OF THE APOCALYPSE (1921). Working closely with director Rex Ingram, June Mathis developed a script that not only satisfied readers of the Ibáñez novel but consciously carved a new niche in the romantic pantheon for their extraordinary discovery. Alexander Walker has outlined the film's canny arrangement of grand emotional episodes, which highlighted Valentino in scenes of aggressive sexuality, seduction, rejection, and reconciliation.[89]

Valentino was not always so lucky in his vehicles, but later the same year his role in THE SHEIK (1921) cemented his claim as king of exotic costume romance. As Theda Bara brought the kohl-eyed vamp into the culture of the teens, so Valentino, riding the crest of an incipient vogue for orientalism, launched the twenties passion for sheiks. The difference was, of course, that to love Valentino was not to die but to be reborn in a paroxysm of liberated bliss. Traditional rules of etiquette were served by clever little plot twists, but who in the audience remembered or cared that Sheik Ahmed Ben Hassan had been a European all along?

When Valentino died suddenly in 1926, he was about to release his latest film, a sequel to THE SHEIK that contained more than a little self-mocking humor. SON OF THE SHEIK (1926) demonstrated that he was quite able to step outside his manufac-tured image, analyze the Valentino mystique with tongue firmly in cheek, and still give the public what it desired. The film proved to be his greatest popular success in years, but how much of this can be traced to his own talents and how much to the outlandish notoriety surrounding his death is still an unresolved question.

Buster Keaton

Many vaudevillians and music-hall comedians were attracted to the cinema during the silent era, from Charlie Chaplin and Harry Langdon to Stan Laurel and W. C. Fields. Most were content to transfer the style or character of their theater work to the screen in relatively unchanged fashion. In Chaplin's case, this meant inserting more mood and characterization into his films than Mack Sennett felt comfortable with. For Langdon or Fields, it was an opportunity to film the most popular of their stage routines. Only Buster Keaton took the trouble to master the essential mechan-ics of the cinema. From the day he first set foot in Roscoe "Fatty" Arbuckle's studio, he began to study the function of the camera in screen comedy. Where other comics were content to record their own performances on film, Keaton involved the camera (and all other technical elements of the cinema) as a key participant, not just an observer.

While an artist and craftsman of consummate skill, Keaton was politically and socially unable to play the Hollywood game. When working conditions were good, he produced the most graceful and hilarious of his films; when conditions were bad, he drew a blank. Control of those conditions was typically shaped by a more experienced friend or associate, one who could set up a production situation within which Buster

Buster Keaton: poster art for THE GENERAL *(1927) by Hap Hadley.*

could operate, thus freeing him from administrative details and allowing him, if he so desired, to continue spending his time on impromptu baseball games.

Arbuckle was the first of these mentors. In 1917 he invited Keaton, who had recently broken up the family act, "The Three Keatons," to join his Comicque Film Company in New York City. Keaton writes in his autobiography:

> Roscoe . . . took the camera apart for me so I would understand how it worked and what it could do. He showed me how film was developed, cut, and then spliced together. But the greatest thing to me about picturemaking was the way it automatically did away with the physical limitations of the theatre. On the stage, even one as immense as the New York Hippodrome stage, one could show only so much (*My Wonderful World of Slapstick*, p. 93).

Showing everything soon became a Keaton trademark. Under Arbuckle's tutelage, Keaton quickly learned to build on the mock violence and knockabout of his vaudeville act. The contained pratfalls of the stage comedian soon grew into the expansive, sweeping trajectories of films like OUR HOSPITALITY (1923) and SEVEN CHANCES (1925), with cinematic time and space completely at the service of extended gag sequences.[90]

It was Joseph Schenck who made it possible for Keaton to develop these skills on his own. Schenck had been producing Arbuckle's films and noted Keaton's growing success in the short films made between 1917 and 1919. When Arbuckle moved to features, Schenck promoted Keaton to head Arbuckle's unit, where Keaton continued to work with much of his familiar technical staff and supporting company. Keaton had married Natalie Talmadge, the sister of Schenck's wife, Norma, and the business relationship took on the cozy familiarity of a family affair. Keaton flourished under this supportive arrangement, and his series of two-reelers quickly established him as the screen's fastest-rising young comedian. During 1921 and 1922, when Chaplin films were few and far between, a new Keaton two-reeler was onscreen every other month. In 1923 Keaton himself moved to features, although not until he released THE NAVIGATOR (1924) did he have a hit of sizable proportions.

Modern acclaim tends to obscure the fact, but in box-office terms Keaton's films were not in the same league as those of Chaplin and Lloyd. Keaton's contract paid him a salary of only $1,000 per week, plus 25 percent of the profits of his pictures, but these were slim and occasionally nonexistent. Keaton was so careless of the economic organization of his own production company that he did not even own any stock in it—Schenck family interests owned most of the shares.[91]

Joseph Schenck became a partner in United Artists in 1924 and president two years later. All of Keaton's features had been distributed through Metro or Metro-Goldwyn-Mayer, but Schenck moved him over to United Artists and gave the go-ahead for Keaton's most ambitious production, THE GENERAL (1927). In his scrupulous account of Keaton's finances, Tom Dardis shows how the film, now regarded as perhaps the single greatest achievement of silent comedy, was both a critical and commercial failure in 1927. Two additional United Artists features, COL-LEGE (1927) and STEAMBOAT BILL, JR. (1928), were nearly as disappointing. Unable to continue backing the sagging Keaton production company, Schenck advised the comedian to move his operation to MGM. In later years, Keaton told Kevin Brownlow (and everyone else who asked) that this move was "the biggest mistake of my life." Here, his old unit dissolved, he was assigned a production supervisor, and MGM screenwriters dared to concoct his scripts. While the first of these films, THE CAMERAMAN (1928), was certainly up to standard, no critics today will defend the later MGM features (1929–1933) against the earlier output. (David Robinson, for example, does not even include the post-1929 titles in his Keaton filmography.) Keaton's lack of involvement is palpable, but his own personal problems, especially his growing alcoholism, must bear most of the responsibility. The chief irony, as Dardis points out, is that most of these films were highly profitable and that Keaton was for the first time earning the salary of a major star, $3,000 per peek. But as Keaton's life continued to disintegrate, his position at MGM grew impossible, and he began a long and ultimately pitiful decline.[92]

Happily, however, Buster Keaton became the first great screen artist to be rehabilitated through film restoration. After decades as a Hollywood ghost, he got a tumultuous reception at the 1965 Venice Film Festival that not only restored his own reputation but helped trigger a wholesale reassessment of the entire silent era, a period that had suffered as much as he had from many years of patronization and neglect.

Harold Lloyd

Harold Lloyd was not only the most popular comedian of the 1920s but, by the close of the silent era, the biggest box-office draw in motion pictures. He far outgrossed Buster Keaton (whose best films, as we have seen, sometimes lost money) and surpassed even Chaplin over the long run, since there was always at least one new Lloyd feature each year. Richard Schickel reminds us that when *Variety* ranked the twenty wealthiest members of the entertainment industry in 1927, Lloyd was the only performer on the list. While his decline in popularity was rapid when the industry converted to sound, it seems strange that Lloyd was so quickly consigned to oblivion in the classic film histories. Lewis Jacobs, for example, mentions Lloyd only in passing in *The Rise of the American Film*, a book that devoted an entire chapter to Chaplin.[93]

In his introduction to the 1971 reissue of Lloyd's 1928 autobiography, Museum of Modern Art curator Richard Griffith suggested an explanation for the dearth of interest:

> The lack of a definitive late book on Lloyd reflects the disesteem in which he has traditionally been held by the movie highbrows. They do not like his optimism. His calculated comedy methods have been labelled "mechanical" and let go at that. His wealth and success have naturally been held against him. But it's the optimism which chiefly sticks in the highbrow craw and accounts for the continued fundamental lack of interest in him and the continued rating of him below Chaplin, Keaton, and even Langdon. *Weltschmerz* is hard to find in him, and *Weltschmerz* is of course essential (*An American Comedy*, p. v).

Griffith wrote this just a few years too soon. Not only would the film-book explosion of the 1970s and 1980s produce several important studies of Lloyd and his work, but

Harold Lloyd (Balaban & Katz Magazine, *1 April 1926*).

the public mood itself began to change dramatically; eventually, it became difficult to find anyone who would hold Lloyd's prosperity and optimism against him. Lloyd's bespectacled "glass" character was the quintessential achiever in the era of Harding normalcy and Coolidge prosperity. Onscreen, he applied wit, perseverance, and guile in an exhausting effort to better himself and achieve the American dream. Offscreen, Lloyd made it clear that comedy-making was a business with him, and in discussing his work with reporters, he concentrated almost exclusively on the mechanics of gag construction. He pioneered "scientific" methods of audience research that included charting gags and plotting viewers' chuckles and titters on elaborate graphs. Using this data to recut and reshape his features, he crafted them into laugh-provoking entertainments of unparalleled efficiency. Lloyd was never the critics' darling, but he did earn the most laughs and the most money. He was the Steven Spielberg of silent comedy.[94]

Of all the major silent comedians, Lloyd was the only one with no prior reputation as a stage comic. In fact, his theater experience was limited to backwater stock companies, and when he entered films it was not as a featured player but as an extra. He fell in with another extra, Hal Roach, who was about to set himself up as a producer on the strength of a small inheritance. When he began working for Roach in 1915, Lloyd looked around at the other comedians onscreen and saw a collection of clowns in funny costumes and makeups. There were remnants of the ethnic stereotypes of vaudeville days, fat comics and thin comics, an assortment of ill-fitting suits and pants, and a forest of pasted-on moustaches. He stole from the best. "Chaplin was going great guns," Lloyd remembered, "his success such that unless you wore funny clothes and otherwise aped him you were not a comedian. Exhibitors who could not get the original demanded imitations." Lloyd created the character of "Lonesome Luke," an inverted Chaplin figure. "All his clothes were too large, mine were too small. My shoes were funny, but different; my moustache funny, but different." This "the same only different" policy was already a Hollywood tradition and served Lloyd admirably. Lonesome Luke earned his niche among the slapstick clowns by the speed and violence of his routines and his willingness to suffer outrageous amounts of pain.[95]

But in 1917 Lloyd and Roach dropped Lonesome Luke, substituting a new character whose mannerisms were completely natural and whose costumes were comfortably off the rack. A pair of black horn-rimmed glasses completed the look, and the famous Lloyd "glass character" was born. With the stylized Sennett tradition already fading, the situation comedy based on realistic characters and events took its place. Lloyd's genius was to shape his character in such a way that it seemed to merge with the postwar generation's developing self-image.

The twenties adopted Lloyd as a special icon. In SAFETY LAST (1923) his character hopes to rise to the top of the department-store business, a dream that comes true when Harold is forced to climb the outside of the building. The shot of Lloyd dangling from a clock face in this film is the most famous image in silent comedy. It prefigures another twenties image of worker and clock in Fritz Lang's METROPOLIS, but with characteristic American humor and optimism. Produced for $120,963, the film grossed twelve times its negative cost, $1,588,545.[96] THE FRESHMAN (1925), Lloyd's contribution to the decade's collegiate mania, earned even more.

Many suggestions have been offered to explain Lloyd's decline after 1928, from poor material to his own inability to continue playing the same character, eternally youthful and optimistic. What has been overlooked is that Harold Lloyd, like the jaunty boater he often sported, was an ingrained element of twenties culture. Depression-era America turned its back on all that, and blotted out its love affair with artists like Lloyd—as Richard Griffith noted, not enough *Weltschmerz*.

Clara Bow

Did film make any real contribution to twentieth-century American culture? Most standard history texts are silent on the issue, but those that do mention the movies have a tendency to emphasize three common points: THE BIRTH OF A NATION, THE JAZZ SINGER, and Clara Bow.[97] For example, in Frank Freidel's *America in the Twentieth Century*, the impact of the cinema is reduced to the following:

> Motion pictures flamboyantly heralded the new moral code and together with tabloid papers helped fabricate false stereotypes of the period. An estimated 50 million people a week went to theaters to see the "It" girl, Clara Bow, the glamorous Rudolph Valentino, comedian Charlie Chaplin, gangster pictures, Westerns, and great spectacles like the first film version of *The Ten Commandments* (*America in the Twentieth Century* [New York: Knopf, 1976], p. 154).

A further line about THE JAZZ SINGER and the obligatory early mention of THE BIRTH OF A NATION are the limit of this text's acknowledgment of the motion picture. Other volumes might alter the supporting players, but Clara Bow, the "It" girl, remains a constant. When she died in 1965, her obituary was carried on the front page of the *New York Times*. "More than any other woman entertainer of her time," the paper wrote, "Clara Bow perhaps best personified the giddier aspects of an unreal era, the 'Roaring Twenties.' "[98]

One would expect to see this importance reflected in numerous critical studies, monographs, and retrospectives, but such is definitely not the case. Clara Bow may be the cultural historians' idea of a silent star, but she rates hardly a mention from most film specialists. Only three years after her death, Kevin Brownlow published his massive, wide-ranging study of the silent film *The Parade's Gone By . . .* , a work that focuses closely on individual careers. Yet Clara Bow is not mentioned.[99]

There seems to be quite a difference of opinion here, and it turns on the real significance of Bow's position as a prototypical flapper. Colleen Moore was certainly the first to establish the screen archetype of the flapper, as early as 1923 in FLAMING YOUTH. She was far more articulate than Bow, and with her own producing company, she had a degree of control over her roles to which Bow never even aspired. But Bow ensured her place in history in more spectacular ways. First, while Colleen Moore led a relatively decorous offscreen life, Clara Bow, in Adolph Zukor's words, "was exactly the same off the screen as on." The rambunctious swath she cut through the film community—one must turn to *Hollywood Babylon* for a full account— seemed a casebook study of the "new moral code" and its "false stereotypes."[100] More important, Bow was targeted by Elinor Glyn as the prime female possessor of "It," a fantastically successful promotional gambit that outlived Glyn and overwhelmed anything else one might say about Bow.

Clara Bow (Balaban & Katz Magazine, *undated*).

Madame Glyn, author of the scandalous best-seller *Three Weeks* (published in 1907 and filmed at least twice, most notably in 1924), had taken on herself the mission of instructing Hollywood society in proper standards of civilized behavior. Appalled by the various levels of vulgarity she found in Hollywood, Glyn formulated the concept of "It," an attractive aura of poise and self-confidence that she found all too rare among American film stars:

> To have "It," the fortunate possessor must have that strange magnetism which attracts both sexes. "It" is a purely virile quality, belonging to a strong character. He or she must be entirely unself-conscious and full of self-confidence, indifferent to the effect he or she is producing, and un-influenced by others. There must be physical attraction, but beauty is unnecessary. Conceit or self-consciousness destroys "It" immediately (quoted in James Robert Parish, *The Paramount Pretties*, p. 65).

For Madame Glyn, Clara Bow, Antonio Moreno, Rex the Wonder Horse, and the doorman at the Ambassador Hotel were the only possessors of "It" in Hollywood.[101]

"It" did nothing for the other three but soon came to dominate the life and career of Clara Bow, which until then had been largely unexceptional. In 1921 she had entered one of many beauty contests then being sponsored by the fan magazines, from which she emerged with a screen test and a part in a real movie. Her scenes wound up on the cutting-room floor, but she eventually came under contract to B. P. Schulberg, a former Paramount executive then operating the "Poverty Row" studio, Preferred Pictures. Schulberg used her in some of his own films and skillfully built up her value by loaning her out to other producers. In 1924 she appeared in eight features, and in 1925 she was seen in fourteen, including Lubitsch's KISS ME AGAIN for Warners. When Schulberg rejoined Paramount late in 1925, he brought Bow with him, and with first-class stories, co-stars, and production values her popularity soared.

Surviving Bow films, especially MANTRAP (1926), KID BOOTS (1926), GET YOUR MAN (1927), and RED HAIR (1928), show a natural comedienne, blending sexiness and humor in a tradition later developed by Carole Lombard.[102] This accessible, home-grown sexuality, radiating the special magnetism that so captured the likes of Elinor Glyn, did offer a new screen vision of the American woman. But the whole "It girl" idea was so bound up with the ethos of the 1920s that Depression-era audiences rejected it, and Bow's career ended in 1933. It seems that the icons of one age can quickly become the "false stereotypes" of the next.

John Gilbert

By the time of Rudolph Valentino's death, the mantle of "great lover" had already begun to pass to a local contender, Metro-Goldwyn-Mayer's popular new star John Gilbert. Gilbert had been working in pictures for a decade, first as a bit player at Inceville, later as a writer and director, and by the early twenties as the lead in a series of inexpensive melodramas for William Fox. But even his elegant performance in John Ford's CAMERO KIRBY (1923) had failed to arouse much public response. In 1924 Gilbert moved to the new MGM, and his sudden acclaim for films such as HIS

WEEK STARTING JANUARY 4, 1926

BALABAN & KATZ
MAGAZINE

Issued Weekly for your Entertainment

In this Issue:

"Colleen Moore Tells How to Win A Flapper's Heart"

John Gilbert (Balaban & Katz Magazine, *4 January 1926*).

HOUR (1924) and HE WHO GETS SLAPPED (1924) made him seem an overnight success. Even his daughter's scrupulously researched biography talks of Gilbert's "meteoric rise," but Gilbert had in fact spent years working his way up from within the industry.[103] His career was no comet.

Release of THE MERRY WIDOW and THE BIG PARADE in 1925 firmly established his popularity as well as his value to MGM. Although his onscreen lovemaking was as dark and passionate as Valentino's, Gilbert projected an entirely different image of a romantic idol. As Alexander Walker has noted, Gilbert was able to appeal romantically to the females in the audience without alienating their male companions. The hearty, good-natured American values that he projected made him the first successful link between the romantic traditions of Valentino and Wallace Reid. Clark Gable, whose early career crossed Gilbert's more than once, would inherit this crown when Gilbert's star faded.[104]

Gilbert himself identified his career with Valentino's, admiring his rival's natural acceptance of fame and adulation.[105] According to King Vidor, who directed five Gilbert features between 1924 and 1926 and was a close friend, Gilbert was never able to handle the emotional stress that came with Hollywood celebrity:

> Jack Gilbert was an impressionable fellow, not too well established in a role of his own in life. The paths he followed in his daily life were greatly influenced by the parts that some scriptwriter had written for him. When he began to read the publicity emanating from his studio which dubbed him the "great lover," his behavior in real life began to change accordingly. It was a difficult assignment to live up to (*A Tree Is a Tree*, p. 134).

Gilbert was not the only Hollywood star to behave in an erratic and self-destructive fashion, but the reasons for his ultimate decline seem directly bound up with his personal and emotional problems. He made more than his share of powerful enemies (most notably Louis B. Mayer), while his romantic entanglements with such stars as Greta Garbo, Leatrice Joy, and Ina Claire, the last two of whom he married, seem hopelessly neurotic and immature. When a crisis in his career developed, he had no professional or emotional support to help survive it.[106]

It is a convention of Hollywood history that John Gilbert's career was destroyed by the talkies, but why this was allowed to happen is still a controversial issue. Critics report that audiences laughed at his lovemaking in the first talkie he released, HIS GLORIOUS NIGHT (1929), but the conclusion that his voice was at fault is no longer generally accepted. Rather, Gilbert seems to have been the victim of inappropriate scripting and direction. As Vidor suggests, "The literal content of his scenes, which in silent films had been imagined, was too intense to put into spoken words." In other words, we can see now that the laughter over Gilbert's repeated "I love you. I love you. I love you" in this film was directed not at his vocal quality but at his dialogue, something not understood at the time.[107]

Supporters of a conspiracy theory lay the blame at the feet of Louis B. Mayer. According to this group, Mayer had sworn to destroy Gilbert as early as 8 September 1926, when the actor assaulted him over an insult to Greta Garbo, whom Gilbert was scheduled to marry that day. When talkies arrived, Mayer took advantage of the confusion to sabotage Gilbert's films and ruin his career. "You make that picture and make it *lousy*," he ordered the director of HIS GLORIOUS NIGHT, at least according to Louise Brooks.[108]

In 1928 Gilbert had renewed his contract for three years, at the fabulous sum of $250,000 per picture, with a guarantee of two pictures per year. Bypassing Mayer altogether, he had made this contract directly with Nicholas Schenck in Loew's New York office. There was no provision for a sound test in the agreement, and it was practically unbreakable. Alexander Walker suggests that Schenck agreed to such generous terms in order to keep Gilbert from going to United Artists. He needed Gilbert on the lot to sweeten the value of the shares he was negotiating to sell to William Fox, then in the midst of his failed attempt to purchase control of Loew's.[109]

If Mayer had wanted to destroy Gilbert's career, why wait two years to begin work? Why not demolish him before contract-renewal time, instead of after? Mayer had a 10 percent share of the profits of Gilbert's films, and Irving Thalberg had 5 percent.[110] Why would these men—and it was Thalberg who supervised production, not Mayer—cut their own throats at a time of chaos in the industry?

The conspiracy buffs attribute too much wisdom and foresight to Mayer. The fact is, most silent stars were very badly presented in their early talkies, even those producing their own films. Pickford, Gish, Swanson, Talmadge, Lloyd, Keaton, and Gilbert were only some of those whose talking picture debuts were far below their usual standard. Only Garbo and Chaney, who chose to make eccentric talkie debuts, came through unscathed.

John Gilbert was a victim of the inability of Hollywood's best minds to predict a method of pushing silent stars into the age of talkies. Any vendetta on the part of Louis B. Mayer was simply another nail in the coffin.

Louise Brooks

> There is one actress who is destined to succeed Gloria Swanson some day in the hearts of movie fans. And, to our way of thinking, that actress is Louise Brooks. Her work in *A Social Celebrity* was a revelation. This girl has charm, experience, looks, personality, and BRAINS (*Exhibitor's Trade Review*, 18 June 1926, p. 2).

In a sense, Louise Brooks did ultimately supplant Swanson in the hearts of movie fans, at least those who combined their nostalgia with a strong taste for the outré and the exotic. But the celebrity that Brooks achieved bears little relation to the Hollywood stardom of Norma Talmadge, Pola Negri, or Gloria Swanson. In her heyday at Paramount (1925–1928) Brooks made few magazine covers, seldom achieved featured billing, and not infrequently appeared in support of W. C. Fields or Wallace Beery.

By no objective standard could Brooks be considered one of the major stars of the silent era, but today her status is unique. What historian Lotte Eisner once called "the miracle of Louise Brooks" became in the 1980s "the phenomenon of Louise Brooks." At a time not especially interested in silent film, a passion for Brooks and her work spread from a small circle of admirers to a broad international public. She became *The New Yorker*'s favorite silent-film star, published a surprisingly popular memoir, and saw festivals of her most obscure work reach museum screens around

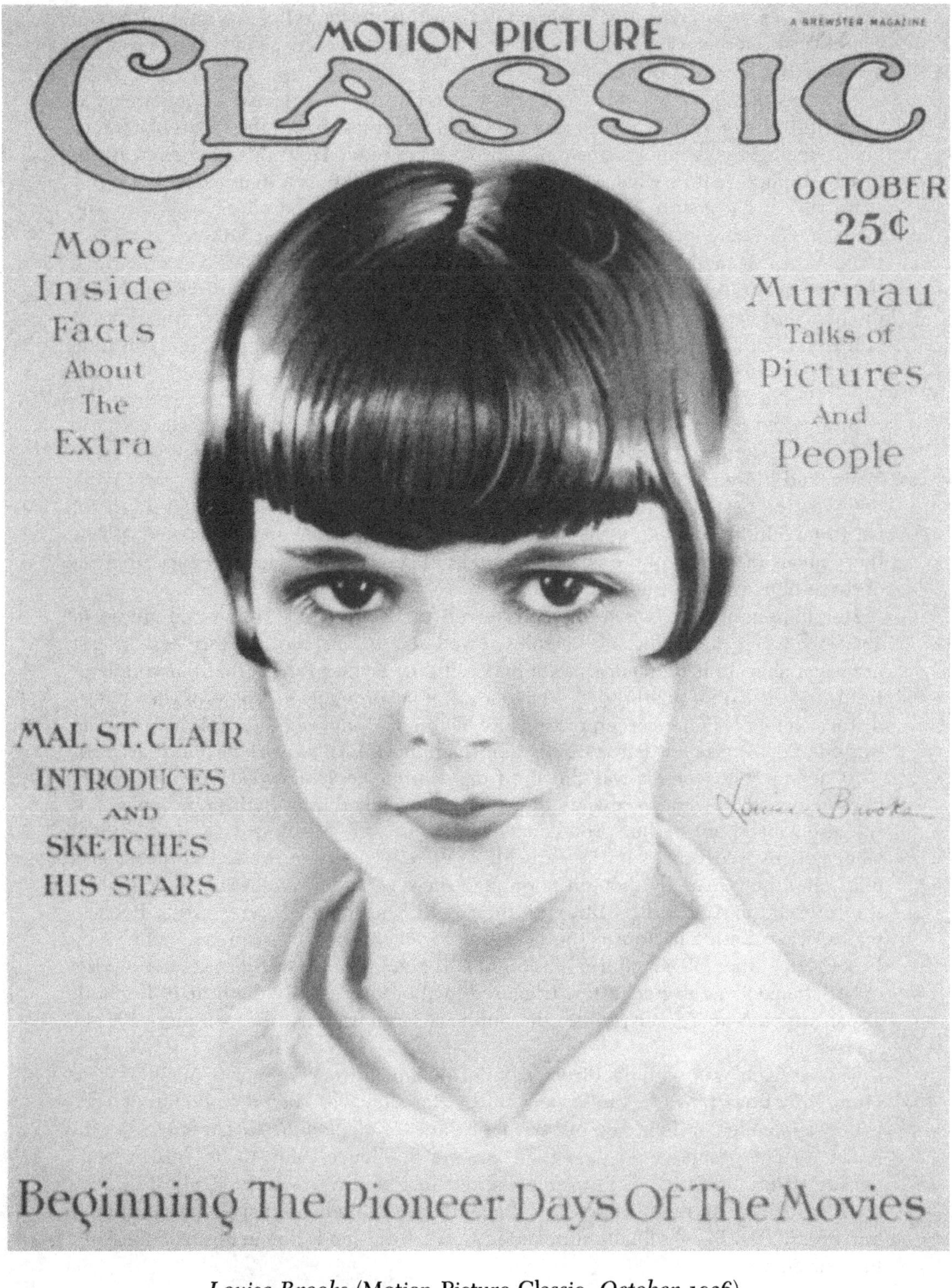

Louise Brooks (Motion Picture Classic, *October 1926*).

the world. In 1989 a 600-page biography exhaustively detailed her on- and off-screen career.[111] Nonetheless, to view the silent film through the image of Louise Brooks is a substantial recasting of history.

Many reputations fall and rise over the years, but Brooks's renewed popularity was a rare instance of a major reordering of critical priorities. From the status of a minor entertainer, Brooks emerged as an icon of the decade. How this happened is not nearly so important as what it means to the study of film as a living art.

Initially, what critical reputation Brooks possessed was based on two films she made in Germany for G. W. Pabst, PANDORA'S BOX (1929) and DIARY OF A LOST GIRL (1929). Heavily censored and never widely released, they were known only to the cognescenti, who treasured the few prints collected in scattered archives. In her discussion of Pabst's work in *The Haunted Screen*, Lotte Eisner appears to give most of the credit for the success of these films to Brooks. "Her gifts of profound intuition may seem purely passive to an inexperienced audience," Eisner wrote, "yet she succeeded in stimulating an otherwise unequal director's talent to the extreme."[112]

Brooks had entered film in 1925. Prior to this she had toured as a dancer with the Denishawn Company (1922–1924), then appeared in Broadway revues for George White and Florenz Ziegfeld. Her first films were made for Paramount in New York, but even the best of them, such as Frank Tuttle's LOVE 'EM AND LEAVE 'EM (1926), fail to take full advantage of her radiant blend of innocence and sensuality. Nor is there much awareness of the character and intelligence in her face and eyes. In most of these films she is a traditional ingenue.

Her films improved when she transferred to Paramount's Hollywood studio in 1927–1928, but the quality of her roles stayed about the same. Howard Hawks cast her as an anachronistic *femme fatale* in A GIRL IN EVERY PORT (1928), and only in BEGGARS OF LIFE (1928) did she have a role that brought out some of the contradictory elements of her screen personality. Tired of Hollywood life and the parts she was offered, Brooks left Paramount when the opportunity to work for Pabst arrived.

At a time when talent was flowing from Europe to Hollywood, Louise Brooks became one of the first to reverse the trend. She walked into the history books, but she also walked out on her professional career. Eisner, Ado Kyrou, and the others who rediscovered Brooks in the early 1950s were not very interested in these early films, and they certainly thought nothing of the few pathetic roles she landed when she returned to America.[113] But with their help, and that of James Card at Rochester's George Eastman House, the new Brooks legend began to spread. Articles by Brooks appearing in such journals as *Sight and Sound* and *Film Culture*, and reports of her strange exile in Rochester, triggered further interest. By the time of Kenneth Tynan's 1979 *New Yorker* profile, the public at large was ready for a Louise Brooks revival.

This acclaim was without direct parallel in film history. Revivals of interest in Humphrey Bogart, W. C. Fields, and Busby Berkeley were based on bodies of work widely applauded in their day, but Brooks had never made more than a minor splash. Artists or composers could pass their careers in silence, only to be "discovered" decades later, but until recently film lacked this kind of memory. Only when the work of scholars and archivists was sufficiently developed could such a reconsideration occur. That Brooks finally supplanted Gloria Swanson is due in no small measure to their efforts.

10

The Envelope, Please

*T*he Academy of Motion Picture Arts and Sciences was formed by Hollywood's silent-film community just as the silent film itself was about to pass from the scene. The announced goals of the Academy were "to develop harmony and adjust differences and grievances within the industry, . . . promote the good repute of the profession and protect it from outside attack, and . . . aid in the advancement of the motion picture in all its arts and sciences."[1] Today the Academy is best known for its annual awards ceremony, but in its initial months it was far more concerned with the threat to industrial "harmony" posed by incipient unionization.

On 29 November 1926 the major producers had finally signed the Studio Basic Agreement, which codified their relationship to organized stagehands, carpenters, electricians, painters, and musicians. Prior to this date jurisdictional quarrels among competing unions had weakened and divided the organized labor force, but when the International Alliance of Theatrical Stage Employees and Motion Picture Machine Operators was finally able to establish its jurisdiction over studio craft workers, industry leaders were forced to capitulate. Hollywood's moment as a non-union haven was over.[2]

The "talent," however, was still unorganized. Honorary societies such as the Screen Writers' Guild of the Authors' League of America or the American Society of Cinematographers did not function as unions. But with the signing of the Studio Basic Agreement, unionization was in the air, and Actors' Equity, which had been trying without success to organize the studios since 1922, announced plans for a new campaign.

Enter the Academy. Within weeks of the signing of the Studio Basic Agreement, Louis B. Mayer had suggested a new industry organization to supplement the activities of the Hays Office, especially in regard to this new labor issue. By March the International Academy of Motion Picture Arts and Sciences had elected its first officers: Douglas Fairbanks, president; Fred Niblo, vice-president; M. C. Levee, treasurer; and Frank Woods, secretary.[3]

The Academy consisted of five distinct branches: actors, directors, producers and production executives, technicians (including cinematographers), and writers. However, it soon became apparent that the producers' branch was controlling the agenda for its own benefit. It coopted the other branches on such tricky issues as the 10

Founders of the Academy of Motion Picture Arts and Sciences. Seated: *Louis B. Mayer, Conrad Nagel, Mary Pickford, Douglas Fairbanks, Frank Woods, M. C. Levee, Joseph M. Schenck, Fred Niblo.* Standing: *Cedric Gibbons, J. A. Ball, Carey Wilson, George Cohen, Edwin Loeb, Fred Beetson, Frank Lloyd, Roy Pomeroy, John Stahl, Harry Rapf.*

percent wage cut of 1927, a threatened blow to non-union labor that the Academy claimed credit for rescinding. With its controlled, invitational membership, the Academy soon became the studio-approved alternative to a real union, a situation that caused immediate grumbling, especially among the actors and writers.[4]

While all this was moving forward, the Academy's committee on merit awards announced a dozen categories that would be the basis for an annual series of citations. Films released between 1 August 1927 and 1 August 1928 would be eligible—in effect, the last year of the silent cinema. Earlier awards had been given by trade papers, fan magazines, and "better films" committees, but what made the Academy's awards interesting were their final two categories. There was no citation for "Best Picture." Instead, Academy members were asked to vote on two production awards:

1. A Distinction Award for the most outstanding motion picture production, considering all elements that contribute to a picture's greatness.
2. A Distinction Award for the most unique, artistic, worthy and original production without reference to cost or magnitude.[5]

It would appear that the Merit Award Committee understood a distinction between art and commerce, and established equal prizes for films that excelled in each area. The award for "outstanding motion picture production" was clearly intended to honor the craft of producing, the domain of one of the Academy's five component branches, while that for "artistic, worthy and original production" suggests the aesthetic criteria of *Exceptional Photoplays*.

This distinction is typical of the age. Even in Hollywood, where a vast industrial structure for the manufacture of film had sprung up in less than two decades, there was a deep regard for the artistic potential of the new medium. The public statements of Griffith, Pickford, Chaplin, Thalberg, Vidor, Gish, and other industry leaders make this clear in a way that would be inconceivable today. On the other hand, only a few radicals (von Stroheim chief among them) felt that there was anything inherently contradictory in the American cinema's dual function as commerce and art.[6]

Films eventually singled out in these two categories reflected these distinctions fairly well: SUNRISE, THE CROWD, and CHANG for "artistic production," WINGS, THE LAST COMMAND, THE RACKET, 7TH HEAVEN, and THE WAY OF ALL FLESH for "outstanding production." That first year the Academy bestowed its two top production awards on Fox's SUNRISE and Paramount's WINGS.

History records this event differently, especially history as written by the Motion Picture Academy. The following year it was decided to combine the two Distinction Awards into one top prize. There are a number of reasonable explanations for this, including the greater economic impact that a single award carries, and the ego problem of designating one group of nominees as "not so artistic." In tracing the lineage of the current "Best Picture" category, however, official histories approved by the Academy consciously elevate WINGS at the expense of SUNRISE. One such volume not only discounts the stature of the "artistic quality of production" award, lumping it with the minor technical citations and special awards, but retroactively changes the name of the award given WINGS to "Best Picture."[7]

No doubt the Academy has its own reasons for ignoring the high award its founders voted to SUNRISE and tracing the lineage of its current top winner directly back to WINGS. Certainly it is no easier today to analyze the rich output of silent American features and rank them according to "best," "outstanding," or "most important." Such a task was attempted by the Royal Film Archive of Belgium as part of a project honoring the American bicentennial, and the results are interesting not so much for how they relate to the Academy's thinking but for how they summarize history's verdict on the films of the 1915–1928 period and their place within the entire history of American cinema.[8]

An international grouping of critics and historians, including 116 Americans and 87 "non-Americans," was asked to list the "most important and misappreciated" American films through 1976. Of the top ten "most important" titles cited, eight were released between 1915 and 1928, a phenomenal number that reflects the high regard accorded films of this era half a century after the demise of silent pictures. Here are the top ten films cited, along with the number of times each film was recognized (out of 205 possible votes):

CITIZEN KANE (1941)	156 votes
SUNRISE (1927)	114
GREED (1924)	106

WINGS (*Paramount, 1927*): *a window card.*

INTOLERANCE (1916)	105
THE BIRTH OF A NATION (1915)	95
SINGIN' IN THE RAIN (1952)	77
NANOOK OF THE NORTH (1922)	77
THE GENERAL (1927)	77
THE GOLD RUSH (1925)	69
THE CROWD (1928)	67

It should be noted that any such poll reflects only the critical thinking of the moment, and not any ideal or even objective pantheon. Nevertheless, the consensus seen here (on the silent films, at least), would have held few surprises for any critic writing since 1930.

As we have seen, SUNRISE was immediately cited by the Hollywood community for its "unique" and "artistic" qualities. A conscious attempt to merge the European art cinema with Hollywood's production and distribution resources, it failed commercially but succeeded as a prestige item for the Fox studio. More important, it suggested a new method of visual discourse to a whole generation of American filmmakers:

> Here is camera technique pushed to its limits, freed from pantomime and parade against a world as motionless as a backdrop. . . . Not since the earliest, simplest moving pictures, when locomotives, fire engines, and crowds in the streets were transposed to the screen artlessly and endearingly . . . has there been such joy in motion as under Murnau's direction (Louise Bogan, "*Sunrise*," *New Republic*, 26 October 1927).

Of the eight silent films on the list, SUNRISE may have been the least important to audiences of the time, but its standing among critics and industry professionals was remarkably high. Karl Struss, one of its cinematographers, found it revolutionary in the way it expressed thought entirely through visual imagery—not just camera movement, but all elements of a carefully preplanned production design.[9] While the American cinema had produced work of great style and substance before this, SUNRISE was able to demonstrate to the Hollywood community specific values that could be gained from a formal, even self-conscious application of purely "cinematic" devices. Criticism of SUNRISE within this group almost completely bypassed the film's story line and focused instead on its incorporation of title cards, the function of its camera movements, and the stylized perspectives employed in its settings. The critical community, meanwhile, was not yet sophisticated enough to fully understand the importance of such elements and spent far more time quibbling about the film's "happy ending" and the alleged corruption of artistic ideals this represented for them. The result was an unjust attack on the Fox hierarchy, and the elevation of Murnau to the status of martyr in Hollywood's long battle between commerce and art.

Erich von Stroheim was an even more flamboyant martyr. While SUNRISE may or may not have been compromised by its ending, the whole of GREED was seen as a bleeding fragment, a two-hour sliver of a masterwork originally prepared by its maker in a nine-hour version. But if SUNRISE earned wide support within the professional community, GREED polarized critics and audiences alike. To Richard Watts,

Jr., it was "the most important picture yet produced in America," a dramatic achievement on a par with that season's great Broadway success *Desire Under the Elms*. On
the other hand, the *New York Times* praised MGM executives for cutting the film,
and even Robert E. Sherwood denounced von Stroheim as "a genius . . . badly in
need of a stop watch."[10]

What all these critics were reacting to was the success of von Stroheim's effort to
find a cinematic equivalent of Frank Norris' literary naturalism. In *McTeague*, Norris
had made the world of his characters a significant, even palpable, force in the drama.
Pages of detailed description created a world that defined and delimited the lives of
his characters. In his screen adaptation, von Stroheim employed deep-focus photography, set decoration of extraordinary authenticity, and a performance style of rare
intimacy and authority. To most viewers in 1924, the screen was not yet ready for so
strong a dose of "realism," but among the critical community such attitudes soon
began to change. GREED, especially its uncut version, quickly became an icon of
authenticity, a "holy grail" whose loss could be blamed on crass studio executives.
This being the case, it is somewhat ironic that none of those voting for GREED in the
1976 poll had ever seen anything but the shortened MGM release—a version completely rejected by its director.[11]

It is not surprising that THE BIRTH OF A NATION and INTOLERANCE should appear
so closely together on this list, since history has often considered these two D. W.
Griffith productions as some sort of matched pair. In fact, one view of INTOLERANCE
sees it as a direct response to the reception of the earlier picture, with Griffith lashing
out at those who sought to censor or suppress his epic of the Civil War and Reconstruction.

The same month that Universal City opened in California, New York audiences
saw the premiere of THE BIRTH OF A NATION. If Carl Laemmle's new studio reflected the rapid industrialization of the motion-picture business, then Griffith's film
served as a similar landmark in the development of the motion-picture product itself.
THE BIRTH OF A NATION had an unprecedented effect on the cinema's economic,
aesthetic, technological, and cultural development. While other films may have
matched it in one or another of these categories, no other work in film history has
achieved an impact so broad, and so deep. Figures on the film's exact earnings are
unavailable, but all research indicates that THE BIRTH OF A NATION was by far the
greatest financial success of the silent era. It was the first feature to attract vast
crowds to theater box offices, and it did so while offering an experience that was
technically and artistically in the vanguard of 1915 production standards. It might be
argued that Griffith did not introduce here the moving camera shots, close-ups,
parallel story development, or lighting effects that so impressed audiences, but he
certainly synthesized them in this film with breathtaking effect. THE BIRTH OF A
NATION should never be thought of as just a movie, however. Rather, it was the first
great film event, the first film to force its way into the national consciousness.
Griffith's picture of the war itself was unexceptionable, but his Reconstruction, peo-
pled with heroic Klansmen, duplicitous mulattoes, and rampaging hordes of freed
Negro slaves, roused unprecedented storms of protest.[12]

If INTOLERANCE was Griffith's answer to this uproar, it was not an apology for his
own position but an attack on the forces that saw fit to restrict his right of free speech.
Griffith lost that battle in the Supreme Court, but with INTOLERANCE he lost at the
box office as well. Far more costly and ambitious than THE BIRTH OF A NATION,

The cover of a theater program for D. W. Griffith's INTOLERANCE *(Wark, 1916).*

INTOLERANCE was rejected by audiences who were unable to focus on its four interwoven narrative lines—the fall of Babylon, the Crucifixion, the St. Bartholomew's Eve massacre, and a modern story of labor unrest.

In retrospect it is clear that Griffith demanded too much of an audience that, only a few years earlier, had been satisfied with two-reel chases and slapstick comedies. Even today the dispersed focus clouds INTOLERANCE for modern audiences. No sooner have they developed an interest in Mae Marsh's struggles in the modern story than they are pulled back to ancient Babylon or the Huguenot episode. An unintended effect of this, of course, is to stress the film's formal dynamics while minimizing that emotional appeal which drives THE BIRTH OF A NATION like a roller coaster. INTOLERANCE is a far more intellectual experience than its predecessor, and even today it is a more amenable subject for classroom analysis. Indeed, during the silent era it had already become a textbook, as young Soviet directors took it apart and reconstructed it, in an attempt to understand how it worked and how its lessons might be applied to their own films.

There is only one film on this list that is not a traditional studio narrative: Robert Flaherty's NANOOK OF THE NORTH. Honored by later generations as a progenitor of the documentary tradition, NANOOK was not the first feature produced on an exotic location, nor even the first to take "reality" as its subject matter. In some ways, NANOOK is very much the nonfiction equivalent of THE BIRTH OF A NATION, for Flaherty was able to win a tremendous audience for his film through his canny manipulation of dramatic devices that had already been demonstrated onscreen by others. The genius of NANOOK was to combine the most basic elements of drama—conflict, character, rising and falling dramatic action—with the "documentary" authenticity of cinematography.

With paint-and-canvas "realism" dominating the American studios, and the expressionism of the German studios the only apparent alternative, NANOOK arrived with a thunderclap:

> In a day of emotional and artistic deliquescence on the screen, a picture with the fresh strength and pictorial promise of *Nanook of the North* is in the nature of Revelation. It may be said to be the first photoplay of the natural school of cinematography. . . . Here at last begins our native screen language, as original in concept as *The Cabinet of Dr. Caligari,* yet as natural as that is fantastic (Frances Taylor Patterson, "*Nanook of the North,*" *New Republic,* 9 August 1922).

The promise remained unfulfilled. Historians once saw film as the inheritor of two traditions, fantasy and reality, stemming from the work of French film pioneers Georges Méliès and Louis and Auguste Lumière. If NANOOK OF THE NORTH seemed to be a new BIRTH OF A NATION, they looked in vain for a subsequent INTOLERANCE, GREED, or SUNRISE. The small number of great nonfiction works that did follow never threatened the prevailing fictional tradition. But even a half-century later, NANOOK OF THE NORTH still maintained this aura of promise for critics around the world, who dutifully ranked it as one of the landmark works in cinema history.

That THE GENERAL and THE GOLD RUSH should stand together on this list underscores one of the great sources of tension between period criticism of silent cinema and its modern counterpart. To put it bluntly, Chaplin was a god to film intellectuals of the 1920s, while Buster Keaton was often considered a likable, if limited, performer with nothing very much to say.[13]

THE GOLD RUSH was revered for its humanity, for its studied mixture of pathos, drama, and slapstick, and for its very existence as the latest example of Chaplin's art. By 1925 what Chaplin was doing pretty much defined the highest aspiration of comedy onscreen. He had so succeeded in capturing the hearts and minds of his generation that other comedians (even unintentionally) were inevitably compared to his standard. Chaplin's films remain as imaginative and affecting as always, but the passage of years since their creation has allowed their flaws to show through as well. The crudities of Chaplin's technical methods were simply not an issue in 1925. His cutting, his camera placement, even his scenic design, seem to later audiences a crude holdover from a simpler age of cinema, a limitation that Chaplin's genius for character and gag construction works to overcome. The cardboard sets of THE GOLD RUSH offer very little help to the star and director of this picture, who seems to care not a whit for the actual ambiance of the Far North and, in the old music-hall tradition, is satisfied to throw up a flat.

To look at Buster Keaton's THE GENERAL, however, is to step back into a re-creation of nineteenth-century life that rivals Griffith in texture and detail. As von Stroheim drew strength from the density of his environments, so Keaton creates his gags from objects, situations, and personalities generated by the period and location with which he is working. Chaplin's hungry cabin-mates might inhabit any frozen clime, but Keaton's characters create a southern landscape with more conviction than most dramatic features of the day.

Yet THE GENERAL was a financial catastrophe of such proportions that Keaton was ultimately forced to give up his own production company and sign with Metro-Goldwyn-Mayer. Critical reaction was not much better. For example, the *New York Times* reviewer, Mordaunt Hall, felt that the picture was lacking in humor and inferior to Keaton's earlier films. The comedian "appears to have bitten off more than he can chew," he wrote. Thirty years later a popular survey of silent cinema was still quite guarded in its assessment, admitting only that the film's "reduced comedy content" is compensated for by its unique narrative strength. All this began to change with Keaton's rediscovery in the 1960s. A new perspective on humor saw value in Keaton's style and sensibility, not just his gag structure.[14]

But as this particular poll shows, Keaton was not elevated at the expense of losing Charles Chaplin. Continued viewing, restoration, and analysis of silent films—not only by historians but by theater audiences as well—has allowed a healthy reevaluation of surviving films of the era. The Chaplin–Keaton contest is probably the most visible aspect of this constant restructuring of pantheon priorities. It tells us that silent film as a performing art still lives, but it also suggests that today's pantheon may be very different from that of a generation hence.

King Vidor's THE CROWD is the most recent silent film on the Belgian poll's "top ten" and was in fact released in competition with the earliest talking films. Shot between December 1926 and March 1927, it was on the shelf for almost a year before being issued by MGM. In retrospect, it is not surprising that studio executives had trouble deciding how to position the film in the marketplace. It avoids the plot constraints and character conventions of traditional silent melodrama and looks instead to the "enlightening influence" of German silent cinema as a model. THE CROWD lacks a villain, a happy ending, an action sequence, or even the traditional silent-movie idea of dramatic conflict. Instead it follows the lackluster career of a lower-middle-class urban office worker and his family. The "star," James Murray, was chosen by Vidor for his anonymity, a position to which he quickly returned in the months following the film's release. Vidor may have been looking back at the German cinema in his use of stylized settings, camera movement, and *Kammerspiel* acting, but much of the film's strength today comes from elements that predict the Italian neorealist cinema, still twenty years in the future. While not quite matching Cesare Zavattini's neorealist ideal of "ninety minutes in the life of an average man," The Crowd comes very close, especially in Vidor's handling of Murray, and his extensive location shooting in New York, much of it filmed with hidden cameras.[15]

MGM might have been uncertain about how The Crowd should be released (they offered it to exhibitors with a choice of endings), but their decision to budget half a million dollars for so nontraditional a film is clearly commendable. The Crowd actually turned a small profit for them, despite competition from films like The Jazz Singer, indicating audience support for high-quality filmmaking in the twilight period of silent film that few have discussed. The Motion Picture Academy even nominated it as "most artistic and unique production," but the competition from Sunrise was too strong.[16]

The eight films on this list are consensus masterworks, unsurprising and even a bit conservative in their selection. Without suggesting this group of titles as a rigid canon, it is worth noting that the consensus reached in 1976 was not so very different from what might have been achieved two generations earlier. These are the silent cinema's official masterworks, films that will live forever behind the walls of museums and universities.

But as we have tried to show throughout this book, the silent cinema was not just a roll of film in a can. It was a complex social, aesthetic, and economic fabric that brought the power of the moving image into the twentieth century. The silent film was not simply Hollywood and movie stars but a system of local theaters linking America's small towns and great cities, not just a list of films and filmmakers but a way of life in which technology, showmanship, and economics were all key determinants.

The end of silent pictures: a warning to aviators posted atop the sound stages at MGM, 1929.

List of Abbreviations

AC	*American Cinematographer*
ETR	*Exhibitor's Trade Review*
FDY	*Film Daily Yearbook of Motion Pictures*
MPN	*Motion Picture News*
MPW	*Moving Picture World*
NYDM	*New York Dramatic Mirror*
NYT	*New York Times*
SMPE/SMPTE	*Transactions* [later *Journal*] *of the Society of Motion Picture* [*and Television*] *Engineers*

Notes

Chapter 1. An Industry and an Art

1. "They're Off to Universal City," *Universal Weekly*, 6 March 1915, p. 12; Terry Ramsaye, *A Million and One Nights* (New York: Simon and Schuster, 1926), pp. 590–593.

2. Richard Randall, *Censorship of the Movies* (Madison: University of Wisconsin Press, 1968), pp. 18–21; "Laemmle on Censorship," *NYDM*, 10 March 1915, p. 23.

3. Seymour Stern, "Griffith, I: *The Birth of a Nation*," *Film Culture*, Spring–Summer 1965, pp. 53–54.

4. "A New Array of Exhibition," *NYDM*, 3 February 1915, p. 22.

5. Anthony Slide, *The Big V* (Metuchen, N.J.: Scarecrow Press, 1976), pp. 62–64; Ben Hall, *The Best Remaining Seats* (New York: Bramhall, 1961), pp. 37–41; "Films in Hippodrome," *NYDM*, 3 March 1915, p. 24.

6. "They're Off to Universal City."

7. *Ibid.*

8. "Homer Croy Writes His Impressions of Coast Trip for *Universal Weekly* and *Laemmle Ledger*," *Universal Weekly*, 20 March 1915, p. 8. Jack Rennert, *100 Posters of Buffalo Bill's Wild West* (New York: Darien House, 1976), discusses the development of this use of poster advertising in the United States.

9. Homer Croy, "Looking into the Grand Canyon," *Universal Weekly*, 27 March 1915, p. 12; "Echoes from Universal City," *Universal Weekly*, 3 April 1915, p. 9.

10. "Ohio Censor Resigns," *NYDM*, 17 March 1915, p. 21; Robert Grau, *The Theatre of Science* (New York: Broadway, 1914); Homer Croy, *How Motion Pictures Are Made* (New York: Harper, 1918); "Here and There with Big U Folks on the Way to Universal City," *Universal Weekly*, 3 April 1915, p. 12.

11. "Here and There."

12. Much of this information comes from early studio histories consulted by the author in the files at Universal during 1976–1977. Some sources give the size of the Taylor ranch as 260 acres, 275 acres, *etc.* The original purchase was 230, but Bernstein immediately added to it.

13. "Indoor Studio Built at Universal City," *Universal Weekly*, 23 January 1915, p. 9.

14. "Flood and Gale Hit Universal City Hard," *Universal Weekly*, 6 February 1915, p. 28.

15. All notices are from *NYDM* the month that Universal City opened: "Santa Barbara Busy," 10 March 1915, p. 24; "Along the Pacific Coast," 10 March 1915, p. 27; "Thanhouser Studio Active," 31 March 1915, p. 25; "Open New Lubin Studios," 24 March 1915, p. 25; "Dollars and Sense," 17 March 1915, p. 22.

16. "Details of Celebration at Universal City," *Universal Weekly*, 27 March 1915, p. 8; "Carl Laemmle Opens Universal City," *Universal Weekly*, 20 March 1915, p. 5. Also original program, opening of Universal City, Special Collections, University of California at Los Angeles.

17. Rufus Steele, "Behind the Screen," *Ladies Home Journal*, October 1915, p. 16.

18. "Carl Laemmle Opens Universal City."

19. *Ibid.;* "Details of Celebration."

20. "Details of Celebration."

21. Nearly sixty years later, Carl Laemmle, Jr., vividly described to the author the crash of the stunt plane and his brief conversation with Stites moments before the takeoff, practically his only memory of the opening (interview with Laemmle by the author, 14 June 1973).

22. Steele, "Behind the Screen"; " 'Big Four' Feature Combine," *NYDM*, 24 March 1915, p. 24.

Chapter 2. Going to the Movies

1. L. C. Moen, "Statistics of the Motion Picture Industry," *MPN*, 2 December 1922, p. 2772. Another 17 percent went for shorts and 15 percent for music.

2. Harold Franklin, "Theatre Management," *SMPE* 33 (April 1928), p. 126. This article is adapted from Franklin's extremely valuable *Motion Picture Theater Management* (New York: Doran, 1927), which details all aspects of theater operation at the close of the 1915–1928 period. For the earlier years, see John B. Rathbun, *Motion Picture Making and Exhibiting* (Los Angeles: Holmes, 1914), especially pp. 96–120.

3. "6 Houses Gross $53,096,369," *FDY* (1928), p. 7.

4. Craig Morrison, "From Nickelodeon to Picture Palace and Back," *Design Quarterly* 93 (1974), pp. 6–9.

5. Neil G. Caward, "Starting a Picture Show," *Photoplay*, October 1915, p. 86.

6. L. C. Moen, "Statistics of the Motion Picture Industry," *MPN*, 16 December 1922, p. 3024.

7. David Naylor, *American Picture Palaces* (New York: Van Nostrand Reinhold, 1981), pp. 24–29; John J. Klaber, "Planning the Moving Picture Theatre," *Architectural Record*, November 1915, p. 540; Frederick A. Talbot, *Moving Pictures: How They Are Made and Worked* (Philadelphia: Lippincott, 1923), pp. 164–165.

8. Carl Holliday, "The Movies in an Average City," *American City*, July 1919, p. 59. Holliday was Phelan's dean at the university and claimed to be a former motion-picture man. He presented to a wider public information that Phelan himself issued as *Motion Pictures as a Phase of Commercialized Amusement in Toledo, Ohio* (Toledo: Little Book Press, 1919).

9. Quoted in William Marston Seabury, *The Public and the Motion Picture Industry* (New York: Macmillan, 1926), p. 277.

10. Thomas H. Dickinson, "Movies Changing Life of the Nation," *NYT*, 1 July 1923.

11. "The Editor's Chair," *American Projectionist*, February 1926, p. 8. "What the Picture Did for Me" was a continuing column of exhibitor comments, generally complaints, instituted by the *Exhibitor's Herald* in 1916. One example: "*The Iron Horse* (Fox). Oh, the print, the print, the print, the print!!! The rottenest I have had since a long time. Why can't Fox buy good prints? The picture was exceptionally fine. Oh but the print . . . !" M. J. Babin, Fairyland Theatre, White Castle, La. (*Exhibitor's Herald*, 28 August 1926, p. 66).

12. "Are the Motion Picture Schools Sucker Traps?" *American Projectionist*, September 1923, p. 10.

13. "Record of Film Fires," *FDY* (1925), p. 346.

14. Norman Clarke, *The Mighty Hippodrome* (Cranbury, N.J.: Barnes, 1968).

15. Quoted in Hall, *The Best Remaining Seats*, pp. 39–40. See also "Million-Dollar Theatre Opens," *MPN*, 18 April 1914, p. 23.

16. H. Lyman Broening, "Presentation Suffers from Bad Projection," *AC*, October 1926, p. 18.

17. See Naylor, *American Picture Palaces*, pp. 37–38. The Loew's Midland in Kansas City, Missouri, incorporated the Oriental Room of the demolished Vanderbilt mansion as its ladies' lounge.

18. Hall, *The Best Remaining Seats*, pp. 183–198, is especially good on the function of movie-theater organs.

19. Douglas Gomery, "The Movies Become Big Business: Publix Theatres and the Chain-Store Strategy," in Gorham Kindham, *The American Movie Industry* (Carbondale: Southern Illinois University Press, 1982), p. 28.

20. Naylor, *American Picture Palaces*, p. 44.

21. *Ibid.*, p. 48.

22. Dennis Sharp, *The Picture Palace* (New York: Praeger, 1969), p. 74; Naylor, *American Picture Palaces*, pp. 68–69.

23. Benjamin Hampton, *History of the American Film Industry* (New York: Dover, 1970), pp. 326–334; Hall, *The Best Remaining Seats*, p. 121; Naylor, *American Picture Palaces*, p. 113.

24. Holliday, "Movies in an Average City," p. 59; Herbert Corey, "Money in the Movies," *Everybody's Magazine*, September 1919, p. 30.

25. Alice Miller Mitchell, *Children and Movies* (Chicago: University of Chicago, 1929), pp. 17, 22, 27, 70–71, 135–142, 159. For a flavorful recollection of exactly the same ruses occurring on New York's Lower East Side, see "I Got Two, Who Got Three?" by Nathan Halper and Benjamin Mandelker[n], *Commentary*, July 1952, pp. 60–64.

26. Mitchell, *Children and Movies*, p. 154; "How Children Are Entertained," *Journal of Education*, 25

February 1915, pp. 207–212, quoted in Garth Jowett, *Film: The Democratic Art* (Boston: Little, Brown, 1976), p. 46.

27. *Educational Screen* survey reprinted in *FDY* (1924), p. 353; W. Stephen Bush, "Scenarios by the Bushel," *NYT*, 5 December 1920; Beth Brown, "Making Movies for Women," *MPW*, 26 March 1927, p. 342.

28. "Problems of an Exhibitor," *FDY* (1925), p. 59.

29. Other theaters in town included the Liberty (1,067 seats), the White (1,000 seats), the Hippodrome (900 seats), the Strand (700 seats), the Bijou (400 seats), the Lyceum (400 seats), and Ryan's (400 seats) (*FDY* [1926], p. 487).

30. H. W. Hepner, "Public Likes, Dislikes," *FDY* (1929), p. 896 (reprinted from *Exhibitor's Herald and Moving Picture World*). Unfortunately, the school and town are not identified.

31. Letters from James Mark Purcell to the author, 31 December 1984, 26 January 1985, 9 November 1986.

32. "Key City Grosses," *FDY* (1929), p. 871 (this useful summary, based on *Variety's* weekly figures, appeared in *FDY* beginning with the 1925 edition); Moen, "Statistics," *MPN*, 25 November 1922, p. 2655, and 16 December 1922, p. 3024. Moen's figures are based on a relatively comprehensive survey, but there is considerable disagreement on the numbers. The *Film Daily's* estimate that 60 percent of exhibitors were changing weekly at this time appears unsubstantiated (*Film Daily*, 23 January 1923, quoted in Seabury, *The Public and the Motion Picture Industry*, p. 278).

33. Seabury, *The Public and the Motion Picture Industry*, p. 277. These figures disagree with those of both *MPN* and the *Film Daily*, but all three sets do at least indicate the same trend toward gradual acceptance of the weekly program.

34. Moen, "Statistics," *MPN*, 2 December 1922, p. 2772.

35. George Theofiles, "A Guide to Collecting Movie Memorabilia," *Collectibles Monthly*, November 1977, p. 1.

36. Steve Schapiro and David Chierichetti, *The Movie Poster Book* (New York: Dutton, 1979), pp. 8, 16. These numbers are from the 1930s and may or may not reflect the size of print runs in the early feature period.

37. See the pressbook for THE FRESHMAN (Pathé, 1925); "Pressagenting the Movies," *NYT*, 3 February 1918. Contrary to what some have written, it is not true that the B or C styles were considered inferior designs.

38. See the pressbook for THE PHANTOM OF THE OPERA (Universal, 1925); Richard Koszarski, *The Man You Loved to Hate: Erich von Stroheim and Hollywood* (New York: Oxford University Press, 1983), p. 41.

39. "Novel Mutual Posters and Their Makers," *Reel Life*, 30 May 1914; see also *MPN*, 24 September 1915, p. 60, and "The True Story of a Poster That Failed and One That Didn't," in the pressbook for THE HEART RAIDER (Paramount, 1923). The most comprehensive discussion of the studios' advertising art departments can be found in Stephen Rebello and Richard Allen, *Reel Art: Great Posters from the Golden Age of the Silver Screen* (New York: Abbeville, 1988).

40. Theofiles, "A Guide to Collecting Movie Memorabilia."

41. For more on Reichenbach, see "The 'Tody' Hamiltons of the Film World," *NYT*, 8 June 1924; Ramsaye, *A Million and One Nights*, pp. 626–627; Christopher Finch and Linda Rosenkrantz, *Going Hollywood* (Garden City, N.Y.: Doubleday, 1979), pp. 270, 271, 282; Harry Reichenbach and David Freedman, *Phantom Fame: The Anatomy of Ballyhoo* (London: Noel Douglas, 1932). Reichenbach quote from *FDY* (1924), p. 489.

42. "Practical Showmanship Ideas," *FDY* (1928), p. 707; "Publix Pepped by Stars' Premium, Lasky Award Won by Charles Amos," *Publix Opinion*, 31 December 1927, p. 3.

43. "What a Live Wire Can Do with a Dead One," *MPN*, 4 December 1920, p. 4245.

44. Moen, "Statistics," *MPN*, 25 November 1922, p. 2644.

45. Hall, *The Best Remaining Seats*, p. 180; Erno Rapee, *Motion Picture Moods for Pianists and Organists* (New York: Schirmer, 1924).

46. George W. Beynon, *Musical Presentation of Motion Pictures* (New York: Schirmer, 1921), pp. 11, 47; Burr C. Cook, "Fitting Music to the Movie Scenes," *Motion Picture Magazine*, October 1916, p. 111. Breil's short opera "The Legend" was performed three times by the New York Metropolitan Opera in 1919 (George Pratt to author, 18 June 1986).

47. Gillian Anderson, "Music for Silent Films (1894–1929): A Guide" (Washington, D.C.: Library of Congress, 1988).

48. Beynon, *Musical Presentation*, p. 12.

49. E. C. Mills, "The Musician, the Movie, and the Music Tax," *Metronome*, 15 September 1926, p. 26.

50. See, for example, the cue sheets for LADY WINDERMERE'S FAN reproduced in *"Image": On the Art and Evolution of the Film* (New York: Dover, 1979), p. 146.

51. Beynon, *Musical Presentation*, pp. 16, 35.

52. "Survivors of a Vanishing Race in the Movie World," *NYT*, 18 January 1920; Junko Ogihara, "The Exhibition of Films for Japanese-Americans in Los Angeles in the Silent Film Era," *Film History* 4, no. 2 (1990).

53. Edith Lang and George West, *Musical Accompaniment of Moving Pictures* (Boston: Boston Music Company, 1920), pp. 31–33. This may be one of the prepared Paramount scores referred to by Beynon. Tourneur seems to have had bad luck with his music. He writes of seeing PRUNELLA "in one of the side-shows in Atlantic City. An automatic piano furnished the musical score, which consisted of popular dance music" (Maurice Tourneur, "Meeting the Public Demands," *Shadowland*, May 1920, p. 46).

54. Moen, "Statistics," *MPN*, 25 November 1922, p. 2644.

55. "Popular Overtures," *Film Daily*, 24 October 1926, p. 9.

56. Hall, *The Best Remaining Seats*, pp. 56–65; Charles Beardsley, *Hollywood's Master Showman: The Legendary Sid Grauman* (New York: Cornwall, 1983), pp. 40–49.

57. "Rivoli's Holiday Week Specialties Win," *MPN*, 4 December 1920, p. 4234.

58. John Baxter, *Sixty Years of Hollywood* (Cranbury, N.J.: Barnes, 1973), p. 54.

59. Robert E. Sherwood, "Poisonous Prologues," *Motion Picture Classic*, November 1925, p. 22.

60. "Universal Presentations: *Outside the Law*," *Universal Weekly*, 29 May 1926, p. 22.

61. Frank Cambria, "Evolution of Presentation in Motion Pictures," *MPW*, 26 March 1927, p. 321. For more information on Cambria and Publix Theaters, see *Publix Opinion*, published weekly by Publix from 24 April 1927.

62. From the opening-week program of the Paramount Theatre, 19 November 1926. See the Theatre Historical Society's *Annual* 3 (1976), a special number on the Times Square Paramount.

63. Eric Clarke, "An Exhibitor's Problems in 1925," *SMPE* 23 (October 1925), p. 46; Lewis M. Townsend, "Problems of a Projectionist," *SMPE* 25 (May 1926), p. 79 (also in *American Projectionist*, June 1926, p. 6); Clarke, "An Exhibitor's Problems in 1926," *SMPE* 27 (October 1926), p. 46; Clarke, "An Exhibitor's Problems in 1927," *SMPE* 31 (September 1927), p. 450; Townsend and William W. Hennessy, "Some Novel Projected Motion Picture Presentations," *SMPE* 34 (April 1928), p. 345.

64. The figures are Clarke's. *FDY* gives the size of the Picadilly in 1926 as only 1,500 seats. In any case, the combine represented nearly all of the largest theaters in Rochester.

65. See Clarke's "An Exhibitor's Problems in 1926," pp. 48–51, and Symon Gould, "The Little Theatre Movement in the Cinema," *SMPE* 27 (October 1926), p. 58. Rothapfel's Radio City Music Hall catastrophe of 1932, where the "balanced program" finally eliminated the film altogether, is well described in Charles Francisco, *The Radio City Music Hall* (New York: Dutton, 1979). Only after Rothapfel's physical collapse on opening night were RKO theater executives able to re-introduce the film, although, ironically, the stage-show tradition continued in this theater for decades.

66. "Regulating the Speed of Pictures," *MPW*, 4 December 1909, p. 792; "Joy-Riders of the Theatre," *Photoplay*, November 1916, p. 72.

67. "Motion Picture Standards," *SMPE* 4 (July 1917); James R. Cameron, *Motion Picture Projection*, 3d ed. (New York: Technical Book Company, 1922), p. 27; F. H. Richardson, "The Various Effects of Over-Speeding Projection," *SMPE* 10 (May 1920), p. 61.

68. "Discussion of Gregory's Paper," *SMPE* 12 (May 1921), p. 82.

69. "Discussion," *SMPE* 17 (October 1923), p. 123.

70. "Report of Standards and Nomenclature Committee," *SMPE* 22 (May 1925), pp. 134–135.

71. Victor Milner, "Speed of Projection," *AC*, July 1923, p. 6; "ASC Advocates Holding 60 Ft per Minute Taking Speed," *AC*, May 1925, p. 20; Dan Clark, "A Mid-Year Cinematographic Review," *AC*, June 1926, p. 12.

72. Kevin Brownlow, "Silent Films: What Was the Right Speed?" *Sight and Sound*, Summer 1980, p. 164; letter from Kevin Brownlow to the author, 9 January 1986. Brownlow admits that his estimates are subjective, however.

73. "Change Over Signals and Buzzers," *American Projectionist*, May 1923, p. 9. A speed of 126 feet per minute equals 33.6 frames per second.

74. Brownlow, "Silent Films"; James Card, "Silent-Film Speed," in *"Image": On The Art and Evolution of the Film*, p. 145; Richard Rowland, "The Speed of Projection of Film," *SMPE* 27 (October 1926), p. 77. Some of the cue sheets were extremely detailed and inconsistent. OLD IRONSIDES was to be run at speeds varying from 60 to 120 (letter from Kevin Brownlow to the author, 10 December 1985).

75. P. A. McGuire, "General Motors Has Nothing on Accuracy of Projector Builders," *American Projectionist*, May 1926, p. 6; Paul Perry, "Cause of Speedy Projections," *AC*, March 1925, p. 7; "Some Objections to Present Methods," *AC*, September 1925, p. 4; John M. Joy, "Film Mutilation," *SMPE* 26 (May 1926), p. 5; Cameron, *Motion Picture Projection*, pp. 636–643.

76. Franklin, "Theatre Management," p. 136; Earl I. Sponable, "Some Technical Aspects of the Movie-tone," *SMPE* 31 (September 1927), p. 458; George Edwards, "The Little Red Wagon," *American Projectionist*, June 1927, p. 15.

77. Clarke, "An Exhibitor's Problems in 1925"; Townsend, "Problems of a Projectionist." See also the commentary on film cutting in George Pratt, *Spellbound in Darkness* (Greenwich, Conn.: New York Graphic Society, 1973), p. 376.

78. Clarke, "An Exhibitor's Problems in 1926."

79. "When a Film Grows Old," *NYT*, 28 August 1921; Earl J. Denison, "My Troubles, Your Troubles, and Our Troubles," *American Projectionist*, July 1926, p. 4; Joy, "Film Mutilation."

80. Arthur H. Gray, "A Few Practical Needs in the Field of Projection," *SMPE* 32 (September 1927), p. 628.

81. Townsend, "Problems of a Projectionist"; Joy, "Film Mutilation."

82. "Poor Prints His Trouble," *MPN*, 4 December 1920, p. 4326.

Chapter 3. The Industry

1. *MPN*, 3 April 1915, pp. 78–83.

2. Slide, *The Big V*, p. 65.

3. Janet Wasko, *Movies and Money* (Norwood, N.J.: Ablex, 1982), p. 11; Horace A. Fuld, "The Fakes and Frauds in Motion Pictures: Getting into the Film Business," *Motion Picture Magazine*, October 1915, p. 107.

4. Kevin Lewis, "A World Across From Broadway: The Shuberts and the Movies," *Film History* 1 (1987), pp. 39–52; Hampton, *A History of the Movies*, pp. 134–135; Ramsaye, *A Million and One Nights*, pp. 712–713; Paul Spehr, *The Movies Begin* (Dobbs Ferry, N.Y.: Morgan and Morgan, 1977), pp. 72, 76, 82, 84–92; Lucien Andriot, in an interview with the author, Palm Springs, California, June 1973.

5. Richard Koszarski, *The Rivals of D. W. Griffith* (Minneapolis: Walker Art Center, 1976), p. 55.

6. Wasko, *Movies and Money*, p. 11.

7. *Ibid.*; Ramsaye, *A Million and One Nights*, pp. 717–718; Kalton Lahue, *Dreams for Sale: The Rise and Fall of the Triangle Film Corporation* (Cranbury, N.J.: Barnes, 1971), p. 25.

8. Lahue, *Dreams for Sale*, pp. 48–49, 89.

9. Hampton, *History of the Movies*, pp. 144–145; Lahue, *Dreams for Sale*, pp. 77–78, 134–135.

10. Diane Koszarski, *The Complete Films of William S. Hart* (New York: Dover, 1980), pp. xv, 34; Lahue, *Dreams for Sale*, pp. 89–90, 162.

11. Iris Barry and Eileen Bowser, *D. W. Griffith: American Film Master* (New York: Museum of Modern Art, 1965), p. 49.

12. Hampton, *A History of the Movies*, pp. 117–120; Earle A. Beatty, Esq., "Summary History of the Motion Picture Industry" (1940), p. 162, unpublished manuscript prepared for the defense in *United States* v. *Paramount Pictures, Inc., et al.*, Eq. 87–273, author's collection.

13. Robert Sklar, *Movie-Made America* (New York: Vintage, 1975), pp. 143–144; Beatty, "Summary History," p. 163; "A $1,500,000,000 Business," *FDY* (1927), p. 738.

14. Jesse Lasky, with Don Weldon, *I Blow My Own Horn* (London: Victor Gollancz, 1957), pp. 122–124.

15. "The Motion Picture Hall of Fame," *Motion Picture Magazine*, December 1918, p. 12.

16. See Seabury, *The Public and the Motion Picture Industry*, pp. 59–63; Howard Lewis, *The Motion Picture Industry* (New York: Van Nostrand, 1933), pp. 142–180; Mae Huettig, *Economic Control in the Motion Picture Industry* (Philadelphia: University of Pennsylvania Press, 1944), pp. 113–142.

17. Gertrude Jobes, *Motion Picture Empire* (Hamden, Conn.: Archon, 1966), pp. 156–158.

18. Hampton, *A History of the Movies*, pp. 174–178.

19. *Ibid.*, p. 177.

20. "Chaplin Signs with Exhibitors' Circuit," *MPW*, 14 July 1917; Hampton, *A History of the Movies*, p. 180. The number of films to be delivered under this contract was later renegotiated.
21. Hampton, *A History of the Movies*, pp. 195–196; Adolph Zukor, with Dale Kramer, *The Public Is Never Wrong* (New York: Putnam, 1953).
22. Hampton, *A History of the Movies*, p. 206; Huettig, *Economic Control*, pp. 32–33.
23. Hampton, *A History of the Movies*, p. 242.
24. Beatty, "Summary History," pp. 163–165.
25. *Ibid.*; Hampton, *A History of the Movies*, pp. 255–257.
26. Huettig, *Economic Control*, pp. 35–36; Seabury, *The Public and the Motion Picture Industry*, pp. 21–23.
27. Lewis Jacobs, *The Rise of the American Film* (New York: Harcourt, Brace, 1939; reprinted, New York: Teachers College Press, 1968), pp. 288–289; Hampton, *A History of the Movies*, pp. 278–280, 363–364.
28. Ramsaye, *A Million and One Nights*, p. 794; Tino Balio, *United Artists: The Company Built by the Stars* (Madison: University of Wisconsin Press, 1976), pp. 3–5; Charles Chaplin, *My Autobiography* (New York: Simon and Schuster, 1964), pp. 221–222; Mary Pickford, *Sunshine and Shadow* (Garden City, N.Y.: Doubleday, 1955), p. 115.
29. Balio, *United Artists*, p. 30.
30. Hampton, *A History of the Movies*, pp. 227–229; Balio, *United Artists*, pp. 25–27.
31. Balio, *United Artists*, pp. 37–39.
32. *Ibid.*, pp. 43, 283. These losses, of course, relate only to the distribution end of the business. Depending on their acumen as producers, the partners could still have been netting considerable amounts of money.
33. *Ibid.*, pp. 52–60.
34. Ramsaye, *A Million and One Nights*, p. 431; Beatty, "Summary History," pp. 99–112, 115–122.
35. Bosley Crowther, *The Lion's Share* (New York: Dutton, 1957), p. 42.
36. *Ibid.*, pp. 46, 48–49.
37. David Pirie, *Anatomy of the Movies* (New York: Macmillan, 1981), p. 296.
38. The formal date of the Metro-Goldwyn incorporation was 16 May; 17 April is sometimes used as the date of the "announcement" of the combine.
39. Crowther, *The Lion's Share*, pp. 70, 80.
40. *Ibid.*, pp. 80–81.
41. Hampton, *A History of the Movies*, pp. 101, 102. *Upton Sinclair Presents William Fox* (Los Angeles: Upton Sinclair, 1933), a study of nearly four hundred pages, devotes practically all its space to a discussion of the attempted buyout, an admittedly topical event. How Fox got to this point in his career is mere prologue. Wasko, *Movies and Money*, pp. 70–76, goes over the same ground from a more modern perspective.
42. Spehr, *The Movies Begin*, p. 94; "New Jersey Capitalists Prepared to Back Fox," *MPN*, 3 April 1915, p. 46; Glenndon Allvine, *The Greatest Fox of Them All* (New York: Lyle Stuart, 1969), p. 86; Hampton, *A History of the Movies*, p. 102.
43. Ramsaye, *A Million and One Nights*, pp. 704–707; *Upton Sinclair Presents William Fox*, pp. 59–61.
44. Jobes, *Motion Picture Empire*, p. 186; Robert Stanley, *The Celluloid Empire* (New York: Hastings House, 1978), pp. 76–77; *Upton Sinclair Presents William Fox*, pp. 68–70; Naylor, *American Picture Palaces*, pp. 80–83, 120; Hall, *The Best Remaining Seats*, p. 112.
45. "New Expansion Work Now Under Way at Our West Coast Studios Is One of Marvels of All Filmdom," *Fox Folks*, September 1926, pp. 15–16.
46. Richard Koszarski, *Universal Pictures: 65 Years* (New York: Museum of Modern Art, 1977), p. 7. "It was evident that the basic idea of motion pictures and Mr. Woolworth's innovation were identical—a small price commodity in tremendous quantities," wrote Laemmle in a 1927 manuscript entitled "This Business of Motion Pictures" (excerpted in *Film History* 3 [1989]), p. 49. A similar series of articles, under the general title "From the Inside," appeared in the *Saturday Evening Post*, 27 August, 3 September, and 10 September 1927. The uncredited ghostwriter of all three pieces was probably Paul Gulick, a Universal publicist.
47. "Quit Using Dope!" *Universal Weekly*, 16 January 1915, p. 3; "Regular Service—or Bust!" *Moving Picture Weekly*, 10 March 1917, pp. 6–7.
48. Anthony Slide, *Early Women Directors* (Cranbury, N.J.: Barnes, 1977).
49. Bob Thomas, *Thalberg* (New York: Bantam, 1970), p. 31.

50. Carl Laemmle to Irving Thalberg, 5 December 1922 (author's collection).

51. Lichtman, quoted in I. G. Edmonds, *Big U* (Cranbury, N.J.: Barnes, 1977), p. 135; Hampton, *A History of the Movies,* p. 321; Beatty, "Summary History," p. 196.

52. "Universal Needs More First Run Houses," *Universal Weekly,* 8 May 1926, p. 8.

53. Hampton, *A History of the Movies,* p. 380; Charles Higham, *Warner Brothers* (New York: Scribners, 1975), pp. 10–11; Clive Hirschhorn, *The Warner Bros. Story* (New York: Crown, 1979), pp. 20–21. For an account of Rin-Tin-Tin's career, see Higham, pp. 32–41.

54. Beatty, "Summary History," p. 175.

55. THE KISS, a Garbo silent that opened on 16 November 1929, made a profit of $448,000. See Samuel Marx, *Mayer and Thalberg: The Make-Believe Saints* (New York: Random House, 1975), p. 256.

56. Horace A. Fuld, "The Fakes and Frauds in Motion Pictures: Getting into the Film Business," *Motion Picture Magazine,* October 1915, p. 107.

57. "Movies as Investments," *Barron's,* 14 April 1924, p. 10; Johnson Heywood, "How 'Movie' Industry Got on Sound Financial Basis," *Forbes,* 1 March 1927, p. 13.

58. Richard W. Saunders, "Finance and Pictures," *NYT,* 7 November 1926; "Industry Statistics," *FDY* (1951), p. 90.

59. Richard W. Saunders, "The Financial Progress of the Motion Picture Industry in 1925," *FDY* (1926), p. 17.

60. "At Least $500,000,000 Invested in 'Movies,' " *NYT,* 2 January 1916.

61. Herbert Corey, "Money in the Movies," *Everybody's Magazine,* September 1919, p. 30; Moen, "Statistics," *MPN,* 18 November 1922, p. 2527.

62. Raymond Moley, *The Hays Office* (New York: Bobbs-Merrill, 1945), p. 41; Will Hays, *See and Hear* (Motion Picture Producers and Distributors of America, 1929), p. 34; *Barron's,* 14 April 1924; *Wall Street News,* quoted in "A $1,500,000,000 Business," *FDY* (1927), p. 738; Carl Laemmle, "From the Inside," *Saturday Evening Post,* 27 August 1927, p. 10; E. E. Quantrell, "The Motion Picture Industry," *Bankers Monthly,* October 1927, p. 12.

63. Jobes, *Motion Picture Empire;* Huettig, *Economic Control,* p. 55.

64. Lucien Lehman, *American Illusion (Le grand mirage U.S.A.)* (New York: Century, 1931). In considering these studies, one might well ask: Why list "Allied Chemical Substances" and "Chemicals Proper" as different industries? Or "Oil and Gas" separately from "Petroleum and Mineral Oil Products"? "Wholesale Trade," "Retail Trade," and "Misc. Wholesale and Retail Trade" are listed as three distinct industries by Huettig, but these figures must duplicate those for other industries appearing elswhere on the chart. And some industries here, such as "Domestic Service" or "Investment Trusts," are not very industrial in the manufacturing sense—obviously, conclusions intended by the Hollywood partisans.

Chapter 4. Making Movies

1. Peter Bogdanovich, ed., *Allan Dwan: The Last Pioneer* (New York: Praeger, 1971), pp. 16–17; Raoul Walsh, *Each Man in His Time* (New York: Doubleday, 1974), pp. 62–67; Charles Higham, *Hollywood Cameramen* (Bloomington: Indiana University Press, 1970), pp. 35–56 (Garmes), 134–154 (Miller); Kevin Brownlow, *The Parade's Gone By . . .* (New York: Alfred Knopf, 1968), pp. 308–311 (Hornbeck); "Dorothy Arzner Interview," *Cinema* (Beverly Hills) 34 (1974), p. 10.

2. J. Vorhies, "Columbia Movies," *Motion Picture Magazine,* August 1915, p. 93; Victor Freeburg, *The Art of Photoplay Making* (New York: Macmillan, 1918); *Pictorial Beauty on Screen* (New York: Macmillan, 1923); Frances Taylor Patterson, *Cinema Craftsmanship* (New York: Harcourt, Brace, 1921), p. v. See also Patterson's *Scenario and Screen* (New York: Harcourt, Brace, 1928) and *Motion Picture Continuities* (New York: Columbia University Press, 1929), perhaps the first film book published by an American university press.

3. Kevin Brownlow, *The War, the West, and the Wilderness* (New York: Knopf, 1978), pp. 119–125; Carl Louis Gregory, "Instruction in Motion Picture Photography," *SMPE* 28 (October 1926), p. 303.

4. Joseph P. Kennedy, ed., *The Story of the Film* (Boston: Shaw, 1927), contains transcripts of the fourteen lectures by various leaders of the artistic and business community of the motion-picture industry. On the amateur film movement, see, for example, Jack Bechdolt, *How to Make Your Own Motion Picture Plays* (New York: Greenberg, 1926), or Morrie Ryskind, C. F. Stevens, and James Englander, *The Home Movie Scenario Book* (New York: Anson, 1927), which offer sophisticated technical advice and sample film scenarios.

5. "Are the Motion Picture Schools Sucker Traps?" *American Projectionist,* September 1923, p. 10; John Emerson and Anita Loos, *Breaking into the Movies* (New York: McCann, 1921), p. 6.

6. Jean Bernique, *Motion Picture Acting* (Chicago: Producers Service Company, 1916); Mae Marsh, *Screen Acting* (Los Angeles: Photo-Star, 1921), p. 16.

7. Horace A. Fuld, "The Fakes and Frauds in Motion Pictures," *Motion Picture Magazine,* November 1915, p. 111.

8. A. Van Buren Powell, *The Photoplay Synopsis* (Springfield, Mass.: Home Correspondence School, 1919).

9. *The Secret of Successful Photoplay Writing* (Los Angeles: Palmer Photoplay, 1920).

10. *The Photoplaywrights' League of America: Its Object and Purposes,* promotional brochure (1921), author's collection.

11. Ernest A. Dench, "Making Money with a Motion Picture Camera," *Motion Picture Magazine,* October 1917, p. 39.

12. See, for example, Carl Louis Gregory, *Motion Picture Photography* (New York: Falk, 1927), or Herbert McKay, *Handbook of Motion Picture Photography* (New York: Falk, 1927). Gregory had been in charge of instruction for the Signal Corps during their wartime program at Columbia.

13. *Historical Statistics of the United States, Colonial Times to 1970,* part 1 (Washington, D.C.: U.S. Department of Commerce, 1975), p. 142; "Are the Motion Picture Schools Sucker Traps?" *loc. cit.*

14. George Blaisdell, "Mecca of the Motion Picture," *MPW,* 10 July 1915, p. 215; Perley Poore Sheehan, *Hollywood as a World Center* (Hollywood: Hollywood Citizens' Press, 1924), pp. 1, 102–115.

15. Kevin Brownlow and John Kobal, *Hollywood: The Pioneers* (New York: Knopf, 1979), pp. 90–107; Sklar, *Movie-Made America,* p. 68. See also Murray Ross, *Stars and Strikes* (New York: Columbia University Press, 1941).

16. *NYDM,* 24 March 1915, p. 26 (Ince; the road was probably Sunset Boulevard); Valerie von Stroheim, in an interview with the author, Los Angeles, June 1978. Actors' Equity claimed that there were only 1,200 actors in the entire state of California at the start of 1915; this number was spread among films, vaudeville, and legitimate theater (*NYDM,* 3 February 1915, p. 9).

17. The lower figure is from *MPW,* 10 July 1915, p. 216; the higher figure, *MPN,* 3 April 1915, p. 39.

18. "The Grand March," *Photoplay,* November 1918, pp. 86–87.

19. In addition to outside pressures, the city fathers also seem to have done their best to rid Fort Lee of filmmakers; see Rita Altomara, *Hollywood on the Palisades* (New York: Garland, 1983). "Sunless Temple of New York's Movies," *NYT,* 7 November 1920 (Griffith).

20. The Mirror studio was a small, independent operation typical of many scattered around the New York area. A number of Johnny Hines comedies were shot there.

21. *ETR,* 25 September 1920, p. 1822.

22. Richard Koszarski, *The Astoria Studio and Its Fabulous Films* (New York: Dover, 1983), p. 8.

23. Edward Van Zile, *That Marvel—the Movie* (New York: Putnam, 1923), p. 216; "Movies as Investments," p. 10; Lasky, *I Blow My Own Horn,* p. 195.

24. For a rare discussion, see Kathleen Karr, "Hooray for Wilkes-Barre, Saranac Lake—and Hollywood," in *The American Film Heritage* (Washington, D.C.: Acropolis, 1972), pp. 104–109. The most attention to these filmmakers can be found in locally produced documentary films such as ALL BUT FORGOTTEN: HOLMAN F. DAY, FILM MAKER, directed by Everett Foster, and WHEN YOU WORE A TULIP, about regional production in Wisconsin, directed by Steven Schaller. Florida is one of the only regional centers adequately discussed. See Richard Alan Nelson, "Florida and the American Motion Picture Industry, 1898–1930" (Ph.D. diss., Florida State University, 1980), as well as various articles by Nelson.

25. "Gossip of the Studios," *NYDM,* 3 March 1915, p. 26.

26. "The Photo Play Market," *Photoplay Author,* December 1914, p. 191.

27. "Colleges Fail in the Test," *NYDM,* 24 February 1915, p. 25. Schools competing were the University of Pennsylvania (58 entries, 2 acceptable), Columbia (32 and 1), Cornell (49 and 2), Harvard (62 and 3), and the following with no acceptable submissions: Yale (48), Princeton (15), University of Michigan (43), University of Chicago (12), University of California (9), University of Wisconsin (14).

28. Gorenflot, "Thinks and Things," *Photoplay Author,* December 1914, p. 183.

29. Douglas Brown, "The Cost Elements of a Motion Picture," *SMPE* 17 (October 1923), p. 141; "Film Rights, and What They Are Worth," *NYT,* 11 August 1920.

30. "High Price of Stories," *NYT,* 30 March 1924.

31. "The Movies: A Colossus That Totters," *Bookman,* February 1919, pp. 653–659.

32. "No Protection for Movie Scenarios," *NYT*, 13 February 1914.

33. Bordwell, Staiger, and Thompson, *The Classical Hollywood Cinema*, p. 136. See the sections on Ince and Sennett in chapter 8 of this volume.

34. "MGM Studio Tour" is available in 16 mm from the Em Gee Film Library, Reseda, Calif., which also has other such promotional reels.

35. "Take away the phoney tinsel of Hollywood and you'll find the real tinsel underneath," Oscar Levant is reported to have said.

36. Cf. Bordwell, Staiger, and Thompson, *The Classical Hollywood Cinema*, p. 137: "those with greater marketability (*e.g.*, Hart) could demand certain working conditions." United Artists, of course, was entirely based on this premise.

37. Frederick James Smith, "The Cost of a Five Reel Photoplay," *NYDM*, 7 July 1917, p. 9; "Movies as Investments," p. 10.

38. Richard W. Saunders, "Finance and Pictures," *NYT*, 7 November 1926.

39. Johnson Heywood, "How 'Movie' Industry Got on Sound Financial Basis," *Forbes,* 1 March 1927, p. 13; "High Costs Halt Production," *NYT*, 27 October 1923.

40. "Present Production Costs Contrasted with Low Figures of the Past," *NYT*, 19 December 1926.

41. "Motion Pictures and Finance," *Barron's*, 19 May 1924, p. 5. The figures are repeated by James Spearing in "A New Phase Opens in the Film Industry," *NYT*, 3 July 1927, and by *MPN* editor William A. Johnson in *SMPE* 32 (September 1927), p. 667.

42. William S. Holman, "Cost-Accounting for the Motion-Picture Industry," *Journal of Accountancy*, December 1920, p. 420.

43. Alfred A. Cohn, "What They Really Get—NOW!" *Photoplay*, March 1916, p. 27.

44. "Star Salaries," *FDY* (1924), p. 299; also "The High Cost of Film Stars," *NYT*, 4 November 1923.

45. "Harold Lloyd Heads List of Huge Earnings of Stars and Directors," *NYT*, 16 May 1926.

46. Fred Balshofer and Arthur Miller, *One Reel a Week* (Los Angeles: University of California Press, 1967), pp. 130, 134. For information on this early period, see John Hambley and Patrick Downing, *The Art of Hollywood* (London: Thames Television, 1979).

47. Mosgrove Colwell, "Something New in Pictures," *Motion Picture Magazine*, August 1916, p. 53 (Kellar); Maurice Tourneur, "Stylization in Motion Picture Direction," *Motion Picture Magazine*, September 1918, p. 101. Universal's MADAME CUBIST, a two-reeler released earlier than THE YELLOW GIRL in 1916, made specific references to the Armory Show in its advertising but used its "futurist and cubist" costumes simply as a fashion parade, unlike the integral design scheme of THE YELLOW GIRL. See *Moving Picture Weekly*, 12 February 1916, pp. 18–19.

48. Even before HUMAN WRECKAGE, a visitor to one Hollywood set wrote, "A liberal use of yellows, reds and blues assaulted the eye, and one ventured if the room was to convey a hasheesh-eaters' paradise" ("A Visit to Movieland," *Forum*, January 1920, p. 16). The requirements of orthochromatic film stock were probably responsible.

49. Leon Barsacq and Elliott Stein, *Caligari's Cabinet and Other Grand Illusions* (Boston: New York Graphic Society, 1976), p. 212; "The Architecture of Motion Picture Settings," *American Architect*, 7 July 1920, p. 1; James Hood MacFarland, "Architectural Problems in Motion Picture Production," *American Architect*, 21 July 1920, p. 65. THE COPPERHEAD is preserved in the archives of the George Eastman House/International Museum of Photography, Rochester, N.Y.

50. Other teams included John Seitz and director Rex Ingram (1920–1926), Oliver Marsh photographing Mae Murray (1922–1925), and Charles Rosher photographing Mary Pickford (1917–1927).

51. Hal Mohr, in an interview with the author, Los Angeles, 10 July 1971.

52. "A Half Century of Loyalty, Progress, Artistry," *AC*, January 1969, p. 46; "An Open Letter," *AC*, August 1926, p. 8; Hal Mohr interview.

53. *NYDM*, 3 March 1915, p. 28.

54. Stephen S. Norton, "Close-Ups," *AC*, July 1923, p. 8; Welford Beaton, "Submerging the Production Under Senseless Close-Ups," *The Film Spectator*, 12 May 1928, p. 7; idem, "Is Eric von Stroheim a Really Good Director?" *Film Spectator*, 17 March 1928, p. 8; "Now the Close-Up," *NYT*, 1 October 1922.

55. "Ideal Directors," *NYT*, 13 February 1921.

56. "Camera Expert Studies Old Masters for Effect," *NYT*, 12 June 1927; Cecil B. DeMille, "Motion Picture Directing," *SMPE* 34 (April 1928), p. 295; Higham, *Hollywood Cameramen*, p. 35.

57. See the discussion of this issue in chapter 5.

58. John Baxter, *The Hollywood Exiles* (New York: Taplinger, 1976), pp. 19–53; Karl Struss, "Dramatic Cinematography," *SMPE* 34 (April 1928), p. 317.

59. Projection through colored filters was also sometimes employed, but this was essentially an exhibitor's technique and not under the control of the filmmakers. For an excellent general discussion of the use of color in motion pictures, see Brian Coe, *The History of Movie Photography* (Westfield, N.J.: Eastview Editions, 1981), esp. pp. 112–139.

60. G. A. Blair, "The Tinting of Motion-Picture Film," *SMPE* 10 (May 1920), p. 45. L. A. Jones, "Discussion of Paper Entitled 'Transmission of Tinted Motion Picture Films,' " *SMPE* 12 (May 1921), p. 101; *Tinting and Toning of Eastman Positive Motion Picture Film* (Rochester: Eastman Kodak Company, 1927), pp. 23, 36.

61. Koszarski, *The Man You Loved to Hate*, pp. 67–70; Eric Elliott, *Anatomy of Motion Picture Art* (Dijon: Pool, 1928), p. 38.

62. "Hand Painting Films," *American Projectionist*, September 1923, p. 3. For an example of Brock's ads, see *FDY* (1927), p. K. In earlier years, other colorists, also based in New York, had also offered their services, notably G. R. Silvera (p. 80) and John Duer Scott (p. 84) in the 1922–1923 edition.

63. William V. D. Kelley, "Imbibition Coloring of Motion Picture Films," *SMPE* 28 (October 1926), p. 238.

64. William V. D. Kelley, "Natural Color Cinematography," *SMPE* 7 (November 1918), p. 38. There were some three-color systems in this period, such as Gaumont Chronochrome, which had no commercial impact and are of importance mainly in understanding later successful three-color systems. Panchromatic stock had already been offered to the trade by 1915. See, for example, the display ad for Harrison-Ramsey panchromatic negative film stock in *MPN*, 21 February 1914, p. 40.

65. D. B. Thomas, *The First Colour Motion Pictures* (London: Her Majesty's Stationery Office, 1969).

66. *Ibid.*, pp. 37–38; William T. Crespinal, "Color Photography—Past and Present," *American Projectionist*, May 1925, p. 4; "Color in the Motion Picture," *AC*, January 1969, p. 80; Kelley, "Natural Color Cinematography"; W. T. Crespinel [*sic*], "Color Photography—Yesterday, Today and Tomorrow," *AC*, March 1929, p. 4. Kelley did originally try Prizma as an additive system but soon abandoned the idea.

67. Carroll H. Dunning, "Color Photography in 1922," *FDY* (1922–1923), p. 17.

68. Kelley, "Imbibition Coloring."

69. The technology behind many of these competing systems was quite similar. Technicolor was sued by Prizma in 1922 for patents infringement, but it was Prizma that soon faded from the scene (*NYT*, 26 September 1922, p. 31).

70. Grant Whytock, in an interview with the author, Los Angeles, 16 July 1971.

71. Kelley, "Imbibition Coloring."

72. Phil Rosen, "Believes Color Will Not Aid Dramatic Cinematography," *AC*, January 1923, p. 4; Ernest Palmer, who shared an Academy Award with Rennahan for BLOOD AND SAND, remembered in an interview with the author that he had had little patience with the Technicolor expert's compulsion to put adequate amounts of light under sofas and in other obscure corners. Pacific Palisades, California, January 1972.

73. For Kuleshov, see V. I. Pudovkin, *Film Technique and Film Acting* (New York: Grove Press, 1960), pp. 166–169.

74. Brownlow, *The Parade's Gone By . . .* , p. 339.

75. "Real Inspiration," *NYT*, 24 June 1923.

76. *The Theatre and Motion Pictures*, Britannica Booklet no. 7 (New York: Encyclopaedia Britannica, 1933), p. 29.

77. Whytock interview with author; "Why Some American Films Prove Failures in England," *NYT*, 27 April 1924.

78. Arthur Lennig, *Von Stroheim* (Albany: State University of New York, 1973), n.p.

79. Buster Keaton, "Why I Never Smile," *Ladies Home Journal*, June 1926, p. 20.

80. Robert E. Sherwood, "The Phantom Jinx," *Photoplay*, January 1926, p. 113.

81. "Mr. Goldwyn Describes Try-Outs of Pictures," *NYT*, 25 October 1925.

82. Eileen Bowser, *"Intolerance": The Film by David Wark Griffith. Shot by Shot Analysis* (New York: Museum of Modern Art, 1966), p. iii.

83. Robert M. Henderson, *D. W. Griffith: His Life and Work* (New York: Oxford University Press, 1972), p. 288. At the Cinémathèque Française a decade later, Erich von Stroheim not only recut THE WEDDING MARCH but inserted stock footage from MERRY-GO-ROUND which he preferred to that used

in THE WEDDING MARCH. This synchronized print is now shown as the standard version (Koszarski, *The Man You Loved to Hate*, pp. 194–195).

84. *The American Film Institute Catalogue: Feature Films 1921–1930* (New York: Bowker, 1971), p. 454 (LOVE); King Vidor, *A Tree Is a Tree* (New York: Harcourt, Brace, 1953), p. 152.

Chapter 5. Technology

1. P. M. Abbott, "Equipment Used for Motion Pictures," *Annals of the American Academy of Political and Social Science*, November 1926, p. 34. A complete discussion of talking pictures can be found in volume four of this series.

2. C. E. K. Mees, "History of Professional Black-and-White Motion-Picture Film," *SMPE*, October 1954, p. 134; Brownlow, *The Parade's Gone By . . .* , p. 213.

3. Thomas, *First Colour Motion Pictures*, p. 13.

4. Earl Theisen, "The History of Nitrocellulose as a Film Base," *SMPE*, March 1933, p. 259, and "In the Realm of Tricks and Illusion," *International Photographer*, June 1934, p. 8; Mees, "History"; "Fifty Years—or More—of Evolving Cinema Technique," *AC*, January 1969, p. 52.

5. R. J. Flaherty, "The Handling of Motion Picture Film Under Various Climatic Conditons," *SMPE* 26 (May 1926), p. 85.

6. "Director Advocates Panchromatic Stock," *AC*, October 1926, p. 6; "Questions and Answers," *AC*, February 1928, p. 21.

7. "Progress in the Motion Picture Industry," *SMPE* 19 (Sept.–Oct. 1924), p. 7; "Panchromatic Used," *AC*, September 1926, p. 8; "Director Advocates Panchromatic Stock."

8. John Grierson, "Putting Richness into the Photoplay," *AC*, October 1927, p. 4; "Films and Emulsions," *SMPE* 29 (April 1927), p. 11.

9. Mees, "History"; *MPN*, 4 December 1920, pp. 4327, 4329; Gregory, *Motion Picture Photography*, p. 135. In the 1920 *MPN*, Bay State Film Sales also advertised American-made film of unknown manufacture, while other, smaller operators quietly serviced the low end of the business.

10. J. G. Capstaff and M. W. Seymour, "The Duplication of Motion Picture Negatives," *SMPE* 28 (October 1926), p. 223.

11. Mees, "History"; Theisen, "History of Nitrocellulose."

12. Carl Louis Gregory, "Motion Picture Cameras," *SMPE* 3 (April 1917), n.p.; Lyman Broening, "The Cinematographer's Investment," *AC*, October 1923, p. 4.

13. Gregory, "Motion Picture Cameras"; "A Cinematographer's Capital Investment," *AC*, November 1926, p. 12; "Must Be a Capitalist," *AC*, December 1927, p. 11.

14. *MPW*, 10 July 1915, p. 409 (ad); Karl Malkames, "The 35-mm Motion Picture Camera from the Beginnings to the 1920s," *SMPE*, June 1981, p. 503; "Milestone Movie Cameras," *AC*, January 1969, p. 79 (shows a Moy with customized external magazines); Henry V. Hopwood, *Living Pictures* (London: Opticians and Photographers Trades Review, 1899), p. 168–169.

15. "Milestone Movie Cameras," p. 78; Gregory, *Motion Picture Photography*, pp. 366–367.

16. "Milestone Movie Cameras," p. 116; Laurence Roberts, "Cameras and Systems: A History of Contributions from the Bell & Howell Co. (Part I)," *SMPE*, October 1982, p. 934; Lescarboura, *Behind the Motion Picture Screen*, p. 82. Historians frequently confuse the 2709 with a more primitive wooden-cased Bell & Howell, which was in use from 1909 at the Essanay studio. Only eight examples of this camera were manufactured, one of which may be examined in the collection of the George Eastman House in Rochester. The fact that the 2709 lacked a cranking-speed indicator has not deterred at least one group of historians from publishing a picture of it: see Bordwell, Staiger, and Thompson, *The Classical Hollywood Cinema*, illus. 20.4.

17. "Milestone Movie Cameras"; Laurence J. Roberts, "The Mitchell Camera: The Machine and Its Makers," *SMPE*, February 1982, p. 141; McKay, *Handbook*, pp. 68–69.

18. "A Camera out of the West," *AC*, 1 October 1921, p. 13; "New Bell & Howell Professional Model Out," *AC*, November 1924, p. 25. See also *AC*, 15 January 1922, p. 8; May 1922, p. 22; July 1922, p. 20, etc.

19. Gregory, *Motion Picture Photography*, pp. 353–356, 367; McKay, *Handbook*, pp. 72–74; "The Akeley Specialist," *AC*, October 1927, p. 7.

20. Laurence Roberts, "Cameras and Systems: A History of Contributions from the Bell & Howell Co. (Part II)," *SMPE*, November 1982, p. 1079; J. H. McNabb, "A New Camera for Screen News Cinematography," *SMPE* 23 (October 1925), p. 77; *AC*, April 1926, p. 5; *AC*, January 1927, pp. 14–15.

21. McKay, *Handbook*, pp. 83–95; "New Automatic Motion Picture Camera," *AC*, July 1925, p. 5. For illustrations showing the use of the motorized Debrie Parvo and the Moy aerial camera, see Koszarski, *The Astoria Studio*, pp. 30, 41.

22. *AC*, September 1925, p. 22 (announcement of cameras and equipment for rent); *AC*, July 1925, p. 22 (Bausch and Lomb ad); "Lenses," *SMPE* 29 (April 1927), p. 16; *AC*, June 1927, p. 15 (ad for Plasmat lenses); Joseph A. Dubray, "Large Aperture Lenses in Cinematography," *SMPE* 33 (April 1928), p. 205; *AC*, 1 February 1922, p. 12 (John Leezar biography); Susan and John Harvith, *Karl Struss: Man with a Camera* (Cranbrook Academy of Art/Museum, 1976), pp. 10–11.

23. "Discussion of Dubray's Paper," *SMPE* 33 (April 1928), p. 211 (those complaining were Lester Cuffe and Dr. C. E. K. Mees); Ernest Palmer interview with author (STREET ANGEL).

24. Fred Archer and Elmer Fryer, "Still Photography in Motion Picture Work," *SMPE* 33 (April 1928), p. 167 (technical aspects). See Shirley Vance Martin, " 'Still' Pictures: How and Why They Are Made," in *Opportunities in the Motion Picture Industry* (Los Angeles: Photoplay Research Society, 1922), pp. 47–54, for a contemporary account, and John Kobal's preface to *Hollywood: The Pioneers* (New York: Knopf, 1979), pp. 10–11, for a collector's reflection on motion-picture stills. Maurice Tourneur's film A GIRL'S FOLLY (1917) offers a revealing example of the studio techniques of stills photographers in this period.

25. Brownlow, *The Parade's Gone By . . .* , p. 213 (Universal); Gregory, *Motion Picture Photography*, p. 213; see also McKay, *Handbook*, pp. 125–128.

26. W. A. D. Evans, "Industrial Lighting with Mercury Vapor Lamps," *Transactions of the Illuminating Engineering Association*, 1915; Gregory, *Motion Picture Photography*, pp. 221–222; Lescarboura, *Behind the Motion Picture Screen*, pp. 134–138; Alfred B. Hitchens, "Artificial Lighting of Motion Picture Studios," *AC*, September 1922, p. 14.

27. Cecil B. DeMille, "Motion Picture Directing," *SMPE* 34 (1928), p. 300; "The Evolution of Motion Picture Lighting," *AC*, January 1969, p. 94; "Recent Developments in Producing Pictures," *NYT*, 6 July 1924. Despite DeMille's claim, an arc lamp is used as a prop in his WHAT'S HIS NAME, filmed six months before THE WARRENS OF VIRGINIA and thus placing the equipment at the studio that much earlier.

28. L. C. Porter, "The 'Kleig Eyes' Question," *AC*, October 1923, p. 9; Harry D. Brown, "Electrical Problems on World's Biggest Set," *AC*, October 1923, p. 5.

29. Higham, *Hollywood Cameramen*, pp. 18–19, 39–40; Charles W. Handley, "History of Motion-Picture Studio Lighting," *SMPE*, October 1954, p. 129; Peter Mole, "The Tungsten Lamp in the Studio," *SMPE* 31 (September 1927), p. 582; Victor Milner, "The Cinema in 1932," *AC*, August 1922, p. 8.

30. Louis Physioc, "Does the Camera Lie?" *AC*, January 1928, p. 21; Peter Mole, "Advance of the Mazda," *AC*, August 1928, p. 26.

31. Higham, *Hollywood Cameramen*, p. 39; "Incandescents," *AC*, February 1928; Mole, "Advance of the Mazda," p. 26; R. E. Farnham, "The Effective Application of Incandescent Lamps for Motion Picture Photography," *AC*, June 1928, p. 30.

32. But today, at the Laird International Studios in Culver City, California, one can still see glass stages constructed by Thomas Ince when he built the lot in 1918–1919. They have long been used only for warehouse space, of course.

33. H. A. MacNary, "Remote Control Switchboards for Motion-Picture Studios," *SMPE* 10 (May 1920), pp. 12, 18–19.

34. McKay, *Handbook*, pp. 165–167; I. Serrurier, "Moviola Film Viewing Machine," *SMPE* 34 (April 1928), p. 558. John Emerson and Anita Loos can be seen playing with one of the early miniaturized viewing machines in an illustration on page 80 of their book *How to Write Photoplays* (New York: John McCann, 1921). See also Robert V. Kerns, "The Malkames Collection," *AC*, May 1969, p. 470.

35. See Gregory, *Motion Picture Photography*, pp. 133–134; McKay, *Handbook*, pp. 142–144; Lescarboura, *Behind the Motion Picture Screen*, pp. 204–208; "Highlights of Lab History," *AC*, January 1969, p. 104.

36. Roscoe C. Hubbard, "Erbograph Machine," *SMPE* 17 (October 1923), p. 163; "Highlights of Lab History"; Roy Hunter, "Developer Perfected," *AC*, February 1928, p. 7; J. I. Crabtree and C. E. Ives, "Rack Marks and Airbell Markings on Motion Picture Film," *SMPE* 24 (October 1925), p. 95.

37. J. I. Crabtree, "The Motion-Picture Laboratory," *SMPE*, January 1955, p. 13; Hubbard, "Erbograph Machine"; Alfred B. Hitchens, "Machine Development of Negative and Positive Motion Picture Film," *SMPE* 22 (May 1925), p. 46; C. Roy Hunter, "A Negative Developing Machine," *SMPE* 33 (April 1928), p. 195.

38. Gregory, *Motion Picture Photography*, pp. 165–176; Laurence Roberts, "Cameras and Systems: A History of Contributions from the Bell & Howell Co. (Part I)," *SMPE*, October 1982, pp. 936–937; Roscoe C. Hubbard, "Printing Motion Picture Film," *SMPE* 28 (October 1926), p. 252; Lescarboura, *Behind the Motion Picture Screen*, pp. 210–214; Gregory, *Motion Picture Photography*, p. 172; Abbott, "Equipment Used for Motion Pictures," p. 40; F. H. Richardson, "The Need for Improvement in Present Practice as Regards Film Reels," *SMPE* 13 (October 1921), p. 116.

39. Laurence Roberts, "Cameras and Systems," *SMPE*, October 1982, p. 937; Denison, "My Troubles, Your Troubles, Our Troubles," p. 4; Dr. Maxwell Vidaver, "Film Examination by Mechanical Means," *American Projectionist*, October 1924, p. 4; Richardson, "Need for Improvement"; Arthur H. Gray, "A Few Practical Needs in the Field of Projection," *SMPE* 32 (September 1927), p. 628.

40. R. P. Burrows, "Fundamentals of Illumination in Motion Picture Projection," *SMPE* 7 (November 1918), p. 74; T. O'Conner Sloane, *Motion Picture Projection* (New York: Falk, 1922), pp. 117–120; Hall, *The Best Remaining Seats*, pp. 102, 201–202.

41. Don G. Malkames, "Early Projector Mechanisms," *SMPE*, October 1957, p. 628; David S. Hulfish, *Motion Picture Work* (Chicago: American School of Correspondence, 1913), pp. 225–240 (this book appeared in an earlier two-volume edition in 1911); *MPW*, 10 July 1915, p. 409 (ad for Motion Picture Apparatus Company), 401 ("Equipment for Sale"); *MPN*, 3 April 1915, p. 99 (ad for Stern Manufacturing Company).

42. Malkames, "Early Projector Mechanisms"; Hulfish, *Motion Picture Work*, pp. 161–188; Cameron, *Motion Picture Projection*; Sloane, *Motion Picture Projection*.

43. Hulfish, *Motion Picture Work*, pp. 189–200; Sloane, *Motion Picture Projection*, pp. 233–238; Malkames, "Early Projector Mechanisms"; Cameron, *Motion Picture Projection*, pp. 636–644; "Grauman's Chinese Theatre," *American Projectionist*, July 1927, p. 6.

44. Malkames, "Early Projector Mechanisms"; Cameron, *Motion Picture Projection*, pp. 472–597; Sloane, *Motion Picture Projection*, p. 229; *American Projectionist*, April 1927.

Chapter 6. The Show

1. See discussion of Universal in chapter 1.

2. "Impressions en Route" and "Producers or Manufacturers," *NYDM*, 3 March 1915, p. 23. In 1922, 37 percent of a theater's film-rental payments were devoted to the non-feature end of the bill (Moen, "Statistics," *MPN*, 9 December 1922, p. 2904.

3. Moen, "Statistics," *MPN*, 25 November 1922, p. 2644 (see also p. 48); Axel Madsen, *William Wyler* (New York: Crowell, 1973), pp. 423–425. The two surviving Wyler titles are THE CROOK BUSTER (1925) and THE TWO FISTER (1927).

4. Robert E. Sherwood, when praising NANOOK OF THE NORTH, discusses it in terms of travel pictures and scenics. See *The Best Moving Pictures of 1922–23* (Boston: Small, Maynard, 1923), p. 3. See also his general discussion of short subjects, pp. 121–133.

5. Anthony Slide, *Early American Cinema* (Cranbury, N.J.: Barnes, 1970), pp. 157–176. By comparison, Kevin Brownlow never mentions serials in either *The Parade's Gone By . . .* or *Hollywood: The Pioneers*, and they are referred to only in passing in William K. Everson's *American Silent Film* and Bordwell, Staiger, and Thompson's *The Classical Hollywood Cinema*. Kalton Lahue, *Continued Next Week: A History of the Moving Picture Serial* (Norman: University of Oklahoma Press, 1964), contains a valuable filmography; *Bound and Gagged: The Story of the Silent Serials* (New York: Castle, 1968), is an expansion of his earlier work. Manuel Weltman and Raymond Lee, *Pearl White, the Peerless, Fearless Girl* (Cranbury, N.J.: Barnes, 1969), is an eccentric but well-illustrated biography.

6. Slide, *Early American Cinema*, pp. 158–159, 172; Joe Franklin, *Classics of the Silent Screen* (New York: Citadel Press, 1959), p. 12.

7. Lahue, *Continued Next Week*, p. 44.

8. See filmography in Lahue, *Continued Next Week*, pp. 153–276.

9. *Ibid.*, pp. 48–50.

10. Raymond Fielding, *The American Newsreel* (Norman: University of Oklahoma Press, 1972), pp. 83–85.

11. Emmanuel Cohen, "The Business of International News by Motion Picture," *SMPE* 28 (October 1926), p. 296.

12. Fielding, *The American Newsreel*, pp. 133–135; Lescarboura, *Behind the Motion Picture Screen*, p. 240.

13. Bob Donahue, "The News Cameraman," in *Breaking into the Movies*, ed. Charles Reed Jones (New York: Unicorn, 1927), p. 188.

14. Fielding, *The American Newsreel*, pp. 141–142; Lescarboura, *Behind the Motion Picture Screen*, pp. 236–237.

15. Homer Croy, *How Motion Pictures Are Made* (New York: Harper, 1918), p. 256.

16. Cohen, "The Business of International News."

17. Kansas City holds a prominent place in the early careers of such animators as Disney, Iwerks, Harman, Ising, and Freleng, but it never became a real production center, and all these men left as soon as they were able.

18. These processes are explained at some length in Leonard Maltin, *Of Mice and Magic* (New York: New American Library, 1980), pp. 7–11, and Donald Crafton, *Before Mickey* (Cambridge, Mass.: MIT Press, 1982), pp. 138–167. The key Bray-Hurd patents are all reproduced in *Film History* 2/3 (September–October 1988), pp. 229–266.

19. Maltin makes this claim in *Of Mice and Magic*, pp. 10, 21–22.

20. Crafton, *Before Mickey*, pp. 179–184.

21. Croy, *How Motion Pictures Are Made*, p. 314; Lescarboura, *Behind the Motion Picture Screen*, p. 306.

22. Joe Adamson, "A Talk with Dick Huemer," in Gerald and Danny Peary, *The American Animated Cartoon* (New York: Dutton, 1980), p. 31.

23. Crafton, *Before Mickey*, pp. 301–346.

24. Leslie Carbarga, *The Fleischer Story* (New York: Crown, 1976). This self-reflexive quality is unique among American film genres of this era and runs from the earliest animated sketches of J. Stuart Blackton through McCay, Bray, Mesmer, Fleischer—indeed, almost the whole of silent animation.

25. Don Shay, "Willis O'Brien, Creator of the Impossible," *Focus on Film*, Autumn 1973, p. 19 (O'Brien's film career dates from 1915); Lescarboura, *Behind the Motion Picture Screen*, pp. 312–322; Crafton, *Before Mickey*, p. 265.

26. Louise Beaudet to author, 9 March 1987.

27. Adamson,, "A Talk with Dick Huemer," p. 35.

28. "Short Subject Releases," *FDY* (1926), pp. 449–456. Ignoring, as much as possible, animated cartoons, novelties, and other miscellany, one can count the following numbers of short comedy releases for 1925: Educational (152 reels), FBO (98 reels), Fox (68 reels), Pathé (187 reels), Universal (156 reels), and another 331 reels supplied by various states rights distributors. See list on p. 48.

29. Kalton Lahue and Terry Brewer, *Kops and Custard* (Norman: University of Oklahoma Press, 1968), pp. 122–123.

30. Lescarboura, *Behind the Motion Picture Screen*, p. 55.

31. Gilbert Seldes, *The Seven Lively Arts* (New York: Harper, 1924), pp. 41–54.

32. David Madden, *Harlequin's Stick, Charlie's Cane* (Bowling Green, Ohio: Popular Press, 1975); Mack Sennett, "The Psychology of Film Comedy," *Motion Picture Classic*, November 1918, p. 20.

33. Arthur Swan, "Greenroom Chitchat," *NYDM*, 7 July 1915, p. 8.

34. Richard Schickel, *Harold Lloyd: The Shape of Laughter* (Boston: New York Graphic Society, 1974), pp. 35–38.

35. David Yallop, *The Day the Laughter Stopped* (New York: St. Martin's Press, 1976), has an excellent filmography, as well as a solid account of Arbuckle's career that is heavy on the scandal and trial.

36. Schapiro and Chierichetti, *The Movie Poster Book*, p. 25.

37. "Harold Lloyd Heads List of Huge Earnings of Stars and Directors," *NYT*, 16 May 1926.

38. See Kalton Lahue and Sam Gill, *Clown Princes and Court Jesters* (Cranbury, N.J.: Barnes, 1970), for a sampling of many of these.

39. Emerson and Loos, *How to Write Photoplays*, p. 21.

40. Peter Milne, *Motion Picture Directing* (New York: Falk, 122), pp. 199–200; Herman G. Weinberg, *The Lubitsch Touch* (New York: Dutton, 1968), p. 317. In fact, those men now considered Lubitsch disciples all owed their careers to their work with Chaplin on A WOMAN OF PARIS.

41. Everson, *American Silent Film*, p. 268.

42. A. Nicholas Vardac, *Stage to Screen* (Cambridge, Mass.: Harvard University Press, 1949), and John Fell, *Film and the Narrative Tradition* (Norman: Oklahoma University Press, 1974), discuss various aspects of the relation between stage and screen melodrama in the early twentieth century.

43. George N. Fenin and William K. Everson, *The Western* (New York: Orion Press, 1962).

44. William L. Slout, "*Uncle Tom's Cabin* in American Film History," *Journal of Popular Film* (Spring

1973), pp. 137–151; Iris Barry, *Film Notes*, ed. Eileen Bowser (New York: Museum of Modern Art, 1969), pp. 36–37 (WAY DOWN EAST). On family melodrama, see Fell, *Film and the Narrative Tradition*, pp. 12–36, and Vardac, *Stage to Screen*, pp. 20 ff.

45. See the illustration of one of these location units in Koszarski, *The Astoria Studio*, p. 51.

46. "Sticks Nix Hick Pix," *Variety*, 17 July 1935, p. 1. See discussion of Vidor in chapter 8.

47. Carlos Clarens, *An Illustrated History of the Horror Film* (New York: Capricorn, 1968), pp. 54–58.

48. Brownlow, *The War, the West, and the Wilderness*, pp. 171–176; Michael T. Isenberg, *War on Film* (East Brunswick, N.J.: Associated University Presses, 1981).

49. DeWitt Bodeen, "Charles Ray," *Films in Review*, November 1968, pp. 548–580.

50. Kathleen Karr, "The Long Square Up: Exploitation Trends in the Silent Film," *Journal of Popular Film* (Spring 1974), pp. 107–128; Kay Sloan, *The Loud Silents: Origins of the Social Problem Film* (Chicago: University of Illinois Press, 1988); Kevin Brownlow, *Behind the Mask of Innocence* (New York: Knopf, 1990).

51. Al Di Lauro and Gerald Rabkin, *Dirty Movies* (New York: Chelsea House, 1976), pp. 47–51, 53. A FREE RIDE, said to be the earliest extant American stag film, already included such conventional iconographic elements as the automobile.

52. Thomas Cripps, *Slow Fade to Black* (New York: Oxford University Press, 1977), pp. 77–83, 170–202. Robeson did appear in the silent BORDERLINE, but this aberrant production was filmed in Switzerland in 1930.

53. *The Most Important and Misappreciated American Films Since the Beginning of the Cinema* (Brussels: Royal Film Archive of Belgium, 1978).

54. THE HOME MAKER is in the collection of the UCLA Film Archives.

55. At the end of the silent period, an entire group of films—WHITE GOLD (1927), THE WIND (1928), and CITY GIRL (1928–1930)—shared the premise of an urban woman who is uprooted and forced to relocate on a farm. In each case, this traditional heart of American culture is pictured as a patriarchal tyranny, with madness and murder the inevitable outcome. For GREED, see Koszarski, *The Man You Loved to Hate*, pp. 114–149; for THE CROWD, see Vidor, *A Tree Is a Tree*, pp. 145–158. While GREED was a dead loss, THE CROWD actually made a little money.

Chapter 7. Watching the Screen

1. Myron Lounsbury, *The Origins of American Film Criticism, 1909–1939* (New York: Arno Press, 1973).

2. "Garden—*Blind Husbands*," *Paterson* (N.J.) *Call*, 20 January 1920.

3. For Ward Marsh, see Dennis Dillon, "The Film Reviewing of W. Ward Marsh of the *Cleveland Plain Dealer*, 1919–1970" (Ph.D. diss., New York University, 1976). See also Walter Conley, "Harriette Underhill," *Silent Picture* (Spring 1972), p. 24. There is nothing as yet on Kitty Kelly.

4. "*Foolish Wives*: A Review of a Picture That Is an Insult to Every American," *Photoplay*, March 1922, p. 70. For an anthology of capsule reviews from *Photoplay*, see Paul A. Scaramazza, ed., *Ten Years in Paradise* (Arlington, Va.: Pleasant Press, 1974), introduction by Anthony Slide.

5. Anthony Slide, ed., *International Film, Radio, and Television Journals* (Westport, Conn.: Greenwood Press, 1985), pp. 383–388. This volume is a valuable source for all film periodicals during the period under discussion.

6. Stanley Kauffmann and Bruce Henstell, eds., *American Film Criticism* (New York: Liveright, 1972), pp. 25–42. For a discussion of trade papers active before 1915, see the earlier volumes of this series.

7. Rita Horwitz, *An Index to Vol. I, 1907, of "The Moving Picture World and View Photographer"* (Washington, D.C.: American Film Institute, 1974).

8. Slide, *International Film, Radio, and Television Journals*, pp. 98–99.

9. "Riddle Gawne," *Wid's Daily*, 18 August 1918.

10. "Greed," *Harrison's Reports*, 13 December 1924.

11. Kauffmann and Henstell, *American Film Criticism*, p. 188. See Welford Beaton, *Know Your Movies* (Hollywood: Howard Hill, 1932); Tamar Lane, *What's Wrong with the Movies?* (Los Angeles: Waverly, 1923).

12. Charles Matthew Feldman, *The National Board of Censorship (Review) of Motion Pictures, 1909–1922* (New York: Arno Press, 1977), pp. 20–26.

13. *Ibid.*, pp. 15, 23–24; Nancy J. Rosenbloom, "Between Reform and Regulation: The Struggle over Film Censorship in Progressive America, 1909–1922," *Film History* 1/4 (1987), pp. 307–325.

14. Feldman, *The National Board of Censorship*, p. 67.
15. Rosenbloom, "Between Reform and Regulation," pp. 316–318.
16. Feldman, *The National Board of Censorship*, pp. 84–85.
17. Richard Randall, *Censorship of the Movies* (Madison: University of Wisconsin Press, 1968), pp. 19–20.
18. "Film Producers Urge Federal Censorship," *MPN*, 3 April 1915, p. 45.
19. THE NIGGER (1915) was a miscegenation melodrama released by Fox before THE BIRTH OF A NATION.
20. Pare Lorentz and Morris Ernst, *Censored: The Private Life of the Movie* (New York: Cape and Smith, 1930), p. 15.
21. Motion Picture Commission to Metro-Goldwyn Pictures Corporation, 25 November 1924, New York State Library, Albany, N.Y. State censorship records preserved here are among the most comprehensive surviving anywhere and date from 1921.
22. Pages 128–142. This book is also valuable for its reprinting of various state and local censorship ordinances, including those of Pennsylvania, New York, and Chicago.
23. Richard Watts, Jr., "A Landmark in Film Annals," *New York Herald-Tribune*, 14 December 1924.
24. Lorentz and Ernst, *Censored*, pp. 17–18.
25. *Ibid.*, p. 84.
26. *Ibid.*, p. 8; "Noticed and Noted," *NYT*, 8 February 1920.
27. Kathleen D. McCarthy, "Nickel Vice and Virtue: Movie Censorship in Chicago, 1907–15," *Journal of Popular Film* 5/1 (1976), pp. 37, 46; "The Pro and Con of Police Censorship," *Photoplay*, March 1915, p. 66; "Ask Wilson to Stop War Film Changes," *NYT*, 29 April 1918 (HEARTS OF THE WORLD). While there were only six state censorship boards, the number of cities and towns with their own censoring authority is uncounted.
28. These titles are taken from the season's releases listed in *Wid's Yearbook* (1921), pp. 292–313.
29. Robert Windeler, *Sweetheart: The Story of Mary Pickford* (New York: Praeger, 1973), pp. 115–118.
30. Feldman, *National Board of Censorship*, pp. 150–151, 171–182, 187–191.
31. "Producers Agree to Reform Films," *NYT*, 15 March 1921. Senator Myers' motion is reprinted in Oberholtzer, *The Morals of the Movie*, pp. 248–251.
32. "Carl Laemmle Summons All Censors to Conference at Universal City," *Moving Picture Weekly*, 30 July 1921, p. 34; "Carl Laemmle Makes Motion Picture History," *Moving Picture Weekly*, 10 September 1921, p. 11; "Censors Approve *Foolish Wives*," *Moving Picture Weekly*, 10 September 1921, p. 12. In fact, Pennsylvania chairman Harry Knapp, serving as spokesman of the delegation, suggested that the film would prove "highly interesting entertainment when it is finally whipped into . . . shape." There was some criticism of the censors for taking part in this circus. Ironically, the effect may have been to increase pressure for federal censorship, since the industry showed that it could easily dazzle members of mere local boards.
33. Yallop, *The Day the Laughter Stopped*, provides the best information on the Arbuckle affair.
34. *Ibid.*, p. 245.
35. Sidney Kirkpatrick, *A Cast of Killers* (New York: Dutton, 1986), offers one solution to the Taylor murder, Robert Giroux another in *A Deed of Death* (New York: Knopf, 1990).
36. "Change *Foolish Wives*," *NYT*, 19 January 1922.
37. Olga Martin, *Hollywood's Movie Commandments* (New York: Wilson, 1937), p. 17; Raymond Moley, *The Hays Office* (New York: Bobbs-Merrill, 1945), p. 58.
38. Moley, *The Hays Office*, pp. 63–64.
39. Lorentz and Ernst, *Censored*, p. 109.
40. Wilton A. Barrett, "Better Films Movement to 1923," *FDY* (1924), p. 499.
41. Barrett, "Better Films Movement," p. 501; Lorentz and Ernst, *Censored*, p. 110.
42. Barrett, "Better Films Movement," p. 499. See also *From Quasimodo to Scarlett O'Hara: A National Board of Review Anthology* (New York: Ungar, 1982).
43. "The National Board of Review," *FDY* (1927), p. 477; Symon Gould, "The Little Theater Movement in the Cinema," *SMPE* 27 (October 1926), p. 58; "National Board of Review Activities in 1927," *FDY* (1928), p. 928 (THE MARCH OF THE MOVIES). There is no apparent connection between this "assemblage" and the similarly titled film produced several years later by J. Stuart Blackton.
44. Vachel Lindsay, *The Art of the Moving Picture* (New York: Macmillan, 1915, 1922; reprinted New York: Liveright, 1970), p. 7–8.
45. Hugo Munsterberg, *The Photoplay: A Psychological Study* (New York: Appleton, 1916).

46. Seldes, *The Seven Lively Arts;* Munsterberg, *The Photoplay,* p. ix.
47. Robert E. Sherwood, *The Best Moving Pictures of 1922–23* (Boston: Small, Maynard, 1923).

Chapter 8. The Filmmakers

1. For period opinions on the power of directors, see Milne, *Motion Picture Directing;* Harry Carr, "The Status of the Directors," *Motion Picture Classic,* November 1925, p. 20; Matthew Josephson, "Masters of the Motion Picture," *Motion Picture Classic,* August 1926, p. 24, as well as the Hollywood-based fan magazine *Motion Picture Director.*
2. Indeed, by the late 1980s, such popular film magazines as *American Film* and *Premiere* were largely given over to recounting the off-screen machinations of such figures.
3. James Agee, "David Wark Griffith," *Nation,* 4 September 1948.
4. Vlada Petric, "David Wark Griffith," in *Cinema: A Critical Dictionary,* ed. Richard Roud (London: Secker and Warburg, 1980), pp. 449–462.
5. Sergei Eisenstein, "Dickens, Griffith, and the Film Today," in *Film Form* (New York: Harcourt, Brace, 1949), pp. 195–255.
6. Edward Wagenknecht and Anthony Slide, *The Films of D. W. Griffith* (New York: Crown, 1975). See Slide's essay on A ROMANCE OF HAPPY VALLEY (p. 106) and John Belton's on TRUE HEART SUSIE (pp. 119–120).
7. See Richard Schickel, *D. W. Griffith: An American Life* (New York: Simon and Schuster, 1984), which is especially useful for information on Griffith's fiscal problems; Louise Brooks, in an interview with the author, Rochester, N.Y., 30 May 1979 (Griffith at Astoria).
8. Janet Staiger, "Dividing Labor for Production Control: Thomas Ince and the Rise of the Studio System," in *The American Movie Industry,* ed. Gorham Kindhem (Carbondale: Southern Illinois University Press, 1982), pp. 94–103.
9. Pratt, *Spellbound in Darkness,* pp. 147–173.
10. Staiger, "Dividing Labor," p. 100; Kalton Lahue, *Mack Sennett's Keystone* (Cranbury, N.J.: Barnes, 1971), pp. 241–249.
11. He made his first feature, THE BATTLE OF GETTYSBURG, in 1913. See the Ince filmography prepared by Stephen Higgins in *Griffithiana* 18–21 (October 1984), pp. 155–220.
12. Milne, *Motion Picture Directing,* p. 139.
13. Higgins filmography, pp. 195–203.
14. For a Keystone filmography, see Lahue and Brewer, *Kops and Custards,* pp. 172–201. Massive amounts of Sennett material, long uncatalogued, have recently been made available by the Academy of Motion Picture Arts and Sciences, Beverly Hills, California.
15. Seldes, *The Seven Lively Arts,* pp. 3–24; Clarence Badger, "Reminiscences of the Early Days of Movie Comedies," in *"Image": On the Art and Evolution of the Film,* pp. 97–99. Kalton Lahue, in *Mack Sennett's Keystone,* makes much of the fact that Sennett's business manager, George Stout, organized the Keystone operation after doing the same for Ince, which would thus imply a direct link between the two systems. See pp. 242–244.
16. Harry Carr, "Mack Sennett—the Laugh Tester," *Photoplay,* May 1915, p. 70 (Carr would later serve as editor of the *Mack Sennett Weekly,* a studio house organ); Lahue, *Mack Sennett's Keystone,* p. 303.
17. Carr, "Mack Sennett."
18. Brownlow, *The Parade's Gone By . . . ,* p. 311; Carr, "Mack Sennett"; Lahue, *Mack Sennett's Keystone,* pp. 280–281.
19. Brownlow, *The Parade's Gone By . . . ,* p. 310.
20. George Geltzer, "Herbert Brenon," *Films in Review,* March 1955, p. 116.
21. Gerald MacDonald, "U.S. Filmmaking Abroad," *Films in Review,* June–July 1954, p. 259.
22. "Great Directors and Their Productions," *NYDM,* July 1916, p. 26.
23. "The King of Jamaica," *Photoplay,* July 1916, pp. 135–137; Ramsaye, *A Million and One Nights,* pp. 705–706.
24. Alison Smith, "Little Journeys to Eastern Studios: Brenon," *NYDM,* 25 August 1917, p. 15 (THE FALL OF THE ROMANOFFS); *FDY* (1929), p. 17. In the associated poll for the best film, SORRELL AND SON finished second, behind Lubitsch's THE PATRIOT.
25. Herbert Cruickshank, "From Fad to Worse," *Motion Picture Classic,* November 1928, p. 33.
26. Elizabeth Peltret, "On the Lot with Lois Weber," *Photoplay,* October 1917, p. 89; Aline Carter, "Muse of the Reel," *Motion Picture Magazine,* March 1921, p. 105.

27. Richard Koszarski, "The Years Have Not Been Kind to Lois Weber," in *Women and the Cinema*, ed. Karyn Kay and Gerald Peary (New York: Dutton, 1977), pp. 146–152 (WHERE ARE MY CHILDREN?); Bertha Smith, "A Perpetual Leading Lady," *Sunset*, March 1914, pp. 634–636.

28. The release continuity of THE HAND THAT ROCKS THE CRADLE is published in *Film History* 1/4 (1987), pp. 341–366. See also Lisa Rudman, "Marriage—the Ideal and the Reel; or, The Cinematic Marriage Manual," in the same issue, pp. 327–339.

29. George Geltzer, "Maurice Tourneur," *Films in Review*, April 1961, p. 193.

30. Maurice Tourneur, "Stylization in Motion Picture Direction," *Motion Picture Magazine*, September 1918, p. 101.

31. For a discussion of this sequence, see Kevin Brownlow's article on THE WISHING RING in *The American Film Heritage*, pp. 144–146.

32. Richard Koszarski, "Maurice Tourneur, First of the Visual Stylists," *Film Comment*, March–April 1973, pp. 24–31.

33. Maurice Tourneur, "Meeting the Public Demands," *Shadowland*, May 1920, p. 46.

34. Dorothy Nutting, "Monsieur Tourneur," *Photoplay*, July 1918, p. 55; Geltzer, "Maurice Tourneur."

35. See Charles Higham, *Cecil B. DeMille* (New York: Scribners, 1973), pp. 19–31, for background on THE SQUAW MAN. The barn had already been renovated for use as a film studio, according to Robert S. Birchard, "Diamond Jubilee for *The Squaw Man*," *AC*, August 1989, pp. 34–39.

36. Higham, *Cecil B. DeMille*, p. 31, claims the film was sold for $43,000, but Birchard, using materials at the DeMille estate, shows a "net producer profit" of $244,700. "Diamond Jubilee," p. 39. Ramsaye, *A Million and One Nights*, pp. 625–626, provides an early version of the film's curious mechanical problems.

37. Hampton, *A History of the Movies*, p. 218.

38. Cecil B. DeMille, "Photodrama: A New Art," *MPW*, 21 July 1917, p. 374. "Lasky lighting" was essentially single-source illumination that produced severe low-key effects, lighting up one side of a face and casting the rest into shadow. DeMille claimed to have introduced it in THE WARRENS OF VIRGINIA (1914). See Cecil B. DeMille, "Motion Picture Directing," p. 300.

39. *The Autobiography of Cecil B. DeMille*, ed. Donald Hayne (Englewood Cliffs, N.J.: Prentice-Hall, 1959), pp. 190–191.

40. Hampton, *A History of the Movies*, p. 221.

41. Jacobs, *The Rise of the American Film*, p. 342.

42. Hazel Simpson Naylor, "Real Folks," *Motion Picture Magazine*, September 1918, p. 34; Milne, *Motion Picture Directing*, p. 226; Wagenknecht, *The Movies in the Age of Innocence*, p. 151; Jack Spears, *Hollywood: The Golden Era* (New York: Castle, 1971), p. 289.

43. Lane, *What's Wrong with the Movies?*, pp. 66–67; Brownlow, *The Parade's Gone By . . .*, p. 270; David Robinson, *Hollywood in the Twenties* (Cranbury, N.J.: Barnes, 1968), p. 92.

44. Spears, *Hollywood*, pp. 279–313. This is the only extended treatment of Neilan's career to date.

45. Milne, *Motion Picture Directing*, pp. 220–221; Marshall Neilan, "Acting for the Screen: The Six Great Essentials," in *Opportunities in the Motion Picture Industry* (Los Angeles: Photoplay Research Society, 1922), pp. 5–11.

46. According to her friend Stephen Higgins, Miss Sweet later characterized Neilan in one sentence: "He was a great director but a lousy husband."

47. Spears, *Hollywood*, p. 291; Brownlow, *The Parade's Gone By . . .*, p. 422.

48. *The American Film Heritage*, pp. 104–109.

49. Vidor, *A Tree Is a Tree*, p. 16. See also Raymond Durgnat and Scott Simmon, *King Vidor, American* (Berkeley: University of California Press, 1988).

50. John Baxter, *King Vidor* (New York: Monarch, 1976), pp. 9–10.

51. Vidor, *A Tree Is a Tree*, p. 85. For more of Vidor's attitudes on the necessity of maintaining one's personal integrity in the face of the studio system, see his article "Rubber Stamp Movies," *New Theatre*, September 1934. Few directors in Hollywood had the courage to go public with such extreme statements.

52. Charles Higham and Joel Greenberg, *The Celluloid Muse* (Chicago: Regnery, 1969), p. 229.

53. Peter Noble, *Hollywood Scapegoat* (London: Fortune Press, 1950).

54. Koszarski, *The Man You Loved to Hate* (production histories of von Stroheim's films); Harriette Underhill, "Von Stroheim's *Foolish Wives* Not So Foolish," *New York Tribune*, 22 January 1922, IV:4 (von Stroheim quote).

55. *The Most Important and Misappreciated American Films*, pp. 145, 150.

56. Koszarski, *The Man You Loved to Hate*, p. 41.

57. Valerie von Stroheim, in an interview with the author, Los Angeles, June 1978.

58. Liam O'Leary, *Rex Ingram, Master of the Silent Cinema* (Dublin: Academy Press, 1980), is the only extended study. Ingram's European career is discussed in Michael Powell's memoir *A Life in the Movies* (New York: Knopf, 1987), pp. 116–172.

59. Lane, *What's Wrong with the Movies?* p. 15. Lane lists these four as the leaders and then attacks them for not living up to their promise.

60. Rex Ingram, "Directing the Picture," in *Opportunities in the Motion Picture Industry*, pp. 27–33.

61. Rex Ingram, "Art Advantages of the European Scene," *Theatre*, January 1928, p. 64.

62. " 'If You Beat Me, I Wept': Alice Terry Reminiscences About Silent Films," in Marshall Deutelbaum, ed., *"Image": On the Art and Evolution of the Film*, p. 183; Grant Whytock, in an interview with the author, North Hollywood, California, 16 July 1971; Milne, *Motion Picture Directing*, pp. 66–67.

63. "The Million Dollar Girl," *Photoplay*, October 1923, p. 63.

64. Robinson Locke Collection, New York Public Library, June Mathis file; June Mathis, "Tapping the Thought Wireless," *MPW*, 21 July 1917, p. 409.

65. Hampton, *A History of the Movies*, p. 310. "The spiritualistic element, absent from the book, has been introduced in the photoplay," noted the *New York Times*, 7 March 1921.

66. See GREED file, MGM Collection, Department of Special Collections, University of Southern California.

67. Brownlow, *Parade's Gone By*, pp. 385–414.

68. "June Mathis Dies While at Theatre," *NYT*, 27 July 1927; "June Mathis in Dramatic Exit," unidentified clipping in Locke Collection. For a recent assessment of Mathis' career, see *Dictionary of Literary Biography* 44, 2d ser. (Detroit: Gale, 1986), pp. 244–250.

69. Sherwood, *Best Moving Pictures of 1922–23*, p. 3.

70. Grierson, quoted in Jacobs, *The Documentary Tradition*, p. 25; Mrs. Robert Flaherty, "The Camera's Eye," *National Board of Review Magazine*, April 1927, p. 5.

71. See Terry Ramsaye, "Flaherty, Great Adventurer," *Photoplay*, May 1928, p. 58; Frances Flaherty, *The Odyssey of a Film-Maker* (Urbana, Ill.: Beta Phi Mu–University of Illinois Press, 1960), p. 13; Brownlow, *The War, the West, and the Wilderness*, p. 475, and also Brownlow's excellent coverage of similar expedition films.

72. Griffith, *The World of Robert Flaherty*, p. 36.

73. Calder-Marshall, *The Innocent Eye*, p. 85.

74. Hugh Gray, "Robert Flaherty and the Naturalistic Documentary," *Hollywood Quarterly*, Fall 1950, p. 47. Some years later, Flaherty's most notorious bit of creativity involved his teaching shark-hunting to Aran Islanders. See Calder-Marshall, p. 150.

75. Christopher M. Lyman, *The Vanishing Race and Other Illusions* (New York: Pantheon, 1982), p. 114. Lyman extensively outlines the methods used by Curtis to achieve his effects.

76. Arthur Marx, *Goldwyn* (New York: Norton, 1976), p. 107.

77. Marx, *Goldwyn*, pp. 11–15, 64–67. See also A. Scott Berg, *Goldwyn* (New York: Knopf, 1989).

78. Ramsaye, *A Million and One Nights*, pp. 752–753.

79. Allene Talmey, *Doug and Mary and Others* (New York: Macy-Macius, 1927), p. 81 (Goldwyn quote). Of the original Eminent Authors group, only Rupert Hughes and Rex Beach had any real success; the rest, including Mary Roberts Rinehart, Gertrude Atherton, and Gouverneur Morris, seem to have actively resisted the requirements of the screenplay form.

80. "Flashes from Eastern Stars," *Motion Picture Classic*, March 1925, p. 52.

81. Marx, *Goldwyn*, p. 96; Hampton, *A History of the Movies*, p. 244; Jacobs, *The Rise of the American Film*, p. 288; Jobes, *Motion Picture Empire*, p. 240; Kevin Lewis, "Include Me Out: Samuel Goldwyn and Joe Godsol," *Film History* 2/2 (1988), pp. 133–153; Johnson, *The Great Goldwyn*, p. 81. See also Samuel Goldwyn, *Behind the Screen* (New York: Doran, 1923).

82. Griffith, *Samuel Goldwyn: The Producer and His Films* (New York: Museum of Modern Art, 1954), p. 6.

83. Walter Wagner, *You Must Remember This* (New York: Putnam, 1975), p. 113.

84. Ramsaye, *A Million and One Nights*, p. 825; Jacobs, *Rise of the American Film*, p. 379.

85. Jacobs, *The Rise of the American Film*, p. 375.

86. *Ibid.*, pp. 378–379.

87. Victor Freeburg, *Pictorial Beauty on the Screen* (New York: Macmillan, 1923); Fenin and Everson, *The Western*, pp. 132–133. For a full discussion of the production problems of THE COVERED WAGON, see Brownlow, *The War, the West, and the Wilderness*, pp. 368–381.
88. Quoted in George Geltzer, "James Cruze," *Films in Review*, June–July 1954, p. 289.
89. "New Film Record Set by *Passion,*" *NYT*, 23 December 1920, p. 28; Hazel Simpson Naylor, "California Chatter," *Motion Picture Magazine*, August 1921, p. 99, quoted in Pratt, *Spellbound in Darkness*, p. 359 (THE CABINET OF DR. CALIGARI). For an intriguing discussion of the Lubitsch maneuver, see Baxter, *The Hollywood Exiles* (New York: Taplinger, 1976), pp. 27–36.
90. Brownlow, *The Parade's Gone By . . .*, p. 134.
91. Herbert Howe, "The Film Wizard of Europe," *Photoplay*, December 1922, p. 28.
92. Milne, *Motion Picture Directing*, pp. 199–200.
93. Jacobs, *The Rise of the American Film*, pp. 354–357.
94. See Herman G. Weinberg, *The Lubitsch Touch* (New York: Dutton, 1968), especially pp. 26–27.
95. See Howe, "Film Wizard of Europe," and Milne, *Motion Picture Directing*, p. 202.
96. *FDY* (1929), p. 9.
97. Talmey, *Doug and Mary and Others*, p. 165.
98. Dorothy Herzog, "How to Be a Producer," *Photoplay*, April 1926, p. 66.
99. Marx, *Mayer and Thalberg*, pp. 25–28.
100. Koszarski, *The Man You Loved to Hate*, pp. 101–108.
101. Lewis Milestone, "The Reign of the Director," *New Theatre and Film*, March 1937.
102. Brownlow, *The Parade's Gone By . . .*, pp. 486–490.
103. Marx, *Mayer and Thalberg*, p. 254 (see financial figures presented here for all the Thalberg films); Thomas, *Thalberg*, p. 373 (Thalberg award).
104. F. W. Murnau, "The Ideal Picture Needs No Titles," *Theatre*, January 1928, p. 72; Alexandre Astruc, "Le caméra-stylo," *L'Écran français*, 30 March 1948, p. 144.
105. Lotte Eisner, *Murnau* (Berkeley: University of California Press, 1973), p. 198.
106. Brownlow, *The Parade's Gone By . . .*, p. 152.
107. For the influence of expressionism, see, for example, the use of distorted settings to represent drug-induced visions in HUMAN WRECKAGE (1923) and dreams in BEGGAR ON HORSEBACK (1925).
108. John Grierson, *Grierson on Documentary* (Berkeley: University of California Press, 1966), pp. 83–85.
109. Brownlow, *The Parade's Gone By . . .*, p. 190 (moustache); Herman G. Weinberg, *Josef von Sternberg* (New York: Dutton, 1967), p. 118 (THE SALVATION HUNTERS).
110. Josef von Sternberg, *Fun in a Chinese Laundry* (New York: Macmillan, 1965), pp. 204–205.
111. Brownlow, *The Parade's Gone By . . .*, pp. 194–195.
112. Weinberg, *Josef von Sternberg*, p. 124.
113. B. G. Braver-Mann, "Josef von Sternberg," *Experimental Cinema* 5 (1934), p. 20.
114. Grierson, *Grierson on Documentary*, p. 60 (the comment dates from 1932).

Chapter 9. The Stars

1. Jowett, *Film, the Democratic Art*, pp. 54–57; "Great Artists Contest," *Motion Picture Magazine*, October 1914, p. 128. Given that J. Stuart Blackton was president of this magazine, one should accept the high standing of Vitagraph stars here with some caution.
2. Hampton, *History of the Movies*, p. 140. Zukor's first group of stars had been acquired at much lower rates.
3. *Ibid.*, p. 194.
4. "The Motion Picture Hall of Fame," *Motion Picture Magazine*, December 1918.
5. Lane, *What's Wrong with the Movies?* p. 134.
6. "The Box Office Test," *FDY* (1925), p. 5.
7. Remember that regional preferences were quite strong. A 1925 survey of its readers conducted by the *Nebraska Farmer* named Tom Mix the favorite star, far ahead of second-place finishers Fred Thompson and Thomas Meighan. Well down the list, Thompson's horse, Silver King, is seen to outpoll Lillian Gish. Women constituted 68 percent of those surveyed (reprinted in *FDY* [1926], p. 9).
8. See Timothy Lyons, *Charles Chaplin: A Guide to References and Resources* (Boston: Hall, 1979), pp. 2–87, and David Robinson, *Chaplin: His Life and Art* (New York: McGraw-Hill, 1985).

9. Jacobs, *The Rise of the American Film*, p. 229.

10. Sklar, *Movie-Made America*, pp. 110–116.

11. Kevin Brownlow and David Gill present unique documentary evidence of Chaplin's process of refining through repetition in their Thames Television series "The Unknown Chaplin" (1981).

12. Inexpensively distributed in poster and postcard form, the one-sheet for the film was commonly identified with Pickford and the entire early cinema. It is, for instance, the only example of a Pickford poster illustrated in Robert Windeler's biography *Sweetheart: The Story of Mary Pickford.*

13. Wagenknecht, *The Movies in the Age of Innocence*, p. 158. Se also James Card, "The Films of Mary Pickford," in *"Image": On the Art and Evolution of the Film*, pp. 121–132.

14. Hampton, *A History of the Movies*, p. 146.

15. *Ibid.*, p. 166.

16. *Ibid.*, p. 192.

17. Wagenknecht, *The Movies in the Age of Innocence*, p. 150, is especially strong on the 1917 Artcraft films. For STELLA MARIS, see Anthony Slide's essay in *The Rivals of D. W. Griffith*, ed. Richard Koszarski (Minneapolis: Walker Art Center, 1976), pp. 12–13.

18. Chaplin, *My Autobiography*, p. 223; Robert Lindsay, "Mary Pickford, Silents Sweetheart, Is Active in Memory and Business," *NYT*, 16 March 1976, p. 37. Pickford never liked Chaplin, and after his autobiography appeared, she violently counterattacked. See the interview with her in Wagner, *You Must Remember This*, where she criticizes Chaplin's business behavior and calls him "a cheap, hamfat comedian, throwing pies and acting in a very undignified manner" (p. 18).

19. Wagenknecht, *Movies in the Age of Innocence*, p. 157, has an interesting discussion of the significance of this hair-bobbing. See also Mary Pickford, *Sunshine and Shadow* (Garden City, N.Y.: Doubleday, 1955), p. 175.

20. Alistair Cooke, *Douglas Fairbanks: The Making of a Screen Character* (New York: Museum of Modern Art, 1940), p. 14.

21. Lahue, *Dreams for Sale*, pp. 57–58; Ralph Hancock and Letitia Fairbanks, *Douglas Fairbanks: The Fourth Musketeer* (New York: Henry Holt, 1953), p. 139.

22. Cooke, *Douglas Fairbanks*, p. 25.

23. James Mark Purcell, in a study of American film grosses, has shown that Fairbanks' United Artists features were always among the top money-earners of their season, with ROBIN HOOD clearly surpassing all other releases in 1922. Of course, high production costs on films like THE THIEF OF BAGDAD sometimes served to narrow Fairbanks' profit margins (letter from Purcell to the author, 26 January 1985).

24. Louis Delluc, *Cinéma et cie* (Paris: Bernard Grasset, 1919), pp. 172–173; René Jeanne and Charles Ford, *Histoire illustrée du cinéma muet*, vol 1 (Paris: Marabout Université, 1966), p. 80.

25. Pearl White, *Just Me* (New York: Doran, 1919). But see Wallace Davies, "The Truth About Pearl White," *Films in Review*, November 1959, p. 537.

26. White, *Just Me*, pp. 99–101. White spent her entire American career in the East and never even visited Hollywood.

27. For her filmography, see Weltman and Lee, *Pearl White, the Peerless Fearless Girl*, pp. 256–266.

28. Grau, *The Theatre of Science*, pp. 242–243.

29. See Lahue, *Bound and Gagged*; Lahue, *Continued Next Week* for discussion of White's dominance of the serial in this period.

30. *Upton Sinclair Presents William Fox*, p. 56.

31. Alexander Walker, *The Celluloid Sacrifice* (New York: Hawthorne, 1967), pp. 19–20.

32. Ramsaye, *A Million and One Nights*, pp. 702–704; DeWitt Bodeen, "Theda Bara," *Films in Review*, May 1968, p. 268.

33. Molly Haskell, *From Reverence to Rape* (New York: Holt, Rinehart, and Winston, 1974), p. 43 (vamp as male fantasy); Roberta Courtland, "The Divine Theda," *Motion Picture Magazine*, April 1917, p. 62 (Freeburg quote); Norman Zierold, *Sex Goddesses of the Silent Screen* (Chicago: Regnery, 1973), p. 15 (Bara quote).

34. "Great Artists Contest," *Motion Picture Magazine*, October 1914, p. 128. Of the six actors just mentioned, only Bushman receives more than cursory treatment in the most extensive study of the period, Kevin Brownlow's *The Parade's Gone By* . . .

35. See especially Richard Schickel's study of Reid in *The Stars* (New York: Bonanza, 1962), pp. 56–57, which matches the sensationalism of Kenneth Anger's *Hollywood Babylon* (Phoenix: Associated Professional Services, 1965).

36. DeWitt Bodeen, "Wallace Reid," *Films in Review*, April 1966, pp. 205–230.

37. Lasky, *I Blow My Own Horn*, pp. 112–114.

38. "Popular Players Contest," *Motion Picture Magazine*, August 1916; Eleanor Wardall, "Wallace Reid at Home," *Motion Picture Magazine*, February 1917, p. 192.

39. Quoted in Bodeen, "Wallace Reid," p. 219 (*Los Angeles Examiner* quote); Walker, *Stardom*, p. 203 (dope ring). Bodeen got the VALLEY OF THE GIANTS story from Dorothy Davenport (pp. 215–216); Brownlow quotes Karl Brown, cameraman on the picture, in *Hollywood: The Pioneers*, p. 11.

40. Ramsaye, *A Million and One Nights*, p. 606.

41. William S. Hart and Mary Hart, *Pinto Ben and Other Stories* (New York: Britton, 1919), p. 23. Hart originally published the poem in 1907 and as late as 1928 made a version for Victor Records. In addition to the book, there was, inevitably, a two-reel film version produced in 1915.

42. Diane Koszarski, *The Complete Films of William S. Hart*.

43. *The Fugitive "Draw" Egan*, budget sheet, Gatewood Dunstan Collection, manuscript division, Library of Congress, Washington, D.C. Reproduced in Diane Koszarski, *The Complete Films of William S. Hart*, p. xv.

44. *Ibid.*

45. Volume in the collection of George Pratt. Reproduced in D. Koszarski, *Complete Films*, p. xxiv.

46. *FDY* (1924), p. 299; Lane, *What's Wrong with the Movies?* p. 144; Adela Rogers St. Johns, "Our One and Only Great Actress," *Photoplay*, February 1926.

47. Mrs. Talmadge published a long-winded and ultimately useless biography of her daughters, *The Talmadge Sisters* (Philadelphia: Lippincott, 1924). See also Anita Loos, *The Talmadge Girls: A Memoir* (New York: Viking, 1978).

48. Jack Spears, "Norma Talmadge," in *Hollywood: The Golden Era*, p. 120.

49. Hampton, *History of the Motion Picture*, p. 324; Schickel, *The Stars*, p. 12.

50. Brownlow, *Hollywood: The Pioneers*, p. 175.

51. For a detailed account of Davies' career, see Fred Lawrence Guiles, *Marion Davies* (New York: McGraw-Hill, 1972).

52. Allen Churchill, *The Year the World Went Mad* (New York: Crowell, 1960), p. 14.

53. Robert G. Anderson, *Faces, Forms, Films: The Artistry of Lon Chaney* (New York: Castle, 1971); Forrest J. Ackerman, *Lon of a Thousand Faces* (Beverly Hills: Morrison, Raven-Hill, 1983). These fan-magazine-style biographies are stronger on illustration than analysis, and Chaney's important role in late silent cinema remains inadequately understood.

54. *Fant'America, 1: Tod Browning, Lon Chaney* (XV Festival Internazionale del Film di Fantascienza, Trieste, 1977). The catalogue of this joint Browning–Chaney retrospective contains fine filmographies and useful texts (in Italian), largely translated from period American sources.

55. Fenin and Everson, *The Western*, pp. 109 ff., 116; Bardèche and Brasillach, *History of the Film*, p. 114.

56. Hampton, *A History of the Movies*, p. 124; Fenin and Everson, *The Western*, p. 115.

57. George Pratt, "The Posse Is Still Riding Like Mad," in *"Image": On the Art and Evolution of the Film*, p. 68.

58. Don Miller, *The Hollywood Corral* (New York: Popular Library, 1976), pp. 2–87.

59. Paul Mix, *The Life and Legend of Tom Mix* (Cranbury, N.J.: Barnes, 1972), p. 193.

60. Talmey, *Doug and Mary and Others*, p. 73; Wagenknecht, *The Movies in the Age of Innocence*, p. 251. For examples of her recent following, see *Lilian Gish* (New York: Museum of Modern Art, 1980), with its admiring essay by Charles Silver and testimonials from Gish's friends and co-workers.

61. Vidor, *A Tree Is a Tree*, p. 132.

62. Gish's autobiography, *The Movies, Mr. Griffith, and Me* (Englewood Cliffs, N.J.: Prentice-Hall, 1969), written with Ann Pinchot, remains the best biographical source.

63. Vidor, *A Tree Is a Tree*, p. 127.

64. *Ibid.*, p. 130; Gish, *The Movies*, p. 285.

65. See the appreciative reappraisal of this film in Alexander Walker's section on Gish in his *Stardom*, pp. 79–81.

66. Louise Brooks, *Lulu in Hollywood* (New York: Knopf, 1982), pp. 85–92; Gish, *The Movies*, pp. 294–295. Only one film, a mediocre talkie called ONE ROMANTIC NIGHT, was made under the United Artists contract.

67. Gish has long promoted the concept of silent films as a universal language. See her essay "A

Universal Language" in the *Encyclopaedia Britannica*, 14th ed., reprinted in *The Theatre and Motion Pictures*, pp. 33–34.

68. Talmey, *Doug and Mary and Others*, p. 22.

69. Gloria Swanson, *Swanson on Swanson* (New York: Random House, 1980), pp. 24–43.

70. Fritzi Remont, "Diving into Drama," *Motion Picture Magazine*, December 1918, p. 102. For plot summaries, see Richard Hudson and Raymond Lee, *Gloria Swanson* (Cranbury, N.J.: Barnes, 1970), pp. 116–119; for Swanson's opinions, see *Swanson on Swanson*, p. 103.

71. Walker, *Stardom*, p. 129.

72. *Swanson on Swanson*, p. 273.

73. See Koszarski, *The Man You Loved to Hate*, pp. 196–238.

74. Remont, "Diving into Drama," p. 103. Swanson died in 1983.

75. See the editorial attack "The Star System" in the trade annual *Wid's Year Book* (1921), pp. 342–343, which echoes these feelings.

76. Baxter, *The Hollywood Exiles*, pp. 34–36. The American response to Negri is very evident in the review of PASSION published in the *New York Times* on 13 December 1920.

77. Note the summary treatment of Negri's American career even in such works as Kevin Brownlow's *The Parade's Gone By . . .* and Edward Wagenknecht's *The Movies in the Age of Innocence*.

78. "Your Opinion Contest," *Motion Picture Classic*, July 1926 (Negri polled 27,599 votes, far ahead of Pickford [18,766] and Swanson [11,462]); Pola Negri, *Memoirs of a Star* (Garden City, N.Y.: Doubleday, 1970), p. 248.

79. Alice Williamson, *Alice in Movieland* (New York: Appleton, 1928), p. 147.

80. Baxter, *The Hollywood Exiles*, p. 46. But Norman Zierold, who seems far less prejudiced against Negri, claims that this carpet was replaced at the last moment by one of more suitable proportions; see *Sex Goddesses of the Silent Screen* (Chicago: Regnery, 1973), p. 119.

81. Negri, *Memoirs of a Star*, p. 315.

82. Zierold, *Sex Goddesses*, p. 90; Maurice Zolotow, *Billy Wilder in Hollywood* (New York: Putnam, 1977), p. 160.

83. Irving Shulman, *Valentino* (New York: Trident Press, 1967). Anthony Slide promotes the Shulman book in "Rudolph Valentino: Latin Lover" in *Close-Ups*, ed. Danny Peary (New York: Workman), p. 131.

84. Lloyd Morris, *Not So Long Ago* (New York: Random House, 1949), discusses the era entirely in terms of radio, the automobile, and motion pictures. For the Valentino funeral, see pp. 119–120.

85. Brownlow, *Hollywood: The Pioneers*, p. 184; Slide, "Rudolph Valentino," pp. 130–134.

86. David Carroll, *The Matinee Idols* (New York: Galahad, 1972), pp. 125–126.

87. *Motion Picture Magazine*, December 1918, p. 12.

88. The ad is reprinted in Brownlow, *Hollywood: The Pioneers*, p. 186. For plot summaries and credits of Valentino's films, see Diane Koszarski, *There's a New Star in Heaven . . . Valentino* (Berlin: Verlag Volker Spiess, 1979), pp. 31–100.

89. Walker, *Stardom*, pp. 153–156.

90. See Robinson, *Keaton*, for a discussion of this conception of "trajectory."

91. Tom Dardis, *Keaton: The Man Who Wouldn't Lie Down* (New York: Scribners, 1979), pp. 113–114. But Keaton did have a coterie of loyal fans, including President Calvin Coolidge, who ran THE NAVIGATOR at least three times in his private screening room on the presidential yacht *Mayflower*. Coolidge was once described in a fan magazine as "the first national executive to depend upon motion pictures as his only recreation." See Ashmun Brown, "President Coolidge Goes to the Movies," *Motion Picture Classic*, January 1926, p. 16.

92. Dardis, *Keaton*, pp. 135–145, 158–159; Brownlow, *The Parade's Gone By . . .*, p. 493.

93. Tom Dardis, *Harold Lloyd: The Man on the Clock* (New York: Viking, 1983), p. 200; Richard Schickel, *Harold Lloyd: The Shape of Laughter*, p. 73; Jacobs, *The Rise of the American Film*, p. 414. In fact, Jacobs treats Keaton in an even more perfunctory manner: a single reference in a 600-page book.

94. In addition to the works by Dardis and Schickel already cited, see Adam Reilly, *Harold Lloyd: The King of Daredevil Comedy* (New York: Macmillan, 1977). For Lloyd's audience research, see Reilly, pp. 106–107.

95. Lloyd, *An American Comedy*, pp. 53–54.

96. Dardis, *Harold Lloyd*, p. 142.

97. Bow's prominence in general American history texts was pointed out to me by Garth Jowett.

98. "Clara Bow, the 'It' Girl, Dies at 60; Film Actress Set Vogue in 1920s," *NYT*, 28 September 1965, p. 1.

99. The best of the specialized works is David Stenn, *Clara Bow: Running Wild* (Garden City, N.Y.: Doubleday, 1988).

100. Colleen Moore, *Silent Star* (Garden City, N.Y.: Doubleday, 1968), p. 135 (FLAMING YOUTH); Zukor, *The Public Is Never Wrong*, pp. 244–245; Anger, *Hollywood Babylon*, pp. 153–161.

101. Zierold, *Sex Goddesses*, pp. 166–167. Glyn quoted in James Robert Parish, *The Paramount Pretties* (New Rochelle, Arlington House, 1972), p. 65.

102. Bow was less effective as a dramatic actress, despite her appearance in such classics as DANCING MOTHERS and WINGS. The film version of IT, as it happens, is not one of her best films.

103. Leatrice Gilbert Fountain, *Dark Star: The Untold Story of the Meteoric Rise and Fall of the Legendary John Gilbert* (New York: St. Martin's Press, 1985).

104. Walker, *Stardom*, pp. 174–175. Gable made one of his first screen appearances as an extra in Gilbert's THE MERRY WIDOW. Later he was given the lead in RED DUST, a film that had been announced for Gilbert and that Gilbert had hoped would revive his reputation. Instead, it established Gable. See Fountain, *Dark Star*, pp. 226–227.

105. Walker, *Stardom*, pp. 174–176.

106. See Fountain, *Dark Star*, for many tales of his emotional problems.

107. Vidor, *A Tree Is a Tree*, p. 138.

108. Fountain, *Dark Star*, p. 130. (The marriage to Garbo never took place; Mayer quoted in Brownlow, *The Parade's Gone By . . .* , p. 576.)

109. Walker, *The Shattered Silents* (New York: William Morrow, 1979), p. 174–176.

110. Marx, *Mayer and Thalberg*, p. 48.

111. Lotte Eisner, *Haunted Screen*, p. 295; Kenneth Tynan, "The Girl in the Black Helmet," *New Yorker*, 11 June 1979, pp. 45–86; Brooks, *Lulu in Hollywood*; Barry Paris, *Louise Brooks* (New York: Knopf, 1989).

112. Eisner, *The Haunted Screen*, p. 296.

113. Ado Kyrou, *Amour-érotisme au cinéma* (Paris: Terrain Vague, 1957).

Chapter 10. The Envelope, Please

1. Frank Woods, "The Academy of Motion Picture Arts and Sciences," *SMPE* 33 (April 1928), p. 25.

2. Murray Ross, *Stars and Strikes* (New York: Columbia University Press, 1941), pp. 13–18. The full history of the relationship between the IATSE and the motion-picture industry is outside the scope of this study. But some indication of its unique nature was suggested by the producer Joseph P. Kennedy, who claimed that "what we are trying to do [with the Studio Basic Agreement] is to maintain an open shop without prejudice to union labor (Joseph P. Kennedy, *The Story of the Films* [Boston: A. W. Shaw, 1927], p. 23).

3. Robert Osborne, *Fifty Golden Years of Oscar: The Official History of the Academy of Motion Picture Arts and Sciences* (La Habra: ESE California, 1979), n.p. The "International" in the new Academy's name was dropped immediately, perhaps because it made the new organization sound too much like the IATSE.

4. Woods, "The Academy of Motion Picture Arts and Sciences" (original branches); Ross, *Stars and Strikes*, pp. 41, 57.

5. "Plan for Awards of Merit," Academy Bulletin 12 (misprinted as 11) (16 July 1928), p. 2.

6. See the many such comments collected in the anthology *Hollywood Directors, 1914–1940*, edited by Richard Koszarski (New York: Oxford University Press, 1976).

7. Osborne, *Fifty Golden Years of Oscar*.

8. Royal Film Archive of Belgium, *The Most Important and Misappreciated American Films*.

9. Karl Struss, "Dramatic Cinematography," *SMPE* 34 (April 1928), p. 317.

10. Richard Watts, Jr., "Landmark in Film Annals," *New York Herald Tribune*, 14 December 1924; "Frank Norris's *McTeague*," *New York Times*, 5 December 1924; Robert E. Sherwood, "*Greed*," *Life*, 1 January 1925.

11. See Herman G. Weinberg, *The Complete "Greed" of Erich von Stroheim* (New York: Dutton, 1973); Koszarski, *The Man You Loved to Hate*, pp. 114–149.

12. Richard Schickel, *D. W. Griffith: An American Life* (New York: Simon and Schuster, 1984), contains a good general discussion of the place of THE BIRTH OF A NATION in Griffith's career. See also *Film*

Culture 36 (Spring–Summer 1965), a special issue on THE BIRTH OF A NATION edited by Seymour Stern.

13. See, for example, the commentary on Chaplin and Keaton in Paul Rotha, *The Film Till Now* (London: Jonathan Cape, 1930; 2d ed., ed. Richard Griffith, New York: Barnes and Noble, 1950).

14. Dardis, *Keaton*, pp. 135–157; Mordaunt Hall, *"The General," New York Times*, 8 February 1927; Joe Franklin, *Classics of the Silent Screen* (New York: Citadel Press, 1959), p. 89. A good example of the more recent approach is Noel Carroll, "An In-Depth Analysis of Buster Keaton's *The General*" (Ph.D. diss., New York University, 1978).

15. MGM art-department log, author's collection (production data); Vidor, *A Tree Is a Tree*, p. 150 ("enlightening influence"); Eric Rhode, "Why Neo-Realism Failed," *Sight and Sound*, Winter 1960–1961, p. 27 (neorealist ideal).

16. *The Crowd* cost $551,000 and earned a profit of $69,000, according to figures supplied in Marx, *Mayer and Thalberg*, p. 255.

Bibliography

Agnew, Frances. *Motion Picture Acting*. New York: Reliance Newspapers Syndicate, 1913.

Aitken, Roy E. *The "Birth of a Nation" Story*. Middleburg, Va.: Denlinger, 1965.

Allen, Robert C. *Vaudeville and Film, 1895–1915: A Study in Media Interaction*. New York: Arno Press, 1980.

Altomara, Rita. *Hollywood on the Palisades*. New York: Garland, 1983.

Anderson, Gillian. *Music for Silent Films: 1894–1929*. Washington: The Library of Congress, 1988.

Anderson, Robert G. *Faces, Forms, Films: The Artistry of Lon Chaney*. New York: Castle, 1971.

Balaban, Carrie. *Continuous Performance*. New York: G. P. Putnam's Sons, 1942.

Balio, Tino. *United Artists: The Company Built by the Stars*. Madison: University of Wisconsin Press, 1976.

Balio, Tino, ed. *The American Film Industry*. Madison: University of Wisconsin Press, 1976.

Ball, Eustace Hale. *The Art of the Photoplay*. 2d ed. New York: Veritas, 1919.

Ball, Robert Hamilton. *Shakespeare on Silent Film*. New York: Theatre Arts, 1968.

Balshofer, Fred, and Arthur Miller. *One Reel a Week*. Los Angeles: University of California Press, 1967.

Bardèche, Maurice, and Robert Brasillach, *History of the Film*. Translated and edited by Iris Barry. London: George Allen and Unwin, 1938; New York: Norton–Museum of Modern Art, 1938.

Barr, Charles. *Laurel and Hardy*. Berekeley: University of California Press, 1968.

Barry, Iris. *Let's Go to the Movies*. New York: Payson and Clarke, 1926.

———. *D. W. Griffith, American Film Master*. New York: Museum of Modern Art, 1940.

Basten, Fred E. *Glorious Technicolor: The Movies' Magic Rainbow*. New York: Barnes, 1980.

Baxter, John. *The Hollywood Exiles*. New York: Taplinger, 1976.

Beardsley, Charles. *Hollywood's Master Showman: The Legendary Sid Grauman*. New York: Cornwall, 1983.

Beaton, Welford. *Know Your Movies: The Theory and Practice of Motion Picture Production*. Hollywood: Howard Hill, 1932.

Bell, Geoffrey. *The Golden Gate and the Silver Screen*. Rutherford: Fairleigh Dickinson University Press, 1984.

Berg, A. Scott. *Goldwyn*. New York: Alfred Knopf, 1989.

Berg, Charles M. *An Investigation of the Motives for and Realization of Music to Accompany the American Silent Film, 1897–1927*. New York: Arno Press, 1976.

Bernique, Jean. *Motion Picture Acting for Professionals and Amateurs*. Producers Service Company, 1916.

Bertsch, Marguerite. *How to Write for Moving Pictures: A Manual of Instruction and Information*. New York: Doran, 1917.

Beynon, George. *Musical Presentation of Motion Pictures*. New York: Schirmer, 1921.

Bitzer, G. W. *Billy Bitzer: His Story*. New York: Farrar, Straus, and Giroux, 1973.

Blesh, Rudy. *Keaton*. New York: Macmillan, 1966.

Bloem, Walter S. *The Soul of the Moving Picture*. New York: Dutton, 1924.

Blum, Daniel. *A Pictorial History of the Silent Screen.* New York: Grosset and Dunlap, 1953.

Bogdanovich, Peter. *John Ford.* Berkeley: University of California Press, 1968.

———. *Allan Dwan, the Last Pioneer.* New York: Praeger, 1971.

Bollman, Gladys, and Henry Bollman. *Motion Pictures for Community Needs.* New York: Henry Holt, 1922.

Bonomo, Joe. *The Strongman.* New York: Bonomo Studios, 1968.

Bordwell, David, Janet Staiger, and Kristin Thompson. *The Classical Hollywood Cinema.* New York: Columbia University Press, 1985.

Brooks, Louise. *Lulu in Hollywood.* New York: Knopf, 1982.

Brown, Karl. *Adventures with D. W. Griffith.* Edited by Kevin Brownlow. New York: Farrar, Straus, and Giroux, 1973.

Brownlow, Kevin. *The Parade's Gone By . . .* New York: Knopf, 1968.

———. *The War, the West, and the Wilderness.* New York: Knopf, 1979.

———. *Behind the Mask of Innocence.* New York: Knopf, 1990.

Brownlow, Kevin, and John Kobal. *Hollywood: The Pioneeers.* New York: Knopf, 1979.

Calder-Marshall, Arthur. *The Innocent Eye.* New York: Harcourt, Brace, 1966.

Cameron, James R. *Motion Picture Projection.* 3d ed. New York: Technical Book Company, 1922.

Campbell, Craig. *Reel America and World War I.* Jefferson, N.C.: McFarland, 1985.

Cannom, Robert C. *Van Dyke and the Mythical City of Hollywood.* Culver City: Murray & Gee, 1948.

Catalog of Copyright Entries, Cumulative Series: Motion Pictures, 1912–1939. Washington, D.C.: Copyright Office, Library of Congress, 1951.

Chaplin, Charles. *My Autobiography.* New York: Simon and Schuster, 1964.

Cherchi Usai, Paolo, and Lorenzo Codelli, eds. *Sulla via di Hollywood [On the Road to Hollywood].* Pordenone: Edizioni Biblioteca Dell'Immagine, 1988.

Coe, Brian. *The History of Movie Photography.* Westfield, N.J.: Eastview Editions, 1981.

Collins, Francis A. *The Camera Man.* New York: Century, 1919.

Cooke, Alistair. *Douglas Fairbanks: The Making of a Screen Character.* New York: Museum of Modern Art, 1940.

Cooper, Miriam. *Dark Lady of the Silents.* New York: Bobbs-Merrill, 1973.

Crafton, Donald. *Before Mickey: The Animated Film, 1898–1928.* Cambridge, Mass.: MIT Press, 1982.

Cripps, Thomas. *Slow Fade to Black.* New York: Oxford University Press, 1977.

Crowther, Bosley. *The Lion's Share: The Story of an Entertainment Empire.* New York: Dutton, 1957.

———. *Hollywood Rajah: The Life and Times of Louis B. Mayer.* New York: Holt, Rinehart, and Winston, 1960.

Croy, Homer. *How Motion Pictures Are Made.* New York: Harper, 1918.

———. *Star Maker: The Story of D. W. Griffith.* New York: Duell, Sloan, and Pearce, 1959.

Daniels, Bebe and Ben Lyons. *Life with the Lyons.* London: Odhams, 1953.

Dardis, Tom. *Keaton, the Man Who Wouldn't Lie Down.* New York: Scribners, 1979.

———. *Harold Lloyd: The Man on the Clock.* New York: Viking, 1983.

DeMille, Cecil B. *The Autobiography of Cecil B. DeMille.* Edited by Donald Hayne. Englewood, Cliffs, N.J.: Prentice-Hall, 1959.

deMille, William. *Hollywood Saga.* New York: Dutton, 1937.

Dench, Ernest A. *Making the Movies.* New York: Macmillan, 1919.

Deutelbaum, Marshall, ed. *"Image": On the Art and Evolution of the Film.* New York: Dover, 1979.

Di Lauro, Al, and Gerald Rabkin. *Dirty Movies: An Illustrated History of the Stag Film, 1915–1970.* New York: Chelsea House, 1976.

Dodds, John W. *The Several Lives of Paul Fejos.* New York: Wenner-Gren Foundation, 1973.

Drinkwater, John. *The Life and Adventures of Carl Laemmle.* New York: Putnam, 1931.

Durgnat, Raymond, and Scott Simmon. *King Vidor, American.* Berkeley: University of California Press, 1988.

Ellis, Don Carlos, and Laura Thornborough. *Motion Pictures in Education: A Practical Handbook for Users of Visual Aids.* New York: Crowell, 1923.

Emerson, John, and Anita Loos. *How to Write Photoplays*. New York: McCann, 1920.

———. *Breaking into the Movies*. New York: McCann, 1921.

Ernst, Morris L., and Pare Lorentz. *Censored: The Private Life of the Movies*. New York: Cape and Smith, 1930.

Esenwein, J. B., and Arthur Leeds. *Writing the Photoplay*. Springfield, Mass.: Home Correspondence School, 1913.

Everson, William K. *The Films of Hal Roach*. New York: Museum of Modern Art, 1971.

———. *American Silent Film*. New York: Oxford University Press, 1978.

Fairbanks, Douglas. *Laugh and Live*. New York: Britton, 1917.

Fell, John. *Film and the Narrative Tradition*. Norman: University of Oklahoma Press, 1974.

Fenin, George N., and William K. Everson. *The Western: From Silents to Cinerama*. New York: Orion Press, 1962.

Fielding, Raymond. *The American Newsreel, 1911–67*. Norman: University of Oklahoma Press, 1972.

Fielding, Raymond, ed. *A Technological History of Motion Pictures and Television*. Berkeley: University of California Press, 1967.

Flaherty, Frances H. *The Odyssey of a Film-Maker: Robert Flaherty's Story*. Urbana: Beta Phi Mu—University of Illinois Press, 1960.

Fountain, Leatrice Gilbert. *Dark Star: The Untold Story of the Meteoric Rise and Fall of the Legendary John Gilbert*. New York: St. Martin's Press, 1985.

Fowler, Gene. *Father Goose: The Story of Mack Sennett*. New York: Covici, Friede, 1934.

Franklin, Harold B. *Motion Picture Theater Management*. New York: Doran, 1927.

Freeburg, Victor. *The Art of Photoplay Making*. New York: Macmillan, 1918.

———. *Pictorial Beauty on the Screen*. New York: Macmillan, 1923.

Gallagher, Tag. *John Ford: The Man and His Films*. Berkeley: University of California Press, 1986.

Giroux, Robert. *A Deed of Death*. New York: Knopf, 1990.

Gish, Lillian, with Ann Pinchot. *The Movies, Mr. Griffith, and Me*. Englewood Cliffs, N.J.: Prentice-Hall, 1969.

Goldwyn, Samuel. *Behind the Screen*. New York: Doran, 1923.

Gomery, Douglas. *The Hollywood Studio System*. New York: St. Martin's Press, 1986.

Grace, Dick. *I Am Still Alive*. New York: Rand McNally, 1931.

Grau, Robert. *The Theatre of Science*. New York: Broadway, 1914.

Gregory, Carl Louis. *Condensed Course in Motion Picture Photography*. New York: New York Institute of Photography, 1920.

———. *Motion Picture Photography*. 2d ed. Edited by Herbert C. McKay. New York: Falk, 1927.

Griffith, Linda Arvidson. *When the Movies Were Young*. New York: Dutton, 1925.

Griffith, Richard. *The World of Robert Flaherty*. New York: Duell, Little, 1953.

———. *Samuel Goldwyn: The Producer and His Films*. New York: Museum of Modern Art, 1956.

Guiles, Fred Lawrence. *Marion Davies*. New York: McGraw-Hill, 1972.

Hacker, Leonard. *Cinematic Design*. Boston: Photographic Publishing Co., 1931.

Hall, Ben M. *The Best Remaining Seats*. New York: Bramhall House, 1961.

Hall, Hal, ed. *Cinematographic Annual*. 2 vols. Hollywood: American Society of Cinematographers, 1930–1931.

Hambling, John, and Patrick Downing. *The Art of Hollywood*. London: Thames Television, 1979.

Hampton, Benjamin B. *A History of the Movies*. New York: Covici, Friede, 1931.

Hanson, Patricia K., ed. *The American Film Institute Catalog of Motion Pictures Produced in the United States: Feature Films, 1911–20*. Berkeley: University of California Press, 1988.

Hart, William S. *My Life East and West*. New York: Houghton Mifflin, 1929.

Hart, William S., and Mary Hart. *Pinto Ben and Other Stories*. New York: Britton, 1919.

Hays, Will H. *The Memoirs of Will H. Hays*. Garden City, N.Y.: Doubleday, 1955.

Henderson, Robert M. *D. W. Griffith: His Life and Work*. New York: Oxford University Press, 1972.

Herndon, Booton. *Mary Pickford and Douglas Fairbanks*. New York: Norton, 1977.

Higashi, Sumiko. *Virgins, Vamps, and Flappers: The American Silent Movie Heroine*. Montreal: Eden Press, 1979.
———. *Cecil B. DeMille: A Guide to References and Resources*. Boston: G. K. Hall, 1985.
Higham, Charles. *Hollywood Cameramen*. Bloomington: Indiana University Press, 1970.
Hill, Laurance L., and Silas E. Snyder. *Can Anything Good Come Out of Hollywood?* Los Angeles: Times-Mirror Press, 1923.
Hochman, Stanley, ed. *From Quasimodo to Scarlett O'Hara: A National Board of Review Anthology, 1920–1940*. New York: Ungar, 1982.
Hoffman, Charles. *Sounds for Silents*. New York: DBS, 1970.
Horowitz, Rita, and Harriet Harrison, eds. *The George Kleine Collection of Early Motion Pictures in the Library of Congress: A Catalog*. Washington, D.C.: Library of Congress, 1980.
Huettig, Mae D. *Economic Control of the Motion Picture Industry: A Study in Industrial Organization*. Philadelphia: University of Pennsylvania Press, 1944.
Huff, Theodore. *Charlie Chaplin*. New York: Schuman, 1951.
Hulfish, David S. *Motion Picture Work*. Chicago: American School of Correspondence, 1913.
Irwin, Will. *The House That Shadows Built*. New York: Doubleday, Doran, 1928.
Jacobs, Lewis. *The Rise of the American Film*. New York: Harcourt, Brace, 1939.
Jacobs, Lewis, ed. *The Compound Cinema: The Film Writings of Harry Alan Potamkin*. New York: Teachers College Press, 1977.
Jobes, Gertrude. *Motion Picture Empire*. Hamden, Conn.: Archon, 1966.
Johnson, Martin. *Camera Trails in Hollywood*. New York: Century, 1924.
Jones, Charles Reed, ed. *Breaking into the Movies*. New York: Unicorn Press, 1927.
Jowett, Garth. *Film: the Democratic Art*. Boston: Little, Brown, 1976.
Kaufmann, Stanley, and Bruce Henstell, eds. *American Film Criticism, from the Beginnings to Citizen Kane*. New York: Liveright, 1972.
Kelley, Albert. *Movies Just Growed*. Woodland Hills, Calif.: Quality Instant Printing, 1976.
Kennedy, Joseph P., ed. *The Story of the Films*. Chicago: Shaw, 1927.
Kerr, Paul, ed. *The Hollywood Film Industry*. London: Routledge and Kegan Paul, 1986.
Kerr, Walter. *The Silent Clowns*. New York: Knopf, 1979.
Kindem, Gorham, ed. *The American Movie Industry*. Carbondale: Southern Illinois University Press, 1982.
Kirkpatrick, Sidney. *A Cast of Killers*. New York: Dutton, 1986.
Klumph, Inez, and Helen Klumph. *Screen Acting: Its Requirements and Rewards*. New York: Falk, 1922.
Kobal, John. *The Art of the Great Hollywood Portrait Photographers, 1925–40*. New York: Harrison House, 1980.
Kohner, Frederick. *The Magician of Sunset Boulevard*. Palos Verdes: Morgan Press, 1977.
Koszarski, Diane. *There's a New Star in Heaven . . . Valentino*. Berlin: Verlag Volker Spiess, 1979.
———. *The Complete Films of William S. Hart*. New York: Dover, 1980.
Koszarski, Richard. *Universal Pictures: 65 Years*. New York: Museum of Modern Art, 1977.
———. *The Astoria Studio and Its Fabulous Films*. New York: Dover, 1983.
———. *The Man You Loved to Hate: Erich von Stroheim and Hollywood*. New York: Oxford University Press, 1983.
Koszarski, Richard, ed. *Hollywood Directors, 1914–40*. New York: Oxford University Press, 1976.
———, ed. *The Rivals of D. W. Griffith: Alternate Auteurs 1913–1918*. Minneapolis: Walker Art Center, 1976.
Lahue, Kalton. *Continued Next Week: A History of the Moving Picture Serial, 1912–30*. Norman: University of Oklahoma Press, 1964.
———. *World of Laughter*. Norman: University of Oklahoma Press, 1966.
———. *Bound and Gagged: The Story of the Silent Serials*. Cranbury, N.J.: Barnes, 1968.
———. *Dreams for Sale: The Rise and Fall of the Triangle Film Corporation*. Cranbury, N.J.: Barnes, 1971.
———. *Motion Picture Pioneer: The Selig Polyscope Company*. Cranbury, N.J.: Barnes, 1973.

Lahue, Kalton, and Terry Brewer. *Kops and Custards: The Legend of Keystone Films.* Norman: University of Oklahoma Press, 1967.

Lahue, Kalton, and Sam Gill. *Clown Princes and Court Jesters.* Cranbury, N.J.: Barnes, 1970.

Lane, Tamar. *What's Wrong with the Movies?* Los Angeles: Waverly, 1923.

Lasky, Jesse L., with Don Weldon. *I Blow My Own Horn.* London: Victor Gollancz, 1957.

Lauritzen, Einer, and Gunnar Lundquist. *American Film Index, 1916–1920.* Stockholm: Film Index, 1984.

Lennig, Arthur. *The Silent Voice: A Text.* Privately printed, 1969.

Lescarboura, Austin. *Behind the Motion Picture Screen.* New York: Munn, 1919.

Lewis, Howard T. *Cases of the Motion Picture Industry.* New York: McGraw-Hill, 1930.

———. *The Motion Picture Industry.* New York: Van Nostrand, 1933.

Lindsay, Vachel. *The Art of the Moving Picture.* 2d ed. New York: Macmillan, 1922.

Lloyd, Harold. *An American Comedy.* New York: Longman, Green, 1928. Reprinted, with an introduction by Richard Griffith. New York: Dover, 1971.

Loos, Anita. *A Girl Like I.* New York: Viking Press, 1966.

———. *The Talmadge Girls: A Memoir.* New York: Viking, 1978.

Lounsbury, Myron Osborn. *Origins of American Film Criticism, 1909–1939.* New York: Arno Press, 1973.

Lowrey, Carolyn. *The First One Hundred Noted Men and Women of the Screen.* New York: Moffat, Yard, 1920.

Lubschez, Ben J. *The Story of the Motion Picture, 65 B.C. to 1920 A.D.* New York: Reeland, 1920.

Lutz, E. G. *Animated Cartoons.* New York: Scribners, 1920.

———. *The Motion-Picture Cameraman.* New York: Scribners, 1927.

Lyons, Timothy. *The Silent Partner.* New York: Arno Press, 1974.

Marion, Frances. *Off with Their Heads!* New York: Macmillan, 1972.

Marsh, Mae. *Screen Acting.* New York: Stokes, 1921.

Martin, Olga J. *Hollywood's Movie Commandments: A Handbook for Motion Picture Writers and Reviewers.* New York: Wilson, 1937.

Marx, Samuel. *Mayer and Thalberg, the Make-Believe Saints.* New York: Random House, 1975.

McCarthy, Mary Eunice. *Hands of Hollywood.* Hollywood: Photoplay Research Bureau, n.d.

McKay, Herbert C. *The Handbook of Motion Picture Photography.* New York: Falk, 1927.

Miller, Virgil. *Splinters from Hollywood Tripods.* New York: Exposition Press, 1964.

Milne, Peter. *Motion Picture Directing: The Facts and Theories of the Newest Art.* New York: Falk, 1922.

Mitchell, Alice M. *Children and Movies.* Chicago: University of Chicago Press, 1929.

Mock, James R., and Cedric Larson. *Words That Won the War: The Story of the Committee on Public Information, 1917–1919.* Princeton: Princeton University Press, 1939.

Moley, Raymond. *The Hays Office.* Indianapolis: Bobbs-Merrill, 1945.

Moore, Colleen. *Silent Star.* New York: Doubleday, 1968.

Morris, Lloyd. *Not So Long Ago.* New York: Random House, 1949.

Morsberger, Robert, et al., eds. *American Screenwriters.* Vol. 26 of the *Dictionary of Literary Biography.* Detroit: Gale, 1984.

Mould, David. *American Newsfilm, 1914–1919: The Underground War.* New York: Garland, 1983.

Munden, Kenneth W., ed. *The American Film Institute Catalog of Motion Pictures Produced in the United States: Feature Films, 1921–1930.* New York: Bowker, 1971.

Munsterberg, Hugo. *The Photoplay: A Psychological Study.* New York: Appleton, 1916.

Naylor, David. *American Picture Palaces.* New York: Van Nostrand Reinhold, 1981.

———. *Great American Movie Theaters.* Washington, D.C.: Preservation Press, 1987.

Negri, Pola. *Memoirs of a Star.* Garden City, N.Y.: Doubleday, 1970.

Nicoll, Allardyce. *Film and Theater.* New York: Crowell, 1936.

Noble, Peter. *Hollywood Scapegoat: The Biography of Erich von Stroheim.* London: Fortune Press, 1950.

Nunn, Curtis. *Marguerite Clark, America's Darling of Broadway and the Silver Screen.* Fort Worth: Texas Christian University Press, 1981.

O'Dell, Paul. *Griffith and the Rise of Hollywood.* Cranbury, N.J.: Barnes, 1970.
O'Dell, Scott. *Representative Photoplays Analyzed.* Hollywood: Palmer Institute of Authorship, 1924.
O'Leary, Liam. *The Silent Cinema.* New York: Dutton, 1965.
————. *Rex Ingram, Master of the Silent Cinema.* Dublin: Academy Press, 1980.
Oberholtzer, Ellis Paxson. *The Morals of the Movie.* Philadelphia: Penn, 1922.
Paine, Albert Bigelow. *Life and Lillian Gish.* New York: Macmillan, 1932.
Palmer, Frederick. *Palmer Plan Handbook.* Rev. ed. Los Angeles: Palmer Institute of Authorship, 1921.
————. *Photoplay Plot Encyclopedia: An Analysis of the Use in Photoplays of the Thirty-Six Dramatic Situations and Their Subdivisions.* 2d ed., rev. Los Angeles: Palmer Photoplay, 1922.
Paris, Barry. *Louise Brooks.* New York: Knopf, 1989.
Parsons, Louella O. *How to Write for the Movies.* Chicago: McClurg, 1917.
Patterson, Frances Taylor. *Cinema Craftsmanship.* New York: Harcourt, Brace, and Howe, 1921.
————. *Scenario and Screen.* New York: Harcourt, Brace, 1928.
————. *Motion Picture Continuities: A Kiss for Cinderella, The Scarlet Letter, The Last Command.* New York: Columbia University Press, 1929.
Peacocke, Capt. Leslie T. *Hints on Photoplay Writing.* Chicago: Photoplay, 1916.
Peden, Charles. *Newsreel Man.* New York: Doubleday, Doran, 1932.
Pensel, Hans. *Seastrom and Stiller in Hollywood.* New York: Vantage Press, 1969.
Phelan, John. *Motion Pictures as a Phase of Commercialized Amusement in Toledo, Ohio.* Toledo: Little Book Press, 1919.
Phillips, Henry Albert. *The Feature Photoplay.* Springfield, Mass.: Home Correspondence School, 1921.
Photoplay Reseach Society. *Opportunities in the Motion Picture Industry.* Los Angeles: Photoplay Research Society, 1922.
Pickford, Mary. *Sunshine and Shadow.* Garden City, N.Y.: Doubleday, 1955.
Platt, Agnes. *Practical Hints on Acting for the Cinema.* New York: Dutton, 1923.
Powell, A. Van Buren. *The Photoplay Synopsis.* Springfield, Mass.: Home Correspondence School, 1919.
Pratt, George. *Spellbound in Darkness: A History of the Silent Film.* Greenwich, Conn.: New York Graphic Society, 1973.
Quigley, Martin. *Decency in Motion Pictures.* New York: Macmillan, 1937.
Ramsaye, Terry. *A Million and One Nights.* New York: Simon and Schuster, 1926.
Randall, Richard S. *Censorship of the Movies.* Madison: University of Wisconsin Press, 1968.
Rapee, Erno. *Motion Picture Moods for Pianists and Organists.* New York: Schirmer, 1924.
Rathbun, John B. *Motion Picture Making and Exhibiting.* Los Angeles: Holmes, 1914.
Rebello, Stephen, and Richard Allen. *Reel Art: Great Posters from the Golden Age of the Silver Screen.* New York: Abbeville, 1988.
Reichenbach, Harry, and David Freedman. *Phantom Fame: The Anatomy of Ballyhoo.* London: Noel Douglas, 1932.
Reilly, Adam. *Harold Lloyd, the King of Daredevil Comedy.* New York: Macmillan, 1977.
Rheuban, Joyce. *Harry Langdon: The Comedian as Metteur-en-scène.* Rutherford, N.J.: Farleigh Dickinson University Press, 1983.
Richardson, F. H. *Handbook of Projection.* 5th ed. 2 vols. New York: Chalmers, 1927.
Riddle, Melvin M. *Pen to Silversheet.* N.p.: Harvey White, 1922.
Robinson, David. *Hollywood in the Twenties.* New York: Barnes, 1968.
————. *Buster Keaton.* Bloomington: Indiana University Press, 1969.
————. *Chaplin: The Mirror of Opinion.* Bloomington: Indiana University Press, 1984.
————. *Chaplin: His Life and Art.* New York: McGraw-Hill, 1985.
Ross, Murray. *Stars and Strikes: The Unionization of Hollywood.* New York: Columbia University Press, 1941.
Rotha, Paul. *The Film Till Now.* London: Jonathan Cape, 1930.
————. *Rotha on the Film.* London: Faber and Faber, 1958.
Rutland, J. R. *State Censorship of Motion Pictures.* New York: Wilson Co., 1923.

Sandburg, Carl. *Carl Sandburg at the Movies*. Edited by Dale Fetherling and Doug Fetherling. Metuchen, N.J.: Scarecrow Press, 1985.

Sargent, Epes Winthrop. *The Technique of the Photoplay*. 2d ed. New York: Moving Picture World, 1913.

Saylor, Oliver M. *Revolt in the Arts*. New York: Brentano's, 1930.

Scaramazza, Paul A. *Ten Years in Paradise. 1921–1930: Concise Film Reviews from a Great Magazine*. Arlington, Va.: Pleasant Press, 1974.

Schickel, Richard. *His Picture in the Papers*. New York: Charterhouse, 1973.

———. *Harold Lloyd: The Shape of Laughter*. Boston: New York Graphic Society, 1974.

———. *D. W. Griffith: An American Life*. New York: Simon and Schuster, 1984.

Scott, Evelyn. *Hollywood: When Silents Were Golden*. New York: McGraw-Hill, 1972.

Seabury, William M. *The Public and the Motion Picture Industry*. New York: Macmillan, 1926.

———. *Motion Picture Problems: The Cinema and the League of Nations*. New York: Avondale Press, 1929.

Seldes, Gilbert. *The Seven Lively Arts*. New York: Harper, 1924.

Sennett, Mack, as told to Cameron Shipp. *King of Comedy*. New York: Doubleday, 1954.

Sessions, Ralph. *The Movies in Rockland County: Adolph Zukor and the Silent Era*. New City: Historical Society of Rockland County, 1982.

Sharp, Dennis. *The Picture Palace and Other Buildings for the Movies*. New York: Praeger, 1969.

Sheehan, Perley Poore. *Hollywood as a World Center*. Hollywood: Hollywood Citizen Press, 1924.

Sherwood, Robert E., ed. *The Best Moving Pictures of 1922–23*. Boston: Small, Maynard, 1923.

Shipman, Nell. *The Silent Screen and My Talking Heart*. Boise: Boise State University Press, 1987.

Sklar, Robert. *Movie-Made America: A Cultural History of American Movies*. New York: Random House, 1975.

Slide, Anthony. *Early American Cinema*. Cranbury, N.J.: Barnes, 1970.

———. *Aspects of American Film Before 1920*. Metuchen, N.J.: Scarecrow Press, 1978.

———. *The Kindergarten of the Movies: A History of the Fine Arts Company*. Metuchen, N.J.: Scarecrow Press, 1980.

———. *Early Women Directors*. Rev. ed. New York: Da Capo Press, 1984.

———. *The Big V: A History of the Vitagraph Company*. Rev. ed. Metuchen, N.J.: Scarecrow Press, 1987.

Slide, Anthony, ed. *The American Film Industry*. Westport, Conn.: Greenwood Press, 1986.

Sloan, Kay. *The Loud Silents: Origins of the Social Problem Film*. Chicago: University of Illinois Press, 1988.

Smith, Albert E., in collaboration with Phil Koury. *Two Reels and a Crank*. Garden City, N.Y.: Doubleday, 1952.

Stenn, David. *Clara Bow: Running Wild*. Garden City, N.Y.: Doubleday, 1988.

Sterling, Anna Kate, ed. *The Best of Shadowland*. Metuchen, N.J.: Scarecrow Press, 1987.

Swanson, Gloria. *Swanson on Swanson*. New York: Random House, 1980.

Talbot, Frederick A. *Practical Cinematography and Its Applications*. London: Heinemann, 1913.

———. *Moving Pictures: How They Are Made and Worked*. Philadelphia: Lippincott, 1914.

Talmadge, Margaret L. *The Talmadge Sisters*. Philadelphia: Lippincott, 1924.

Talmey, Allene. *Doug and Mary and Others*. New York: Macy-Masius, 1927.

The Theater and Motion Pictures. Britannica Booklet no. 7. New York: Encyclopaedia Britannica, 1933.

Thomas, D. B. *The First Colour Motion Pictures*. London: Her Majesty's Stationery Office, 1969.

Thompson, Kristin. *Exporting Entertainment: America in the World Film Market, 1907–1934*. London: British Film Institute, 1985.

Tibbets, John C., ed. *Introduction to the Photoplay*. Shawnee Mission, Kans.: National Film Society, 1977.

Tinting and Toning of Eastman Positive Motion Picture Film. Rochester, N.Y.: Eastman Kodak, 1927.

Tuska, Jon. *The Filming of the West*. Garden City, N.Y.: Doubleday, 1976.

Van Zile, Edward. *That Marvel—the Movie*. New York: Putnam Sons, 1923.

Vardac, A. Nicholas. *Stage to Screen: Theatrical Method from Garrick to Griffith*. Cambridge, Mass.: Harvard University Press, 1949.

Vidor, King. *A Tree Is a Tree*. New York: Harcourt, Brace, 1953.

von Sternberg, Josef. *Fun in a Chinese Laundry*. New York: Macmillan, 1965.

Wagenknecht, Edward. *The Movies in the Age of Innocence*. Norman: University of Oklahoma Press, 1962.

————. *Stars of the Silents*. Metuchen, N.J.: Scarecrow Press, 1987.

Wagner, Rob. *Film Folk*. New York: Century, 1918.

Walsh, Raoul. *Each Man in His Time*. New York: Farrar, Straus, and Giroux, 1974.

Ward, Larry Wayne. *The Motion Picture Goes to War*. Ann Arbor, Mich.: UMI Research Press, 1985.

Wasko, Janet. *Movies and Money*. Norwood, N.Y.: Ablex, 1982.

Weinberg, Herman G. *Josef von Sternberg*. New York: Dutton, 1967.

————. *The Lubitsch Touch: A Critical Study*. New York: Dutton, 1968.

————. *The Complete "Greed" of Erich von Stroheim*. New York: Dutton, 1973.

————. *The Complete "Wedding March" of Erich von Stroheim*. Boston: Little, Brown, 1974.

Weltman, Manuel, and Raymond Lee. *Pearl White, the Peerless Fearless Girl*. Cranbury, N.J.: Barnes, 1969.

Williamson, Alice M. *Alice in Movieland*. New York: Appleton, 1928.

Windeler, Robert. *Sweetheart: The Story of Mary Pickford*. New York: Praeger, 1974.

Wright, William Lord. *Photoplay Writing*. New York: Falk, 1922.

Yallop, David. *The Day the Laughter Stopped*. New York: St. Martin's Press, 1976.

Zierold, Norman. *Sex Goddesses of the Silent Screen*. Chicago: Regnery, 1973.

Zukor, Adolph, with Dale Kramer. *The Public Is Never Wrong*. New York: Putnam, 1953.

The amount of published material dealing with the silent-feature period is vast. The bibliography above includes only book-length studies of direct value in the preparation of this volume. Relevant periodical articles are indexed in much more sophisticated fashion than full-length works and can easily be located in various standard indexes. These include *The Film Index*, 3 vols. (New York: Kraus International, 1985); Richard Dyer MacCann and Ted Perry, eds., *The New Film Index* (New York: Dutton, 1975); John Gerlach and Lana Gerlach, eds., *The Critical Index* (New York: Teachers College Press; 1974); Linda Batty, ed., *Retrospective Index to Film Periodicals, 1930–1971* (New York: Bowker, 1971); Mel Schuster, ed., *Motion Picture Directors: A Bibliography of Magazine and Periodical Articles, 1900–1972* (Metuchen, N.J.: Scarecrow Press, 1973); Patricia King Hanson and Stephen L. Hanson, eds., *Film Review Index*, Vol. 1, *1882–1949* (Phoenix: Oryx, 1986); and the annual editions of *International Index to Film Periodicals* (since 1972) and *Film Literature Index* (since 1973).

Among the most important journals used in the research on this volume were *American Cinematographer, American Projectionist, Exhibitors Trade Review, Film History, Motion Picture Magazine, The Motion Picture News, Moving Picture World, New York Dramatic Mirror, New York Times, The Silent Picture, Transactions* (later *Journal*) *of the Society of Motion Picture Engineers*, and *Universal Weekly* (sometimes called *Moving Picture Weekly*).

Background for many of the chapters has been provided by oral-history interviews conducted by the author with the following silent-film–era workers. Transcripts of most of the interviews are on deposit with the American Film Institute or the American Museum of the Moving Image.

- Lucien Andriot, cinematographer
- Gertrude Astor, actress
- Constance Binney, actress
- Louise Brooks, actress
- Harry Burke, groundsman
- J. J. Cohn, production executive
- Stanley Cortez, cinematographer
- Herb Edelman, cinematographer

- George Folsey, cinematographer
- David Garber, art director
- Lee Garmes, cinematographer
- Tay Garnett, director
- Burnett Guffey, cinematographer
- Irving Heitzner, cinematographer
- Harold Henderson, location scout
- H. R. Hough, production executive
- James Wong Howe, cinematographer
- Paul Ivano, cinematographer
- Ted Kent, editor
- Paul Kohner, production executive
- Rudy Koubek, projectionist
- Carl Laemmle, Jr., production executive
- Ann Little, actress
- Anita Loos, screenwriter
- Mary MacLaren, actress
- William Margulies, cinematographer
- George Marshall, director
- Samuel Marx, story editor
- Ted McCord, cinematographer
- Lewis Milestone, director
- Hal Mohr, cinematographer
- Ernest Palmer, cinematographer
- Ray Rennahan, cinematographer
- George Robertson, prop man
- Joseph Ruttenberg, cinematographer
- Karl Struss, cinematographer
- Gloria Swanson, actress
- Henry Tiedmann, gaffer
- Charles Van Enger, cinematographer
- Valerie von Stroheim, actress
- Grant Whytock, editor
- Irvin Willat, director
- Fay Wray, actress
- William Wyler, director

Access to manuscript sources has expanded tremendously, even during the course of this research. Many archives and libraries have published catalogs of their own holdings, but for general collection surveys see Linda Mehr, ed., *Motion Pictures, Television, and Radio: A Union Catalogue of Manuscript and Special Collections in the Western United States* (Boston: Hall, 1977); Kim N. Fisher, ed., *On the Screen: A Film, Television and Video Research Guide* (Littleton, Colo.: Libraries Unlimited, 1986); and *International Directory of Film and Television Documentation Centers* (Chicago: St. James Press, 1988).

Picture Sources

American Museum of the Moving Image: 17, 35, 60, 71, 101 (both), 103 (both), 117, 118, 119, 121 (below), 151, 153, 154
American Society of Cinematographers: 123
Robert S. Birchard: 65
David Bradley: 185
Culver Pictures, Inc.: 27, 149, 165
William K. Everson: 240
Hirschl & Adler Galleries, Inc.: 55
Diane Koszarski: 42, 280
The Museum of Modern Art/Department of Film Stills Archive: 32, 88, 226, 242
Theatre Historical Society: 50
Marc Wanamaker/Bison Archives: 3, 6, 8, 57, 74, 78, 81, 83, 99, 109, 144, 156, 176, 182, 207, 215, 217, 245, 252, 316, 324
All others from author's collection

General Index

Italic numerals signify illustrations.

Index of Films

CPSIA information can be obtained
at www.ICGtesting.com
Printed in the USA
JSHW061002260722
28563JS00005B/115